A Margin of Hope

BOOKS BY IRVING HOWE

Celebrations and Attacks

Leon Trotsky

The Critical Point

Decline of the New

Steady Work: Essays in the Politics of
Democratic Radicalism, 1953–1966

Thomas Hardy: A Critical Study

A World More Attractive

The American Communist Party: A Critical History
(with Lewis Coser)

Politics and the Novel

William Faulkner: A Critical Study

Sherwood Anderson: A Critical Biography

The U.A.W. and Walter Reuther
(with B. J. Widick)

BOOKS EDITED BY IRVING HOWE

How We Lived
(with Kenneth Libo)

The World of the Blue-Collar Worker

Essential Works of Socialism

The Seventies: Problems & Proposals
(with Michael Harrington)

Voices from the Yiddish
(with Eliezer Greenberg)

A Treasury of Yiddish Poetry
(with Eliezer Greenberg)

The Idea of the Modern

The Basic Writings of Trotsky

The Radical Imagination

Edith Wharton: A Critical Collection

The Radical Papers

A Treasury of Yiddish Stories
(with Eliezer Greenberg)

IRVING HOWE

A
MARGIN
OF
HOPE

An Intellectual Autobiography

A Harvest/HBJ Book
Harcourt Brace Jovanovich, Publishers
San Diego   New York   London

Requests for permission to make copies of any
part of the work should be mailed to:
Permissions, Harcourt Brace Jovanovich, Publishers,
757 Third Avenue, New York, N.Y. 10017

The epigrams by J. V. Cunningham on pages 189–90
are reprinted with the permission of
the Ohio University Press, Athens.

Library of Congress Cataloging in Publication Data
Howe, Irving.
A margin of hope.
1. Howe, Irving.   2. Jews—New York (N.Y.)—Biography.
3. Jewish radicals—New York (N.Y.)—Biography.
4. Critics—New York (N.Y.)—Biography.   5. New York
(N.Y.)—Biography.   6. New York (N.Y.)—Intellectual
life.   I. Title.
[F128.9.J5H59   1984]   974.7'1004924024   [B]   83-18549
ISBN 0-15-157138-4
ISBN 0-15-677245-1 (pbk.)

Printed in the United States of America
First Harvest/HBJ edition 1984

B   C   D   E

TO ILANA

Contents

A Margin of Hope

1

In the Movement

When, asked Ignazio Silone one summer evening in Rome, did you first become a Socialist? We were having the usual difficulties in starting a conversation, though we knew we shared many ideas and some experiences. I had become a Socialist, I told him, at the advanced age of fourteen. "You too"—he started laughing—"it was the same with you!" He in the Abruzzi and I in the Bronx, some thread of shared desire had linked our youth. And what, he started to ask, had made me turn to a politics not exactly popular in the United Sta— But he caught himself, as if the answer were self-evident.

For him, it was. Others may wonder, and that has prompted me also to wonder. I find it hard to give assured answers, though perhaps that is no reason for chagrin, since about the most important matters in our lives we seem fated to remain uncertain, torn between the rival claims of will and circumstance. Let me start with circumstance.

The East Bronx, when I lived there as a boy, formed a thick tangle of streets crammed with Jewish immigrants from Eastern Europe, almost all of them poor. We lived in narrow five-story tenements, wall flush against wall, and with slate-colored stoops rising sharply in front. There never was enough space. The buildings, clenched into rows, looked down upon us like sentinels, and the apartments in the buildings were packed with relatives and children, many of them fugitives from unpaid rent. These tenements had first gone up during the early years of the century, and if not quite so grimy as those of the Lower East Side in Manhattan or the Brownsville section of Brooklyn, they were bad enough. The halls on the ground floor leading to the staircase always seemed dark and at night spooky; even in my middle teens, when I was trying to brace myself to visions of political heroism, I would still feel a slight shudder of nerves whenever I started up the staircase.

Hardly a day passed but someone was moving in or out. Often you could see a family's entire belongings—furniture, pots and pans, bedding, a tricycle—piled up on the sidewalks because they had been dispossessed. In my part of the East Bronx, where the main streets were Boston Road and Prospect Avenue, it was rare for a building of red or tan brick to break the monotony of muddy browns and grays; what I remember of these streets is notable for flatness of color, sameness of shade. If you wanted to see a "modern" building—one that had an elevator, parquet floors, and French doors—you had to take a trolley across the borough to the newer sections of the West Bronx. Streetcars, some with overhanging cables, cut through the length and width of the borough. Milk came in the morning by horse and wagon, and one of my first lessons in the hardness of existence was watching horses slip on the winter ice and being whipped back to work.

In the early thirties—by then I was entering my teens—the East Bronx was still a self-contained little world, lacking the cultural vivacity that had brightened the Lower East Side of Manhattan a decade or two earlier but otherwise, in custom and value, not very different. Yiddish was spoken everywhere. The English of the young, if unmarred by accent, had its own intonation, the stumbling melody of immigrant speech. A mile or two from my building —I did not know it then—there lived a cluster of Yiddish writers who would gather on Sundays near a big rock in Crotona Park, where I would go to play ball or wander around. At the corner newsstands the Yiddish daily, the *Forward*, sold about as well as the *News* and the *Mirror*, the two-cent tabloids with crime stories, pictures, gossip. The *News* had a feature called "Embarrassing Moments" that I continued to read avidly even after I made the acquaintance of Shelley and Marx. The *Times* did not prosper in such neighborhoods, and while I had heard of it before entering high school, I certainly had not read it with any regularity. Only at the prompting of culturally ambitious or politically sensitive teachers in high school did I start looking into the *Times* (it seemed almost as weighty an act as starting to read Shakespeare). I would feel self-conscious about carrying that large paper in the subway. To read the *News* meant that you belonged, it was a paper for plebeians on the run; to read the *Times* signaled alien yearnings, perhaps some vision of getting away. No one made such things explicit, no one needed to.

Two or three blocks from where we lived stood the peeling McKinley Square Theatre, in which a company of Yiddish actors, as mediocre as they were poor, tried to keep alive. You had to patronize them once in a while with a thirty-five-cent ticket, said my father, because it was a scandal to see fellow Jews "dying of hunger three times a day." (Blessed Yiddish: no one just dies of hunger, you die three times a day.) The nearest synagogue, in a once baroque structure, was also struggling through the Depression, and as if to acknowledge reduced circumstances my own bar mitzvah took place not there, since that would have cost too much and probably made us feel uncomfortable, but in a whitewashed storefront *shul*, ramshackle and bleak with its scattering of aged Jews. This sort of penniless congregation no longer exists in Jewish neighborhoods, but its equivalents can still be found among the more exotic black denominations. A few blocks past the synagogue, on Wilkins Avenue, stood the loft in which a secular Yiddish school was run by the Workmen's Circle, a fraternal order more or less socialist in outlook. My father, though hardly pious, would not let me go there because he felt ill at ease with the bluntly secular. It was as if he knew what "the real thing" was in Judaism, even though himself gradually slipping away from it. That loft on Wilkins Avenue turned out to be more important in my life than any synagogue.

An inexperienced eye moving across the East Bronx would have noticed little difference between one part and another. That eye would have been mistaken, for the immigrant world had its intricate latticing of social position. All through the years of the Depression our neighborhood clung to its inner supports of morale, its insistence upon helping its own in ways that were its own—which meant keeping as far as possible from the authority of the state, suspect as both gentile and bourgeois. Many people in the East Bronx would have starved—and perhaps some did a little—rather than go on "relief." The psychology of the *shtetl* householder in Eastern Europe, with his desperate improvisations to appear independent, had an odd way of recurring among these garment workers, some of whom still dreamed of managing their own little businesses, even if no more than a candy store with its shuffle of pennies across the counter. Almost everyone dreaded "charity."

The gradations of status in this immigrant world were hardly visible to anyone but its own people. Once things had really become bad for my family, in 1931 and 1932, my father would say with his grim humor, "At least we're not on Fox Street." Fox Street he regarded as our private Bowery, the bottom in poverty, a surrender to that demoralization which over the centuries Jews had learned to fear at least as much as hunger. The few times I actually got to see this Fox Street it did not seem much worse than our own Jennings Street, yet everyone in the East Bronx would immediately have understood what my father was getting at. In later years, when things were sometimes hard for me, though never so hard as during the thirties, I would frighten myself or try ironically to cut my fear with remembered pictures of Fox Street: twisted, narrow, dirty, a place slipping out of the discipline to which respectable poverty must cling.

In our neighborhood many of the women went to work. They would stand long hours at the counters of grocery and candy stores or join their men in the forty-five-minute subway ride to the garment center, a trip that made your bones ache even before starting to work. Even when the women went downtown, the family remained the center of life. Sometimes the family was about all that was left of Jewishness; or, more accurately, all that we had left of Jewishness had come to rest in the family. Jewishness flickered to life on Friday night, with a touch of Sabbath ceremony a few moments before dinner; it came radiantly to life during Passover, when traditional dignities shone through its ritual. Our parents clung to family life as if that was their one certainty: everything else seemed frightening, alien, incomprehensible. Not that they often talked about these things. Speaking openly would have been still more frightening, a shattering of defenses. Only in moments of crisis could that happen—as in those hysterical scenes that broke out when adolescents tried to slip away into lives of their own.

In the worst of times, between 1930 and 1934, there were still hours of happiness, many of them. An infection of hope had seized these Jews, not really for themselves (a possibility their sardonic realism taught them to discount), but hope at once passionate and abstract, fixed equally upon America and their children. Whatever their faith or opinions, they felt that here in America the Jews had at least a chance, and as it turned out they were right. Once I went with my mother to see the movie *All Quiet on the Western Front*, and watched the tears stream down her face as the butterfly moved across the final frames; another time I went with my father to Yankee Stadium and sat a few dozen yards from Babe Ruth, the greatest man in the Bronx. Both these expeditions, linking our little world with the great one outside, signified my parents' unspoken readiness that I start my journey out of the immigrant milieu, a journey that they feared almost as much as they desired it. Yet the best times were at home, in the comfort of our innerness, as on those Sunday evenings when there was enough money to indulge in delicatessen, or once in a while when my mother went off on a visit and my father and I sat quietly in the kitchen dipping bits of apple into glasses of hot tea.

Home meant snugness and deprivation, a place and a feeling I kept to myself. It could not be part of one's new life. The thought of bringing my friends home was inconceivable, for I would have been as ashamed to show them to my parents as to show my parents to them. I had enough imagination to suppose that each could see through the shams of the other, but not enough courage to defend one against the other. Besides, where would people sit in those cramped apartments? The worldly manner affected by some of my friends would have stirred flames of suspicion in the eyes of my father; the sullen immigrant kindliness of my parents would have struck my friends as all too similar to that of their fathers and mothers; and my own self-consciousness, which in relation to my parents led me into a maze of superfluous lies and deceptions, made

6 | A Margin of Hope

it difficult for me to believe in the possibility of a life grounded in simple good faith.

Immigrant Jewish life left us with a large weight of fear. Fear had seeped into Jewish bones over the centuries, fear had become the intuitive Jewish response to authority, fear seemed the strongest emotion that the very world itself, earth, sky, and sun, brought out in Jews. To be Jewish meant—not this alone, but this always—to live with fear, on the edge of foreseen catastrophe. "A Jew's joy," says the Yiddish proverb, "is not without fright."

Meanwhile we were poor. We were never really hungry, but almost always anxious. During the summers I would try to find some work, but who in 1934 or 1935 needed a stringbean of a boy with glasses? Once I carried rolls of linoleum for a storekeeper who suffered from a hernia, but after a day or two he fired me, saying in his kindly-sour way that there was no need for me to get a hernia, too. Another time I found a few days' work distributing circulars for a supermarket, but again was fired because the manager suspected (rightly enough) that some of the circulars were ending up in sewers. Mostly, the summers would float by in a soft, foggy daydream: reading, wandering the streets, staring (after a time not so innocently) out of back windows.

It was in the summers that one grew into problems, began to fumble toward self and sex. If I had had to wait until my parents told me how the human race perpetuates itself, I still would not know. Passionate about most things public, the immigrants were shy about everything private. Many were intensely romantic, their escape from religious orthodoxy having been facilitated by sentiments adapted from European romanticism; but it was a romanticism shy of words, a reticent turning toward the idea of personality. And it was guarded by a decorum more rigid than shame.

To be poor is something that happens to you; to experience poverty is to gain an idea of what is happening. When my father's grocery store in the West Bronx went bankrupt in 1930 and he became a "customer peddler" trudging from door to door to offer modest credit to Italian and Irish housewives, we were really poor, crowded into a small apartment with aunts, uncles, and grandmother in order to save rent. The move from the West to the East

Bronx came to no more than a few miles, but socially the distance was vast. We were dropping from the lower middle class to the proletarian—the most painful of all social descents. This unsettled my sense of things: I was driven inward, toward book and dream.

At the age of thirteen I caught scarlet fever, then a serious disease, and stayed in bed for six weeks. I sent my father to the local library to bring me the collected poems of Milton, Words-worth, and Keats, names that had been mentioned by a teacher I admired. The librarian must have stared at my father, but perhaps she knew something about these immigrant Jews and their crazy kids. Lying in bed a little feverish, I read through the entire work of these poets: the clipped eloquence of *Samson Agonistes* and the candied richness of "The Eve of St. Agnes" remaining for decades in memory. Exactly what this was all about I am still not certain: some monstrous craving, some eagerness for cultural appropriation drawn from sources deeper than myself. In any case, stuck now in the East Bronx, I began to cultivate—this is not a rare combination —both a heightened social awareness and an adolescent cultural snobbism. Later I would tell myself, trying to make it all a joke, that I had a kinship of sorts with American writers like Hawthorne and Melville, who had also known the shock of suddenly reduced circumstances.

My parents became workers. They labored in the dress trade, my mother an operator, my father a presser. It was my mother— strong, humorless, enclosing—who held us together, not by a mere idea but through energies out of her depths. She was the kind of woman who blooms through sustaining others. At first she would come home with a paycheck of twelve or fifteen dollars a week, tired and troubled, yet gripping in her hands the life of everyone near her—helping my father overcome his shame at having failed in business, helping me adjust a little to the roughnecks of this new neighborhood in the East Bronx, helping my grandmother keep house, helping relatives in distress. After my father found work he often came home, especially in the summers, with blisters on his body, the result of hours spent over a steaming press iron, and my mother would apply a soothing mixture of baking soda and water to his skin. They held together, the two of them, through good times and bad, but how hard they had to work! How desperately hard everything was for them and the thousands of others like them in our immigrant streets!

Then came the great strike. In 1933 the International Ladies Garment Workers Union, which all through the twenties had been reduced to feebleness, took the risk of calling out the entire dress trade. Immediately, though they had never before shown any class militancy, my folks joined the picket lines. For a Jew to scab was as unthinkable as to become a Christian convert. Once the strike was won, life became easier: we could now have meat more often, my parents started to squirrel away a few dollars in a savings account, and once my birthday came round my mother bought me a few "grownup" shirts. When it comes to a passion for shirts I stand side by side with Jay Gatsby, and for quite as good a reason.

After the strike my parents rarely attended union meetings, though they paid their dues faithfully and would respond immediately if the union issued a strike call. The garment unions were an essential part of immigrant life, helping to ease its hardships and giving our people a fragment of dignity. In later years, whenever I heard intellectuals of the Right or Left attack unionism, I would be seized by an uncontrollable rage that then gave way to frustration: how to explain to young people what the strike of 1933 had meant, how to find words to tell of the small comforts the union had brought, meat on the table and "grownup" shirts?

We were still poor, but it was no longer a grinding, desperate poverty (though only romantic fools or children of affluence can suppose that being poor is anything but hard). Until the age of fourteen or fifteen, and by then the worst was over, I had little sense of being a victim of social injustice. It was simply that in my early teens, for reasons hard to grasp, things had changed unpleasantly. Only after I started high school did the idea of poverty come to me with any force; only then did I see it with the familiar blend of outrage, shame, and ambition. I began to read a magazine that printed Sherwood Anderson's quavering reports about North Carolina textile workers who had been on strike for months, and these articles brought tears of indignation to my eyes. Was I aware that I might also have been feeling sorry for myself? Probably not. It was easier to feel sorry for others.

The realization of what it meant to be poor I had first to discover through reading about poverty; the sense of my own deprivation grew keen after I learned about the troubles of people I did not know. And this was typical of many other boys and girls in my generation, in whom family trouble and intellectual stirring joined to create a political consciousness. It all served, in any case, as preparation for the crucial experience of my youth: it prepared me for the movement.

Radicalism in our part of the city seemed more than marginal exotica, and in the city as a whole more than an alien import. It had a place and strength of its own. It was still the belief of a minority, but a minority that kept growing. Socialism, for many immigrant Jews, was not merely politics or an idea, it was an encompassing culture, a style of perceiving and judging through which to structure their lives. So diffused had the socialist idea become in the immigrant world since the days of Debs and Hillquit that socialist organization tended in consequence to be weak: almost everyone seemed to be a Socialist of one sort or another. This was not really true, it was a mistake easy to make. Even in the "outside" neighborhoods where the gentiles lived, radical sentiments were starting to gain a foothold. In 1934, why not?

We had a few Republicans in the East Bronx, or so the election returns indicated, but they were rarely to be seen in any organized form. A Republican street meeting was treated as a genuine curiosity; "Look, fer crissakes, de Republicans!" (Perhaps they had gone "underground"?) But the Democratic machine, firmly Irish, held power in the borough and won support, as well as moral luster, from Roosevelt's New Deal, which would quickly gain the hearts of a large section, Socialists included, of the Jewish population. Still, among those who cared intensely about politics—those who linked themselves into "circles" of debaters in the park, or went to meetings in the halls, or stopped at almost any outdoor rally to discuss, argue, and kibitz—there was a strong conviction that capitalism had reached a point of final collapse. Something radically new was needed—almost everyone agreed to that! Later we learned that this had not been quite the universal persuasion we supposed; but when your own mind is charged with an idea, you cannot always bother to look into other minds.

Many of the boys and girls growing up in my neighborhood tried to pretend that all was normal, the Depression had not struck, their parents were not jobless, expectations of a future still made sense. They looked for work. They hoped for a modest career, maybe as accountants or schoolteachers. My father's fondest dream was that I should become a high-school teacher, for in those days high-school teachers earned about forty dollars a week, enough for reasonable comfort. I felt all along that I would never reach that goal because, so legend had it among us, in the oral examination for teachers you had to pronounce "Long Island" without sounding a hard "g"—clearly a trick for eliminating Jewish candidates. It took a few decades before I overcame a distaste for that neck of land.

Among young people the one political idea, perhaps the one idea, that had real power was radicalism. Only radicalism seemed to offer the prospect of coherence, only radicalism could provide a unified view of the world. Grownups often said that in America radicalism was just a daydream that would distract us from the hard business of getting ahead, but seldom did they argue that radicalism was wrong. The psychology of individual striving had been called into question, but it had a strong grip even upon those who rejected it. Traditional American myths, often taken over with naive eagerness by the very immigrants critical of American society, could still rouse flickers of hope. A hope of finding a little corner, a little job, a little business, which meant in effect to continue along the ways of one's parents. If one regarded this as a delusion or as morally unworthy, there remained only a choice in modes of rebellion.

So I stumbled into socialism. I stumbled into it with about as much foreknowledge of what it would mean to me as I would stumble into other experiences later in life. I was eager, I was afraid, I was a little rapturous—not very different from other young people of the moment. For this was a time profoundly disorganizing in its effects upon the young; there was no longer that intuitive transmission of cues by which social existence is regulated. We were adrift and needed definition, meaning, platform, anchor. We were still dutifully going to high school and college, partly because we knew of nothing else to do, partly because we liked to read books, and partly because our parents clung stubbornly to the dream of education. We had a burning need for order—yes, even in our middle teens: a sure sign that the society was in deep disorder. We needed order both in our lives and in our view of life, and we thought to gain a semblance of the former by imposing an ideology on the latter. For a while it worked.

There were no breadlines in the Bronx that I knew of, but there were people in need of bread. Once or twice I went so far afield as to glimpse Hooverville, the colony of shacks thrown up by the unemployed along Riverside Drive. And all the time there were voices of anxiety at home, worried about "slack," the season without work, or complaining about cuts in piecework rates in the shops. One terrible day in the early thirties we heard that the Bank of the United States—Jewish-owned!—had failed, and I sat in our apartment listening to my aunt and grandmother wailing over the loss of the few hundred dollars they had scraped together. Still with a mite of humor, my aunt told of passing a line of depositors at a nearby branch of the bank—people vainly, sometimes hysterically, trying to retrieve their money—and of the woman friend who cried out at the doors of the shut bank: "Meester politzman, meester politzman, loz mikh arein, let me in!"

Things had gone profoundly wrong. No later discounting of the radicalism of the thirties can wipe away this simple truth.

Things had gone wrong not only in America but still more in Europe. Whatever the provincialism of immigrant Jewish life, it was far less provincial than most other segments of America in responding to the tragedies of Europe in the thirties. We were still, in some deep sense, part of Europe, and it was right for us to be so. Even the least political among us knew that the rise of Hitler would sooner or later tear apart our lives. When the Socialists of Vienna tried vainly in 1934 to put up military resistance against the repressions of the Dollfuss government, I would hover around the newsstands—that was an important part of life in the thirties, people hovering around newsstands—to read the headlines with a grief I could barely have explained. Later I would feel the same grief when the Fascists approached Madrid. European society was breaking up, and the conclusion we drew from this fact—too simple, no doubt—was that all possibility of mending or patching was done with, that the time of apocalypse had come, that everything would now depend on whether socialism could, in one last victorious upsurge, repel the barbarians. We saw no other choices, and the time did not encourage any.

Things had gone wrong, an intense need for order, the prospect of coherence: these are the keys to understanding why at least some young people became radicals in the thirties. I put all this in a high-minded way, aware that in our age of moral depreciation we have learned to suspect such talk. Very well, let us be more skeptical. No doubt one reason for turning to the socialist youth movement was that in my family's slide from modest lower-middle-class security to anxious working-class poverty I had suffered a loss of psychological comfort. Life disarranged had become vulnerable; vulnerable people look for shelter; shelter can be found in political movements possessing a world view. The movement eased my loneliness, gave me a feeling of place, indulged me in the belief that I had scaled peaks of comprehension. Could all this have occurred without the historical shock of the Depression? Perhaps. But so frequently and with such depths of fervor? Probably not. Efforts to explain radical politics by psychological deviancy founder on circularity, triviality, and impudence, especially when they ignore the circumstances of history. Perhaps what needs to be explained is not why some of us became radicals in the thirties, but why others did not.

Explain then (a skeptical voice presses harder) why you became a Socialist and not a Communist? I cannot really claim that I was already wise to the outrages of Stalinism, for at the time not many grownups were. The distinctions, fine or coarse, between radical movements were usually discovered only after joining one of them: they were dinned into your ears as a kind of inoculation against raiding by political opponents. Perhaps what made me a Socialist rather than a Communist was that the Socialists reached me first, through some students at my high school who were sons of old-time officials in the garment unions. But it must have been more than that. Perhaps I would have been afraid to become a Communist, since that involved a higher ratio of risk, severe battles with parents, fear of ostracism in school. Perhaps I sensed that I could not adapt to the stringent demands of the Communists, for while I had a sharp hunger for the coherence of disciplined thought, I also felt strong resistance to the discipline of coherent organization. Anyway, whether through a failure of nerve or some youthful intuition, I was never tempted.

There I was, then, fourteen years old, walking up the stairs to the Yiddish school on Wilkins Avenue where the Young Peoples Socialist League (YPSL) held its weekly meetings on Sunday night. Another eight or nine such groups met in the Bronx, each having between twenty and fifty members. The organizer of my YPSL "circle," a chubby, good-humored boy named Louie, spoke well, with a friendly, uplifting voice, as he sketched out the week's assignments—outdoor meeting, literature distribution, visiting "contacts." A few years later I would conclude that Louie couldn't string together two consecutive thoughts, but at the time I was struck by his articulateness. Other young comrades spoke about their work, and they too spoke well. The atmosphere was serious, but not at all forbidding. At the end of the business meeting, Louie gave a two-minute sermon about recruiting new members, but he did this in a humorous way. Then came "the educational," a discussion of Nazi Germany led by a slightly older fellow from another circle. He too spoke well.

The second week (or was it the seventh?) there was a debate among the members, suddenly fierce, two speaking in favor of a united front with the Communists and two against—my first bite into the bittersweet fruits of factionalism! I began to detect different styles: some of the young comrades were, as I'd now put it, empirical, hard-headed, bored with theory, the kind who would end as officials of unions or Jewish organizations; but others were bookish, ambitious to display a fringe of Marxist vocabulary, starting to move from social democratic pragmatism toward facsimiles of Leninism. Some spoke too loudly, others used words I couldn't understand. My capacity for judgment soon began to crowd my feelings of admiration, yet I felt awed by this outpouring of language. Some heritage of Jewish sensibility or incipient trace of intellectuality led me to find here a home of sorts. I joined.

My parents objected to my politics, of course, and warned me about troublesome consequences, but both objections and warnings were weak. Why? Perhaps because life had been steadily wearing my parents down and they no longer had much energy for battle, perhaps because they knew some friends whose children had become Communists and felt that by comparison they were getting off lightly. I also see a deeper reason. As immigrants they had already lost a good part of their authority over me; indeed, they were themselves partly responsible for this loss. The more we native-born boys and girls made our way into American spheres of school and work, the more our immigrant parents grew uncertain about their right to command. They felt lost. They were overly impressed by the articulateness of their children, even though in moments of exasperation they could be wildly savage about it. My entry into the little world of socialism must have struck my parents as part of the estrangement that had to be accepted whenever a boy or girl went out into "the real world," the world of the gentiles. During the next few years—it would be comic if it weren't so sad—they objected more to my late hours, a result of wandering the streets with cronies after meetings, than to the meetings themselves. I exploited their innocence shamelessly, though there were moments when I felt a little ashamed.

Sliding into the socialist milieu, I was overcome by a sense of enlargement and discovery. Day-to-day activities of the movement might be boring, but its life was aglow with the promise of meaning. Nor was this a result of any foolish optimism about the prospects of victory. We knew that in Europe our side had taken crushing defeats and that in America we were very weak. No, our excitement came less from hope than despair. It came from a conviction that history had reached a point of final conflict. It came from a belief that the "death agony of capitalism" was now at hand—by no means a fatuous conclusion in the thirties, only a mistaken one. The odds against our enterprise were overwhelming, yet it was precisely this that made it seem a moral imperative.

Comparisons between radical politics and religious practice are likely to be glib, especially when used to dismiss the substance of the radical case; yet in thinking back to these years I'm forced to recognize, not very comfortably, that there were *some* parallels between the two. Everything seemed to fall into place: ordered meaning, a world grasped through theory, a life shaped by purpose. Is that not the essence of conversion? Not that anything really did fall into place: socialist thought after the triumph of Hitler was in severe crisis, the movement in America was fragile, and the torments of adolescence kept breaking through the routines of politics. Yet there were pleasure and sustenance to be found in shared work, in that bonding fraternity which is both the most yearned-for and most treacherous of twentieth-century experiences. Political life was often drudgery: attending tiresome meetings where democracy required that nudniks be allowed to drone on; hawking papers in the streets when few noticed and fewer bought; collecting petitions; distributing leaflets. But all this could release emotions of high purpose such as many political movements inspire, but left-wing movements, with their scored visions, seem especially to elicit.

So I found myself drawn into a routine of activity, discussion, conflict, ambition. How could school or college compete? How could a teacher of history, so open to our scorn as Professor Facing-Both-Ways, keep our attention, when we had Norman Thomas booming out in his rich, passionate voice a call to "socialism in our time"? Constantly, there were things to do. There were speeches to make, my first trembling venture a debut comparable in anxiety to the first time I saw my name in print. There were the sacred texts to struggle with—not the socialist primers we soon recognized as threadbare, but the *Communist Manifesto*, the *18th Brumaire of Louis Bonaparte,* even the first volume of *Das Kapital* two or three years later. There were people to admire—the leaders of the socialist youth, who seemed enviable in their authority. Weighty-sounding terms began to roll off our tongues, "surplus value" and "rate of profit," "the road to power" and "fetichism of commodities," this last bringing a special tilt of pleasure, so nicely did it vibrate with paradox and mystery.

Analysis, theory, ideology: these became the substance of what we saw and thought, shadowing reality, sometimes overpowering it. They told of historical disaster, and with a logic seemingly inexorable. There were moments, however, when the actuality of this disaster broke through analysis, theory, ideology, and then we knew ourselves abandoned, lost. We felt that we were living in a terrible time, and perhaps the most terrible part of it was that "out there" a great many people were going about their business undisturbed. Didn't they know, hadn't they heard the bad news? History became our secret sharer, secret fright. I would yield to fantasies, was sometimes shaken by dreams about Jews and radicals in Hitler's camps, or old Bolsheviks locked away in the Arctic, and wondered if I would be able to stand the privations and tortures to which they were being subjected. Of course not, for I knew my inner measure of cowardice, being unable even to bear the pain of a hot bath. In later years, talking with old friends, I learned that these had been shared fantasies and dreams, causing a similar despair. It was knowledge that brought comfort of a kind.

There had been a considerable growth of American socialism since 1929, an adherence of gifted, energetic people, some from trade unions, and this promised a revival after the lean years of the twenties. Internally a younger group of "Militants" was turning leftward, while the "Old Guard," hard-bitten veterans of the Jewish garment unions, clung to a fixed social democratic ideology. About all this I knew nothing when I joined up on Wilkins Avenue, but in a few months I saw myself as quite an expert. Almost together with my membership card, I was handed a pamphlet by Haim Kantorovich, a Polish-Jewish theorist who spoke for a growing leftward trend within the Socialist International, arguing that the humiliating collapse of the German Social Democracy before Hitler's thugs constituted final proof of how hopeless was the reformist perspective in an age of crisis. What we needed now, said the Militants, was a turn to a more combative (some added, revolutionary) socialism, minus the authoritarian encumbrances of Leninism. In 1935 it was very hard for a young Socialist who kept even one eye on Europe to have much faith in gradualism.

Two problems—real ones—were tearing the movement apart. The domestic problem was, what attitude should Socialists take toward Roosevelt's New Deal or, as we've since come to call it, the welfare state? The international problem was, how were Socialists to analyze and respond to the growth of totalitarianism in the Soviet Union? In this dispute the outstanding leader of the party, Norman Thomas, sided mostly with the Militants.

For several decades European Socialists had been struggling to work out a political response to liberal governments enacting welfare reforms (social security, unemployment insurance, public works, pensions, and so forth) within capitalist society. For American Socialists this had hardly been a problem, since the welfare state—or what passes for one among us—came here later than in Europe. The far right of the European social democracy virtually blended into welfare liberalism, contenting itself with modest reforms. The far left, while not opposed to such reforms, saw them as mere palliatives and tried to maintain a revolutionary perspective. Between these polar tendencies wobbled the social democratic center, dominant in most of the parties, which favored reform programs while maintaining—sometimes only on Sundays—a commitment to basic change. Similar divisions now flared up in the American movement, and all through the early 1930s they took a fierce, even ugly form. The problem was new to American Socialists, who had often contented themselves with sweeping denunciations of "the system." The very smallness of the movement in America made it almost certain that ideological disputes would be fought to the edge of death.

The younger leftist leaders of the Militant group, winning Norman Thomas to their outlook, criticized the New Deal with some cogency. They pointed out that it had not really ended unemployment or changed the basic situation of the worker in capitalist society. True, as far as it went. But the socialist officials of the Jewish unions, laden with the experience of decades, knew that with Roosevelt's policies something crucial *had* changed. Tens of thousands of workers were being recruited by the unions. New contracts were being signed, gains registered, future victories made possible. Roosevelt became an adored figure in the unions, so much so that some of his shameful acts—such as conniving in the refusal to admit Jewish refugees from Nazi Germany and maintaining an embargo on arms to loyalist Spain—would be virtually ignored. Soon the reforms associated with his name came to seem, for many radical workers, a workable replacement for the flickering goal of socialism.

The Militants included not only unripe "theoreticians" in New York, but some gifted trade union leaders such as the Reuther brothers in Detroit, who were caught up in the excitement of organizing industrial workers into the CIO. These people seemed exactly the sort that a socialist movement in America needed: idealistic yet practical, touched by native iconoclasm yet a little sophisticated in the ways of Marxism. By contrast, there was something sour about the Old Guard: they had suffered too many blows in the twenties, trying to keep their unions intact against the simultaneous assaults of American prosperity and fanatical communism. Most of the young Socialists could never feel any tie with these people.

By 1936 the inner struggle in the Socialist Party had become so bitter that a split was inevitable. When it came, the Old Guard took the Jewish unions and a considerable minority of the movement with it, proposing now to end socialist isolation and attach itself to the New Deal coalition. The Thomas wing hoped to build a fresh, uncompromising party.

Retrospective wisdom, never in short supply, would suggest that there might have been a more flexible strategy for American Socialists, one that acknowledged the New Deal as a step toward humanizing capitalism, but still affirmed the need for a basic socialist critique. Even electoral support of Roosevelt, which concerned the Old Guard most, might have been combined with agitation for extending the welfare state, which concerned the Militants most. But such a nuanced policy was unavailable to either side. Nerves were strained, feelings hurt. I used to think, and not I alone, that if only we got rid of those old, worn-out pinochleplayers who made the party headquarters into a mere hangout but never did much work, then our path would be clear. Pitiful illusion, so characteristic of a whole arc of socialist experience! Soon the path was cleared, but hardly anyone remained to take it.

More was finally at stake than an immediate response to the New Deal. For the Old Guard, especially its core of unionists, Roosevelt came along as a savior, enabling it to abandon an ideology in which it had gradually been losing faith. With no great trouble they adapted themselves to the status quo, functioning as devoted unionists. In later decades, when I would meet them at some conference, they would still find it hard to give up entirely the socialist label, even though they had largely given up the socialist content—so powerful is the faith of one's youth. As for the Militants, they were driven mainly by a conviction that a worldwide socialist transformation was on the historical agenda, and once it became clear that they had badly miscalculated, they too suffered doubt and disintegration. Most of the socialist activists in the CIO who had sided with Norman Thomas soon left him, following the Old Guard toward conciliation with New Deal politics; indeed, if they wanted to retain influence within their unions, they seldom had any choice.

About the other major issue dividing the movement—Stalinism—the Old Guard was by and large the more prescient. It took a principled stand of opposition to the communist regime, insisting that democracy was essential to any society presuming to call itself socialist. In the early thirties some Militants flirted briefly with the "Soviet experiment," but within a year or two all began to attack the Soviet dictatorship out of both humane revulsion and socialist principle.

Ideology counts in politics, especially left-wing politics, but other things also come into play, less easy to specify or control. The Militants were young, many of them just out of college. Some, like the witty, fast-talking Gus Tyler, were making a leftward tour through Marxism on the way to other interests; others, like such forgotten intellectuals as Maynard Krueger, were marked by a rather ingenuous American utopianism, employing a rhetoric that thirty years later the New Left would favor in its early "participatory democracy" phase.

For decades the movement had been bedeviling itself with a search for ways to become "more American," ways of sloughing off European accents, outlooks, styles. "More American" the Militants certainly were. But this was by no means an unqualified advantage, for in American socialism there has always been a strand of native sectarianism, striking a posture of unbending, almost apolitical righteousness. The Old Guard, by contrast, though often speaking with Yiddish or German accents, was canny, sharp, increasingly attuned to those maneuvers of local politics that all trade unionists must master if they are to survive. The few intellectuals siding with the Old Guard, men like Algernon Lee and James Oneal, knew their Marxism perhaps better than the green leftist youth who mocked them; but they were terribly scholastic, fixed into the conveniences of their sect. The Old Guard had become dry in spirit, terribly embittered, punch-drunk from bloody fights with the Communists. There is something unattractive about a right-wing Social Democrat who has found his bureaucratic niche and makes a safe politics out of anticommunism, correct as that anticommunism may be. He has lost that larger sympathy for the oppressed, that responsiveness to new modes of rebellion that a Socialist ought to have.

Norman Thomas had it. Pure in spirit, brave, selfless to a fault, and wonderfully free of the public man's self-importance, Thomas was in some ways too large for the movement in behalf of which he spoke. With his crackling voice and rapid wit, he would often rise to an eloquence that could sway even skeptics and opponents. This was no demagogue or soapbox ranter. He spoke with logic, he marshaled arguments and facts, he came out with comely sentences and paragraphs. Through the sheer sincerity of his yearning, he made it seem that "socialism in our time" was no mere phrase—it was coming soon. Hearing his rasping eloquence, as he brought us the good tidings, we felt proud to be his comrades. Meanwhile we knew he was very different from those who merely spun theories. Did Boss Hague of Jersey City try to institute a vest-pocket fascism, or Governor Paul McNutt of Indiana propose informally to repeal the Bill of Rights? Thomas was there to say it couldn't be done, at least not without the embarrassment of arresting him. When desperately poor sharecroppers in Arkansas formed the Southern Tenant Farmers Union in 1934, he kept going down South, risking his neck, defying vigilantes, winning the affection of people who had never before dared speak for their rights.

In the mid-thirties I didn't yet know him personally, for he was a great man and I just another YPSL. But I loved to hear him speak. As he shambled up to the podium, he would pull together the segments of his body that seemed to move on different planes of space; he would laugh along with us when he needled opponents, those sardonic thrusts being, we knew, the mere sharp edge of his fundamentally good nature; and then he would lose himself, either from craft or passion, in rapid, stammering perorations.

There was already talk that Thomas did not function nearly as well within the party as outside it. He wasn't single-minded or devious enough to be a strong party leader; he couldn't content himself with the snap formulas of "left" or "right"; he made the "mistake" of revealing to anyone who cared the mounting intellectual doubts that bothered him. He was badly torn between the imperatives of morality and the devices of politics, between all that had made him a Socialist and whatever it might be (who really knew?) that in America could yet make socialism a political option. If he partly shared the feeling of his younger comrades that recent events in Europe had shown the helplessness of reformism, he also knew in his bones that in the United States "revolutionary" politics could lead only to the sterility of the sect.

He was a superb tribune and would have made a great popular

leader, if there had been a popular movement behind him. As it was, he allowed himself to be torn apart by the socialist dilemmas of the thirties. He let himself be excessively influenced by the sectarian-academic young Marxists who had been "radicalized" at a pace somewhat more in tune with debate at City College than life in the United States. I think he really knew better, but he went along with the young leftists, partly because they flattered him—not in any crude personal way, but through appeals to his idealism—and partly because they were his, all he really had. They loved him, at least until the moment came, as it almost always did, when they abandoned him out of what they cried was overwhelming need and some of us muttered was simply opportunism. Even when these leftists of yesterday shamefacedly avoided him, Thomas would rarely show bitterness, only a sort of caustic exasperation. It might have been better for American socialism had he been a little less responsive to his followers, a little readier to stick by his own perceptions.

Suppose he *had* stuck by his own perceptions, avoiding both the sterilities of the Old Guard and the excesses of the younger "revolutionaries." Would it have made any real difference? I doubt it. Precisely what was most attractive about American socialism in the early thirties—its good feeling, its freshness, its lack of ideological fixity—made it peculiarly susceptible to raids from the New Deal and assault by the Communists. Perhaps it was inevitable that American socialism destroy itself against the reef of the newly emerging welfare state, quite as decades earlier the German sociologist Werner Sombart had predicted it would shatter itself against "the reef of apple pie." Perhaps it was "fated" too that in the distraught thirties the authoritarian simplicities of the Communists would attract more people, not least of all intellectuals, than Socialists ever could. People wanted certainty and that we could not give them. Steadily, with a self-destructiveness arising largely from good faith, American socialism was letting slip through its fingers the second great opportunity that history had presented it. Steadily, the movement kept shrinking, with some prominent figures sliding into the milieu of New Deal politics and trade union leadership, others dropping away through disgust with factional bickering, and a small but significant number surrendering to one or another Far Left group, notably the Trotskyists.

American socialism was not yet a sect, but day by day it was getting closer.

Back in the Bronx, though vibrating keenly to the nuances of factional dispute, we remained faithful to the daily tasks of the movement. We still kept trying to reach out to the workers, mostly Jewish workers, who for the first time in years were enjoying a certain improvement in their conditions as a result of unionization. Their radicalism was slowly being weakened by their appreciation of Roosevelt's reforms, and while we strove to demonstrate how feeble these reforms were, citing figures on continued unemployment and theories about the nature of capitalism, the Jewish workers had enough hard sense to recognize that in their constricted lives even small improvements meant a lot.

During warmer months we would go out a few times a week to· hold street meetings. Today the institution of the street meeting is almost forgotten, but in earlier decades it formed a vivid part of the city's political life. It was at once a mode of agitation, an inexpensive form of popular entertainment, and a training school where young speakers could learn to talk quickly and to cope with skilled hecklers.

Six or seven of us, armed with a platform, an American flag, and batches of socialist literature, would set up at a busy intersection of the East Bronx. Inept speakers—that is to say, most of us—could shout themselves hoarse in ten minutes; a skillful soapboxer could keep on for three-quarters of an hour, gathering a crowd of 150 people and bringing it all to a climax with a good sale of literature and an exciting question period. It was in the question period that you could tell the difference between mere ranters and real speakers. A candidate for debate would always rise up in the audience, sometimes a "rugged individualist" brandishing the one idea he remembered from high-school economics, who would ask on what ground we proposed to deny John D. Rockefeller or Henry Ford the right to pass on his wealth to his descendants. There followed a cascade of refutation, from sarcasm about the extent to which Rockefeller's or Ford's descendants ever did an honest day's work, to impassioned descriptions of how terrible were the labor conditions in the mines of Rockefeller and the plants of Ford (and they *were* terrible).

More ambitious speakers would take a crack at rough simplifications of the theory of surplus value; indeed, to be able to popularize Marxist economics, and thereby show one's comrades that one knew those points well, was a source of pride. Other questions might come from the Stalinists, who at that time were pretty thick in the Bronx. Their tone depended on the party line of the moment, sweetly coaxing or murderously hostile. If they asked about left-wing united fronts, we were prepared—really prepared!—with crushing replies about Stalinist duplicity in pre-Hitler Germany and the insane Stalinist theory of "social fascism" (that Social Democrats were "really" a wing of fascism). If they asked whether we were naive enough to suppose the bourgeoisie would be the first ruling class in history to surrender power without armed resistance, we found that harder to answer, since we weren't so sure ourselves.

As a street orator I was a total failure. Within a few minutes I could disperse a crowd that another speaker had taken an hour to bring together. If I spoke first, "to warm things up," I would start shouting at the top of my lungs and then look around with bewilderment: why was the street so empty?

In the East Bronx we had a comrade named Irving Panken who in a few minutes could achieve a magical rapport with a street audience. This other Irving had a high, reedy voice that cut through street noises like a blade; he seemed to pour into his oratory all the passion of his soul, a passion that did not otherwise emerge very easily. A feeling for the sheer outrageousness of life, the pain that gripped the years of the workers, broke through his rhetoric. The grief and anger that floated along with his spittle would shake people; a hush would come over the street, in a collective recognition that this boy was touching some tissue of experience that all of them knew to be tender. Some of these listeners were expert at judging street speakers, quite as their fathers had been at judging cantors, and when the other Irving finished, you could hear a murmur, "Dos haist a redner" (That's what I call a speaker!). That he spoke in English did not lessen their admiration, for they cared less about vocabulary than melody and dialectic. If at this point someone was rash enough to start heckling, the other Irving, his passion spent, would break out with an aria of bitterness, his replies quick and crushing. We never won much of anything else, but we were good at winning debates.

Most of our meetings were held in Jewish neighborhoods, since that was where we lived; but sometimes, remembering that our task was to reach the American proletariat, we would prod ourselves to reach out to the gentiles. A handful of white kids, we'd go to Harlem and set up a platform on 125th Street and Lenox Avenue. Except for an occasional drunk or religious fanatic, we were never molested. Nor did we feel any sense of risk. The spectacle of white kids obviously well-spoken and sincere in their attacks on racial discrimination must have struck our audience as worth at least a few minutes of attention. Or maybe they were just bemused by the whole thing. Rarely did we encounter the kind of surging black anger that was to break out in the sixties. Far more dangerous were our occasional ventures into Irish neighborhoods, usually near Fordham Road in the northwest Bronx. Tacitly sharing, I suspect, the Jewish persuasion that the Irish are a violent people, we knew that there were numerous followers of the fascist Father Coughlin in these neighborhoods, and our fears were often warranted. We seldom got through such an evening without a scuffle, sometimes a rush of street toughs breaking up our meeting. Since our sense of beleaguerment was already acute enough, we usually avoided confrontations with our Irish brothers.

It was different in the Jewish neighborhoods. Attitudes of tolerance, feelings that one had to put up with one's cranks, eccentrics, idealists, and extremists, pervaded the Jewish community to an extent that those profiting from them did not always stop to appreciate. The Jewish labor movement had established a tradition of controversy and freedom, so that even when some groups like the Communists willfully violated this tradition, it still exerted an enormous moral power in the immigrant streets. Trotskyist meetings were sometimes broken up, but never spontaneously, only by decision of the Communist Party. Most of the time the Jewish neighborhood was prepared to listen to almost anyone with its characteristic mixture of interest, skepticism, and amusement. Not that these audiences were easily taken in by our grandiose speeches. You might be shouting at the top of your lungs against reformism or Stalin's betrayals, but for the middle-aged garment worker taking a stroll after a hard day at the shop you were just a bright and cocky Jewish boy, a talkative little *pisher*.

Even among the Stalinists, Jewishness counted in surprising

ways. I remember one evening in the late thirties when a Trotskyist street meeting was being harassed by a gang of Stalinists and a screeching lady heckler jostled a girl I knew, causing her glasses to fall and break. The girl—with how much guile or sincerity I could never say—started bawling that her mother would punish her for breaking the glasses, and the Stalinist lady, suddenly sympathetic, took her to a store to get a new pair. For the Stalinist lady, my friend had a few minutes earlier been a "fascist," but when trouble came and the glasses were broken, she must have seemed just a nice Jewish girl.

To speak at a street meeting was an art not easily mastered. It required either a complete abandonment to feeling or the canny manipulation of rhetorical devices. A speaker like the other Irving gave himself up to the inner flow of his passions and the result was trancelike. Other speakers were more calculating. Once, when there was a strike of bakers in the East Bronx, my YPSL circle rushed to the scene, eager to help the working class. It was a chilly fall night, the street dark, the bakery shut. Getting up on the platform, I felt overcome by a sense of desolation: a handful of comrades, a blackened bakery, not a soul in sight. I started to shout but soon stopped, my voice dwindling to a whisper. Then an old-time Socialist, August Claessens, got up to speak, and as if out of nowhere people started to gather. With an endless fund of amusing stories, all adapted to a simple socialist message, Claessens conversed rather than orated. The other Irving drew people through the ferocity of his emotions, Claessens relied on skills of intimacy.

About a week later, one night at dinner, my father turned to me with a velvety sarcasm and asked, "What do you have against that baker? A poor man tries to make a living, and you tell people not to buy his bread." Speechmaker though I now fancied myself, I found not a word to say. How had he learned about that meeting, a good fifteen blocks away? It turned out that a *landsman* of his had been passing by and had hurried to report to my father the carryings-on of his errant son. As for the question itself, I answered it about as well as I would answer all his other questions.

We were living in New York and New York was said to be part of the United States. Yet, at least in our imaginations, we were making New York over into another country, a place apart from the Old World and the New. It was a New York cast in tropes of extremity. It was New York as both imperial city and center of action, the powerhouse of capitalism and crucible of socialism. Like everyone else trying to survive in this city, we were pummeling it into the shape of our needs, but what we saw was not wholly delusion; it contained bits and pieces of reality. Years later, writing about the New York of his imagination, the critic Lionel Abel joked that in the thirties it "became the most interesting part of the Soviet Union . . . the one part of that country in which the struggle between Stalin and Trotsky could be openly expressed." This New York also shaded off into myth, but usefully, for that was how some of us needed to see the city: enemy of philistines, antithesis of hayseed, proudly internationalist in vision. So it was, a little.

Our sense of America was less hostile than embarrassed, and sometimes it even gave way to sentimentality. I was always susceptible—others too, I think—to movies about small towns with hayrides, chummy homes, roomy, passionate cars, and rosy cheerleaders. Our socialist girls were vivid, bright, sometimes beautiful, but none looked like the prairie creamcakes whose pictures reached us from Hollywood. These movies, with their enticements of space and ease, formed a kind of Depression pastoral. One summer I fell into reading American farm novels by Hamlin Garland, Ruth Suckow, and Willa Cather, and in our airless Bronx apartment I suffered anxiously, waiting for the rains that alone could spare the crops and save the farms. When once in a rare while I traveled by train, I loved to sit up late into the night watching through the window the lights of towns and villages, seemingly lost forever in the native distance. And when I read Sherwood Anderson's *Winesburg, Ohio*, that fragile classic of another America, I saw that while its central figure shared with me emotions of loneliness, there was also a distance between us, for he was out there in alien territory while I belonged, hopelessly and forever, to New York.

The New York we knew was not just a vital metropolis brimming with politics and confusion; it was also brutal and ugly, the foul-smelling jungle Céline would evoke in *Journey to the End of Night*. New York was frightening, not in the way it later became, as a place of violence and crime, but as a social vortex into which you might be dragged down, forever beyond rescue. So many people seemed lost here, pinned to the line of subsistence. New

York was also the embodiment of that alien world which boys and girls raised in an immigrant home had been taught to regard with suspicion. It was "their" city in ways that one's parents could hardly have explained and probably didn't need to; later, once I had conquered the arcane knowledge of Marxism, it became "their" city in a new, supposedly deeper, way.

The provinciality of New York in the thirties, which regarded a temporary meeting of ethnic subcultures and social crisis as if it were an eternal fact of nature, led us to suppose that only here in this city could one bear to live at all, though if one weren't in utter revolt against society, we thought, life in New York could only be constricted, mean, intolerable. In the mythology of the movement New York took on a sheen of glamor, for it was always "the party center," no matter which party it might be. Here you could listen to the leaders and intellectuals, here it was usually possible to fill a fair-sized hall with comrades and critics.

There were places in New York I knew intimately. In our very distance from the city—caused less by a considered "alienation" than by an unacknowledged shyness beneath our claims to bravado —we made for ourselves a kind of underground city, a series of stopping places where we could ease our restlessness, forget a little about our politics, and feel indifferent to our lack of money. In the winter there were "socials" given by branches of the movement to raise funds for their headquarters, and I would go to them shyly and dutifully. There were the free concerts at the Metropolitan Museum where—it was a matter of pride to know—the music was not very good but we found comfort on the marble floor, huddling together in our winter coats, trying to resist a little the romantic surges of Beethoven and Schubert. There were the movies on Forty-second Street, where amid clouds of steam and stench we let our political virtue be compromised by European art films. Here we saw Renoir's *Grand Illusion*, which shook us beyond control or reasoning. Half-heartedly we tried to criticize the absence of a class approach, Renoir's stress upon endurance rather than revolt, but I think we were moved precisely by what we said was its weakness. We were moved by its vision of a solidarity beyond class or nation, resting on a pacifism of friends.

We thought of ourselves as exposed to the coldest winds in the coldest capitalist city, and in many ways we were, but we were still living in a somewhat sheltered place. Not only because the movement had a way of turning in upon itself, finding security in the very isolation our speeches deplored, but also because our life, for all our desire to cut ourselves off from official society, was shaped by the fact that in New York the Jews still formed a genuine community reaching into a dozen neighborhoods and a multitude of institutions, within the shadow of which we found protection of a kind.

Being protected could also mean getting roughed up a little. What you believed or said you believed did not matter nearly so much as what you were, and what you were was not nearly so much a result of decision as you wanted to suppose. If you found a job— but who expected to?—it was likely to be in a "Jewish industry," and if you went to college it was still with Jewish students. We did not realize how sheltering it was to grow up in this environment, just as we did not realize how the "bourgeois democracy" we railed against made it possible for us to speak and survive. It was all part of our mania, perhaps the century's mania, for *willing* a new life.

There were other shelters. Legends about the thirties center, reasonably enough, on City College, but I think it was really the high schools that gave New York a good part of whatever morale it managed to keep during the Depression years. There were some good, solid high schools and I went to one of them, De Witt Clinton in the northwest Bronx.

Midway through high school I decided to become a crackerjack agitator—not so easy for a quiet, reflective boy. I joined a demonstration in the school's lunchroom organized by the communist and socialist student groups, several of us getting up on chairs to shout rhythmically, "Lower lunchroom prices!" (We had read that you reached the masses through economic demands.) We were hauled before the school principal, who asked me whether I ever bought my lunch downstairs. Sheepishly I had to admit that for the past two years I had been bringing jelly and cream cheese sandwiches from home in a paper bag. I muttered something about the principle of the thing and the old grouch, as I imagined him, smiled faintly—maybe he was glad his teachers were knocking *some* idea of principle into our heads. He answered that the lunchroom was running at a loss, and that if I wanted to take it over he would try to arrange that, but I quickly saw through this bourgeois trickery and turned him down flat. He let us go with a reprimand and I felt relieved that news of this misadventure would not reach my parents, for I was decidedly less afraid of getting suspended from school than of having to explain it all to my father. And the suspicion began to wriggle its way into my head that we socialist kids had been dragged into a piece of foolishness by our communist rivals, who were then—the Popular Front had not quite arrived— taunting us to become more militant. We did join with the communist students in more serious demonstrations, this time against ROTC on campus, and these brought police on horseback to the campus. There, I think, we had some right on our side. Hatred of militarism was a feeling shared by many students, including some who didn't think of themselves as radical: it was a hatred that had become an ingrained part of the culture, an echo of the intense revulsion against the butchery and lies of the First World War.

Our teachers worked hard trying to drive some knowledge, even a few ideas, into our heads. Apart from algebra and gymnasium (where, between knee bends, I endured political harangues with an anti-Semitic flavor), there was pleasure in the work of learning.

I had already been exposed to a good mind during my last year of junior high school, when an English teacher named Mr. Solomon strode into the classroom booming out in a gravelly voice, "It is an ancient mariner . . ." I was scared out of my skin—what was this maniac up to? A good forty years later I can still hear that thundering recital whenever anyone mentions the name of Coleridge. With this impassioned teacher we read *The Odyssey* in verse translation, *A Tale of Two Cities, Hamlet, The Rime of the Ancient Mariner*, and *Ivanhoe*—the last, he snarled, "for the babies." Being thirteen or fourteen years old, we did not dare show a lack of appreciation and thereby, through Mr. Solomon's intimidating solicitude, came to appreciate.

Each week we wrote a composition—never, thank heaven, "creative," and aways done in class, since Mr. Solomon grinned wickedly that he was tired of reading pickups from encyclopedias. Once, looking over a notably pretentious paper of mine, he called me up to his desk and whispered in my ear (it was just for me, really a sign of affection), "You have a gift for bullshit—cut it out!" I blushed, perhaps more for the word than the message, and I tried to cut it out. When the class was "bad," or Mr. Solomon thought we needed some mental exercise, he made us diagram sentences. Now and then I find myself trying to remember what an "adverbial objective" is.

The teachers at De Witt Clinton were not equally inspired, but many were very good. One English teacher talked too much about the Popular Front, but since she also got me to read *Jude the Obscure*, a novel I fell in love with, I forgave her politics. Another English teacher, Mr. Stone, was a muscular WASP who had been an IWW man in his youth, and that lent him a reddish halo. He wasn't very reddish in class; in fact, he had an exasperating way of assigning us reactionary tasks. He made us read Edmund Burke's *Speech on Conciliation with the Colonies*, and for five or six weeks we analyzed the arguments and structure of this great piece of writing till I loathed Burke as if he had done me a personal wrong. Years later, in preparing for a political debate, bits of remembered language and modes of argument would suddenly come back to me from those cool dissections of Burke's rhetoric.

There was an air of intellectual openness and eagerness in that school, a feeling that we were being led, gently or roughly, into experiences somehow good for us, though it was only natural that as young human beasts we should resist them. Once, in a class on European history, the teacher asked me to explain dialectical materialism and, child of folly that I was, I explained. That teacher may have lured me into this trap with sly motives, yet in a way he was right: one of the things that happen in a good school is that young people are encouraged safely to overextend themselves.

In the thirties the educational institutions of the city were still under the sway of a unified culture, that dominant "Americanism" which some ethnic subcultures may have challenged a little, but which prudence and ambition persuaded them to submit to. Our high schools combined legends of Horatio Alger with plays of William Shakespeare, being innocently persuaded of their compatibility; even those radical teachers who proposed to criticize this linkage did so in the name of a superior version of the commonly accepted culture.

The culture of New York was then still a culture of the word. For many young people the public library was still a place of refreshment and pleasure. Daily newspapers were numerous, not yet challenged by other "media." Theaters presented plays with acknowledged scripts. Serious magazines really influenced educated opinion. Men with free time gathered in cafeterias and parks to discuss politics. Political campaigns meant speechmaking, not just handshaking. A high-school graduate would have read at least a novel by Dickens and a play by Shakespeare. There was a shared belief in the value—indeed, the honor—of gaining a high-school diploma, even among many who did not stay long enough to get it. This was not utopia, far from it. But the city did have a unity of culture, and that unity has since been broken.

Once a political movement starts to falter, its decomposition takes on a life of its own. You feel as if you have been invaded by some mysterious sickness, a Hardyesque fatality. Leaders lose their power to persuade; the bonds of fraternity crack; the very aroma of the movement—the air in the office, the mood at a meeting—turns bad. It's no longer a pleasure to go down to the party headquarters, to kibitz and gossip with comrades. At meetings everyone seems to be counting the house. For the few to whom it matters, this decline can be agonizing, like a secret, nagging pain. Two or three times now I have lived through this experience, and I've become, I suppose, an expert at spotting the symptoms. When I recognize them I feel ashamed, the way one does upon noticing that a friend has begun to show the pallor of disease. I want to flee.

One major symptom, by 1936 or so, was that many of the "practicals" were dropping out of the party. These were good people, usually Jewish trade unionists who still wanted to reconcile their daily work in the garment center with being stirred now and then by a socialist speech. They had little patience with Marxist theorizing; they had worked, sometimes hard, for the party; their bias, half through weariness, was toward day-to-day tasks.

Between the "practicals" and the aspiring young intellectuals there was an unavoidable clash. Each attacked the other and drew blood. "They" seldom bothered to reflect on the crisis of socialism, lacked concern with ultimate goals, failed to understand our obsession with the Russian question. "We," said our opponents, were sadly cut off from the realities of American politics and were letting socialist thought congeal into scholasticism. In a large movement two such groups might find space to live together, but in a movement shriveling into isolation they simply got on each other's nerves.

I may be darkening the picture somewhat. In 1936 the several thousand people remaining in the Socialist Party were by no means simply despairing. To be sure, Norman Thomas's Presidential vote had gone down from 884,781 in 1932 to 187,572 in 1936, and segments of the party had all but collapsed. But we consoled ourselves with the thought that many people were voting for Franklin D. Roosevelt not because they had turned against socialism, but because they saw him as "the lesser evil" (while evading the fact that our political system always puts a heavy premium on "the lesser evil").

Ideology, in all its fierce allure, was reaching us as rarely before in the history of American socialism. Theoreticians, most of brief tenure, kept springing up. We were discovering the excitement of theses and documents, platforms and polemics, "fresh starts" and "shaking off dead weight"—all those devices by which actual losses can be made to look like possible gains. Factions multiplied. From little ones emerged littler ones.

The major cause of socialist decline could be put in one word: Roosevelt. That canny politician, half savior and half confidence man, ruined us. He was saving capitalism through modest reforms. We Socialists were right, for all the good it did us, in pointing out that unemployment was not seriously eased until the country turned to war production. In a nation, however, where the myths of individualism and free enterprise continued to grip the popular imagination, even Roosevelt's small steps toward the welfare state met violent opposition from the Right. So it was hard to tell our friends that the social and labor legislation for which we had campaigned so long were inconsequential, just because enacted by a Democrat; harder still to make persuasive the argument that it made no difference whether Roosevelt or some Republican became President. When more cautious, we said it made no *fundamental* difference, but most people felt that there could be a lot of important differences short of fundamental.

In the socialist ranks there persisted an old-style Debsian rectitude, morally admirable but not really able to cope with the complexities that Roosevelt was introducing into capitalist society. Veteran Socialists had insisted upon voting only for the party ticket —I held to this "principle" even years after I had stopped thinking it essential, so that the first time I pulled a lever for someone not on a socialist line I felt sick. By the late thirties the Socialist Party was not really a party anymore, if by a party one means a national organization various in composition, requiring loyalty only to a general set of principles, and by no means fixed into an ideological stance. The socialist movement was now trapped somewhere between party and sect—really a society of friends that enjoyed neither the flexibility of a party nor the firmness of a sect.

If we needed one last push toward annihilation, it came from the several hundred Trotskyists who entered the Socialist Party in 1936 and remained there fourteen months, until August 1937. Virtuosos of ideology, fancying themselves a resurrected bolshevik vanguard, the Trotskyists brought with them a mixture of intellectual rigor and destructive quarrelsomeness. A few of them undertook the entry out of a sincere wish to create a new left-wing, anti-Stalinist alignment; the majority saw it as a maneuver to chip away left-wing Socialists.

The political differences between left-wing Socialists and Trotskyists were then barely visible to anyone but a learned expert. The leftward-moving Socialists were at the border posts of Leninism, though in style and character still largely shaped by the world view of social democracy. Similar tensions between idea and attitude could be found among left-wing Socialists throughout the world, but in America, being few in number and without much self-confidence, we were peculiarly susceptible to Trotskyist lures.

Between someone moving leftward within a socialist space and someone, however heretical, emerging from the communist milieu, there really are major differences—less in formal ideology than in conduct and values. These differences became clear only with time, and in those hectic years, when we had reason to think that the world was heading toward utter destruction and socialism seemed the one transforming hope, we wanted to brush aside such differences. It seemed the left thing to do. The Trotskyists brought with them an aura of certainty, a quickness in referring to Marxist texts, a pride in factional strife, a system of relationships resembling the internal arrangements of a religious sect. Precisely this insistence upon their assured historical future as the vanguard of tomorrow's vanguard, made it all but impossible for them to fuse with any other group. Yet precisely these qualities of their behavior also aroused in us a grudging admiration. The Trotskyists were the people who *knew*. They knew why the Russian Revolution had succeeded, they knew why it had been betrayed, they even knew how it might recur. They seemed professional, though it took some time before we understood that they were merely monolithic. They had "positions" on every conceivable question. They bore an air of pride as the last true voice of October. They carried with them the tragic aura of the great fallen leader whose word they passed on through print and whisper. They held fast to a claim for revolutionary purity, and was this not what we, in our amateurish way, had been searching for all through the thirties?

Some of the Trotskyist leaders, men like Max Shachtman, James Burnham, Joseph Carter, were indeed brilliant intellectuals: brilliant with the blinders of system, brilliant at polemic, nuance, and hair-splitting. They overwhelmed some of us the way the Russian Bolsheviks must have overwhelmed European radicals in 1920–21. The first time I heard Max Shachtman speak, I was stunned. He came to City College in 1937 to debate the Moscow trials with Morris Schappes, a Stalinist who had recently been fired from his job as English instructor. Even someone less wooden in speech than Schappes would have had trouble coping with Shachtman's staccato devastation. He races through a list of defendants at the Moscow trials, recalling their roles in the October Revolution— political leaders, army commandants, members of Lenin's Central Committee. Is it conceivable that these men could be accomplices of Hitler? He picks up Schappes's unfortunate analogy to Benedict Arnold, showing that the true analogy would be to Arnold seizing power and destroying Washington, Jefferson, Madison, Franklin. He tears to pieces the "evidence" presented at the trials, with a savage, sardonic contempt for the falsehoods of Stalinism. I feel exhilarated. This is what it means to be a Marxist leader, cut from strong bolshevik cloth—not the flimsies of our faltering Socialists! Politics could be tournament, deep knowledge, high-wire virtuosity, opera, circus, all brimming with passion and assault.

By the time the Trotskyists were kicked out of the party, they had done their work. They took with them two or three times as many people as they had come in with, and as their leader, the wily James P. Cannon, later said, "The Socialist Party was put on the sidelines. This was a great achievement, because it was an obstacle

in the path of building a revolutionary party." Of such achievements the history of American radicalism has had no lack, though
Cannon never quite managed also to put bourgeois society or
Stalinism "on the sidelines." I myself was one of a tiny group who
at the last minute went along with the Trotskyists, enchanted cap-
tives heading straight into the hermetic box of a left-wing sect.

2

Life in a Sect

If I know your sect I anticipate your argument.
—EMERSON

For two or three years I was an almost total believer. Whatever powers of skepticism—never very great—were available to a young radical in the thirties, by now had been all but snuffed out. A little did remain, and it showed itself mostly as a hesitant opposition that a few friends and I put up against an effort to transform the Trotskyist youth organization from a lively, talkative league of bright kids into a disciplined "legion" of junior revolutionists. This effort was foolish, perhaps reckless, though it came about through the promptings of Trotsky himself, the "Old Man," as we called him. He was still using political lenses ground in 1917, and what they allowed him to see of the American landscape was sadly blurred. He did not understand that a "vanguardist" youth movement had neither place nor possibilities in America. Some of us chose to suppress our residual doubts, not about Marxism itself, which seemed powerful and valid, but about the full-scale application of Marxism to America. We spoke of adapting Marxism to American circumstances, without considering that the more serious the adaptation, the less there might remain of Marxism. But if my resistance was feeble to that clammy encirclement through which a sect secures its converts, it may have had some value in preparing

36

me for later heresies. There really is no such thing as an "almost total believer"—the "almost" either expands or contracts.

We have had hundreds of left-wing sects in America, but they have seldom thrived. When you think about it this seems odd, since there is a long history of religious sectarianism among us. The heritage of Protestantism, with its increasingly extremist sects splitting away from one another, has probably contributed a touch of rigidity to our radicalism. So too the tradition of moral dissent in the line of Emerson and Thoreau, with its counterposition of individual rectitude to ordinary politics. Even Debsian socialism in its brief flare-up contained a strong sectarian current: the unbending children of the dawn. Yet our political sects have withered while the religious ones flourished. Sometimes there has been a crossing of energies, bringing little good to either religion or politics. The fundamentalist temper, in fact, has been a recurrent disaster in American radicalism.

The sect creates a life apart, casting aside the imperfections of the world as given and hoping, through disciplines of withdrawal, to establish its own "little world" as a haven for the elect. It is chosen to be the vanguard of History, a vessel of the Idea. Eventually it will triumph over enemies and skeptics, but meanwhile it has to huddle in its own bit of space. It endures a hibernation of waiting. Its members know they must suffer the pain of helplessness, and in time they learn to celebrate this pain as a sign of vindications to come.

Between the religious sects, strong in America, and the political sects, merely numerous, there is a curious symmetry of traits. The sociologist Lewis Coser remarks: "The religious sect, as distinct from the Church, which contains within its fold both saints and sinners, consists of the visible community of pure saints; the political sect, as distinct from the political party which aims at encompassing a high proportion of the mass of the electors, consists of specifically qualified members, 'professional revolutionists,' certified Marxists. . . . The party is inclusive, the sect exclusive."

A religious sect can content itself with waiting. After all, the validity of its faith does not depend on a head count of the faithful. The religious sect requires only that the vision of the Second Coming remain strong—the Coming itself need not be near. But things are harder for the political sect because it claims to be engaged with this world, not another. The political sect may decline into that damp stagnation which many religious sects find comfortable, but because of its ideology the political sect must keep trying to bring its isolation to an end. The political sect has to *remind* itself not to slump into that withdrawal from the world which often seems its natural condition, perhaps even its deepest desire.

Both kinds of sects say they look forward to universal acceptance. But until that happy moment the religious sect can get along pretty well, while the radical sect must drive itself to step out in front of the toiling masses, to become their brain and fist. The masses seldom listen: they are mired in "false consciousness." For the political sect the October Revolution looms as a glorious memory, but also an irksome reminder of failure: why can't what was done once be done again? Done again, if only the right strategy is found?

The Marxist sect seems doomed to a state of perpetual inner warfare between what it is and what it supposes it wants to be. It tears itself apart in a search for deviations, those rents in the political line that might explain why it has failed to achieve its "historic mission." The more the political sect slips into the comforts of isolation—real comforts, by the way—the more its conscious members must chafe against them. There is no peace.

What holds a sect together is mostly the brittle paste of doctrine. A religious sect can get by on exemplary faith, it has eternity on its side, but the political sect has to pin everything on the rightness of doctrine. The party line becomes its most precious good. To call into doubt even an inch of that line is to endanger its survival, so that, in a way, it is quite right to cast out heretics. In a sect, heresy is never incidental.

These are observations of retrospect, purchased at the price of error. Other people had seen as much decades earlier, but in politics it's rare for anyone to learn from predecessors. In any case, once the Trotskyists, now reinforced by a batch of young recruits from the shattered Socialist Party, set themselves up in 1938 as an independent organization, they were no longer quite a "pure" sect. Gains in membership threatened purity of character. At the core of the new organization, called the Socialist Workers Party (SWP), there remained a Trotskyist cadre, grizzled and redoubtable; surrounding it was a crowd of eager socialist kids. Some of the Trotskyist veterans, expelled from the communist movement in the late twenties, were sharp-witted arguers who knew in part of their minds that early American communism had been—what? A jungle? A circus? Yet it was the communist milieu that had made them what they were, and many looked back with nostalgia to the old days of "heroic" factional struggle within the CP. By now they could also look back to their own Trotskyist faction fights, which newcomers like me were invited to regard with awe.

Those had been the days! The days when Marxists were steeled to firmness of will, when speeches lasted for hours, when factional debates, unspoiled by proletarians having to get up early the next morning, spilled over into the stretches of night. No movement is more conservative in its feeling for tradition than the revolutionary. I have heard stories that sometimes, when newcomers were recruited by Marxist sects, they would be given as their first reading matter old "internal bulletins," those yellowed records of obscure factional disputes; but nothing of the sort ever happened to me. Perhaps these are just legends from legendary times.

The newly formed party had some trade unionists trying to act as radicals in their unradical setting. The Trotskyists had built up a concentration of strength in Minneapolis, where they controlled Local 544 of the teamsters' union and had recruited a few dozen honest-to-goodness American workers. They boasted of the Dunne brothers (especially the formidable Vincent Dunne), both active party members and talented union leaders. Young people had come into the SWP eager to work for socialism, and on a number of campuses we had articulate groups. There were also some intellectuals in the ranks who cared about the questions to which intellectuals devote themselves. James Burnham, a philosophy professor haughty in manner and speech, was a major spokesman: logical, gifted, terribly dry. Other intellectuals like Sidney Hook and the editors of *Partisan Review*, Philip Rahv and William Phillips, had come close to the party. Happy to have won such converts and allies, the Trotskyists felt a little nervous about the ideological contaminations that might follow—nervous in the bristling style that self-educated people affect in the presence of trained intellectuals.

Some of our leaders were "pure" sect types, functionaries burrowing like moles in their dinky pasteboard offices, maneuvering for petty advantage or personal gratification, seldom emerging into the sunlight of ordinary existence. It was as if the sect were the world. The two main leaders, James P. Cannon and Max Shachtman, seemed more complex. A stony-faced Irishman, Cannon wore an air of resoluteness suggesting that, if only lucky enough to have been born a Russian, he would have been one of those Old Bolsheviks, silent and unbending, who kept forever faithful to Lenin. He had been an IWW organizer in his youth, then a founder of American communism, and later the first of its leaders to respond to Trotsky's call. He commanded a measure of organizational shrewdness, though not much of the gift for theory that Marxists admire. Holding a small group together can be harder than leading a mass party, and Cannon did this partly through a posture of self-assurance: the kind of man who has been in strikes, who went to Moscow, who knew about real life. Not one of your theory-spinners from City College; no, a pragmatic, almost an American Bolshevik who, if not handicapped by ideals, would have made a powerful trade union leader. And when it came to politics he could always fall back, as he did, on the notes, letters, theses that flowed continuously from the Old Man in Coyoacán.

Shachtman, by contrast, was a New Yorker to the bone, quick of speech, adoring jest, cosmopolitan in taste. His mixture of irony and passion, so familiar to Jewish intellectual life, was not always appreciated by the Midwestern proletarian comrades who took earnestness as proof of devotion. In Shachtman's appearance there was nothing impressive, certainly nothing of that steely manner Cannon cultivated. His was a face you'd expect to find in a bazaar or a diamond center: swarthy, expressive, shrewd. To some, Shachtman never seemed a true leader, for a true leader was not the sort of man who made people laugh or loved crazy jokes. In a large movement he would have found a place as writer and speaker—he was a superb though cruel debater; but in the cramped quarters of the sect he seemed uneasy as ideologue and leader. Every once in a while he showed alarming signs of thinking for himself, as if his large store of Marxist-Leninist knowledge cried out for independent use.

Both these men, though for sharply different reasons, chafed now and then under the bonds of the sect, yet the logic of their politics held them fast within it. The Trotskyists were trying sincerely to act like a political party, even if a tiny one—they ran candidates, issued a popular paper, the *Militant*, and worked hard in the unions. But the center of their concern, given the imperatives of the century, had to remain ideological. And the paradox of it all was that, try as they might to transform themselves into a party, the Trotskyists mattered only insofar as they remained a sect. In "the labor of the negative," to twist Hegel's phrase, they performed brilliantly, advancing Trotsky's critique of Stalinism, exposing the Moscow trials, partly breaking the hold upon the intellectual world of those befuddled writers who praised Stalin's dictatorship as a "higher form of democracy." None of this was easy. It meant putting up with the hatred of Stalinists and their influential friends; it meant bearing the ridicule of liberals who sneered at "paranoid accusations" against the "Soviet experiment"; it meant accepting isolation and contempt. To feel that one has a grip on an essential truth which most of the world prefers to ignore—this is a stance with large risks of self-righteousness. It was only natural that now and again we should succumb to this risk. To certain liberals, intent upon seeing at least two sides to every question and notably cheerful about one major form of European despotism, the Trotskyists seemed tiresome scolds. Tiresome or not, they were among the few people in the thirties telling the truth about Stalinism, or at least part of the truth.

Yet once the Trotskyists ventured on a politics of their own, trying in the America of Franklin Delano Roosevelt to resurrect the tired bones of Leninism, they shrank to a historical oddity. They might spur themselves to "mass work" in the hope of emerging as a proletarian vanguard, but they mattered only insofar as they kept to ideology. Their passion, but also their single possibility, was to testify against the monstrous violation of that Soviet "socialism" to which millions had pledged themselves.

For a brief moment it did seem as if they might break out of their isolation. In 1938 the Nazis announced a meeting in Madison Square Garden, but the Jewish community failed to respond in any dramatic way. An SWP leaflet calling upon people to demonstrate at the Garden was reproduced in the *Daily News*. A leader of the Minneapolis teamsters, Farrell Dobbs, came to New York to instruct us in the arts of street combat (wear a hat and thick jacket, carry a rolled, heavy newspaper). The night of the Nazi rally thousands of people were milling about the Garden. We hoisted "the other Irving" and then Shachtman onto our shoulders; their piercing voices cracked the air with denunciations of Nazism; a parade of thousands stormed through the streets. Rapport with the masses, a path to their desires!

Alas, it was not so. The masses cared only about demonstrating against the brown shirts, nothing about the programs of those who had called the demonstration. The SWP gained perhaps a dozen members from this "mass action"; the "revolutionary lessons" it drew interested no one but itself. Soon fevers cooled; we were back in our familiar isolation.

To yield oneself to the movement—really a sect, but we called it "the movement," and out of courtesy to the past so shall I—was to take on a new identity. Never before, and surely never since, have I lived at so high, so intense a pitch, or been so absorbed in ideas beyond the smallness of self. It began to seem as if the very shape of reality could be molded by our will, as if those really attuned to the inner rhythms of History might bend it to submission. I kept going through the motions of ordinary days: I went to college, had a few odd jobs, dated girls occasionally, lived or at least slept at home. But what mattered—burningly—was the movement, claiming my energies, releasing my fantasies, shielding me day and night from commonplace boredom. (Later, no longer burning so fiercely, I found boredom to be a hateful intimate, my secret sharer, for what could again be so exciting, what could rouse comparable visions of triumph and martyrdom?) The movement gave me something I would never find again and have since come to regard with deep suspicion, almost as a sign of moral derangement: it gave my life a "complete meaning," a "whole purpose." I learned to walk the hedgehog's rigid tracks, vain in their straightness.

Saturdays I would take the subway down from the Bronx to our headquarters on University Place and Thirteenth Street, a ratty little red-brick building, sometimes to talk at meetings, sometimes to crank out leaflets, mostly to hang around for gossip and debate. Saturday evenings a gang of the dedicated young would meander through the city, eating at the Automat (hamburger three nickels, baked potato two nickels, milk one nickel, lemonade free if you were ingenious), and usually end up at a Forty-second Street movie. Sometimes we were in luck, a comrade had access to an apartment, that precious rarity in New York, and we hurried over for the pleasures of retreat and privacy.

There were bright and strong girls in the movement, students very much ahead of their moment and ahead also of their own self-regard. They were determined to behave as if our proclaimed belief in sexual equality had been realized, while in fact of course it was not. They would have regarded collective action by women within the movement as beneath their pride, perhaps as a demand for special indulgence, and that is one reason they could not mobilize themselves to counter the subtle and not-so-subtle sexual condescension to which they were subjected.

The movement had pretty much the same spectrum of personal conduct and sexual attitudes as the outer world, though in decidedly less crude forms and often with a strain of idealistic aspiration. Among young people a good-natured camaraderie prevailed, boys and girls working together, pairing off for a time, and suffering personal wounds with a severity that politics could neither explain nor assuage. At the far edge of the movement there was a bohemian fringe that from my little peak of rectitude I looked down upon. The truth is, I was afraid of it. I was afraid of the rumored dissoluteness of these bohemians who moved in and out of one another's apartments—that wasn't how we had been taught to live in the Bronx. To have been raised in a working-class family, especially a Jewish one, means forever to bear a streak of puritanism which, if not strong enough to keep you from sexual assertion, is strong enough to keep you from very much pleasure.

Among the leaders of the movement there were a handful who used their status for sexual conquest in rather ugly ways, and some of our girls behaved like vanguard groupies. But most of the leading comrades led reasonably stable lives, captive to the values of conventional romanticism. Women who became the wives or lovers of party functionaries had to expect a hard time—poverty and uprootedness—unless they themselves had good jobs; but they found some compensation in being close to the milling talk of the party leadership.

Most admirable of the women in the movement was a group of students who were seriously interested in politics and culture, intent upon battling for place and definition, and trying also to be sexually attractive in the styles mandated, more or less, by American society. I admired them and feared them. They must already have been encountering the problems that "advanced" young women would be struggling with a few decades later, but they didn't yet have the feminist vocabulary or sense of solidarity that might get them through rough times. They seldom complained, at least openly. They typed stencils, gave out leaflets, became organizers, spoke with a flaring eloquence. They declared themselves ready for a new and free life, partners in the adventure of socialism, even though back home their families, with whom they still usually had to live, were putting constant pressures upon them. We all knew that those of us not yet able to leave home had to put up with the nagging of anxious parents who worried that our politics would get us into trouble. Yet there was a tacit agreement that it would be bad form to say much about such unpleasant realities, as if it might dampen our ardor or deflate our claims to freedom.

Didn't the women feel they were suffering discrimination within the movement? Weren't they irked by our readiness to fall back onto the modes of condescension that prevailed in the outer world? Didn't they ever come together just by themselves, like the characters in Doris Lessing's *The Golden Notebook*, for searing, intimate talks, an exchange of sardonic notation? If they did, the rest of us knew little about it, and, what is still more telling, we seldom thought to ask.

Decades later I did ask and was told that young women in the movement had now and again talked among themselves, disturbed by feelings of their own inadequacy and resentful of the roles to which they were often confined. Yet they had not complained openly or strongly—why? Because it was unrealistic to hope to change everything; because it would be unsporting to make trouble in those difficult years; because it seemed possible that some of their deficiencies were their own fault.

Perhaps, before people can feel deeply about a problem, it has to be publicly defined in some harsh, even excessive manner. Perhaps the women in the movement felt that, in the fearful late thirties, it would have been a luxury to speak of their needs and desires. They were Marxists, but they were also American girls taught that it's only right to make it on your own.

Still, it's embarrassing to think back on the complacence that many of us showed toward the feelings of women comrades. The root of the matter may have been that we were programmatically untrained to engage with personal experience at all. The fate of the world hung heavily on our shoulders, yet we asked few questions about the lives, feelings, inner thoughts of those who were supposed to be our partners in making a new society.

Back in the Bronx, on nights after branch meetings, we often relapsed into a kind of male bonding: a retreat from the pressures of politics and sex, happily innocent of any underline of meaning. Five or six of us would troop off to a cafeteria, then take a long hike across the waist of the borough. These were "Max's boys," admirers of Shachtman's wit, tied at some unspoken level to his skepticism and willing to see everything—politics, New York, themselves—as comic spectacle. Mostly unemployed, they kept apart from the more stable comrades. One was an ill-favored curmudgeon, scarred in the face, crushed with ugliness by an unkind God but growlingly acute. He could quote Catullus as readily as Trotsky, loving Latin tags almost as much as his distribution of cruel nicknames (my first was "Skelly," for my extreme thinness, and my second "Fangs," for an ugly eye tooth). He in turn was known as Benny the Ape, and much as he must secretly have hated it, he could hardly object, so caustic was he in naming others. An utterly lost soul, he seemed the perfect candidate for a radical sect.

As if in planned contrast there was another loner, less likable and certainly less learned, named Abe, startling for the violence of his language, a terrorist of diatribe, a nihilist before we even knew the word. For him the movement had become the score for arias of mockery. Usually "the other Irving," sulking passionately, would tag along, as would a delicate fellow whom Benny called "Sister Herman," all splatter of approving laughter when the talk grew especially warm. Once in a while a loner even among these loners would show up, "English Charlie," speaking perfect Cockney in our pure Jewish streets. Where did we ever find this raggle-taggle of displaced creatures, half out of Damon Runyon, half out of Saul Bellow, with their spray of epigram and malice?

We'd set off at midnight, I the youngest of the unlikely half dozen. Now everything had hushed into quiet, no one was in sight.

All seemed carefree in the night, away from family and politics, though some secret anxiety always remained with me that I would get home too late and have to face hysterical scenes with my parents. Our walks were best in the springtime: the nights grew cool, a fraternal expansiveness came upon us, our enemies slept, the world was ours. We would listen with a half-guilty pleasure to Abe's panting malice. We would glide along in our Melvillian freedom, without any clear destination, away from the frustrations of the movement and, for me, the dreary thought that tomorrow morning, with some coins from Mama in my pocket for carfare and lunch, I would be taking the subway to City College or, if school was over, wandering through the streets of the Bronx, stopping at the library to read the liberal weeklies, passing the time in a haze of daydream and books.

What were we doing in those night rambles? I think we were improvising a "double plot," finding for ourselves the relief of grotesquerie and cynicism to parallel our public belief. All that free-floating talk constituted a sort of psychic steam discharging feelings and perceptions that our daytime political selves found hard to acknowledge. Making our passage through the empty streets, we were more honest, more desperate at night.

Once, walking through the drab center of the Bronx, then a patch of territory without either proletarian definition or middle-class pretension, I was heatedly arguing with a friend named Miltie Sacks, a really fierce young Marxist. We passed by a little candy store whose owner had been sitting up in wait for a sale, and my friend, who always seemed to have a few pennies more than the rest of us, treated me to an ice cream soda. Finished with his soda, he returned to the storekeeper for a little more seltzer in his glass. The man stared at him in dismay, and Miltie, no longer the steaming theoretician but a roly-poly Jewish boy, said in great earnestness: "But I *always* get more seltzer with my sodas . . ." The storekeeper turned wearily to his fountain, shrugging his Jewish shoulders as if his fragment of profit, the reward of his night's vigil, had just been dissolved in the bubbling glass.

This memory has stayed with me for some forty years, emblematic, in ways I cannot pretend to understand, of those years of revolt and submission.

*   *   *

The ritual of assuming a new identity began with a choice of "party names," pseudonyms of proposed rebirth. An odd sort of comedy! This movement at the farthest edge of American society, living closer to the turmoil of bolshevism than the travail of America, was now trying to will itself into a native cast. One supposed reason for taking "party names" was that we had to protect ourselves against informers, though I doubt that it really served this end. Taking a new name, as Lewis Coser has said, is to be "understood as an outward symbol of newly-achieved elite status and a decisive break with the outside world of one's past." Another reason we gave ourselves was that if we were going to penetrate the ranks of the American working class, it would surely be a little easier not to come bearing Jewish names. In fact, those Jewish comrades who did "colonize" in Midwestern industrial towns were rarely able to disguise themselves—and for that matter didn't need to, perhaps because anti-Semitism was not very strong among American workers, perhaps because those workers expected radicals to be Jewish anyway. We were caught up in a historical charade, trying to don the costumes of a resurrected bolshevism. The costumes didn't fit. Unacknowledged motives were also at work, having less to do with Marxist strategy than our own confused and unexamined feelings about Jewish origins.

Years later I learned that it was a common practice for Zionist leaders in Israel to change their names from the Yiddish-sounding ones they had been given in Poland and Russia to others that would sound more Hebrew. These people were not trying to escape Jewishness, only a certain kind of Jewishness. But for Ben Gurion, Eshkol, and Allon a new political role also required a new name. The comparison with the Zionists didn't relieve me of the embarrassment I felt when recalling the name-changing induced by American radicalism; but at least it made clear how uneasy has been the spiritual history of even the most "affirmative" of Jews in the twentieth century.

Since the movement yielded so few public gratifications, active members found themselves increasingly absorbed in its internal life. Feverish discussions, regular faction fights, a reasonably accessible hierarchy of leadership: these held our interest. Altogether, there were only a few of us—perhaps by 1939 a thousand members—in the Trotskyist youth group. Yet in being so few, were we not precious in the eyes of History, trainees for the grandeur of the future?

I was bright, eager, hard-working. I learned to speak with some fluency, and soon mastered the tricks of the polemicist—mobilize aggressive impulses, lie in wait for an opening, pounce! That was a path to becoming a leader, and precisely to the extent that we had few followers, we placed a high premium on leadership. Being a leader didn't mean that you sat back in a plush office, exempt from the dull tasks of organization. We were too small, too poor for that. I handed out thousands of leaflets, cranked mimeograph machines, carried platforms in the street, sold party literature, gladly surrendered my youth to the routine of meetings. To an outsider I seemed just a skinny kid who talked fast, but the insiders knew I was being groomed for leadership despite my bouts of skepticism, my petty-bourgeois intellectuality. Marks of status were valued, and at times we fought over them with a ferocity we would have been ashamed to acknowledge.

All this had its innocent side, not so different from elections to a student council. But there was also an ugly side: maneuvering by ambitious "youth" leaders, elaborate games (Marxist Monopoly) for nonexistent power, learning to mask commonplace ambition with high-minded talk. If you wanted to be elected to a leading committee, it wasn't enough that you enjoyed marks of distinction or desired some reward for your work; no, you had to present some "position" on this or the other question. Much of this is common to all youth organizations, but with us, just because we were so scornful of smaller human motives, there grew up a peculiar grandiosity. In a few instances genuine psychotics rose to leadership, young men projecting fantasies of domination and strutting about in a quasi-military style as if behind them stretched regiments of rebellion. The talk was of creating a "vanguard," but the practice, at times, was embarrassingly close to that of a cult. I disliked the "youth leaders" intuitively but could not yet make clear the grounds of my opposition. I disliked their interminable "documents" about the critical world situation, their circles of admirers serving as a kind of bodyguard, their high-flown speeches full of misused big words (a few old friends still joke about one such speech in which bourgeois society was denounced as a "succulent quagmire"). Alas, I didn't yet realize that my political disagreements might more cogently have been expressed as clinical insights. Decades later I heard stories about these aged "youth leaders," no longer in politics but now comfortable as functionaries in trade unions or communal organizations, still using the same grandiose methods they had perfected in the movement. Doesn't this prove the transferability of powers of delusion?

These, of course, were extreme instances. Most of the young people in the movement were not very different from young people elsewhere. Many of us kept a sense of the ridiculous: during our Saturday night wanderings, and sometimes even bluntly at meetings, we poked fun at the little Lenins and the pocket-size Trotskys. And yet, there was ambition . . . Tremendously devoted to the movement I certainly was; completely selfless, no. I wanted to distinguish myself, to be noticed, to become a leader.

To become a leader meant not only to work hard but to absorb the doctrines of the movement and learn to defend them in public speech. And we did learn. Decades later the conservative ideologue Irving Kristol, whom I confess to having recruited to the City College Trotskyist youth group in 1938, would generously acknowledge that from reading the Trotskyist theoretical journal, the *New International*, one could learn how to recognize and perhaps even compose a disciplined intellectual discourse. Kristol was right. The training we received in the movement was narrow—a training in the explication rather than examination of texts, in games of debate rather than play of mind. It was not very different, I suppose, from the training yeshiva students or Jesuit novices have been given over the centuries. It taught us to grasp the structure of an argument, the tactic of logical maneuver. It taught us, within limits, to speak and think, and to value discipline of mind.

I learned to read with an almost Talmudic care. I learned that serious study of a text required a pencil in hand—how much pride that pencil carried! I struggled through the turgid pages of Lenin, delighted in the brilliance of Trotsky. I became a sort of surrogate Russian, easy in references to the disputes between Lenin and Martov or the problem of when Stalinism declined from Thermidor to Bonapartism. Some of this was mere parroting, but some was the groundwork of real knowledge, not very different from young people of a later generation repeating the phrases of Marcuse or Leavis or Trilling. To command the Marxist doctrine became a badge of pride. If Shachtman, during one of his marathon speeches, made a joke about Karl Radek or threw out a fleeting mention of "the August bloc," those of us in the know felt as gleeful as a philosophy graduate student pouncing on a subtle point in a Wittgenstein blue book.

Some people thrived in this intellectual atmosphere, though later I came to feel that they were also crippled by it. During the late thirties I admired a fellow named Hal Draper, several years older than I, who had also come out of the Socialist Party. He was genuinely learned in Marxism, with a mind that marched from one theorem to another as if God were clearing his way. For him Marxism consisted of a set of axioms—by no means just to be repeated and indeed open to fresh interpretation, yet in the end irrefutable axioms. His mind was like a superb machine, and after a time one knew exactly how that machine would work. Still a pure Marxist-Leninist disdaining the wretched compromises to which people like me had sunk, Draper in the seventies published a book on Marxism superior in learning to most academic work on the subject; but even then he wrote as if almost everything remained as we had seen it thirty-five or forty years ago through the lens of anti-Stalinist "revolutionary socialism." He remained an *aficionado* of first principles.

The hermeticism of the movement was not just a result of habit or circumstance; there was a theory—there always is—to justify it. Despite all their efforts to break out of sect confinements, the Trotskyists still accepted the idea that in an era when Stalinism had largely destroyed the revolutionary heritage, it was impossible to build a mass movement and therefore necessary to speak mainly to "advanced workers." This usually meant, speak to the left-wing groups, and also accept as necessary, even purgative, the fratricidal bickering that obsessed the sectarian Left. It made possible a high level of esoteric discourse such as any group of specialists can reach; but the price was severe.

The movement was my school in politics, my school in life. When I'd meet certain professors of sociology or political science in later years, I fancied I could always tell they had come out of one or another radical group: they strained toward comprehensiveness of grasp, they spoke with a quick aspiration to theory. The same held even for certain trade union leaders, those who threw occasional phrases into their speeches about "social responsibility," phrases that did not come spontaneously to the lips of most union officials. The movement taught us skills that turned out to be useful in the bourgeois world. It imbued us with a fascination for the idea of history. It made us facile in the arts of ideological justification. And not always by intention, it brought us to a strong feeling for democracy, if only because the harassment we suffered at the hands of the Stalinists taught us to value freedom of thought rather more than our ideas would otherwise have allowed. Yes, the movement taught us to think, but "only along too well-defined lines." I take this last phrase from a comment that a City College teacher once made on a Marxist composition of mine, a "class angling" of Spenser's "Epithalamion," which I had inanely found to be a symptom of "social decay." That all-too-gentle comment burned itself into my mind as a salutary shaming, and the thought of it can still make me blush.

Clever enough in responding to familiar cues, we had little capacity for turning back on our own premises. Against opponents sharing Marxist premises we could argue well, but against those who did not we were sometimes bewildered. We had a keen sense of intellectual honor, but only a feeble appetite for intellectual risk. That is why we seldom grew disturbed when a comrade questioned a political tactic, but felt alarmed if he or she began to doubt an abstract tenet of Marxism. Consider anthropology. At some point in the late thirties the bad news reached me that Morgan's theory of ancient matriarchy, which Engels had relied upon in writing about the state and family, was now disproved. My own interest in anthropology has always been slight, and I still don't know who disproved Morgan or whether in fact he was disproved. Nor does the case for socialism quite rest or fall on any theory of ancient matriarchy. Still, I felt uneasy, as if a chink had been cut out of my world view, thereby perhaps threatening the whole of it. And in a way I was right—provided one has to have a system of universal application.

Still more serious was a brief encounter with Robert Michels's classic work on political parties, which left me with a permanent sense of disturbance, then doubt, regarding the problem of bureaucracy. (Nor was that doubt stilled by the two or three feeble sentences in Bukharin's book on historical materialism, to which I was sent for refutation.) The very need for coherence that enticed one into a complete intellectual system made total belief increasingly hard, once a flaw was revealed. Adherents of religion had for many centuries been noticing the same trouble.

Our main task in life seemed at times to be the "taking of positions." In the radical world a "position" is a very serious matter, accorded a value akin to that which mystics give to revelation. A "position" meant more than just taking a stand on some issue; it meant working up an elaborate theoretical analysis.

We took positions on almost everything, for positions testified to the fruitfulness of theory. Theory marked our superiority to "vulgar empiricist" politics, compensated for our helplessness, told us that some day this helplessness would be dialectically transformed into power. We took positions on the New Deal, the class nature of Stalinist society, strategies for Indian liberation, the "four-class bloc" proposed by the Chinese Communists, tactics for the French Left, the need for a labor party in the United States. Ideally a Marxist movement should have positions on everything, but since that wasn't really possible, it was good to have sister sects throughout the world that could fill in the positions that remained.

Consider the civil war in Spain. We favored "critical support" for loyalist Spain, since we wanted to see the fascists defeated while finding much to criticize in the politics of the Republic. But of course there was no real support that we could give, critical or otherwise. Yet how we hated the thought that our "positions" didn't make any difference! How we scorned it as "vulgar," pointing to examples of earlier Marxist groups that had taken the proper positions and thereby grown strong.

Sometimes common sense would break through, a triumph of nature over convention. A comrade might make a speech—one or two always did—pointing out that we had no adequate position on the American farmers, though it would have been more to the point to remark that we had no farmers. Did we favor nationalization of the land, cooperatives, the breakup of large farms, or what? Here glimmers of realism finally did break through. Cannon or Shachtman would remark sardonically about our "lack of cadres" in the farm belt, and we would all laugh with relief.

Most of the time, however, we discussed, debated, and did

battle about matters beyond our reach. It was a tribute to the power of the word, as if a correct formulation could create a desired reality. Theses, resolutions, programs would transform idea into substance. To take a sufficiency of positions was to complete the universe.

But it was not just ideology that bound us to the movement. Ideology mattered, though only the more ambitious among us really tried to master the intricacies of Marxist thought. Nor was it just the magnetic pull of group life that held us. Sooner or later we would all rebel against the exhausting routines of political activism. No, what drew young people to the movement—I'm tempted to say, to almost any movement—was the sense that we had gained not merely a purpose in life but a coherent perspective upon everything happening in the world. The movement gave us a language of gesture and response. It felt good to "know." Even in our inexpert hands Marxism could be a powerful analytic tool; we supposed we enjoyed a privileged relation to History. There was a keen pleasure in picking up a copy of the *New York Times* and reading it with that critical superiority, that talent for giving a "deeper" interpretation of events that we felt justified in claiming.

There is still another reason, perhaps the strongest of all, for the appeal of the movement. Marxism advances a profoundly dramatic view of human experience. Its stress upon inevitable conflicts, apocalyptic climaxes, inevitable doom, and glorious futures gripped our imagination. We were always on the rim of heroism; the mockery we might suffer today would turn to glory tomorrow; our loyalty to principle would be rewarded by the grateful masses. The principle of classical drama—peripeteia, or the reversal of fortune—we stood on its head, quite as Marx was supposed to have done to Hegel. The moment of transfiguration would come, if only we held firm to our sense of destiny.

A movement that raises in the imagination of its followers the vision of historical drama must find ways of realizing the dramatic in the course of its history. Since meanwhile we had to suffer the awareness of our fragility, we found excitement, that poor substitute for drama, in the recurrent faction fights that the taking of positions inevitably led to.

These disputes often concerned issues of genuine importance, with the movement groping toward problems that more conventional analysts would confront only decades later. Sometimes these disputes produced vivid writing and speaking in which the talents of leaders, blocked from public outlet, were released through wit and invective. But the faction fights surely had another purpose we could not then acknowledge: they were charades of struggle, substitute rituals for the battles we could not join in the outer world.

In the course of these fights, all energies were mobilized. The movement came to resemble a medieval convocation of theologians locked into months of debate on a proper interpretation of doctrine. People have been burned for less, but we could not burn, nor did many of us want to; so we hurled documents, speeches, polemics against one another. Special discussion meetings were held in downtown halls, Irving Plaza mostly, and when midnight came and we were still carrying on, both factions would chip in to pay the caretaker something extra so he wouldn't throw us out. The factions, now really parties within parties, met regularly. Language took on flame. Internal bulletins, bulging with thought and bluster, came out regularly.

The discussion meetings were like dialectical tournaments, with each faction presenting a squad of speakers prepared in advance, like knights arrayed at both ends of the field. One's capacity for endurance played an extraordinary role in these war games, and there were old-timers who prided themselves on battle scars from the legendary faction fights of the past. (My friend Manny Geltman reports that in one factional dispute a Greek comrade chased him with a knife because Manny called him an Albanian. Surely the comrade had sufficient provocation!)

Amid these bizarre rituals, intellectual life flourished. Power being utterly out of our grasp, the debaters could indulge in theoretical flights of untroubled purity, a refusal of the faintest pragmatic alloy. A man like Shachtman gave startling displays of virtuosity, some of it theater but some real thought. He excelled in destroying an opponent's use of citations from holy texts by restoring them to their proper context; he was devilish in his mockery of pretension and false learning. His shrill voice would rise to flourishes of passion, then suddenly bank to an utterly Jewish taste for the ridiculous. Even his opponents could not always suppress their delight in his skills.

There was comfort in it all. Fantasy spun: not more than two or three hundred people might be present at a discussion meeting, but who did not feel that in pulverizing opponents and smiting dunderheads there was just a touch of Lenin recalled, of Trotsky reenacted? Yielding ourselves to the delusions, as also to the serious issues of the debate, we could forget the coldness of the outer world.

An astonishing battery of skills came into play, and an unmeasured range of impulses also. There were the genuine pedants, the self-absorbed ranters, the sly Talmudists, the factional whips and thumpers invoking vanguard patriotism. And there were genuine seekers after truth.

A ritual combat has to be conducted properly, in accord with fixed rules. If at a discussion meeting a maverick wished to speak apart from the contending factions, democracy required that he be given the floor. Always there were one or two such spoilers, especially a man named Ed Friend, with a variant opinion of his own, who banged away in a ferocious voice though he himself, like Dickens's Mr. Boythorn, was gentle as a canary. Sophisticated adherents of the two factions would share an impatience to get such individualists out of the way, so that we could settle back into the orderly buffeting of dispute.

Both sides gained pleasure from watching these disputes move forward step by step, from jocular argument to deadly attack, from amiable introduction to split or near split—a drama in which the main fighters seemed bound by the fatalities of an action quite as much as the protagonists of a classical play. Sometimes, as in one great faction fight, things got a little out of hand: James Burnham, in his fish-cold style, remarked that his opponent, James P. Cannon, "liked to drink . . ." Here the crimson-faced Cannon rose up, so that we thought there might be a fist fight between the two Irishmen, until Burnham quietly finished his sentence: ". . . milk." But mostly, there was a decorum even in vituperation.

Some deviations from that decorum were permitted. One ardent factionalist was a fellow named Burt Cochran, who affected a tough-guy "proletarian" style. Rumor had it that Cochran had once been an aspiring concert pianist but, if true, this was a youthful blemish we all agreed to overlook, since some of us bore similar blemishes. As Cochran swaggered up to the rostrum, those of us in the opposing faction felt that the rules of decorum requiring us to listen, more or less, to even the most tiresome speaker of the other side could safely be suspended. No sooner did he open his mouth than some of us started shuffling out of the hall, whispering loudly, "Pee time." Even Cochran's factional pals took a fairly tolerant view of this, since they had their candidates among our speakers for their own "pee time."

You might suppose that skills acquired in factional debate would be like skills acquired in graduate study of literature: good mostly for more of the same. But not so. Years later, meeting old friends who had dropped out of the movement and risen to prominence in universities and trade unions, I would watch with amusement how they put to use the rare devices learned in the school of the factions. Listening to Michael Harrington or myself make a speech, I could hear the striving cadence of Shachtman's voice. In the factional tournaments of the thirties we learned to think under pressure, speak with pride in the shapeliness of our speaking, pounce on openings for devastation. It was by no means the most thoughtful kind of thought. It did not encourage that lucidity of self-questioning I would meet among such younger friends as Michael Walzer and John Rawls. It taught us the skills of vicarious conquest, but insufficiently the conquest of self.

Not by politics alone. Indeed, one of our ideas was that to live by politics alone was gross. The impulses that had led us to political radicalism also made us responsive to avant-garde culture.

In the Socialist Party of the mid-thirties the dominant cultural style had been a middlebrow amiability, drawn from the tradition of nineteenth-century progressivism. One virtue of the Socialists was that they didn't feel obliged to have opinions on everything, or demand that everyone have the same opinion, so that within their ranks you could find strict highbrows, good-natured readers of nineteenth-century novels, and happy lowbrows who avoided all print except the New York tabloids. At the age of sixteen I was lent a copy of Edmund Wilson's *Axel's Castle* by a YPSL friend in the Bronx. This was probably the first book of literary criticism I read through from start to finish, even though I had only a skimpy acquaintance with the writers Wilson discussed. Something about Wilson's moral gravity moved me. It always would, though in 1936 I could not yet know I had encountered one of the figures I would come to regard as an intellectual model.

Passing through the Trotskyist movement a year or two later, I began to hear about literary topics Socialists had seldom noticed. We were now reading the great modernist writers—Joyce and Proust, Mann and Yeats—with almost the same attention we gave to Marx and Lenin. We devoured the concluding chapters of Trotsky's *Literature and Revolution*, where he polemicizes against the notion of a distinctly "proletarian culture" and ends with a lyrical rhapsody celebrating the heights that "socialist man" would scale, beyond even Goethe, Beethoven, and Marx. In my mature years I came to dislike this untempered utopianism; there were many things Socialists ought to strive for, but the vision of an age of universal genius was hardly one of them.

The movement tilted toward highbrow culture. Trotsky set an example through his own skillful literary criticism and his friendship with André Breton and Diego Rivera. The first American follower of Trotsky had been the talented writer Max Eastman, and the main spokesmen in America were Shachtman and Burnham, both intellectuals. Furthermore, our fondness for nuance and casuistry predisposed at least some of us to the problematic modes of modernist literature. Trotskyism was marked by an abundance of intellectual pride: truth to the testing, faithfulness to the severities of Marxism. We came to feel superior because we were reading Joyce and Proust, and we made it a point of honor not to smother them in vulgar sociology.

Modernist writers we admired on principle. It seemed only right that we of one vanguard should tip our hats to the giants of another. Still, these writers were not easy to approach: they had not yet been domesticated by the Academy, they still bristled with difficulties, they invited neither confidence nor comradeliness. We could admire them, but only from a distance. With T. S. Eliot, however, I fell crazily in love, more with the rhythms and music of his verse than its meanings. I knew he was a reactionary but didn't really care. The opening lines of "Prufrock," the first stanzas of *The Waste Land*, the haunting melody of *The Hollow Men* ("This is the dead land/This is the cactus land") made me dizzy with excitement. Here was a poetry of the barrenness of our time, the loneliness of our cities. Eliot meant his poems mainly as reflections on the sterility of a faithless age, while I read them mainly as reflections on the decay of bourgeois civilization. A liberal, a Stalinist—so I thought, and not with complete foolishness—could never appreciate Eliot, never respond to his despair as we did. He was our poet, just as he was the poet of those mad Southerners in Nashville about whom we were starting to hear. No doubt, as Eliot would snap a little later, people like ourselves misunderstood him; but it seems just possible that our misunderstanding brought us closer to one strand of feeling in his work than could the understanding of his disciples. For was there not something in his poetry that enabled us to read him as we did? Something that in his later Christian certainties he preferred not to recall? In any case, I loved his poetry with all the ardor of youth. May he, in the heaven that must now be his, forgive my misapprehensions.

The writers who seemed close to us, the ones we felt we alone could understand, were political novelists like Silone, Koestler, Malraux, and a bit later Orwell. We read Koestler's *Darkness at Noon* with a tremendous excitement, moved by its evocation of the sufferings endured by Stalin's victims and irritated by its simplistic explanation of the Moscow trials. One incident in the novel remained uncomfortably in my memory, troubling me in ways I did not understand till many years later. When the bolshevik leader Rubashov is thrown into prison, he hears from a nearby cell the tappings of another inmate. These tappings the experienced Rubashov translates into words; they come from a monarchist, a relic of the miserable Romanovs, long locked away and now fantasizing about a woman's thighs. There is nothing heroic or admirable about this prisoner, yet even Rubashov, long involved in the brutalities of the regime, comes dimly to recognize that this too is a victimized creature like himself. That tapping from a man whose only claim to sympathy is that he *is* a man, that tapping would take me some time to decode.

In the movement, among ourselves, we had a lively experience of culture, sometimes threatening the authority of politics. We would go to concerts at Lewisohn Stadium, putting down our twenty-five cents to hear Jascha Heifetz play the Mendelssohn concerto to the accompaniment of airplanes. And we were lucky to have as one of our comrades Noah Greenberg, a lumbering, good-natured fellow who was an accomplished musician temporarily suppressing his gifts in behalf of politics. Saturday nights we often ended up at his apartment on East Fourteenth Street, where he would play records of compositions we had never heard of and declaim sternly that among pianists only Schnabel was worth serious consideration, while Serkin was a mere miserable tinkler (a prejudice I've never quite shaken off). Noah would hop and dance around the room like a vast bear, noticing subtleties of performance the rest of us lamely pretended also to hear; yet what mattered was not the subtleties or the pretending, but the idea of them, the lesson that there were lessons to be learned. The life of culture could be a high calling, and it could yield pleasure and value short of politics, even despite politics. Noah was then active in the seamen's union, waging a hopeless battle against an entrenched Stalinist leadership; later he gave way to his deeper interests and became director of a group specializing in medieval music. But we had his youth, the years of his fervor and discovery.

If we were clear in our feelings about culture, we were in greater difficulties with regard to "bourgeois thought." Political thought before Marx, we were persuaded, had mattered mainly insofar as it prepared the way for his ideas, and most later political theory was feckless in its efforts to refute those ideas. Bourgeois scholars might accumulate useful information, but they lacked the coherence and cogency that only Marxism could provide. So we said, but less and less often, and with decreasing conviction as the years went by. We were scornful of the idiocies that Stalinism advanced in opposing "bourgeois thought," and as heretics we began to suspect that all was not so neatly ordered as the more stringent Marxists supposed. Besides, if Trotsky could admire Freud, why could we not admire Charles Beard and Vernon Parrington, perhaps even, a little later, John Stuart Mill and Max Weber?

A critical point came in my own intellectual development when I began to see that certain elements of traditional political theory simply could not be reduced to categories of class analysis. The stress of *The Federalist Papers* on the need for countervailing powers in a democratic society represented an important truth, not rendered any less so by Madison's conservative opinions. When Bukharin had fearfully whispered in the late twenties, and Trotsky had openly written in the mid-thirties, that the fundamental sophism of the Stalinists was their identification of party with state or state with society, they were saying something not so very different from what the conservative Madison had said more than a century earlier. Small heresies lead to larger ones. Precisely because we constituted a tiny, persecuted group trying seriously to cope with such major new problems as the nature of Stalinism, the movement had a way of secreting heresies from the very center of its orthodoxy.

3

City College and Beyond

Politics as a function of pure mind, as "autotelic" as the literary criticism proposed by some theorists a few decades later: this I found at City College. In class, lunchroom, and corridor ideology grew wild, a gorgeous weed flourishing without sun or air. Tests of reality? Buffetings of the outer world? No aspiring theoretician in the abundance of his pride would concede an inch to such coarse pragmatism. We lived by the word, steadily on watch for its transubstantiation. Like steeled Marxists we talked about "the road to power"; like godforsaken Talmudists we loved the power of talk.

At City College, which I attended from 1936 to 1940, I had a mediocre record, except for an occasional course that lured me into unplanned enthusiasm (I once wrote an eighty-page paper on the literary criticism of Max Eastman, stuffed with as much nonsense as Eastman's own criticism.) Some poor grades were not entirely my fault. I experienced an unmanageable fright before differential and integral calculus, then a required full-year course, and was left helpless, a mere infant babbling formulas, by the mechanical way it was taught—taught rather like dialectical materialism in the Soviet Union, as a sequence of mysterious signs. (Years later, when suffering bad dreams, I found myself back in that college setting, just before a calculus test for which I would be desperately trying to memorize a mound of incomprehensible equations, until I'd wake up soaked from sweat but relieved that I was in bed and not at school. Even in nightmare, it seems, I am committed to a realistic aesthetic.) But mostly I got poor grades because I spent little time in class and less doing homework. Who could bother to study when next month the world was going to blow up? So I'd go to class, sit impatiently for a few minutes until the roll was called, slip out, head for the lunchroom where a political argument was waiting, and at the hour's end race back to get the books I had left in the classroom. It was a pretty sad way to get an education: whatever a professor said in the first or last few minutes of the class I retained, the middle I seldom knew.

City College was a wonderful place in those years, at least for young radicals, but not because it had a wonderful faculty. Most of the teaching was mediocre and only after I myself became a professor did I understand why. Teaching schedules were punitively high: a fifteen-hour load, if taken with any seriousness, meant a sixty-hour week, and that left no time for reading or intellectual growth. Still, there were a few great teachers like Morris Raphael Cohen, and some gifted ones like Abraham Edel. I took a course in philosophy with Edel in which he pleasantly used the Socratic method, so much so that for years I could remember his questions while never getting to the answers. No harm—in those days I wasn't short of answers.

Morris Cohen's last years at City College coincided with my first two, and I sat in on one of his philosophy classes. It was an experience of salutory terror, listening to this master of the cleansing negation. Like Ronald Colman in one of those movies where he played an elegant Britisher taking on the natives with a gleaming sword, Cohen would take on students to his left, students to his right, ripping open their premises, cutting down their defenses. You went to a Cohen class in order to be ripped open and cut down. The tough-spirited boys who took his classes—many didn't have the courage—knew Cohen meant nothing personal when he said one of them had been speaking foolishly; he said it to adults, too. The students who adored and feared him knew that he cared mostly for an honest struggle in behalf of truth and just a little for the vanities of dialectic. Socrates may also have been a bit of a showman.

In my alleged "subject," English, the teaching at City College was quite poor. Many of the professors were drained out, coasting along on memory and decayed notes; some never had much to give. Their inadequacy didn't bother us much, though it damaged us more than we knew, since the lack of strong adult guides left too many openings for our hubris. We went off on our own, reading in disorderly spurts. A friend named Earl Raab came to love the allegorical silkiness of Spenser's verse, and disobeying my sterner Marxist self, I also found some pleasure in *The Faerie Queene*. Word was starting to get about that Max Weber was a formidable intellectual competitor to Marx, so somewhat nervously we dipped into a few of the sociologist's pages. Some of our more heterodox young radicals, though not alas I, were searching out old pamphlets by Rosa Luxemburg and Julian Martov, which led them to question the whole of bolshevism.

An impressive course that has stayed in memory was given by a professor named Stair, with whom we read Aristotle's *Poetics* line by line. I loved this sort of dragging, affectionate exegesis, though I rewarded Stair with that wretched composition about Max Eastman. He took me to task for my bad spelling and wisely said nothing about the content. In another course—one of those *Beowulf*-to-Virginia-Woolf surveys since become unfashionable but really essential for starting out on a literary education—I encountered a number of poets, like Crabbe and Landor, whose work pricked my imagination and to whom I intended year after year to go back. It was hop, skip, and jump in this sort of course, with a ladling of textbook filler about neo-classicism, romanticism, and the rise of the middle class; but in retrospect I value its historical stress. I learned that Dryden came before Pope, a piece of information comfortable in its own right and useful at the Ph.D. oral examinations I would attend in later years. The teacher of that survey course required us to memorize a Shakespeare sonnet—how I cursed this imposition on my freedom!—but decades later I still take pleasure in summoning the first few lines of "Let me not to the marriage of true minds/Admit impediments."

The social sciences we took to be hopeless. I had an economics course with a fool named "Steamboat" Fulton, whose stock in trade was lyrical rant about twin divinities named Supply and Demand. There were better teachers than "Steamboat," yet little that reached us in the classroom was bold enough in speculation or rigorous enough in method. It was really all right, the formal side of a City College education, but it was not enough for the time or for us. Our professors could not satisfy our hunger for meaning and direction, for some way of grasping the lostness of the life we saw everywhere about us. So I preferred courses that yielded a bit of culture, since about the great world itself, that broken-down mechanism of profit and suffering, I felt I knew more than most of the social science professors.

The real center of life at City College was in our Alcove 1, dark-stained, murky, shaped like a squat horseshoe, one of perhaps ten along the edge of the lunchroom. Alcove 1 was the home of heresy, left sectarianism, independent thought, and—to be honest —a share of fanaticism and intolerance. Here gathered Trotskyist, Socialist, Lovestonite students with their books, pamphlets, ragged overcoats, and cheese sandwiches. Also, one or two deviants from deviancy who were sharp enough to criticize our view that things had started going bad in the Soviet Union mostly with Stalin's usurpation of power. Nearby, in Alcove 2, gathered the far more numerous and powerful Stalinists. The Young Communist League must then have had about four hundred members at City College, while the quarrelsome anti-Stalinist Left, all groups together, had perhaps fifty. The YCL controlled the student paper, using it to print editorials defending the Moscow trials. Closely knit, the YCL had a major advantage in possessing secret allies within the faculty —perhaps a dozen party members.

You could walk into the thick brown darkness of Alcove 1 at almost any time of day or evening and find a convenient argument about the Popular Front in France, the New Deal in America, the civil war in Spain, the Five-Year Plan in Russia, the theory of permanent revolution, and "what Marx really meant." Anyone could join in an argument, there was no external snobbism; but whoever joined did so at his own risk, fools and ignoramuses not being suffered gladly. Each political group spread some of its pamphlets and papers on the alcove table. Here ideas simulated the colors of reality, here we defended the "correct line," that mystic pride of Marxism. I can remember getting into an argument at ten in the morning, going off to some classes, and then returning at two in the afternoon to find the argument still going on, but with an entirely fresh cast of characters. The more versatile among us prided themselves on being able to carry on more than one argument at a time, like chess players before two boards; but maybe this was just boasting. One friend, Izzy Kugler, had a large body of knowledge and near knowledge. In a clash with a Stalinist boy whom we had lured across the border into Alcove 1, Izzy bombarded him with figures about British imperialism, and when the poor fellow expressed disbelief, Izzy sternly directed him to the library where he could "look it up." It was characteristic of City College that even a Stalinist hectored by his worst enemy would dutifully troop off to the library to "look it up." A fact was a fact. But had Izzy really been hammering him with facts? I asked about those statistics and he answered with a charming smile that, well, he had exaggerated a little (which is to say, a lot), since you had to do *something* to get those Stalinist sluggards to read a book!

They weren't all sluggards, of course, and once a few of them came over to our side we thought them bright enough. But they were imprisoned by their "party discipline" and under strict orders not to "fraternize" with us. Alas, they couldn't always obey. Sometimes in anger or frustration a YCLer had to take up the gauntlet. Not an ordinary YCLer, but a leader for whom it was acceptable to violate the ban on fraternizing—leaders, as Moscow made clear, being above ordinary proscriptions. The two sides would start hammering away at each other, a crowd of onlookers would gather, we would charge that they had abandoned revolutionary principles and they that we failed to understand the historical crisis forcing them to change their line. Mutual exhaustion, a furious retreat to the dull safety of Alcove 2, chortling in Alcove 1, a breakup into four or five subarguments: so it would end.

To bring about the historic journey from Alcove 2 to Alcove 1 was a special delight. When arguing with Communists, we seldom had to venture onto the perilous ground of first principles, needing only to prove that their movement had abandoned the axioms of Marxism. Once we noticed a YCLer weakening, we'd turn our "big guns" on him, especially Miltie Sacks, a rotund theoretician who sometimes, I suspect, "broke" Stalinists by reducing them to a state of sheer exhaustion. All this may now seem comical: what did it matter, after all, whether a nineteen-year-old remained in the YCL or not? Well, it did matter. The struggle to loosen the grip of Stalinism on the international Left has been a crucial political experience of our century—even now by no means finished or completely successful—and we felt we were making our own little contribution to it. The YCL from its own point of view shared our estimate that something important was going on. In the thirties City College was the center of student politics; defections there could lead to bigger losses elsewhere.

When we could not get to "them"—those ideological addicts of Alcove 2—we settled into a quieter condition, talking among ourselves, at times in a more contemplative vein than polemic allowed. We quarreled, of course, but with a touch of fraternity, an edge of respect that there was little reason to accord to Alcove 2. Sometimes an honest-to-goodness liberal would wander onto our turf, regarded by us as a rare specimen requiring shelter in a museum. Old-time Socialists seldom interested us: they seemed too slack for our apocalyptic temper. Most irritating, yet somehow also fascinating, was the handful of independent leftists who took anti-Stalinism for granted but kept chopping away at our Marxist and bolshevik assumptions. I found them hard to cope with, for while I did not know this, they formed a kind of presentiment of where some of us were going to end politically.

And where, meanwhile, were the twenty thousand students of City College? Some, utterly indifferent to radical or any other politics, kept faithful to their studies, perhaps hoping for a better future than seemed probable at the time. Some juggled an array of part-time jobs in order to keep going to school, though why they wanted to keep going was not always clear. Some were hopeless careerists (especially, we thought, the engineers), determined at any cost to "make it." Another interesting group had been stained with the skepticism and sadness of the moment, drifting along year after year at City College because it seemed a little better than hanging around the streets. As always, the politically active students formed a minority, but a minority aggressive and articulate. In Alcoves 1 and 2—more, I fear, in the latter—there was at least an appearance of decisiveness: young people who imagined they had a rendezvous with History.

We worked hard. We distributed thousands of our leaflets, a new one every two weeks or so, sometimes in response to a campus event, sometimes as little essays in politics. To put out a thousand copies of a leaflet cost about sixty cents—thirty-eight cents for smeary yellow paper (two reams), fifteen cents for a stencil, and a dime for our share of the ink at the party office. We'd collect nickels from comrades and sympathizers in Alcove 1, though it was a real sacrifice for these boys to give a nickel, since it meant a portion of their lunch. I must have written and then mimeographed dozens of these leaflets: my own equivalent to the three-hundred-word composition required in introductory English courses.

My prose was pungent and purple, meant to attract quick notice—you couldn't write a leaflet in the style of Ruskin. Once, enraged at an editorial in the student paper endorsing the Moscow trials, I let loose with a leaflet entitled "Yellow Journalism on the Campus." Izzy Kugler approved the text, but felt a decorative touch was needed. Thumbing through Bartlett's, he came up with a juicy couplet from Pope: "Destroy his fibs and sophistries in vain / The creature's at his dirty work again." Happily, we made Pope our subhead. When we distributed the leaflet the next morning—it meant getting to school half an hour early and posting ourselves at four or five entrances—it caused a flurry of amusement in the English department, though I didn't know it at the time. The professors we regarded as fuddyduds were pleased that their cantankerous radical students should be quoting Alexander Pope. Perhaps they had not taught entirely in vain? Years later, when I came back to City College, an old professor recognized me and slyly murmured those lines from Pope. It made my heart thump with pleasure.

In the spring the campus began to bristle with activity, a restless overflow from lunchroom to street, especially before the annual Student Strike against War in April. The anti-Stalinist leftists, suddenly aware of their fragility, huddled together in a bloc of sorts, picking up a few allies among liberals and a Socialist-Zionist group called Avukah, which had about a dozen members and was led by Seymour Melman, later a peace activist but already notable for a high-spirited nature and a voice of astonishing resonance. We thought him ideologically deficient but entirely trustworthy, and we valued that voice of his, which in a few minutes could scare up a crowd near Alcove 1. In my first two years, if I remember correctly, we held the antiwar rally together with the boys from Alcove 2, but by 1938 we parted company, thinking of them as warmongers who had abandoned the principles of internationalism.

For some reason the college administration wanted only one student strike. Too weak to hold a rally by ourselves, we agree— but on condition that one of the speakers be ours, the Trotskyist leader and NYU philosophy professor, James Burnham. The very thought makes Alcove 2 recoil with horror: five full minutes of "counterrevolutionary" contamination! An impasse in negotiations; the college assigns Professor Cohen, who might better have been occupied elsewhere, to mediate; we meet in his office, two from each alcove. Listening to our claims, he turns with a grimace to the YCLers: "If you agree to a joint meeting, isn't it only fair that both sides have their own speakers?"

Only fair—the very words, a token of liberal innocence, make the Stalinists gag. We too, though with a greater sense of complication, think it appropriate to be scornful, while prepared of course to take advantage of Cohen's remark. Well, an accommodation is patched up, we have our speaker, the meeting ends. As we're walking out I feel someone touching my arm. It's Cohen, he wants me to stay a minute. And then, in that wonderful Yiddish accent of his, he says: "All right, so you boys want your own speaker. But tell me, why do you have to choose such a bad philosopher?" He grins, I gulp. I mumble something about politics mattering more than philosophy and Burnham being good at politics. He smiles, I flee. Alas, no occasion will later present itself to tell Professor Cohen: you were right.

Through the four unbalanced and overwrought years we spent at City, we educated and miseducated ourselves. Between the kinds of students who made Alcove 1 their home and most of the professors there was a gap seemingly beyond bridging. Perhaps some of the teachers shared our sense of having been cast into a historical abyss, but if so they were seldom able to persuade us. Writing this, I feel uneasy: was not precisely the same complaint made by New Left students in the late sixties when I was a professor? No, not the same complaint. What troubled us as students in City College was not that our professors were excessively devoted to intellectual work, but that they were not devoted enough. The students of Alcove 1, and others too, were intellectual to a fault, entranced by abstraction and deficient in the graces of life. Inevitably, upon encountering the New Left students in the late sixties, all the graduates of Alcove 1 *had* to feel a certain impatience with the sentimental vagueness now passing for radicalism.

We made our dark little limbo of Alcove 1 into a school for the sharpening of wits. Irving Kristol has remarked, "If I left City College with a better education than did many students at other and supposedly better colleges, it was because my involvement in radical politics put me in touch with people and ideas that prompted me to read and think and argue with furious energy." And there is justice in his criticism also:

We in Alcove 1 were terribly concerned with being "right" in politics, economics, sociology, philosophy, history, anthropology, etc. It was essential to be "right" . . . lest a bit of information collide with a theoretical edifice and bring the whole structure tumbling down. So all the little grouplets that joined together to make Alcove 1 their home were always in keen competition to come up with startling bits of information—or better yet, obscure and disorienting quotations from Marx or Engels or Lenin or Trotsky—that would create intellectual trouble for the rest of the company.

Ideas had to fall into systems, systems to envision power— though about power we knew very little. Between the politics about which we talked and the clawed reality of the politics that men experience, there was a relation somewhat like that between the casuistry of seminary and the institution of church. But this was good. For education ought to enable the young to practice the arts of both reflection and governing, the modes of both citizenship and insurgency. Education should be a game like, but not merely of, reality. The boys of Alcove 1 would scatter in every way, yet a common tie, more than nostalgia, held them together. It was the memory of the days when we reached for the gift of lucidity and stumbled into the life of the mind.

In the spring of 1940 I graduated from City College. At Lewisohn Stadium I sat in my absurd black gown next to Irving Kristol and Earl Raab, and we listened to the commencement speaker, an official from the League of Nations who gravely assured us that our generation, unlike an earlier one, would not have to go to the battlefields. We laughed, we scoffed; nearby, some of our fellow graduates whiled away their boredom by rolling dice.

* * *

Once beyond the campus, there were plenty of signposts to reality. Let me mention only one. Wherever the independent Left turned, we found ourselves blocked by an increasingly strong Stalinist movement, and while extremely frustrating, this served to hold in check the tendency of ideological movements to become grandiose.

For several years since 1934 the Communists had been trying to build an alliance with liberals in the name of antifascism, now portraying themselves not as revolutionary Leninists but as native "progressives" brimming with moderation. This policy was notably successful, being on the face of it closer to the realities of American society than the verbal leftism to which Trotskyists and many Socialists were prone. By the late thirties, before the Hitler-Stalin pact brought down the whole Popular Front edifice, the Communist Party had approached the status of a mass movement in a few parts of the country: New York, California, perhaps Detroit and Chicago. It would soon elect two of its leaders, Pete Cacchione and Benjamin Davis, Jr., to the New York City Council. It was gaining control of powerful unions, among them the West Coast longshoremen, the New York transit workers, the East Coast maritime, and District 65, that catchall for the wretchedly paid shipping clerks of New York.

Attacking the CP from the left, we criticized it for retreating to social democratic "class collaboration"—a charge only superficially accurate, since we did not yet understand that neither in its "left" nor "right" phases could Stalinism be usefully assimilated to more traditional political movements: it was something new historically, requiring new categories of analysis. Our criticism was beside the point in another respect: there was neither a revolutionary situation nor much possibility of soon having one in the United States, so that what we were saying had only an abstract relevance in terms of "first principles." Meanwhile, the claim of the Popular Front—the need for common action against the fascist menace—had its obvious plausibility.

More to the point, we criticized the CP for duplicity. We called the Popular Front a masquerade of convenience: should it please the leaders in Moscow, the whole Stalinist apparatus in America would quickly abandon the entire policy. This is precisely what happened in 1939, so here we were talking sense. But insofar as our criticisms proceeded from Leninist assumptions, they could touch only a tiny remnant of communist old-timers. Insofar as they proceeded from democratic values, however, we were somewhat more cogent—though we had not yet measured, nor had anyone else, the extent to which those values had suffered decay in bourgeois society, a decay the Stalinists learned to exploit with virtuoso brilliance. Worse still, our effort to combine Leninist and democratic modes of criticism trapped us in an excess of complexity and confusion.

The Communists called us "Fascists" and "counterrevolutionists." Did they really believe this nonsense? Were they really gullible or stupid enough to think Trotsky had made a secret deal with Hitler and Hirohito? Perhaps some of the rank-and-filers, addicts of faith, were ready to believe it; perhaps one way of describing certain Stalinists was as people ready to believe anything. When we went out into the streets to hawk our paper at union meetings, we knew that those who roughed us up a little, with a shove here and a push there and sometimes even a bloody nose, were organized as CP goon squads. You could expect nothing else from them. But what about party intellectuals like Joseph Starobin and Theodore Draper: did these sophisticated fellows really believe the lies pouring out of Moscow?

It's hard to say. In later years, when I would ask them, they would stare at me with a sort of mild pity, as if I could not understand the shade within shade of rationalization they had perfected in their days as Communists. Of course they didn't believe that Trotsky held secret negotiations with the Nazis or the Japanese; they knew the accusations at the Moscow trials were, let's say, exaggerated. But they were also convinced that the politics of the anti-Stalinist Left were "objectively" counterrevolutionary. The Soviet Union seemed to them in so precarious a condition during the thirties that anything helping its defense had to be justified. Without using such language, they really held to a version of Sorel's notion that the masses, forever sunk in superstition, need a myth to which they can yield themselves—in this case, the myth that Trotsky was working to betray the "socialist fatherland."

And there was something else. It is hard for those who have

never gone through an ideological movement, especially the Stalinist variety, to imagine how self-contained its life can be. Ideology and organization fuse to create a wall that shields those within the inner precincts from doubt, skepticism, and dangerous books.

Sometimes it was physically dangerous to get too close to Stalinist-controlled institutions. The more proletarian the institution, the more dangerous. Workers won over to the CP could be selfless and brave, but were hardly notable for a devotion to tolerance. When we gave out leaflets at meetings of District 65, which the Stalinist youth ran both as an effective union and a fertile source of recruitment, we ran up against proletarian toughs inflamed by YCL leaders. Using skills they had picked up in the garment center, those toughs would push us around with a jab here, an elbow there; they knew how to inflict hurt without leaving marks. Unwilling to turn to the police for protection, since that—heaven forbid!—would have meant resorting to the bourgeois state, we found ourselves invoking the claims of . . . democracy. *Democracy*, did you bastards say *democracy*? Peals of laughter from the Stalinist bravos: didn't we claim to be Marxists and didn't we know the Marxist line on democracy? Well, we thought it was a good deal more complicated than what the CP had been teaching them. But try to argue when you are being shoved away from the doors of the Manhattan Center, and nearby are the cops, unseeing or amused.

These toughs were teaching us the virtues of democracy, or at least a richer Marxist view of it. For just as Trotsky, in denouncing the Stalinist purges, found himself invoking such supraclass categories as honor and integrity, so we spoke—to whom? perhaps no one but ourselves—about fairness. And what was this "fairness" but a term in the vocabulary we had rejected as mere liberalism? First blows, then lessons.

Less dangerous physically though more exasperating to the spirit were our frequent brushes against the Stalinists in the student movement. Clever YCL leaders like Celeste Strack, a creamy young woman with a heart of steel, and shrewd fellows like James Wechsler, then passing himself off as a liberal though secretly high in the YCL ranks, would appear at meetings of the American Student Union, a group formed in 1938 out of a merger of communist and socialist student societies, and speak there with a round-eyed ingenuousness in the vocabulary of liberalism. It was all masquerade. We knew it and they knew it, but hardly anyone else did. That's what most "leftist" politics consisted of in those years—a masquerade of innocence!

That masquerade grew intolerable when, at student conferences, a contingent of Vassar girls would show up, patrician and prim, yet somehow always following the Stalinist line. For better or worse, the Trotskyist and socialist youth were hopelessly plebeian, New Yorkers caustic in speech and often uncouth in manner, while those young ladies from Poughkeepsie seemed blithely to combine a fellow-traveling politics—some, it turned out, were secret members of the YCL—with an air of WASP condescension. It was hard to bear. We were reacting, of course, as children of Jewish immigrants, though we would have been furious if you had told us that. The combination of upper-class coolness and Stalinist politics was *too much*, and except in private mockery we didn't really know how to cope with it. But it brought us one benefit: we learned to appreciate a little more warmly our own Brooklyn and Hunter girls, so much livelier and rougher, so much more passionate.

If we tried at these student meetings to suggest that the Young Communist League was a prime manipulator behind the scenes, we would be beaten back with charges of "redbaiting." Such accusations almost always turned out to be effective with the small contingent of genuine liberals. But if we tried to argue the issue of, say, the Popular Front "on its merits," we were often crippled in advance, since one of our main criticisms was the lack of authenticity, and to support this we had to bring up the matter of communist control. At these sessions of the American Student Union, Hal Draper would speak for us with a razored lucidity; but at most we were a thorn in the side of the Stalinists, raising perhaps a few doubts in a few minds. History seemed to lie in their hands.

Once, at a meeting in Washington of the American Youth Congress, a youth "holding company" skillfully engineered by the young Communists, I managed to get the floor for three minutes. It was a great event, and before you smile, try to imagine it: at least two thousand young people packed into a large hall, the majority of them prepared to look upon someone like myself as a "disrupter" or worse. I, all of nineteen years old, skin and bones, intense, proud, scared as hell. Before anyone can think up some maneuver to deny me the floor, I rush to the microphone and pour out a cascade of overcharged but still (it's a matter of pride) grammatical sentences: a critique of the Popular Front, stressing that it means reliance on bourgeois institutions and states very far from dependable in their resistance to fascism, and that it also means abandoning support for oppressed colonial peoples like those in India struggling against imperialism.

Leave aside the flaws of argument one may find in this speech: the mere fact of being able to make it against an array of sneering faces represented something of a victory. Bathed in sweat, trembling from my exertion, chagrined that I had omitted "a few points" (in three minutes!), I get back to my little circle of comrades, all of whom secretly understand the strain I've gone through. Our theoretician of the moment, Miltie Sacks, is kind in his judgment of my speech, kinder than he might be in other circumstances, for he too has surely noticed the omission of "a few points."

The debates of later years about the strength or weakness of communism in America have always seemed to me strangely out of focus. That the CP never came close to being a major force in American political life, that it had at most seventy or eighty thousand members, and that in some parts of the country it continued to suffer isolation and assault even during the Popular Front years— all this is true. But it's not the entire truth. For if you look at the major social institutions, those "intermediary structures" sociologists describe as a mainstay of democracy, then a more complex judgment is required. In many such institutions, from the trade unions to student groups, from fraternal immigrant societies to the YWCA, the Stalinists had entrenched themselves through their activism, selflessness, and tokens of plausibility. Coherent minorities, firm in purpose and ready to sacrifice time and energy, can gain far more political power than a mere counting of heads would possibly suggest.

The true relationships of power within the Left revealed themselves most clearly in regard to the Spanish civil war. Within this country the CP was probably the most persistent agency behind the movement to help loyalist Spain. It formed the Abraham Lincoln Brigade, which sent hundreds of Americans to fight on the Spanish battlefields. The picture of the Spanish civil war held by the majority of enlightened Americans during the late thirties and for many years afterward was essentially that produced by the Popular

Front: a struggle between a heroic, beleaguered democracy and a brutal, insurgent fascism. It was a picture with a large share of truth, but a truth vulgarized, omitting both the revolutionary and repressive sides of the war. Revolutionary, in that the workers of Catalonia, led by the Anarchists and the anti-Stalinist Marxist party called the POUM, had seized factories and land with the intention of moving toward socialist reconstruction. Repressive, in that the small Spanish CP and its Russian backers were able, because of Russian arms, to initiate undemocratic, sometimes terrorist measures against left-wing dissidents within the loyalist camp. So lyrically single-minded was the support given loyalist Spain by American radicals and liberals, it became quite impossible to suggest there might be anything wrong with "our side."

Nor was the anti-Stalinist Left of much help. Trotsky's writings on Spain are among his least impressive. His handful of Spanish followers was reduced to sterile carping because the POUM had taken the "class collaborationist" step of entering the Catalonian government. More cogent was his argument that, in order to arouse the masses for a prolonged struggle against fascism, it was necessary to give land to the peasants, control of factories to the workers, and a promise of independence to Spanish Morocco that might evoke rebellion among Franco's Moorish soldiers.

To many antifascists in both Spain and America, all this seemed too abstract. They argued that the revolutionary pattern Trotsky was sketching did not fit the Spanish actuality, being too evidently cut from Russian cloth. They felt he was focusing too much on the political aspect of things, whereas the real problem was military—a large influx of arms from Nazi Germany and fascist Italy.

The most cogent of the issues raised by the anti-Stalinist Left had to do with democratic rights within loyalist Spain, the way the NKVD, the Russian secret police, had taken over an increasing share of police powers. We were saying what George Orwell would say in *Homage to Catalonia*—a book that earned him a hail of scorn. Our criticism had a moral rationale but was politically very difficult, perhaps impossible, at a time when fascism had taken over most of Europe and the socialist spirit was in full retreat. We were complicating the Spanish question in ways that seemed insufferable. That the loyalist Spain which so stirred hearts could also be guilty of allowing the NKVD to kidnap and murder Andrés Nin, the POUM leader, was simply too much. People could not bear to hear that La Pasionaria, the flaming defender of Madrid, was also a ruthless Stalinist persecuting political opponents. People could not bear to hear that even in loyalist Spain there was reason for dismay, cause for grief.

Spain showed us finally that the thrust of history was not going to be diverted even by the most brilliant of critiques. It was Stalinism, and only Stalinism, that commanded power on "the Left," just as it was fascism, and only fascism, that commanded power on "the Right." These rival yet symmetrical monsters would consume our century. We of the independent Left could write and cry out; we could play the role of critics declaring outrage to a world gone deaf. Surely there was honor and usefulness in doing this. Still, it was the YCL boys who went to fight in Spain: disastrously, as misused victims, yet heroically too, determined to set their bodies as a bulwark to the fire coming from the guns of Hitler and Mussolini. Nothing else reveals so graphically the tragic character of those years: that the yearning for some better world should repeatedly end in muck, foul play, murder.

The strain of those years was unbearable, especially for a little sect that aspired to both intellectual grasp and political strength. What could not be vented on the world, we vented on one another. We cast about for new theories, new feats of comprehension, as if the act of knowing could make up for the reality of helplessness. The lacerating factional dispute that broke out in the American Trotskyist movement in late 1938 was the predictable result; a year and a half later it ended in a split.

Since the late twenties, the independent Marxist groups had been tearing themselves apart in an effort to cope with the "Russian question." What kind of society had emerged under Stalin's terror? Why had the revolution turned so bad? Was the root of disaster to be found in particular circumstances or the original conceptions of bolshevism? Among some American liberals the preoccupation of leftists with such questions evoked much merriment, as a perfect example of Marxist scholasticism. But the liberals were wrong, for Stalinism represented a new phenomenon, probably the most important historical novelty of the time. Our debates were held, it's true, in the ghastly language of Marxist scholasticism; still, we were grappling with urgent matters that later political thinkers would also be obliged to turn to.

Challenged by gifted disciples, Trotsky threw himself into the debate with all his energy. From Mexico came a barrage of documents, caustic in tone and elaborate in structure, defending his theory that Stalinist Russia remained a "degenerated workers' state." A minority, speaking mostly through Shachtman and Burnham, kept inching toward the view that Stalinism represented a new historical phenomenon that it called "bureaucratic collectivism."

Trotsky, I think now as I thought then, was wrong, yet in looking over the materials of this debate several decades later I find myself impressed by a methodological sophistication behind his dogmatism. On the face of things, we were quarreling about language: what to *call* the Stalinist dictatorship we all abhorred. But as usual, quarrels over language mask, and sometimes reveal, quarrels over world view, and this Trotsky understood completely. He understood that our seemingly modest proposal for a change of nomenclature opened large possibilities for changes of idea. Not being exactly shy in debate, he pressed the point repeatedly.

Starting with the premise that Stalinist Russia represented a historical phenomenon almost sure to be short-lived, Trotsky called it a "degenerated workers' state," not because he was so naive as to suppose the Russian workers had anything to do with its policy-making, but because the regime had preserved nationalized property forms that were a "conquest" of the 1917 revolution. Soon, he argued, it would have to give way to either bourgeois restoration or a new proletarian uprising. For the Stalinist bureaucracy to constitute a new class—as the minority suggested—there would have to be, continued Trotsky, a "virtual liquidation of the planned economy" and of nationalized ownership. That had not yet occurred. Nevertheless, there were signs toward the end of his life that Trotsky was seriously modifying his views. In 1939 he wrote a suggestive article, "The USSR in War," in which he said, "The USSR minus the social structure of the October Revolution [nationalized industry and planned economy] would be a fascist regime." Cogent enough, though how to reconcile a fascist "super-structure" with the social base of a "workers' state," no matter how "degenerate," was something of a problem.

In the same article Trotsky showed an awareness of the methodological difficulties in the debate:

> Our critics have more than once argued that the present Soviet bureaucracy bears very little resemblance to either the bourgeois or labor bureaucracy in capitalist society; that, to a far greater degree than does the fascist bureaucracy, it represents a new and much more powerful social formation. This is quite correct and we have never closed our eyes to it. But if we consider the Soviet bureaucracy a "class," then we are compelled to state immediately that this class does not at all resemble any of those propertied classes known to us in the past; our gain consequently is not great. We frequently call the Soviet bureaucracy a caste, underscoring thereby its shut-in character, its arbitrary rule, and that haughtiness of the ruling stratum, which considers that its progenitors issued from the divine lips of Brahma whereas the popular masses originated from the grosser portions of his anatomy. But even this definition does not of course possess a strictly scientific character. Its relative superiority lies in this, that the makeshift character of the term is clear to everybody, since it would enter nobody's mind to identify the Moscow oligarchy with the Hindu caste of Brahmins. The old sociological terminology did not and could not prepare a name for a new social event which is in process of evolution (degeneration) and which has not assumed stable forms. All of us, however, continue to call the Soviet bureaucracy a bureaucracy, not being unmindful of its historical peculiarities. In our opinion this should suffice for the time being.

For Trotsky's critics, it did not suffice. We argued that the total loss of political power by the Russian working class meant that it no longer ruled in any social sense. (I leave aside the question whether it ever really had.) As a propertyless class, the workers could rule only through political power and not in those indirect ways—through the influence of property and wealth—that served the bourgeoisie in its youthful phase. As a result, we continued, democracy was a sine qua non for any society that could usefully be called a workers' state. Stalinism showed no signs of producing from within itself a bourgeois restoration, such as Trotsky had mistakenly foreseen. The bureaucracy had actually become a relatively stable ruling class, with interests of its own in opposition to capitalism and socialism. The traditional Marxist dichotomy of capitalism/socialism to which Trotsky clung had been shown to be mistaken; nothing in history "decreed" such an either/or. There was now a third possibility which we called "bureaucratic collectivism." This bureaucratic collectivism was a statified economy barring private property, and it was dominated by a new ruling class that used totalitarian methods to modernize the backward Russian society through an unprecedented "planned" exploitation. It was a society more reactionary than capitalism, since it deprived the working class—indeed, the population as a whole—of elementary rights that in Western society had been won early in the nineteenth century.

Whether bureaucratic collectivism was a mere transient phase of Russian development or a possible new worldwide social order, the dissident minority did not yet attempt to say. The force of our analysis lay more in its rejection of Trotsky's theory than in a prognosis for the historical future. We were right in insisting upon the novelty of the society that had sprung up in Russia, one resembling neither the reality of capitalism nor the idea of socialism; but we could not go very far in developing a theory of what this new society signified.

Trotsky was quick to pounce on the problems that followed. He feared that our dissidence called into question the entire revolutionary perspective upon which the movement rested. We denied this, and in good faith; but he was right. For if the Soviet bureaucracy represented a new social order neither bourgeois nor proletarian, there arose at least the possibility that its life span would not be brief at all. It might stabilize its rule through a mixture of modern repression (not necessarily terror, but a terror-in-reserve) and a modernized economy. There was the further possibility that the whole perspective of socialism might be called into question, for while those of us advancing the theory of bureaucratic collectivism remained convinced socialists, our new ideas left open the question of whether the working class would be able to fulfill the "historic tasks" assigned to it by Marxism. Even if the workers made a revolution, could they hold power for long without yielding to a new usurping bureaucracy of party leaders and economic managers? Did they possess the social cohesion, discipline, and vision to create a free, humane socialism? We were hardly ready as yet to face such questions, but sooner or later we would have to. Meanwhile, what we had gained in theoretical comprehension we lost in political assurance. In our rickety little boat we had launched ourselves onto the dangerous waters of the problematic.

Who could tell where those waters would take us? Once the split was completed in 1940, our minority group, numbering perhaps a thousand, formed its own organization. With the grandiosity that marks beginnings, we called ourselves the Workers Party, no doubt because we had so few workers among us. At the very start James Burnham dropped away. He had been revising his ideas far more drastically than he had troubled to let us know, and in a few years would be developing his theory of the "managerial revolution," which posited the coming to power in modern society of a new stratum of managers overwhelming both the bourgeoisie and the proletariat—a theory that met with devastating criticism from George Orwell and Dwight Macdonald. The defection of Burnham hurt us badly, since we were not overly blessed with intellectual talent. But there was no turning back, so we pumped our legs as if marching ahead. We started a weekly paper, *Labor Action*, and maintained the theoretical magazine, the *New International*. Within a few years, chastened by our inability to emerge from sect isolation, we dropped the pretense of being a party and renamed ourselves the Independent Socialist League. Within the radical milieu we were simply the Shachtmanites.

Of all the left-wing groups I've known over the years, this was by far the most interesting and troubled, perhaps the most interesting because the most troubled. We wanted at first to show that we remained good Marxists, but every time we thought about a problem, we moved farther away from Leninism and closer to social democracy. Keeping some of the old language, we twisted it to new ideas. Isn't that how most people change their ideas, insisting that they are still faithful to old verities and merely introducing a few adjustments? Our political style was, in truth, very different from that of the Trotskyists. We were less sure of ourselves. We were softer in tone and texture. We were returning to our true selves, though only through the journey of return could we discover what those true selves really were.

(In 1948 I had a conversation with Elliot Cohen, then editor of *Commentary*. With provocative irony he said to me, "You're really a Social Democrat, you know, at least you have the social democratic temperament." I bristled: me, a Social Democrat? I argued heatedly, but his remark stuck in my memory, one of those casual insights that can place the turning of a life.)

Our group began to function during the early years of the European war, when the American economy was booming under the impetus of defense production. Even as we were edging toward unorthodox ideas, we still wanted to establish ourselves as a rooted "working-class tendency," and since most of us were anything but proletarians (being their children is, in America, a very different matter), we began a campaign to plant our younger members in the factories.

On a miniature scale, this was our own "cultural revolution." It was a willing of self-transformation. There were mixed motives behind it all: a large quotient of genuine devotion, drawn from the premise that a socialist organization had to establish itself in the working class if it was ever to amount to anything, and once in a while some touches of personal opportunism, since defense workers did get draft deferments.

The dream of "colonizing" is as old as the radical movement itself, entailing a history of sacrifice, delusion, and frustration. In Russia during the 1880s idealistic young Populists "went to the people," the brutish peasants whom they hoped to stir into rebellion; sometimes they succeeded, but more often they were repulsed as intruders or godless Jews. In the United States the Communist Party, making limitless demands on its cadres, sent thousands of young people into the factories, many of them sticking it out for decades and some becoming important union leaders. Others, more fastidious or nervous, never managed to complete the transformation (or denial) of identity that colonizing required.

I did not join this trek to the proletariat: some inner resistance, some hard grain of sense, kept me in New York. After graduation from CCNY I had looked around for work, and together with two friends, Al Nash and Oscar Pascal (both later to be active in the UAW), found a job in a factory in Long Island City manufacturing pinball machines. Not exactly heavy industry, but still heavy work. Oscar and I got sixteen dollars a week, Al seventeen because, said our foreman, he was married: one of my first encounters with the generosity of free enterprise. I worked a drill press, my muscles aching and my mind sick with monotony. As good Socialists, within a few weeks we started talking union to the other men in the shop. We weren't very skillful, and word must have reached the management. Suddenly, out of nowhere, there appeared one lunch hour a "union" representative (from a "union" no one could locate) who told us he already had a contract with the boss and promised, not wage increases, but that our dues "would be taken care of." As greasy as anyone's stereotype of a con man, this fellow was obviously a plant of the employer. The other workers, a little bewildered, remained silent, but Al, enraged at the idea of a "company union," started peppering him with sharp questions. A few days later, the three of us were summarily fired. We left ashamed of our ineptitude but delighted to be free of the shop.

The "proletarianizing" of our political group was a more serious affair. Dozens of our people settled in Detroit and Buffalo, where they found jobs in auto plants now shifting to defense production. Others went into defense plants in their own cities: New York, Philadelphia, Los Angeles. These were mostly young men and women recently out of college, often with strong intellectual interests, who found it hard to adapt to factory life, its physical strain, its monotony, its discipline.

Our people were bright, articulate, good-spirited; they threw themselves into union work, mostly in the UAW, with their whole hearts. Especially in the more progressive locals, our comrades soon won the confidence of local leaders, shop stewards, and rank-and-file members. They did not function as a tightly disciplined caucus, in this respect breaking with the traditions of both Stalinists and Trotskyists. Once they got over the foolishness of making big political speeches, they proved themselves first-rate unionists. Many became local leaders. They could structure their thoughts into sentences; they knew the rules of parliamentary procedure; they were honorable in combatting racial prejudice.

But finally, it didn't work. Writing years later about this experience, Al Nash remembers that the "proletarianized" members of our group "were able to speed the process of integration by aiding whites to understand the immoral meaning of segregation, by helping blacks to become leaders. . . . Articulate at union meetings and in the plant, and at UAW conventions, we served to make the union more democratic." But, he continued, "we failed mainly in expressing major socialist ideas. . . . We rarely if ever indicated, even to those closest to us in the plant or union, that we were socialists. We were fearful of appearing to hold views that were radically different from those of the constituencies we represented [as local leaders]. In a sense, we became prisoners of the social milieu we sought to change."

That last sentence speaks to a central difficulty of American radicalism. There were also subtler difficulties. Rank-and-file union-ists shrewdly sensed that these college boys and girls were not really *of* them, even if they were *for* and *with* them. Our people were "different." They read the *New York Times*, even if not in the shops. After work they wanted to go home and read books or listen to Beethoven, and if they sometimes went bowling with their shopmates they did so uneasily, self-consciously. Pure-spirited as they were, they could not transform themselves completely. Shop workers they could become, but they couldn't assume the psychol-ogy of men and women who had no choice but to be shop workers.

Deep clashes of style and value came out precisely when our people tried to draw close to the more militant unionists. To have overcome the differences would have required an almost complete self-effacement on the part of our people: it would have required that they give up their personal tastes, their cultural interests, their intellectual styles. They remained in the shops and the unions through the years of the war and for a time afterward. Once it became clear that individual careers were open to them as unionists but that the political possibilities were meager, most drifted home to New York and there fell back into their "natural" modes of life.

Because I had shown a flair for journalism, I served the Shacht-man group as a writer in New York. I loved this work, its illusion of engagement with the affairs of the world; but it also brought dis-comforts. What I did was appreciated well enough, but my friends felt uneasy about my unformed aspirations toward intellectuality. Marxists had always regarded intellectuals as "unstable"—desirable allies, but inclined to vanities of independence. Had I been clear about my own ambitions, knowing whether I wanted to be a politi-cal leader or a free-lance writer, I could have taken one path or another. But wanting to be both—that just could not work. Truth to tell, I was still very far from being an intellectual, only a few mild symptoms of that condition having revealed themselves. Of all the left-wing groups I've known, the Shachtman group was surely the least anti-intellectual: it strove toward a high level of thought, it often achieved an atmosphere of genuine tolerance. But there seems to be something inherent in socialist and perhaps all political movements that provokes them to repeated outbursts of anti-intellectualism, and the more genuinely American they are, the more they incline toward such outbursts.

A radical movement forms a fraternity proclaiming that all brothers and sisters are equal, but the intellectual, no matter how sincere his egalitarian convictions, has to claim that he knows some things better than other people. The intellectual deals with ideas, those mysterious values radical groups also claim as their own. Yet insofar as they aspire to a collective "line," these groups can never be quite comfortable with free-lance writers and thinkers who work as individuals. As a result, the intellectual in politics must always be in an uncomfortable position, suspect as much as admired, often wanted but seldom embraced. He irritates the activists. He seems arrogant and elitist, he holds himself above the petty tasks of organization, he focuses upon complications of analysis when the "burning need" is action. But these political brothers and sisters of his aren't quite ordinary people either. They glisten with good will, they reach moments of thoughtfulness, but they can seldom avoid dropping into simplification.

The activists are at least as ambivalent toward the intellectuals as the intellectuals toward them. The activists shift between an excessive respect for intellectuals and an irritable hostility; they want some intellectuals in the ranks, but as a decorative auxiliary, to be used or brushed aside as convenient. Between genuine workers and genuine intellectuals there sometimes starts up an odd, amused sort of friendliness, each side at ease in its distance from the other; but intellectuals and semi-intellectuals rub each other raw.

None of this was very clear to me in 1940. I thought of myself not as an intellectual but as a political person with somewhat wider cultural interests than prevailed among my friends. For a time, taking the role of journalist helped put aside such inner conflicts of feeling. At the age of twenty-one I became the editor of *Labor Action*. For some eight or nine months, until drafted into the army, I lived by the excitement of turning out this four-page weekly. The paper had been edited by Manny Geltman, a man with a natural gift for language, but now he was going to Los Angeles to become an organizer and I replaced him. It was the best training of my life and one of the happiest periods, too.

Leaders of our group would write political articles, analyzing the progress of the war, commenting on union events and struggles, polemicizing against other left-wing groups. But a good part of the paper, sometimes as much as half, I had to write myself. Prolific and cocksure, brimming with energy and persuaded I had a key to understanding the world, I needed only the reams of yellow paper on which I typed and the *New York Times* from which to draw facts. (Blessed *New York Times*! What would radical journalism in America do without it?)

We were trying to put out a popular paper within reach of "advanced workers," union militants who had some interest in politics, so I cultivated an easy style, aiming for short, crisp sentences, clear and vivid phrasing, and a minimum of political jargon. Reading over, a mere thirty-eight years later, what I wrote in *Labor Action*, I blush at the ready-made assurance with which I wrote; but having encountered in the intervening years a full share of intellectual and academic pomposity, I feel a bit better about the way in which I wrote.

I put in an intense four-day week. Sundays: a few all-purpose editorials, likely to be usable as long as capitalism survives; some amusing or indignant fillers; and editing the cumbersome prose of the political "heavies," trying to lighten their style in a way they won't notice. Mondays: copy arrives from "the field," usually knowledgeable stories about the inner life of unions. I meet with "Carlo," our charming, feckless artist who does a weekly cartoon for the front page: heavy lines, bold chiaroscuro, often caustic, sometimes witty. Give him a tip, a theme, and he quickly converts it into an image. Half the paper should be done by now, but seldom is. Tuesdays: the heavy work starts. I must write "to fill," that is, churn out enough copy according to the need of space. Sometimes it's very little, just a "lead" agitational piece, and sometimes it seems endless.

Wednesdays: in the printshop by 8:00 a.m. handing in the last batches of copy, starting to read proofs and write headlines; an hour later a fine old woman named Ruth, who's been a radical for almost half a century, comes in to take over the proofreading. I start "pasting up," that is, laying out the cut-out strips of proof onto an old issue of the paper, adjusting spaces for cuts, headlines, and boxes. If there's too much material, I have to juggle: it might be good to hold over till next week a heavy piece by our labor expert E. R. McKinney on the War Labor Board, but I don't relish the thought of his growling, were I to do so. Lunchtime: twenty minutes in a little café on West Fourth Street where week after week I sit a few feet away from a man with a heavily lined face who keeps poring over a book: it's W. H. Auden, some of whose poetry I've read. I'm yearning to talk to him: "Look, Mr. Auden, I'm a writer too, sort of a writer . . ." But I'm too shy. Fool! Why doesn't it occur to me that he too might be lonely and glad to talk to a young admirer who puts out a socialist sheet?

By late afternoon our printer Max—a booming Falstaffian character, drinker, gambler, womanizer, and veteran of 1920s communism who half loves us and half wishes we'd disappear from the face of the earth, since we're always behind on our bills—starts shouting that he's ready and by God I'd better be, too. Now comes the utter happiness of an old-fashioned print shop. In imagination I'm a *jour* printer, like Mark Twain and Walt Whitman, only more up-to-date politically. Lift the type out of the long metal trays. Violating union rules, insert corrections and even make up the simpler heads on a type stick. Carry the type to the large platform, called "the stone," where Max follows my pasted-up "dummy." (God help me if it doesn't work out right: "A dummy made by a dummy," he roars, "and a socialist dummy, too!") With quick, delicate movements he inserts thin metal rules and wedges of cardboard to adjust the spacing. The whole thing is held together in a frame that printers call a "chase"—an equilibrium of tension and yielding. If there's too much type I have to decide quickly where to cut, because Max is in a hurry, his woman is waiting in the office. Then, the wet page proofs, the sheer sensuous pleasure of beating out an impression on large sheets of rough paper. Tired but game, Ruth and I read the page proofs, trying to keep corrections to a minimum lest they lead to new errors. And then, about 9:00 p.m., the work is done.

Thursday mornings, I take the subway up to Times Square and go to a late morning show at the Paramount for forty-four cents. Big bands—Benny Goodman or Tommy Dorsey—are playing there, though at the first show, around noon, they are about as bleary as I am after the week's exertion. Still, I like to sit in the enormous half-empty theater, half listening to the saxophone and half looking at the movie. Fridays, the paper comes out and I examine it with a cruel eye, cursing the blunders I've made, hoping the comrades in the office will give me a word of praise. Good-hearted people, they often do.

Don't you know there's a war on? And so there was, in what must, I suppose, be called the real world; but a very strange sort of war. After Hitler's conquest of Poland, there followed a prolonged, eerie stalemate along the Western front, and we socialists speculated that a new balance had been worked out, a division of Europe favorable to Hitler but also avoiding a large-scale war. We saw little reason to have much confidence in the powers of resistance that the bourgeois democracies might show toward Nazi expansionism: not after Munich, not after the takeover of Czechoslovakia. Our speculation was wrong. We underestimated the ferocious urge to total domination characterizing Nazism. We were still thinking about Nazism as the last, desperate convulsion of German capitalism, and had not yet recognized that the society created by the Nazis was something qualitatively new in its monstrousness. Nor did we anticipate that even in the "flabby" bourgeois democracies, so pliant until now in relation to Hitler, there would emerge an enormous popular will to resist, a deep, spontaneous conviction that the Nazi regime had to be destroyed at all costs.

Like those French military strategists who planned the Second World War according to the technologies of the First, we were a war behind in our thinking. We still clung in our formal theories to the "Zimmerwald" tradition of those Socialists in the First World War who had refused to support either side on the grounds that the war was a struggle of rival imperialisms. We argued that capitalism was largely responsible for the rise of fascism; that the Western bourgeois democracies had proved to be anything but reliable opponents of Nazi Germany; that bourgeois democracy (by 1940 visible only in England and America) was unlikely to survive the strains of a prolonged war; and that the "only way" to defeat fascism was to move toward a socialist reconstruction that could give new fighting energy to the European masses. Some of these points contained an element of truth—for instance, the connection between the decay of European bourgeois society and the rise of fascist terrorism. But most were utterly wrong, such as the expectation that democracy would not survive a prolonged war, and all were painfully scholastic and beside the point.

In actuality we recognized what our formal "third camp" position failed to acknowledge adequately: that there was a deep truth in the feelings of most people that Nazi Germany signified a social evil far greater than that of traditional capitalism, and that the one had to be disposed of militarily before the other could be confronted politically. So while sometimes clinging foolishly to traditional radical categories, we functioned according to a more realistic and nuanced politics. We joined with those segments of the trade union movement, symbolized by the Reuther brothers, that tried to defend the rights of workers and the civil liberties of minorities (e.g., the Japanese Americans) even in wartime. We moved, I suppose, to what Marxists called a position of "critical support" for the war, though we didn't make this explicit—and I don't want in the least to deny the deep error of not making it explicit. We were trapped between an inherited ideology and a perceived reality. During the war years our organization came under occasional government surveillance but suffered no serious harassment—certainly a sign that American democracy retained its tolerance even in times of war.

What did we really feel about the war in Europe? The early triumphs of the Nazi army were frightening, and we began to speak among ourselves about the terrible possibility of a triumph of totalitarianism throughout Europe, perhaps the world. Nor were these irrational fears. True, our simplistic notions—"socialism or barbarism"—gained reinforcement from these fears, probably signifying a sense of hopelessness. Day by day (for there was no choice), we went along with the routine of our lives, within the small circle of left-wing politics, just as other Americans went along with their routine, within the small circle of family. We tried to buoy ourselves with talk about holding fast to the line of socialism, but felt we were slipping deeper and deeper into apocalypse; the thought of surviving to old age seemed an implausible vulgarity. Personal life, private feelings, all seemed trivial. I heard the news of Pearl Harbor while walking along Fourteenth Street: a large crowd had gathered in front of a radio store, the news of the Japanese attack came in the neutral tones of a professional announcer, and a strange hush fell upon the crowd, as if there were nothing to say—all was fatality.

For several months longer I continued to put out our paper, until one morning a long-expected notice arrived in the mail. A few weeks later I was on the way to Camp Upton on Long Island. No longer a socialist writer, simply one conscript among others, twenty-two years old, nervous, almost anonymous, and with the novel awareness that for a time, perhaps forever, my life was no longer in my own hands. I would be the name and number stamped on my dog tags.

4

In the Army

Lightly or heavily, those dog tags hung around my neck for almost four years. The army pressed one into physical closeness with hundreds of men, some from distant, alien parts of the country; the army, knowing its business, broke down persuasions of privacy, shame, and fastidiousness; the army imposed hardship and humiliation. Still, it didn't quite break one's spirit if one struggled shrewdly enough to keep it, so that even in recurrent stretches of depression, while zombying through close-order drill or lying empty on a bunk, I would still feel a bit of satisfaction at having stayed in the ranks and not having wanted to become an officer. Finally the army brought a lengthy exposure to solitude, that straining of nerves and pin's worth of knowledge which comes from being locked into one's self.

Army ways are mysterious and opaque: why it sent me to places where there was no active fighting I would never discover. I learned nothing about the dangers men in combat face, and little of those intimations of solidarity they are said to enjoy. Whether one lived or died, fought in the mud of Europe or dozed in an Alaskan barrack, was largely a matter of chance. Idling or shuffling papers in a headquarters company, picking up cigarette butts on parade grounds, standing guard like an iced scarecrow, seeing over and over again the syphilis horror film with its well-profiled chancres, taking basic training three times (once as an "armament specialist," though I hardly knew the difference between a machine gun and a howitzer)—to get past this bulking tedium was to be driven to a severity of inwardness that nothing in my previous years could have prepared me for. Yet others had it far worse.

My last two years in the army I spent at Fort Richardson, a post near Anchorage, Alaska. It was a landscape at once beautiful and barren. In the distance rose great mountain peaks, forever white; in the foreground lay a stubbled, chill terrain. During the long winter the days lasted no more than six hours. The cold reached thirty below, ripping into one's flesh like a drill, hard and dry. Nature here was pronounced sublime, but I found it without solace; the wonders of Alaska were not for a soldier's condition. I would wear three or four layers of outer clothing, puffed out like a clown, though in fairness I'll admit I never got sick. The germs, we used to say, were too clever to follow us up there.

All that bleakness and cold, also the stripped-down familiarities of the barrack, imposed a new order of awareness—perhaps in the way a prisoner studies a crack in the wall, bugs on the ground. Divisions of time grew blurred, then fell into neglect. Having no end of time while living in fear of its end, we did not know how to deal with mere days and weeks. One learned to attend the longer rhythms, living in the sweep of months—or sometimes, in a heightened moment, from the spark of a thought, the pang of a letter. But which day of the week it was—how could that matter if all were alike in their boredom?

By any obvious calculation I was lucky to be up there in Alaska, away from the killing, safe and sluggish, almost indifferent to ego, sex, or thought of the future. I had only to get through a minimal routine: occasional details assigned by a sergeant; Monday morning hikes across the snow; aimless fussing with blanket corners for Saturday inspection; faked urgencies of some dimwit lieutenant about keeping rifles oiled. No one cared much anymore. In this refrigerated asylum it was only natural that army standards relax to a slouchy humaneness.

Our chores done, we could enjoy a bit of freedom. It was a freedom from both risk and possibility, and it left time for reading and, once again, looking into the abysses of one's life—something like watching a picture on a screen when the projector has gotten stuck. The idea of an inner life took on new force, though I could not make up my mind whether it meant growth or decline. I had to accept anonymity in all its starkness and relief. I no longer had a "role" such as civilian life gave, even my odd sort of civilian life. But there was also comfort in this experience of "merging," this yielding to serial numbers. With luck, it might provide a culture for selfhood; at the least, it made one less of a nuisance. And now and again, more prosaically, I would be afflicted with guilt for having been dropped into safety by the military hand that might have dropped me to death.

I had a strange job. In the first years of the war there had been some fighting along the outer Aleutian Islands, which came under the Alaskan command. The Japanese had penetrated a few islands and then, in battles made peculiarly horrible by rain and fog, been driven back. A number of combat units were sent home or disbanded on the spot, and in their haste to get away from the dismal Aleutians, or from some equally dismal spot in Alaska, they had often left their records behind, helter-skelter. Now these records were being collected and shipped to Fort Richardson, where it became my task to "process" them, deciding which should be preserved and which destroyed.

I worked in an abandoned mess hall about half a mile from any other building; it stood there, a brown smudge, like one of those outposts you sometimes see in a Western movie. On bad days, when the wind cut through the camp, it took an effort to get to work: *Don't daydream,* I'd tell myself, *at least not till you take shelter.* Once during a storm, when really not daydreaming, I was hurled by the wind against the side of the mess hall. Bruises, cuts, curses. But safely there, I had the place all to myself. No one was likely to "drop in." What had been the kitchen now became an office, heated by a potbellied stove into which I stuffed discarded records; to keep the fire going was a steady inducement to work. I sat there alone day after day, working a little, reading a lot, sometimes talking out loud to myself and the walls.

Once every few days a friend named Ira, a clever New Yorker who also had a tedious job on the post, would phone me and our conversations, rambling into hours, might concern his wife's letter about a book she had read, lascivious recollections of pastrami sandwiches, or anything at all, just as long as it was not *immediately* personal, which is to say, too sensitive and painful. Once every two weeks I would be visited by the officer nominally in charge of my work, a somewhat nutty captain who cared nothing about records, sorted or unsorted. He used to launch half-serious, half-comic rants about his wife's unfaithfulness—she had apparently seduced most of the civilian males in Illinois—and then come to a climax of outrage not so much about her delinquencies as his failure to "get my share." I was appropriately sympathetic, for in the army one mode of grousing was very much like any other. But even these harmless visits came to seem a flaw in the perfection of my retreat: I had become fanatical about making the place foolproof, beyond surprise by intruders.

Hundreds of boxes of records were stored in the mess hall proper, and to get to my office in the kitchen you had to enter at the other end of the building and walk through a gloomy maze of shelves. Usually I could hear footsteps in time to put away my book or letter and hurry back to "studying" the records. But to prevent any slip-up, I talked it over with friends in the barrack, and three or four of them, amused by the whole idea, came over one Saturday and skillfully put down a "carpet" of a tinny metal. Stepped on, this metal gave off a crackling noise, like the sputter of firecrackers. Now I was king of the kitchen. (Years later, listening to a discussion of "workers' control of production," I reflected privately that only in my Alaskan job had I ever seen anything resembling it.)

There was no way to measure the work I did, nor did anyone care to. The Pentagon had put out a manual giving instructions on the disposal of records, written in a blinding jargon. Picking up this manual, my captain stared at it with a look of horror and barked out—it was his only direct order in our twenty-two months together—"Throw the fucking thing into the fire!" I didn't "throw the fucking thing into the fire," suspecting a moment might come when it would be handy to display on my table. So, as the months slid by, I pretty much made up my own rules about which records to keep and which to burn. I kept whatever had historical interest, all medical papers that might help a GI sue for a pension, and sometimes odds and ends just because I took pleasure in reading them. A lingering sense of conscience prompted me to work about two hours each morning, long enough to accumulate the pile of paper that would keep my fire going for the rest of the day.

Leafing through the records, mostly official junk, I noticed that one kind kept appearing more and more frequently—psychiatric reports. I soon became an addict, reading these with a fanatical attentiveness to symptom and therapy. Up there in Alaska I got my first intimate sense of psychiatric practice, something different from—more of an improvisation than—the psychiatric theory on which it was presumably based. The "psycho" rate in the Alaskan command was high, second only to that of the Persian Gulf, enforced tedium being harder for many soldiers to bear than even the dangers of combat. One army psychiatrist, a Major Z from Brooklyn, had spent a good many months on Adak, one of the largest of the Aleutians and by all accounts utterly dreary. This Major Z wrote reports at once passionate and dry. A poet of the case history, he made each one into a tense, sometimes even tragic narrative, so that a listing of symptoms grew into an exposure of suffering. As he concluded his stories of crackup, Major Z would almost always recommend that his soldier patients be sent back to the States for rest and treatment. Was it a sign of professional rigor? Or a measure of personal kindness?

I studied his reports with intense care, greater than I would ever give to a literary text, but no answer came. Each scrupulous account ended with an admission of limits; more we do not know or cannot say—as if he wanted to dramatize the helplessness of our knowledge. It was from this Chekhov of the Aleutians that I first learned about the magnitude of human disorder. Then one day, while thumbing through a batch of records, I saw something that made me jump from my chair and start shouting to the walls: a report, this time by another psychiatrist, describing "psychoneurotic symptoms" of Major Z and urging that *he* be sent home in turn! Why, at that moment, didn't Thomas Mann miraculously appear to whisper his knowledge that the true doctor must be the secret sharer of his patient's sickness? Those reports of Major Z, it turned out, had had their source in a communion of weakness. I never read another word from his pen nor have I ever heard what became of him after the war. A theorist of sickness, a mere routine success, a lost practitioner in some obscure upstate town? To me it hardly mattered, for he has remained intact in memory, the unmet teacher and healer of the papers I saved from fire.

Other knowledge came during those years. Never before or since have I read in so wonderfully purposeless a way. The camp library had a few serious books in each of a range of subjects, which encouraged learning and discouraged specialization. In the lapse of freedom the army enforced, it hardly mattered whether one read in anthropology or economics, history or literature. I would work my way through five or six books in a field, warmed by hidden lights of knowledge, without the faintest thought that my reading could ever be of practical use. For sheer disinterestedness of mind, no university I later knew could equal these months in Alaska. There was a world of thought, or what I could grasp of it, and there was my mind, linked in a purity of exercise. I read Boris Souvarine's biography of Stalin, which helped disabuse me of the Leninist myth. I read Gibbon for the sheer pleasure of his sentences and the therapy of his skepticism. I read Merle Curti's book on American democratic thought, not a first-rate work but good enough to persuade me that I knew little about the country in which I had been born. In later years, driven by ambition or trying to fill gaps in my knowledge, I would read in a quick, grasping way, vulgar with purpose, but here I could read for the unalloyed pleasure of knowledge. I read about the Maoris and Matthew Arnold's critical thought, the Bolshevik Revolution and the decline of Rome. In nearly two years in Alaska I must have read 150 solid books, more and better ones than any time before or since.

Enforced isolation and steady reading, together, brought about a slow intellectual change. I remained passionately caught up with politics, but increasingly it became an abstract passion, like a remembered love, and it was crossed by a multitude of new interests leading to that taste for complication which is necessarily a threat to the political mind. It was not my ideas that changed so much, it was my cast of thought. The results would not fully show up until seven or eight years later, but it was here in Alaska that I lost the singleness of mind that had inspired the politics of my youth. To see this as an unambiguous gain would be easy—and fashionable—but I don't think it was. Intellectuals, like most castes, protect themselves by celebrating their habits; the world, however, needs other modes of thought as well, and even the singleness of mind that liberal sophistication teaches us to scorn has its value. Once lost, however, it can never be regained.

As I read without scheme or purpose, I was discovering "what everyone knew." "What everyone knew" is the very substance of education, regained in each life. I was discovering there was far more in the world—more thought, knowledge, even uncertainty—than my earlier convictions had led me to suppose. I became enchanted with language in its own right, starting to wonder why the narrative rhythms of Roger Martin du Gard held my imagination, how Chekhov's unbrilliant paragraphs could move me so deeply (I still don't know), or what it might be about Edmund Wilson's sinuous sentences that enabled them to encircle one's mind. Not once did the idea of becoming a writer, let alone a literary critic, occur to me. The helplessness of being a soldier yielded a certain purity of feeling, though a grinding frustration, too.

Evenings were hard. Loneliness came to a pitch, the very presence of the other men in the barrack serving only to aggravate my sense of being cut off from life. About half an hour before "lights out" a saddened hush would fall across the barrack, as if everyone were slipping back into memory. During spring and summer the Alaskan evenings are splashed with sun, and one July evening we played baseball after midnight, an ecstatic game with wild shouts bearing thoughts of home and freedom. But the long months of cold also meant long hours of darkness, and there was little to do but lie evening after evening on one's bunk, dozing or reading.

Bringing a book into the barrack sometimes created problems with the other men. They were a decent lot and some understood that you might want to read "deep" books in, say, physics or accounting for later advancement. They also understood that you might read Westerns or comics or even "good novels" (Somerset Maugham, J. P. Marquand) in order to kill time. But to read without professional purpose and in a wide range of fields, to hop from "deep" to "deep"—this bewildered them. A little prematurely I came be to known as "the prof," and while there was respect behind that label, it also carried a charge of hostility, not violent but nervous, expressing a fear of difference. Once, on a stormy Sunday, a few of the men got into a sharp argument; the sharpness had its own momentum, almost unrelated to the subject they were talking about. They came to me for a judgment: "What's a cornea? Where is it? What does it do?" I had never made any claims in physiology, but if you were a "prof," by God, you were supposed to know. I tried to answer. I stumbled. Cries of delight: "The prof don't know! The prof don't know!" Some, in seeming good nature, start doing an Indian war dance near my cot. For at least a week I'm teased mercilessly, for in the army an event, no matter how trivial, can hang on for days, perhaps because events are so few. Finally, it all comes out well: my ignorance about the cornea restores me to the common lot, I regain the good feeling of the barrack.

Thrown together month after month in the closeness of barrack life, forced to watch one another dress, sulk, and defecate, we had to work out some rudiments of order. We improvised, perhaps inherited tacit rules that resembled the beginnings of civilization. If someone was physically sick, you had to come to his rescue immediately. If someone lay depressed on his bunk, in emotional pain, you were expected to leave him strictly alone, unless he asked to talk with you. The three or four feet around a bunk formed a precious cordon of privacy, and everyone knew why it had to be respected.

If someone shirked common duties like the Friday night "GI party" (cleaning up the barrack), then he became a target of harsh verbal attack. Standards were improvised for keeping a balance of sorts between a mode of life excessively public and our need for a margin of privacy. This required a delicate sensibility at times. I would be surprised by the way rough men, dull men, men who had little language, could respond to needs and griefs of others. A touch on the shoulder, a word in jest, the gift of a cookie received in the mail, all these spoke of quiet friendships, unasserted sympathies as part of our common effort at "making do." Being in the army might easily destroy sentimental illusions about "the masses," but there was no reason it should lead to contempt.

I made friends with a Southern boy who slept in the next bunk, a good-hearted, unworldly Baptist. We used to talk about racial equality, cultural difference, sometimes religion, talk softly and carefully like scouts feeling out terrain. Some of the other men would come by to listen and that was all right, sanctioned by the code of the barrack. But they rarely interfered, since it was understood that our mild disputes constituted a bond that it would be tactless to violate.

The strongest impression during those years was made by the Southerners. I had never been south of Washington, D.C., and thought all Southern whites were bigots and reactionaries (as many were). Almost by instinct I saw them as threatening, certainly beyond the reach of my understanding. Yet I was repeatedly struck by the ways in which even the least educated Southerners, hard-spirited as they might seem, still were in command of language, still could reach to a coarse or even obscene sort of oral poetry, a *debased* poetry, such as Northerners had either lost or never possessed. And though I could never learn to feel at ease with them, I was sometimes stunned by their gift for tenderness, breaking past the invisible lines of separation we all felt it necessary to preserve, and speaking openly of loneliness, lostness, yearnings. I did not understand this and perhaps still don't, but it left a mark on my memory and enlarged my learning; it helped me unlearn a little the things I had already learned.

About a year after I arrived in Alaska there moved into the end room of the barrack, usually reserved for the highest ranking noncom, a white-haired, leathery sergeant who was obviously older than the rest of us. He talked very little but had an elaborately courteous manner—startlingly, even comically different from anything usually seen in the army. I recognized him as Dashiel Hammett, whose books I admired more than his politics. Not yet knowing that famous people can be as shy as young ones, I hesitated to approach him. We did talk two or three times, mostly on indifferent topics like army routine and the journalism he was writing for the army. I suspect he would have welcomed a stronger approach, but this may be the sheerest imagining, as I, approaching old age, have come to understand how the shyness of the young can be as deadly a barrier as the aloofness of the well-known. At once hopelessly withdrawn and visibly kind, Hammett had a touch of natural aristocracy I had rarely seen before. Enigmatic, sometimes drunk, inspiring respect for reasons hard to name, he slipped away as quietly as he had come—a connection missed, a friend not made —and I settled back into our common routine.

* * *

And the war itself? Was that a matter of intense concern, a subject discussed and debated, in the barrack? I'm afraid not. Most of these men, a notch or two above the average in army intelligence, did not follow the war news very carefully. They rarely discussed strategy or policy. They were so far from the centers of decision, nothing they might do or feel could possibly have any impact on the war. They had, of course, a general sense of how things were going in Europe and the Far East—a sense for which the army word snafu usually sufficed—but they were singularly free of military romanticism or geopolitical considerations. Had anyone made even a squeak as armchair strategist, he would have been laughed out of the barrack.

In the army you absorbed a strong dose of realism, which meant a strong distaste for rhetoric. (One reason our soldiers were immune to the propaganda of the enemy was that they were immune to our own.) And then there always lurked the thought that some of us might suddenly find ourselves in places where shells were falling—which also made for reticence. During my years in Alaska I had a few spurts of ferocious concentration on the European military campaigns, following the battle strategies without a taint of ideological preconception. Such spurts could last for three or four weeks and then I'd lose interest, turning away from the maps and succumbing to lethargy, or something a shade different from lethargy, since it was marked less by indifference than by a protective resignation or withdrawal. Sick people in hospitals sometimes transform their confinement into the totality of their existence, not because they have forgotten but because they remember all too vividly the outer, real world.

One morning toward the war's end, I woke up to tumult in the barrack. "We," the United States, had dropped an atom bomb on a Japanese city and thousands of people had been killed! For the next few days we talked about the possibility that this would bring the war to an end, hardly at all about the larger significance of the bomb. Narrowness of vision, moral apathy? Perhaps so. But I think something else was at work—a hard, unglorious realism concerning the experience of soldiers. No one stopped us from saying what we liked in the safety of the barrack, but in his bones everyone knew we were not free, we lived suspended in a social limbo, and this hardly encouraged anyone to think and speak as a citizen in a democracy is supposed to. The same, I must confess, more or less held for me. In time I would share the anxiety that serious people have felt about the bomb, and I strongly agree with those who felt that President Truman's decision to drop the second bomb on Nagasaki lacked whatever justification there might have been for the first one. (Didn't one atom bomb "make the point" sufficiently?) But these thoughts came only later. In the days immediately after Hiroshima and Nagasaki, I did feel a certain heaviness of spirit, a hovering fear, but I could hardly have said why. In the barrack it was certainly possible to think about one's inner life, far more so than ever in the past. It was possible also to think occasionally about abstract ideas. But this did not seem the place to grapple with the problems of the world.

The barrack was one part of army life, another consisted of a friendship with Ira, the man who used to phone me at work. With him I was able to retrieve a few fragments of New York culture. Together, we could remind ourselves who we were, New Yorkers, Jews, and I at least a radical. Salvaging this modest "difference" meant keeping alive a sliver of identity. Sundays we would set off for Anchorage, walking the two or three miles if the weather allowed, and have a meal of lamb chops at the town diner, taste the cake baked by the Anchorage ladies for the USO, and head back. The town looked like a set for a Western movie, with a gray, slack Main Street that chilled the heart: you almost expected Gary Cooper to swing out of a saloon. Once, during a visit to entertain the troops, the comedian Joe E. Brown had called that street "the longest bar in the world." Our Sunday excursions formed a sedate routine, the equivalent I suppose to chamber-music concerts back home. We talked about family and books in a careful, low-keyed way. (Ira's wife was a compulsive Proust reader, starting up again as soon as she finished the series: I came to measure the seasons by her reported progress from Swann to Charlus.) But we rarely fell into private feelings, still more rarely into self-pity. Not that we weren't susceptible, heaven knows, to self-pity; it was just that we knew how crucial was the need to resist it. By keeping a discipline of limits and not, in that ghastly phrase, "letting it all hang out," we helped each other survive.

Back at the camp we had a friend who worked for the army radio station, a civilian, one of those American autodidacts who constantly amaze with their blend of knowledge and ignorance. In the evening he had to keep playing popular songs and hillbilly tunes for the men who had returned to the barracks, but during the day no one cared what he did. There was a prearranged signal: he would play the opening bars of the slow movement of Haydn's 102nd Symphony, which meant that it was all right to call in and ask for classical music. On the records promptly came, heard probably by no one but the three of us.

Those months of sitting alone in that kitchen office of mine exacted a price, reinforcing an already strong tendency to distraction and withdrawal. The staleness of days, the loneliness of evenings, the fear that youth was being wasted drop by drop, ate into my nerves. I hated it, passionately. So, with barely an exception, did the men in the barrack, though it was rare for any of them to say this openly, not because of fear but because it would have seemed pointless or, what came to the same thing, melodramatic. That less fortunate men were dying on the battlefields was a thought that could not prevent me from experiencing my own smaller but quite real suffering; it could only make me ashamed of it. In Alaska I learned why prison, even the most benevolent, must be a terrible ordeal: for certain temperaments the constraining of will comes to be a torture. Once or twice during these Alaskan years the monotony was broken, as when about a hundred of us went off in trucks one autumn for a long weekend to work on farms in the nearby Matanuska Valley. Picking and sorting potatoes, we gained an acute pleasure in work that seemed to have some value. We slept in a barn, ate fatty bear steak, and came back flushed with twenty-five dollars apiece and a taste of freedom.

Finally, the army forced me to acknowledge my "difference," though not in the expected ways, for whatever anti-Semitism I encountered was seldom vicious or even personal. It hurt less as a wound to my feelings than a moral puzzle I could not make out. I had known that many Americans disliked Jews—try not to know it! I had heard Father Coughlin give his anti-Semitic rants over the radio. I had encountered the occasional ugliness of New York streets. For all of these I had explanations social, historical, and psychological, so grandly scaled they almost blotted out the reality. But here, in my own barrack, among men I liked?

When one of the men made a nasty remark about Jews, he would say it in abstract and remembered tones, as if reciting a worn catechism. It bore the same mechanical rhythm as an obscenity, serving apparently as nothing more than a filler of speech. Yet once it came, it stung. Precisely the impersonal character of the anti-Semitism troubled me, raising for the first time the question whether anything could eradicate a contempt so rooted in ancestral myth. I don't want to overstate the matter: anti-Semitism was not a major difficulty in the war years, at least not for me. Nor do I want to claim that I had already come to understand what later would be a central theme in reflection about the Holocaust: that the mass killing of Jews, while entailing plenty of sadism, proceeded initially from some horrifyingly abstract notions. Nevertheless, in my own rather mild confrontations with folk anti-Semitism, it was precisely the lack of personal intent—what might be called its mythic inclusiveness—that made me feel especially helpless.

Five or six bunks from me slept a soldier from Alabama. He would occasionally make a wisecrack about Jews; they were sharp dealers or loved money. Yet he also wanted to be my friend, since he saw me as one of those interesting fellows who read "deep" books, and something within him yearned for what he thought those books—or at least the people reading them—could give him. (The same jumble of generalized hostility and personal amiability I later encountered in the novels of Thomas Wolfe, a writer who could not bear to think of Jews as ordinary.) When I once grew angry enough to protest these slurs, this Southern soldier seemed genuinely upset: how could I even suppose he wanted to hurt me? The Jews were . . . the Jews, but I was his buddy, for whom he would risk his life. And that was true—he would. Not that he put these feelings into words. Had he been able, he probably would not have needed to. But the confusion and dismay my rebuke produced in him lay stamped in red across his face, so that finally there was nothing to say, all my precious words were useless, and I had to lapse into a silence of frustration.

Alaska was my graduate school, where I patched together the foundation, skimpy and unaccredited, for whatever learning I could acquire. Here began the habit of mumbling to oneself that is an occupational disease of intellectuals. Here I came to see a little of what I really was, rather than what I had tried to will myself into becoming. Words held me; so did ideas. They brought complications a public man could not readily endure. Of course there's a touch of comedy in all this, since the kind of public man I had envisaged myself becoming—a socialist tribune or leader—couldn't expect much of a public role in America. What I was left with was ambivalence, and ambivalence would be my condition for many years. In time I would be overcome by a yearning for the excitements of public speech; I would crave again the life of movements and meetings. But more often a pull inward, a reticence or even shyness would take over, apparently my deeper self.

Those were my years in the army, benign and damaging, sluggish and nervous, an education by chance and a waste of youth. Before the war there had of course been the usual irruptions of need, grasping, and desire as the gross picturings of self. These irruptions one had to tame or suppress or conciliate. Now there were more nuanced ways of thinking about the self; indeed, of deciding how and whether to "have" one. It was not, apparently, a boon dispensed upon birth; it was something one might choose to nourish or to starve. The self need not be a mere docile shadow of one's doings in the world. It might be the very medium of existence, the residence of life. For such modest discoveries the army was far from an ideal place, and the cost in youth and temper ran pretty high. But as the more reflective, or is it the more resigned, characters in the novels of Henry James say: there it was.

5

Into the World

Knowing we will stay alive makes us wild to live. The day Japan surrenders we flip from resignation to crazy impatience. Night after night we sit on our cots counting "points," as if to conjure enough of them to flee the next morning. The months limp.

I board a ship to Seattle, one of those disheveled steamers that chug along the Canadian coast, and clutching the deck rail, stare moodily at the receding Alaskan waste. Preposterous tears fill my eyes. A last melancholy look, part of my youth buried here, I'll miss it even if I hated it. Enough, idiot, go home!

Back in the Bronx, back to its solacing grayness, I visit my parents. My father has become old, bent from his years over the press iron; my mother is visibly sick, yellow with cancer. They know I will be leaving soon, but ask if I would stay "for a few days, maybe," and all I answer is no, I cannot. To oblige them would be a scandal to the heavens. With about two hundred dollars in my pocket, I join two friends to find an apartment on East 107th Street, sufficiently proletarian. Just before moving in, I take a trip back to the Bronx and "steal" a folding chair from my parents' apartment—a chair I'll keep for several years. They don't need it, but why do I? This chair, which wouldn't bring a dollar from a junkman, this last battered token of our immigrant years—do I have the slightest awareness of what prompts me to take it?

The city is wonderfully unimproved. To be able to go into a greasy spoon simply because I want to seems a precious freedom. At first I long only for utter sameness, the New York grime, the sectarian cave, friends fixed in memory. But the women in the movement—they seem to have changed. Working in defense plants, rattling money in their pockets, assuming political responsibilities with a stylish ease, they are more independent than before the war, harder to place, harder to please.

Like many returned soldiers—it seems almost a moral obligation—I join the "52–20 club" (a year's unemployment insurance at twenty dollars a week). This enables me to contribute a year without pay to our socialist weekly. Back to the typewriter banging out articles, some mere set pieces I could have done four or fourteen years ago but others, like one after the Stalinist coup in Czechoslovakia, shadowed by new emotions of gloom. For about six months it all seems exactly as I had remembered and wanted: the past recaptured in every tint, every shape. But it does not work. One must learn that the past is not subject to the reach of will, and soon a metamorphosis of thought and feeling sets in: hesitant, feared.

During the war our little movement had prospered a bit. Those who remained at home had taken good jobs in basic industries, entrenched themselves in a few unions, especially the UAW, and recruited some honest-to-goodness workers. It looked, for a while, as if we were moving ahead, though in truth we were entering hard times. Now we were all a little older and the question of earning a living, once so jauntily brushed aside, took on an urgency it could not have had in the Depression years. Meanwhile our political expectations were crumbling. The capitalist world, by no means in its "final crisis," was entering several decades of economic expansion, so that whatever remained of American radicalism was bound to suffer confusion. The Marshall Plan, which only the most doctrinaire Marxists could dismiss as a scheme of American imperialism to consolidate its hold over Europe, would soon help countries like France, Germany, and Italy start upon a period of relative prosperity. The Resistance movements in Europe, which we had hoped would "deepen" into socialist politics, dissipated their energies in dispute and nostalgia. The European working class, conservative in its very radicalism, clung to traditional loyalties and refused to abandon either social democracy or Stalinism.

In Eastern Europe, Stalinism was showing itself to be not just the singular excrescence of a broken revolution in a backward country, but a new historical force that appeared to be both stable and expansive, powerfully linking military resources with political appeals. And the mounting reports of the Holocaust evoked not just horror but a new and unspoken bewilderment as to the possibilities of the human creature—possibilities, after all, upon which the hope for socialism must ultimately rest. Had we been the unbudging Marxists of eight or nine years earlier, we would simply have papered over these confusions with the formula that had long served radical movements: "correct about basic trends, mistaken about the timing of events." Being less dogmatic, we were more honest. Only for a very little while can nature tolerate so perverse a creature as a *critical* sect.

Still, even in its doldrums the movement offered a few pleasures. One came in 1950. As soon as international Stalinism had taken a "left turn" with the start of the Cold War, Earl Browder, the leader of the American Communist Party, was brutally expelled. This drab, owlish man, once a powerful figure, adviser to influential unionists, recipient of weighty messages from Moscow, honored with wild applause when he appeared at communist mass meetings, now was left with a dozen followers who straggled to meetings with their mimeographed leaflets, just like any other sad little sect. So we challenged Browder to debate Max Shachtman, the head of our group. Rashly Browder agreed, though when leader of the CP he would not even have answered our letter. The world at large continued to go about its business, but for everyone on the Left this debate held a blazing interest: our first chance to enter a face-to-face confrontation with the detested spokesman of Stalinism!

For hours we sat in our dingy Fourteenth Street headquarters discussing what Shachtman should say in the debate. I'm sure it was all perfectly clear in his head, but like other, more powerful leaders, he pretended to uncertainty on the chance that someone might come up with a new idea. I did. Treat Browder, I said, as if he were an East European communist leader slated for show-trial and purge. Shachtman grinned.

The evening of the debate, chaired with reasonable impartiality (as much as flesh could bear) by the radical sociologist C. Wright Mills, some twelve hundred people crowded into a hall, most of them one or another sort of anti-Stalinist. We were eager, metaphorically speaking, for blood. Browder spoke in his usual leaden style, periodically glancing up to the balcony, as if to savor once again the cheers of the faithful. But no cheers came. It was a tonic experience for Browder, this entry into the common fate. Shachtman spoke with repressed fury, as if years of waiting for this moment had perfected a rare discipline. Mounting to a tremulous climax, he started reciting the names of Stalin's victims, leaders of the Polish Communist Party, leaders of the Bulgarian, the Rumanian, the Hungarian, the Czech, all victims of a frame-up, all shot in obscure cellars—but there's a sudden interruption; he has gone past his time and the chairman, trying hard to be fair, asks him to sit down. Shachtman brushes Mills aside—no mere rules are going to interfere with *this* climax. His list of victims concluded, Shachtman wheels toward Browder, stretches a finger of accusation, and cries out: "There but for an accident of geography sits a corpse!" The effect is terrifying: Browder turns ashen. Shachtman sits down and, noticing me at the press table, winks—the only way he can acknowledge his debt. It's enough, that wink, now and forever: one of the better moments of my life. On such symbolic victories we managed to subsist.

It kept growing harder each day. A sect can withstand almost any trouble except the loss of inner certainty. Our little group was trying to adjust its premises to the visible social reality. We wanted to maintain *some* version of Marxism while recognizing that both the Europe and the America of the postwar years seldom matched the expectations of the Marxist mind. We struggled hard to think our way through these difficulties, but each small advance in thought brought a large increase of difficulty. We tried to stay within the confines of a Marxism "stretched" more elastically than we had ever supposed possible, but thereby we lost the support that inelastic doctrine can provide. Still, all this had some use. Our somewhat abstruse discussions were now leading to basic revisions of thought: we were beginning to see that for us the prime value was democracy, and that without it we could not even imagine a desirable socialism. The casual talk about "revolution" one might still occasionally hear was a mere verbal hangover. We were becoming Social Democrats or, if you prefer, democratic Socialists. Thought, at least in moments of crisis, moves faster than the categories containing it.

Yet it was this very process of rethinking that tore us to pieces. Shachtman had a keen mind, but lacked the courage of his conclusions: he had a curious habit of wrapping fresh ideas in stale Marxist paper, causing discontent among both those who disliked the ideas and those who disliked the paper. Some dropped out of our group with lengthy statements—left-wing statements *have* to be lengthy—and others departed quietly. I hung on, uneasily.

There were other signs of trouble. People of proven good nature grew irritable. A solid rank-and-filer who for years had collected dues now disappeared without a trace. It's unnerving: he simply stops coming to meetings, a dead soul. Next comes the turn of the nudniks. Each has a set speech starting with "only if" and ending with guarantees of salvation. "Only if" we become fully Leninist or drop the last vestige of Leninism; "only if" we acquire an indigenous American style (but what is that? how do you get it?); "only if" we recognize that the Soviet Union is not "bureaucratic collectivism" but a new mode of "state capitalism" (and suppose we do, will manna fall?); "only if" we blinker ourselves with one great single truth, can we reach the shores of success.

It becomes an ordeal to attend a meeting. You meet people you like yet can hardly bear to look at. Like votaries of a lapsed religion, we go through the routines of "business" and "discussion." We count our losses. We watch from the corners of our eyes to see who is dropping out. We console ourselves with injunctions to "stand fast." We meet less frequently—a help for the nerves. And the more we apply intelligence, the less it conforms to desire.

There are worse symptoms still. Disturbed people have a remarkable gift for sniffing out movements in trouble. Here is a new comrade, almost speechless: what is he doing with those boots and belt? The organization is crumbling and he declares himself "ready for action." What action? No matter, he's ready. Who is this figure of farce and menace, a provocateur shipped in by the FBI or just a sincere lunatic? We try to shuffle him away, wanting not to hurt his feelings yet fearful of what his fantasies might lead to.

I recall a story told by David Spitz, who belonged to the Columbus, Ohio, branch of the Socialist Party in the days when there still was one. A quiet young man joins the branch (*they are always quiet*). One day he calmly announces he has a cellar full of dynamite. Wearily a member makes a motion to expel, it's passed unanimously, and five minutes later the man with the dynamite is out. (Does he really have dynamite?) There is a common notion that such a fellow is likely to be a bloodstained European imported from Marseille or Sofia. Not at all. He is often a native, a cowboy of revolution, one of those American isolates smoldering with fantasies of the deed. For American socialism he is sheer poison and somehow, whenever things start going bad, he turns up "ready for action."*

In 1947 a young writer named Isaac Rosenfeld, who together with his friend Saul Bellow had briefly been a member of our movement in Chicago, published a story in *Kenyon Review* called "The Party." Drawing upon Rosenfeld's political memories, the story paints a semigrotesque picture of the sect:

> Behold our trademark: ends never meet. . . . Unless we raise two thousand new subscribers by next November our paper, *The Vanguard*, must fold. This is true. Nevertheless, we fail to get subscribers, even lose a few, and still the paper comes out. Perpetual suspension, deferment, a sublet of time. . . . Hardly the thing to expect of the only true party, the movement to which, when the false directions have been taken and all the mistakes made, the working class will of necessity turn. Necessity should cut a somewhat neater figure.

---

* The day after President Kennedy was assassinated, I felt I "knew" Lee Oswald. I wrote:

> A man who embodies the disorder of the city, an utterly displaced creature, totally and proudly alienated, without roots in nation, region, class. *He cannot stand it*, but what it is he cannot stand he does not know. A semi-intellectual, he picks up phrases and bits of ideology the way a derelict picks up cigarette butts. . . . An absolutist of drifting, he is intelligent enough to be in rebellion but sour, compulsive, repressed, seething with *ressentiment*. . . . Liberal society cannot reach or understand him, and he scorns it from the depths of chaos—or, as he comes to believe, from the heights of history. Dostoevsky was a friend of his.

There is a dissident faction calling itself the Ennui Club:

They met after hours in cafes to draw up their program of action, which they called a program of inaction. It was impossible to change the course of events; all existing parties were either bent on evil, or were futile, like our own. . . . It was necessary to go underground within the party. . . . Their objective—I find it almost too fantastic to mention. It was "to bore from within"—miserable pun; the party would change only when it was thoroughly bored with itself. It was to produce in the members a state of boredom so great that they would be unable to attend their own meetings.

The narrator, an (almost) true believer, clings to the faith, the word:

To us has been willed also a fortune; as yet it has no value except in our own circle. . . . But what a fortune—the whole world! Some day the world may actually fall into our hands! Then where would we run?

Like a finger pressing secret wounds, Rosenfeld's story hurt to the point of rage, perhaps because we knew that in its fantastic way it was scraping against the truth. Could we have dismissed him as an enemy it might all have been easy, but we knew he was not an enemy and that made the pain worse.

The time had come to break out. I needed to find some nourishment in the common air, refreshment in the world as it was, a world as badly flawed, no doubt, as we had always said, but still the only one at hand. Grateful as I felt for what the movement had taught—even mistaught—me, it was a crutch I could no longer lean on. It was morally bracing to see myself as an ordinary young man who had to earn an ordinary living. I had few marketable skills, the demand for former editors of socialist weeklies being rather limited in the United States. And I kept staring at the example of older "functionaries" who had given their years to the movement, only now to stagnate, bitterly or sadly, in a state of dependence.

Whenever in later years I heard James T. Farrell remember how hard it had been to leave the Catholic Church, or Joseph Clark on the nervous disorders afflicting some of his comrades after quitting the Communist Party, or Israeli acquaintances describe their guilt upon escaping the claustrophobia of the kibbutz, I would feel a twinge of understanding. Radically different institutions, these all shared a sentiment of coherence that people who left them would miss for a long time, maybe forever. I suppose most human beings have a need to cluster in circles, grasp hands, and praise the warmth they generate. The hunger for community has been one of the deepest and most authentic of our century, partly because so little fulfilled; but it has also been easy prey for charismatic swindlers and authoritarian cannibals.

To quit a movement in which one has invested one's strongest feelings can be terribly painful—at least as painful as leaving home or starting a divorce. At first I tried to maintain connection by keeping a distance. I would come to meetings only occasionally, I would write a piece once in a while for the paper, I would send a check. Had this brought upon me a barrage of accusation, it might have been easy to bear. But my friends were themselves being shaken by old doubts and new thoughts, so that in part of myself I felt it admirable that they should cling to our crumbling organization—just a little longer, in the hope that something might turn up. They even took a qualified pleasure in the modest success I was starting to have as a writer for intellectual journals: qualified because they feared this would lead, as it had with earlier intellectuals, to estrangement.

There were people in the movement I loved and respected—rank-and-filers, and one or two leaders gritting their teeth as they tried to think their way to a fresh politics while keeping the ranks together. I felt guilty. I accused myself of opportunism—and who, looking within himself, will fail to find it? But neither could I shed the conviction that the time of the sect was at an end. Nor deny the charge of my own desires, the persuasion that I was a young man with energy, ambition, perhaps talent. My friends—most of them—did not judge me: it was their understanding that tormented me.

I started hesitantly making my way into the outer world. The bourgeois, the philistine, the intellectual, the commercial world, a foul place, an attractive place with its money, fame, power, guilt—just say, the world! Not that I had much reason, as yet, to be disturbed by the prospect of success or to indulge in those reflections about its final emptiness with which successful Americans often console themselves. When I did think about getting on in the world I felt bad, but less because of what lay ahead of me than what I was leaving behind. I knew that in essential goodness of soul nothing I might ever find "out there" was likely to surpass my parents and my comrades. Nothing ever has.

Drifting away from a movement that has held one's deepest feelings entails far more than abstract decision. It means a wrench of faith. It means to abandon, perhaps betray, those who remain loyal. That I was gradually slipping out of the movement because (I told myself) I wanted to engage freshly with socialist ideas hardly eased the pain, since what stayed like a blow in memory were the faces of friends, troubled and sad. And even if the act of leaving were undertaken in evident good faith, one still had to wonder about inner motives. Only a dunce would not. Such moral discomforts can of course mask a ripe vanity, as if to say: how will they possibly get along without me? Still, my guilt hung on like a dull ache, and not because I thought I was doing wrong, but because I thought I was doing right. The worst kind of guilt is that which comes out of persuasions of necessity.

Perhaps in my awkward way I was reenacting the story of the young man from the provinces which is our legacy from the nineteenth-century novel. Perhaps the East Bronx formed a province, too.

In late 1946 I picked up a novel by Isaac Rosenfeld, *Passage from Home*. What drew me to it was probably the fact that its author had once been in our movement: I was curious about the terms of his passage. The novel itself, sluggish as story but bright with intelligence, described the inner experience of a Jewish boy, "sensitive as a burn," breaking out of family and entering selfhood: from dark to dark. Upon me it made an overwhelming impression, no doubt because it touched elements of my own experience that I had willed to suppress.

The day after finishing the novel, I sat down and wrote two thousand overwrought words about it. I wrote with hardly a thought of publication, pouring out unused feelings that the book released, as if the circling return of this young writer to the days of his adolescence in an immigrant family made it legitimate for me to venture a smaller, less-considered return:

I recall with emotion, for it impinges upon my own life—as so many other Jewish readers will feel the book does—a scene at the end of the novel where, after Bernard's return [from a flight from home], his father faces him in judgment and confession. . . . "He got up from the bed and walked about the room, stopping before the bookcase and looking at my books. He always seemed to regard them as strange and remote objects, symbols of myself, and thus related to him—it was with his money that I had bought them—and yet as alien and hostile as I myself had become. My father ran his hand along a row of books. . . ."

Nobody who has been brought up in an immigrant Jewish family and experienced the helpless conflict between the father, who sees in his son the fulfillment of his own uninformed intellectuality, and the son for whom that very fulfillment becomes the brand of alienation . . . can read this passage without feeling that here is true and acute perception.

I took the piece to Clement Greenberg, then an editor at *Commentary* and already famous for his art criticism. Some need to trip up my own ambition, together with an unwillingness to recognize that for me the writing of this little review had a large symbolic import, drove me to "explain" to Greenberg that I wanted to publish the review because I needed the money. It was a stupid and aggressive thing to say, and Greenberg, who was far from stupid though not exactly deficient in aggression, was quick to understand me. If I felt ashamed about appearing in a "bourgeois" journal, he wasn't going to assuage that feeling. "I don't care *why* you want to print it," he growled. "All I care is whether it's any good."

A few days later, now as close to kindliness as lay within his reach, Greenberg told me that *Commentary* would take the review and asked me to write other things. Once the review appeared I got a note from Isaac Rosenfeld, scrawled in pencil on brown butcher paper, saying I had shown that "the Marxist method" could be used with undogmatic flexibility in literary criticism. I was as bewildered as I was pleased. Not only was I now pronounced a literary critic, but I even had a "method," though when writing the review I had merely released some personal responses, without a thought of "using" Marxism or anything else. So it would continue through the decades, a cultural misunderstanding that chafed my vanity, but to which I had to resign myself.

For the next few years I wrote a number of things for *Com-*

mentary, mostly under the guidance of Greenberg, a hard man with a strong mind. I did an impressionistic piece called "The Alienated Young Jewish Intellectual," indulging a fashionable taste for Jewish self-scrutiny through talk about "alienation" and putting down some troubling memories that saved me from complete sentimentalism. (As a boy, when I played in the streets too long, my father would come from his grocery store, wearing a white apron, to find me. He would shout "Oivie," and his pronunciation of my unloved name, together with the apron, so embarrassed me that I would run home ahead of him, as if to keep a distance. Half a century later, I still feel shame.) Badly written but with lively patches, the piece attracted some attention. At a party I was approached by a giant of a man who looked like a pirate, complete with a game leg. In a rasping voice he said: "You'll write better ones." From Harold Rosenberg, encouragement of sorts.

A "better one" was a 1947 essay in *Commentary* about the novelist Daniel Fuchs, who during the thirties had published three novels set in a Jewish slum in Brooklyn. I liked all three, especially the high-spirited *Homage to Blenholt*. At the time he wrote them Fuchs was working as a substitute teacher in a Brighton Beach school, and though genuinely distinguished, his books brought him next to nothing in money. An offer came, tainted salvage, from Hollywood. He accepted it and there he has remained. Even as I was praising his work I couldn't refrain—since in a young radical there's often a big prig—from jabbing at Fuchs for having abandoned literature for Hollywood. Why didn't Greenberg protect me from this smugness? Why not suggest that I might be unloading on Fuchs my own unresolved problems? Soon after the piece appeared, a letter came from Fuchs asking in the gentlest way whether I knew what it meant to have written three novels and still not be able to make a living? What would I have had him do? I never answered, because I never could.

Half in the movement and half out, starting to write but still frightened of being a writer, I needed some work and money to keep me afloat. I found more work than money with Dwight Macdonald, who had belonged to our political group for a time but had left it, ostensibly because he disagreed with our analysis of Nazism, probably because he could not adjust his journalistic talent to a sectarian milieu. During the war years Macdonald had started to publish a monthly called *Politics*. Sharp and amusing, feckless and irritating, *Politics* for most of its short life was the liveliest magazine the American Left had seen for decades. It exposed political and moral hypocrisies of the Allied powers during the war; it took jabs (I wrote one) at the increasing sedateness of *Partisan Review*; it conducted guerrilla polemics against Marxism; it became a stopping place for independent leftists who were bored with Marxist sects yet refused Cold War conservatism. Its energy came mostly from Macdonald himself, a brilliant journalist. In my own political milieu *Politics* was read with a nervous fascination, for while we were troubled by its accumulating "deviations," it was still a magazine one could actually read, which was more than could usually be said for our *New International*. Who, for example, could resist Macdonald's high-spirited attack on Henry Wallace?

Wallaceland is the mental habitat of Henry Wallace plus a few hundred thousand regular readers of *The New Republic*, *The Nation*, and *PM*. It is a region of perpetual fogs, caused by the warm winds of the liberal Gulf Stream coming in contact with the Soviet glacier. Its natives speak "Wallese," a debased provincial dialect.

Without a party line (sober or drunk, Macdonald could not walk a straight one), the magazine grew increasingly "unreliable" in its ideology, slipping off into various quasi-syndicalist utopianisms, and provoking people like myself precisely because we too were becoming "unreliable," though at a different pace and in other directions.

Macdonald needed an assistant and there I was, ready to assist. I did editorial chores, reworking pieces, and writing a "Magazine Chronicle" praising or attacking articles in other magazines. Macdonald bestowed on me the pen name of Theodore Dryden, who was, he said, a "ferret breeder in Staten Island." All this for fifteen dollars a week!

Macdonald was a hard boss, charmingly irascible, at once bright and silly. He had a deadly eye for dead prose, especially the weighty sort of deadness I brought with me, but he was insensitive to styles not immediately transparent or journalistically "clean," like Harold Rosenberg's epigrammatic prose. Dwight was a little stingy, too, so that some weeks I had to remind him of my precious fifteen dollars. That I was now working for *Politics* made some friends in the movement uneasy, as hard-shell Baptists must feel when a congregant succumbs to soft-shells. It was solemnly agreed —such are the distinctions spun in sects!—that I could work for *Politics* as a technical aide but not an editorial collaborator. Macdonald was kind enough not to tease me about this; perhaps he saw that I was already heading down the slopes of apostasy and there was no need to push.

Toward its end *Politics* became boring, for much the same reasons earlier Marxist journals and the later *Dissent* could sometimes be boring. Macdonald's stay in the radical movement had left him with delusions of theory, and in 1946 he published a long essay, "The Root Is Man," which created a stir on the Left. An effort to demonstrate that "Marxism is no longer a reliable guide to action or understanding," the essay was also "partly a discussion of . . . scientific method, partly some rather desperate suggestions for a new kind of radical approach—individualistic, decentralized, essentially anarchist." The scientific method emerged unscathed from Macdonald's handling, and Marxism he criticized along anarcho-liberal lines familiar enough. His main contribution came in the department of "desperate suggestions," the struggle to find some absolute ethical grounding for an undogmatic radicalism contrasted to Marxist historicism and relativism. The essay was in many ways a poignant expression of the plight of those few intellectuals— Macdonald, Nicola Chiaromonte, Paul Goodman—who wished to dissociate themselves from the new turn to *Realpolitik*, but could not find ways of transforming sentiments of rectitude or visions of utopia into a workable politics. It was also a leftist rationale for a kind of internal emigration of the spirit, with some odd shadings of similarity to the Salinger cult of the late fifties. One need not be a Marxist to suspect that such ideas will usually lead away from politics entirely.

The danger in Macdonald's effort was that finally it would come to little more than a striking of fine moral attitudes that left unanswered the question of what politics, if any, remained for the non-Stalinist left. Still, there was something admirable in his over-reaching. His work drew upon a trend in Western intellectual life during the forties when, in revulsion from the brutalities of Stalinism and the rigidities of anti-Stalinist Marxism, a number of European intellectuals, especially in France, tried to plant a radical politics in the soil of humanist sentiment and ethical value. This effort produced better literary work than political guidance, since it was hard to get beyond stirring injunctions that means should be closely aligned with ends. These injunctions, fine as they were, still left us staring helplessly at the world as it was; they could at best tell us what to be or become, but very little about what to do. The Marxists, impatient with the moral frettings of writers like Camus, Silone, and Chiaromonte, pointed to the necessary gap between assertions of value and necessities of practice; but the Marxists, or most of them, were blind to what was authentic in the gropings of these intellectuals. Ethical consciousness could not be a substitute for politics, yet without it politics had come to seem intolerable.

Acts of reconsideration—with their backing and filling, their spurts of aggression, their finicky nail-biting—can be one of the finer modes of intellectual life; but except for those immediately engaged, they can also be boring. Growing more earnest, *Politics* became less captivating. Its last few issues were choked with lengthy polemics, including attacks on Macdonald by me and my friend Lewis Coser, a socialist refugee from Europe. We "corrected" Dwight, all right, but our polemics helped sink the magazine. By 1947—his patience, energy, and perhaps money giving out—he called it quits, with a likable statement that blamed neither the spirit of the times nor the unaroused proletariat. He was, he said, tired. And there went my fifteen bucks a week.

Working for Macdonald's magazine brought in a few dollars and provided a touch of intellectual novelty; writing for *Commentary* brought in a larger number of dollars and helped spread my name a little. But the vibrant center of our intellectual life was *Partisan Review*, its prestige still high in the late forties. So, as if again to deceive myself about my own desires, I wrote a slashing attack on *Partisan Review*'s postwar retreat from Marxism and sent it off, with a curt note, to one of its editors, Philip Rahv. Whatever else, this was hardly the customary way of breaking into his pages. Perhaps amused by my cheekiness, perhaps still responsive to Marxist war cries, Rahv asked me to drop in at the magazine's office.

I went up to the *PR* office thinking it was a big event in my life and, well, it was. With his low gurgle of a laugh—even his laughter seemed a political act!—Rahv gave me back my article: "You don't really think we're going to print an attack on us, do you?" Then came what he took to be a neat thrust: "After all, you're a Marxist, so you ought to understand why we don't want to act against our own interests." In a gesture I later recognized as his way of opening a conversation, Rahv started poking his finger into my chest, establishing a tradition in which mockery served as a token of friendliness. I tried to answer that Marxism spoke of the clashing interests of social classes, not of editors and writers. He brushed that aside. As I was leaving, he asked if I'd like to review a book for the magazine. Stacks of review copies were lying around, and without grasping the significance of my choice I took a collection of Sholom Aleichem stories. Rahv smiled. Even among big talkers, some things don't have to be made explicit.

In those days *Partisan Review* paid, as I recall, two dollars a printed page. It brought more glory than groceries, but that did not keep serious writers from wanting to appear in its pages. Though the editors, William Phillips and Philip Rahv, had the reputation of being brusque toward young writers, they were as kindly and encouraging to me as a beginner could hope for. One reason, I suspect, was that we all came out of the left-wing milieu, so that Rahv and Phillips must have felt more at ease with me than with, say, a young poet like John Berryman. This did not keep them from occasionally trying to channel my work to suit their narrow polemical needs. I succumbed once or twice—it's very hard for a young writer not to; but after a time I learned that editors will survive very nicely if you deny their schemes. Rahv was shrewd in proposing topics modest enough for my capacities—reviews of books that took me, in miniature, on the journey from politics to literature, and Phillips helped trim my prose of bombast.

For a young writer, nervous with insecurity and ambition, there can hardly be anything more exhilarating than the thought that a literary group stands ready to welcome him. It need not be an unqualified welcome; it can consist of a mere conditional testing, enough to cut the loneliness of youth and nourish dreams of solidarity. Among us in America there has of course been another, stronger line of feeling about the literary life. Circumstances having imposed a stringent isolation on our writers, it was only to be expected that isolation come to be regarded as a sign of moral purity. We have cherished the image of the writer as a lone cowboy "holing up" on a ranch and emerging a few years later with a thousand overwritten pages. Now this may in fact be the way some novelists have started their careers, but it won't do for the critic or social commentator, who cannot survive without those pressures of the past we call tradition and that interplay of voices we call community.

When I began publishing my little pieces in *Partisan Review*, I swelled with a secret pride, feeling I had made my way into the best literary magazine in America. It seemed to me that I was stepping into "another world," a community bright with freedom, bravura, and intimate exchange. I also feared this world, suspecting it might weaken my already weakened political commitment. And I was by no means sure that, in the range of intellectual sharpshooters like Philip Rahv, Sidney Hook, and Harold Rosenberg, I could hold to my bit of space.

By the time I really got to know the New York intellectuals—we might as well agree to call them that—they were going off in many directions. Having come together to quarrel as friends, they were now separating to quarrel as enemies. As if to parody the left-wing sects, each *Partisan* writer, or at least the more aggressively political ones, seemed to constitute a political faction. A writer like Harold Rosenberg or Lionel Abel presented himself as a sort of free-lance guerrilla ready to take on all comers. The only time all the *Partisan* writers came together, except for a rare meeting to draft some statement of protest, was at the parties Rahv or Phillips gave two or three times a year, gatherings of seventy-five to a hundred people that resembled a bazaar more than a social event. Here alliances were struck up or down, deals clinched, quarrels reheated. Turkish boundaries separated men and women, and were crossed only by those women who wrote on their own and thereby had a "right" to share in intellectual conversation. Milling about in the large, drafty rooms of the West Village, the *PR* writers distributed pieces of gossip, weighed prestige ratings, fought over politics.

Semioutsiders were not sure what to make of these gatherings, "important" though we felt them to be; they were too tense to yield much pleasure, yet too chaotic to be regarded as meetings (there was no chairman). I spent one evening staring at a beautiful young woman who had come with the poet Delmore Schwartz, though I was much too shy to say anything to her. Years later, after she had become Schwartz's wife, I told Elizabeth Pollett about that evening, and in mock despair she berated me for not approaching her since she too had been shy and miserable. For someone like Elizabeth, who bore the freshness of America on her face, it must have seemed that she had wandered into a brilliant madhouse, promising wonders of cultivation and heartache.

Was that world of intellectuals *really* there? I mean, really there as a community both substantial and coherent, or was I, out of the clamor of will, "myself creating what I saw"? Later writers would grow sentimental about this *Partisan* milieu, as if once there had been a golden age, or at least a golden minute, in which writers shared ideas and ideals, read each other's work, fought together against Stalinist *apparatchiks* and middlebrow philistines. Since then, goes the myth, there has been a fall, perhaps fortunate, perhaps disabling. It's a nice story, but while I witnessed the fall, I'm not sure there was ever a garden.

I do not know of any occasion when the *Partisan* writers seriously discussed with one another work in progress. They were like-minded in deep, unspoken ways, especially those who shared memories of having grown up in immigrant neighborhoods or who, in irregular sequence, had fled the Stalinist stockade. A grunt of approval from Rahv, a kind word from Lionel Trilling meant more than high praise from outsiders, for one knew that *Partisan* writers seldom rushed to celebrate, indeed, found it far more congenial to attack. But of visible community there were few signs that I could see. This was a gang of intellectual freebooters whose relations with one another more closely resembled the jungle of Hobbes than a commune of Kropotkin. Writers who were usually identified, either by friend or foe, as members of the *Partisan* group would hotly deny that such a group so much as existed, or if it did exist that they—*they!*—would be so docile as to be part of it. Some, like Lionel Abel and Harold Rosenberg, were never very strong in sentiments of fraternity, and Rosenberg, in a polemic against other New York writers, would later coin a memorable phrase, "the herd of independent minds." A newcomer knew he had been accepted once he received the gift of criticism. This was not at all a bad apprenticeship, if only one could pretend to have a thick skin.

But a visible community of mutual learning and help? That was mostly an idea in my head, an unquenched yearning, soon to become suspect as a lapse into sentimentality. Or it was an alluring myth which the *Partisan* writers, perhaps because it still moved them, could acknowledge only through mutterings of denial. In Europe it had often been a matter of pride for writers to say they had once been close to the Bloomsbury group or the *Scrutiny* circle. To have attended Mallarmé's Tuesday evening receptions was a mark of high glory. In New York that sort of feeling, though it existed, was seldom free of a nervous aggressiveness. Contentious, plebeian, and necessarily insecure in their relation to American culture, the New York intellectuals formed, at most, a loose and unacknowledged tribe. Still, members of a tribe are likely to know one another at depths beyond language. The *Partisan* writers might become political enemies and quarrel angrily, yet their half-hidden links were never to be quite broken. The attention, by no means always kindly, that people with a shared past accord one another—this formed a subtle bond that a newcomer could hardly be expected to see.

If there ever had been a coherent group sharing a world view and doing its work together, that must have been during the first five or six years after *Partisan Review* established itself in 1937 as an independent anti-Stalinist organ. But perhaps that too is an illusion? Another instance of our weakness for moving the golden age farther and farther into the past? As early as 1944 William Phillips was complaining that the gifted new writers—he named Randall Jarrell, Elizabeth Bishop, Saul Bellow, Mary McCarthy—"are isolated figures, lacking the elan and confidence of a movement." If so, when *had* there ever been one?

Movement, community, solidarity: it seems always to have been there the day before yesterday, always to have broken up only yesterday morning, always to have left the "young ones" unfortunate in not having known the great days. An unshakable myth calling upon our deepest desires: it was just as well to impose the myth on *Partisan Review* as on anything else. Perhaps, as with so many literary groups, the New York writers had come together mostly in order to drift apart. Perhaps they were closest to one another precisely at the moment of separation, closest with a sense of solidarity rekindled by the hardness of ending.

But that is not how I saw things at the time. In the late forties the morale of the *Partisan* writers was high, some were starting to win fame, and their earlier sense of fighting a defensive action against hordes of philistines and Stalinists was giving way to the feeling that "we" were getting closer to the center of American cultural life, there to bedazzle, instruct, and punish, and to test our powers.

Another amendment: if there was no visible community of New York intellectuals in the sense of people engaged in an active fraternal collaboration, there were filaments of sensibility, persuasions of shared outlook and condition. After all I, a mere novice, within a year or two had established professional relations, and sometimes a little more than that, with Macdonald, Greenberg, and Rahv. These were intellectuals of consequence: Macdonald a gifted publicist, Greenberg the author of such major essays as "Avant Garde and Kitsch," Rahv a powerful critic and editor. A community may consist of people holding sentiments and ideas in common, even if they bristle whenever they approach one another. And for someone making a foray into the intellectual world, it was a piece of good fortune to encounter these editors, critics, hecklers, and teachers.

All these little forays were nothing at all, if it was the world I really wanted to enter. So far I had merely been visiting uncles and aunts, amiable ironic older cousins living down the street. In 1948, however, I did take a step that brought me just a little closer to centers of money, power, and misuse.

I had published in the *Nation* a savage review of a historical novel by the German-Jewish writer Lion Feuchtwanger, a book that draped "progressive" sentiments over spicy contents. Two or three weeks later came a note from T. S. Matthews, editor of *Time* and in an earlier incarnation himself a savage reviewer: if I could write such acid reviews for the *Nation*, why not do some for *Time*? Balzac's Lucien dizzy before the Parisian fleshpots, Dickens's Pip yielding to London snobbery, and now I—also, as it were, a boy from the country—lured by Satan's finger of gold. Everyone I knew held *Time* in contempt for its chauvinist pomposities and abuse of language, and everyone was right.

But I went. In Rockefeller Center the Time-Life Building loomed up as if to command the world, and in a big office I met the stony Matthews, who offered his temptations while no doubt being amused by (since he quite understood) my discomfort. I did a trial review of Van Wyck Brooks's *The Times of Whitman and Melville*, praising its pastel colorings of the native past but criticizing its neglect of our tormented literary radicalism. With few cuts and no changes, the review appeared. Again, Satan's finger beckoned. Would I take a part-time job as a book reviewer, asked Matthews, which meant doing one piece of no more than 800 words a week for seventy-five dollars? My financial troubles would be over; I could do the review at home and then have at least half a week for "my own work." But how could I enter that den of the devil—I who had declared myself a Socialist and in literary pieces appropriated the stance of the uncompromising highbrow? And meanwhile, whom could I ask for advice? My old comrades, affecting a superior realism, suggested that since you had to sell your labor power, you might as well sell it to whoever paid the most. This bringing little comfort, I turned to the Commander of the Partisans, Philip Rahv. The Commander laughed at me. It was better, he mumbled, while that finger of his started poking at my chest, to do dirty work for one boss who paid well than for a dozen who paid badly; free-lancing was a wretched business—he was surely right about that!—and it was still more wretched to be supported by a wife or lover drudging away in an office.

I took the job, comforting myself with the thought that I would not be asked to write political reviews, which indeed I never was. Without a Ph.D. I had no hope of finding the skimpiest instructorship in a university—and who, in those years, wanted that sort of job anyway, who so much as even thought of it? Imagine being locked away in some drab university town, swallowing martinis with waspish English professors and "teaching" Emerson's essays to bored lunkheads! As for liberal magazines like *Commentary* and the *New Republic*, they were usually willing to print my pieces, at least the literary ones, but would not consider me for a staff opening, since it might be a nuisance to have a socialist colleague. *Time* was rather more tolerant of, or indifferent to, my politics even during the McCarthy years. All it wanted from me was a few hundred "literary" words each week, bright, quick, and conspicuously authoritative.

I worked as a *Time* reviewer for about four years, my virtue besieged but not, I liked to think, quite fallen. Virtue, it turned out, was a quantity not so fragile as I had been led to suppose: it could take a good deal of pummeling. Among both friends and enemies I sometimes became an object of fun, and for this I had only myself to blame. Out of embarrassment, I had insisted to an acquaintance that I was working "only part-time" for *Time*, so it seemed reasonable or amusing for friend and foe to ask, can you sell yourself "part-time" to the devil? Isn't a sale a sale? I had meant that I was giving the devil a part of myself in order to gain freedom for the other part. Unless a writer had an inherited income or could turn out best sellers, wasn't that the way of the world? If only I hadn't been so foolish as to "explain" my situation, I would have managed a good deal more comfortably.

I became friendly with a group of literary men who also worked for the magazine—some of them, poor creatures, full-time! One was Robert Cantwell, a talented "proletarian novelist" during the thirties, who became for me the prototype of a figure I would meet again and again: the burned-out ex-Communist, touching in his exposed humanity, seemingly unable to regain his footing as an ordinary person in the ordinary round of life. Cantwell used to slip into the office like one of those Hawthorne characters who bear a stigma of guilt neither they nor anyone else can explain. Painfully nervous, unnervingly gentle, panting like a wounded creature, he would take a book and flee. He wrote turgidly, as incapable of cleverness as of lying, and soon I realized he was being kept on out of institutional generosity. *Time* often damaged its writers but seldom discarded them.

Among the reviewers were Robert Fitzgerald, a gifted poet; Nigel Dennis, soon to be a first-rate satirist; Louis Kronenberger, a cultivated man of letters who covered theater; and James Agee, who had won recognition for *Let Us Now Praise Famous Men*, a lyrical evocation of the life of Southern sharecroppers, and wrote about the movies. All these men felt disdain for *Time* and some discomfort at working there. It became deeply absorbing for me to watch how they coped with these problems: perhaps I could learn from them, since all were writers meriting respect.

Agee seemed to suffer most, though it's quite possible he would have suffered most in any setting. He seemed a figure of utter desperation, a romantic in whom "the Southern quality" had been raised from provincialism to style. Everyone wanted something from him, some revelation of grace or sign of wisdom, yet he himself was by then deeply stricken with self-doubt, and whenever he had to do a "cover story" about the movies he went through the torments of hell. He seemed unable to establish distance from the work he did for *Time*, he couldn't tell himself it was just a living, he punished himself by taking it seriously and then taunting himself for being fool enough to do that. When I met this princely man in the corridors, he would smile at me wanly, distractedly, as if to acknowledge a chafing fraternal link, but what that link might be he did not say, nor did I ask.

At the Friday book conferences Robert Fitzgerald tried to keep his poise, or just his sanity, by assuming an air of unbroken gravity, as if he were a monk bound hostage to a gang of heretics. Needing someone with whom to share my discomfort, I would focus on his immobile, handsome face, hoping that eventually life would also teach me the uses of façade. Our sharing was mainly a sharing of silence.

Nigel Dennis's mask was at an opposite extreme: the sardonic wildness of an Englishman to whom all things American, its magazines especially, must seem absurd. A serious man, he did what he had to, as a professional does, without tears or hand-wringing. He must have thought Fitzgerald and me, in our different modes of embarrassment, more than a little ridiculous. Dennis was a master at turning out flip notices of historical novels which carried just the air of knowing superiority the editors of *Time* adored. Fitzgerald had far more trouble with his copy, and so did I, probably because we were clamped by self-consciousness and sometimes even foolish enough to try to write something serious. At least half the reviews I wrote were never printed.

Each Wednesday morning I would sit in my bedroom, trying to squeeze out a few hundred glistening words, always postponed to the last possible minute, while aware that soon they might be printed simultaneously by giant presses across the country. I had enough sense not to write "Timese," the supercilious style of the magazine's earlier years, but I would try to come up now and then with a "sparkling" phrase. Once, to Matthews's delight, I described Henry Miller's prose as "dithyrambling." That probably assured my job for a year.

Fitzgerald and I got most of the "highbrow stuff." Slick middlebrow magazines like *Time* were eager to "keep up" with Niebuhr and Jaspers, Kafka and Pound; the editors of the magazine were sufficiently self-intoxicated to think they had "intellectual obligations." Dennis used to laugh at Fitzgerald and me when, against our lower judgment, we would take a book of poetry or literary criticism to review; he knew that the books one cared for were precisely the hardest to write about. The magazine wanted to boast of the intellectuals in its stable, it wanted to be the first to notice gifted new writers. We were never asked to write down, only to be "accessible" and "vivid." But of course a sufficient measure of simplification had to slide into vulgarization. There were some things—a nuance of feeling, a complication of judgment, an uncertainty of response—that couldn't be smoothed into the glassy surface of journalistic prose. I wrote reviews of Ezra Pound, William Carlos Williams, and Henry Green in ways that did little violence to my opinions but much to my responses. In reviewing a first novel one admired, it was possible to slip in a single qualification; but two or more meant risking that the editor would say, why bother if it has so many flaws? Doubt, the signature of intellectuals, had to be reserved for other places.

Yet I learned something at *Time*—to write on demand. It is very hard to evoke the quality of a novel in a few paragraphs, harder still to give even the barest version of its plot. Transitions had to be rapid, judgments filed down to simplicity, sentences clipped—though an occasional bravura passage could boast elaborate structure.

During the several years I worked at *Time*, I wrote intently on my own, somewhat as a young professor tries to write his way out of a provincial university. Together with an old political friend, B. J. Widick, I published a book on Walter Reuther and the United Automobile Workers Union; I did a critical biography of Sherwood Anderson; and I began to write the essays that would make up *Politics and the Novel*, the book in which my political and literary interests were able, I think, ardently to fuse. But my somewhat schizoid existence grew more troubling each month. It became harder to think of some phrase that might create the illusion of liveliness in the few hundred words I turned in to *Time*, harder to write as if this sort of factitious liveliness were a supreme value.

Once Robert Fitzgerald left *Time* upon inheriting some

money, I found it harder still. We had not been friends. Perhaps we behaved a little like two respectable gentlemen embarrassed at meeting in a place both disapproved of. Still, his presence had made it easier for me. Now he was gone and I had no crony with whom to share silence. I had to escape, one way or another, and in 1953, when invited to join the Brandeis English department, I did. Perhaps there was even some warrant for my unspoken belief that by working on the time provided by *Time*, I managed to break loose from its grip—indeed, from all it symbolized.

By 1950 I knew I was going to spend the rest of my life as a writer. I had been accepted, with a restrained though sufficient warmth, into the milieu of the New York intellectuals. It seemed extraordinary. Was it really so easy to launch a literary career? So easy to announce oneself a critic, without tests, credentials, or testimonials? Apart from whatever talent one might bring or nurture, the main thing about becoming a writer was apparently to *declare* oneself a writer, imposing one's self-definition on editors and whoever else might care. This was very far from the whole story and not at all the most important part, but to a young man—one whom a distinguished literary lady had just declared to be a "Jew-boy in a hurry"—so it seemed.

6

Literary Life:
New York

By 1947 it seemed the quarrels of the thirties were done with: we had apparently won, we leftist and liberal anti-Stalinists. Too young to have experienced personally the literary-political wars of the thirties, I sometimes felt as if I had lived through them, participant by courtesy of inherited myth and judgment.

How strong had Stalinism really been in the American intellectual world during the thirties? Was it, as becalmed liberals liked to say, a mere marginal eruption confined to a few big cities—the very cities, as it happened, in which our cultural life was concentrated? Or was it true that communist cadres had often taken control of major cultural institutions?

There are no reliable statistics, and the quantitative approach is mostly beside the point. Only a tiny minority of American writers openly announced themselves as Communists; only a somewhat larger minority came under the sway of the sentiments and institutions of cultural Stalinism. The real question is this: where in the intellectual experience and cultural life of the thirties could you find the strongest energies? Where, as the colloquial phrase nicely puts it, was "the action"? To ask the question is to answer it: at least until the Hitler-Stalin pact of 1939, cultural Stalinism had become a significant power in the United States, not unchecked or unchallenged, but exerting far greater influence than its numbers might suggest.

Speaking in the name of the oppressed and invoking the inner rhythms of History, the communist movement tapped both idealism and guilt among intellectuals. It elicited their yearnings for a better world; it exploited their readiness to kneel before an ideological church—both of these together, strength and weakness, rebellion and submission.

In 1932 John Dos Passos said: "Becoming a Socialist right now would have just the same effect as drinking a bottle of near-beer." Sherwood Anderson asked himself what the difference was between Socialists and Communists, and answered: "I guess the Communists mean it!" In its very transparency this sentence helps explain why so many writers in our century have yielded themselves to authoritarian values: *The Communists mean it!*

At least as troubling was the need felt by serious people for a ritual abandonment of intellectual independence—indeed, for a ritual abasement before the brutalities of power. The sensitive literary critic Newton Arvin wrote to his friend Granville Hicks in 1932:

It is a bad world in which we live, and so even the revolutionary movement is anything but what it "ought" to be: God knows, I realize this . . . and God knows it makes my heart sick at times; from one angle it seems nothing but grime and stink and sweat and obscene noises, and the language of the beasts. But surely this is what history is. . . . Lenin must have been (from a conceivable point of view) a dreadful man; so must John Brown and Cromwell and Marat. . . . I believe we can spare ourselves a great deal of pain and disenchantment and even worse (treachery to ourselves) if we discipline ourselves to accept the proletarian and revolutionary leaders and even theorists for what they are and must be: grim fighters in about the most dreadful and desperate struggle in all history—*not* reasonable and "critically-minded."

These words form a classic instance: the belief in some ultimate Reality which only Communists possess; the initial idealism of a scholar taking upon himself the alien role of ruthless fighter; the ease with which he smothers problems of political choice by invoking "historical necessity"; the suspicion that politics is rendered authentic by the weight of violence attached to it; and still, the urgency with which he speaks truth about the desperateness of modern life.

Sometimes by speaking truth, sometimes by shows of brilliance, sometimes by sheer nerve, *Partisan Review* had clawed its way to cultural strength. The magazine could now hoist reputations, push a young writer into prominence, and deal out punishment to philistines, middlebrows, and fellow travelers. Because it stood for something, *Partisan Review* gained influence. It evoked fear among opponents, rage among academics. William Dean Howells had once joked that anyone can make an enemy, the problem is to keep him. This skill *Partisan Review* had mastered.

At the thought of "those characters out there"—that is, beyond the Hudson—cursing and fearing him, Philip Rahv, the dominant editor of the magazine, used to chortle with pleasure. (My image of chortling is of his large body weaving up and down, in appreciation of the discomforts of others.) Rahv ran the magazine like a party leader or parliamentary whip, spinning threads of maneuver so complex they sometimes sped past their intended victims. Whenever I met him, he would propose that I write something to "smash them." Always there was a "them," from Stalinists to New Critics. Rahv cultivated a Marxist style without its political context, and among our "opponents" only Allen Tate responded satisfactorily, for in his splendid Southern manner he was always ready to charge into battle. No wonder Rahv and Tate became good friends: nothing but ideas stood between them.

Most of the New York writers were still young. "Veterans" like Hook and Rahv, Phillips and Schapiro, Rosenberg and Clement Greenberg were in their forties. Younger people, very talented, kept appearing: Randall Jarrell, Elizabeth Hardwick, John Berryman, Saul Bellow, Robert Warshow. Not all of these sympathized with *Partisan* politics, but most felt at home with its homelessness. The magazine had a heady cosmopolitan air in those days, with contributions from T. S. Eliot and George Orwell, André Gide and Jean-Paul Sartre. Anti-Stalinist leftism created a fragile bond across borders: one felt a kinship with writers like Orwell, Silone, and Camus without having ever met them. There was a visible pride in the capacities of mind. There was an impatience with that American tradition which regards writing as the outpouring of untainted intuition. There was a spirit of arrogance that kept out lesser souls, smaller talents.

Now that Hitlerism was destroyed, intellectuals felt they had to reach out for new ideas, new modes of sensibility fitting the postwar world. Dissatisfied or bored with Marxism, many *Partisan* writers started to shake off the very idea of system. In spring 1946 the magazine put out a remarkable issue, "New French Writing," that included Sartre's powerful essay on anti-Semitism, Camus's reflections on the myth of Sisyphus, and the work of other French writers—some, like Malraux, already famous and others still unknown, but all testifying to the upheaval caused by war, captivity, and resistance.

What now began to absorb the New York writers was a search for some principle by which to order the world after Hitler, culture after the Holocaust. The idea of centrality replaced the ideology of Marxism, though the idea can be seen as a stepchild of the ideology. To be central meant to engage with questions that gave our time its peculiarly terrible character. T. S. Eliot in his poetry had been central; Trotsky had for a time been central; and in the postwar years Kafka seemed central, if only in the purity of his desolation. The idea of the central was slippery—that was what made it attractive.

In the late forties Lionel Abel wrote a piece challenging the older assumption of the centrality of modernist culture and radical politics; that was no longer true, he said, though what had replaced them he could not say. No, said Harold Rosenberg. He believed the historical crisis that had spawned modernism was so persistent, so unrelenting, "there is no place for art to go but forward." Why so? Hadn't we been saying the same thing about politics, and didn't political life somehow not go "forward"? Still, if (as I now believe) Abel was right, the question remained: what might come after modernist culture and radical politics? No one quite foresaw the benefits of several decades of relative affluence and reconsolidated democracy in Western society. No one foresaw it until the Marxist lenses, or blinkers, were lowered. So a race broke out, some of the

Partisan sprinters heading straight for the castle of centrality while others were distracted by sideshows of novelty.

A year or two after the war one began to hear about existentialism, associating it mainly with the names of Sartre and Camus and thinking of it not as a formal philosophy but as a testimony springing from the ordeal of Europe. It seemed more attractive in voice than doctrine. It swept aside the rigidities of deterministic systems, the Left's traditional reliance on "historical forces." It sought to implant a new strength in the *sentiment* of freedom, not by claiming for it transcendent validation or even historical grounding, but by placing it at the heart of our need, perhaps our desperation. "We had arrived," wrote Nicola Chiaromonte, "at humanity's zero hour and history was senseless; the only thing that made sense was that part of man which remained outside of history, alien and impervious to the whirlwind of events. If, indeed, such a part existed." That "if" was transformed by desire into an "as if," becoming the burden of Camus's rebel.

In America existentialism led to no literary groups or schools, but it forced writers back to an apprehension of some essential, naked man: a mere idea of man, if you wish, but an idea rich in salvage. I can't remember anyone I knew declaring himself an existentialist except William Barrett, a recent addition to the *Partisan* circle; yet in some unsystematic way the writings of Sartre and Camus left a strong mark. Of the two, Sartre had the more powerful mind, but politically and "personally" (though I never met him) I felt closer to Camus. Sartre seemed an unresting machine for the manufacture of theories, while Camus, in his veiled bewilderments and unveiled vanities, struck one as more humane. You might learn from Sartre, but you could talk with Camus. And in Camus there were two saving presences: the individual person, a stranger stammering with doubt, and the physical world, shore, ocean, sun. There was also a disturbing softness in Camus, a weakness for noble rhetoric. Still, I thought of him as a comrade, as I could not think of Sartre. It was Camus who said: "The great event of the twentieth century was the forsaking of the values of freedom by the revolutionary movements. . . . Since that moment a certain hope has disappeared from the world and a solitude has begun for each and every man." That was how I felt in those years, though I would not have put it quite so grandly, with quite so much assurance about the "solitude" of "each and every man." But then, I told myself, Camus was French.

Ideology crumbled, personality bloomed. Perhaps there was a relation between the two? The New York writers, unmoored and glad to be, began to take pleasure in constructing elaborate public selves. The *Partisan* group had done its best work during the late thirties and early forties; now its scattered members, tasting the sweets of individuality, were beginning to do their best individual work. In the search for centrality, they yearned to embrace (even crush) the spirit of the age.

Do I delude myself in thinking there was something peculiarly Jewish in this need to wrestle with the hovering *Zeitgeist*? "For two thousand years the main energies of Jewish communities . . . have gone into the mass production of intellectuals"—so Harold Rosenberg had once written. Here now, with appropriate flair and chaos, were a number of them, cut off from traditional attachments either Jewish or American, casting themselves as agents of the problematic, straining for high thought and career.

The first New York writer with whom I became friendly was a recent arrival from Chicago. *Wunderkind* grown into tubby sage, Isaac Rosenfeld radiated a generosity that melted the crustiest New York hearts. It was easy to imagine him, as his childhood friend Saul Bellow recalled, getting up at a debating club in school, still in short pants, and reading an essay on Schopenhauer; it was not hard to imagine him in a Vilna yeshiva, elucidating points of Talmud. Owlish and jovial but with sudden lilts of dignity, loving jokes even more than arguments, he had a mind strong at unsystematic reflection, though he never quite found the medium, in either fiction or essay, to release his gift. He was also a delicious mimic. Visiting Isaac, I would beg him to do his Yiddish version of Prufrock—"ikh ver alt, ikh ver alt, un mayn pupik vert mir kalt" (I grow old, I grow old, and my bellybutton grows cold)—or his devilish skit about Rahv and Phillips, now deflated to Weber and Fields, spatting over who should go downstairs to buy stamps. Isaac seemed a literary offspring of Sholom Aleichem but his mind had succumbed to Kafka—not, as it turned out, a happy affair. Still, he was our golden boy, more so than Bellow, for there was an air of yeshiva purity about Isaac that made one hope wildly for his future.

Profligate with his being, his time, his thought, he lacked only that cunning economy that enables writers to sustain lengthy careers.

I learned from Isaac the possibility of a life unflinching in restlessness, chained to some absolute of the *luftmensh*. Chaos besieged his orderly mind, engulfing his Jewish reasonableness. He became a wanderer, physically and intellectually, out of step even with his own dybbuk. He played minor parts for a time in a third-rate Yiddish theatrical troupe; he closed himself into a Wilhelm Reich orgone box to grasp superior energies; he wanted to get past his skepticism and stretch beyond known definitions of person and place. Jewish to his bones, he sought a way of leaping beyond those constraints that in our time signify Jewishness, and all that stood in his way was his body, his country, his time. At thirty-eight he died, in lonely sloth.

When I knew him, in his few happy years after the war, Isaac made me feel the world was spacious. There was room for him and for me. Our friendship didn't last long: he must have smiled at my opinions, while I fretted at the splashing away of his gifts. All we had in common was being young, Jewish, in love with English words, and a rationalism that no one can escape whose childhood has been soaked in Yiddish. Isaac chose to move beyond that rationalism, as I could not, but even while fearing the price he must pay, I envied his staggering freedom. Little remains of this flawed, noble spirit: a minor first novel, some fine critical miniatures, and a legend of charm and waste, a comic intelligence spent upon itself.

I visited Isaac as friend but attended Harold Rosenberg as audience. Never have I known anyone who could talk with such unflagging manic brilliance, pouring out a Niagara of epigrams. In the late forties Harold was not yet a famous art critic, and the consciousness of public power that shadowed—perhaps overshadowed—him was not yet a barrier. Whatever fears may have assailed him, he surely could not have known the fear of running dry that haunts so many writers. He was always available, and always nothing but himself. Harold was Harold as granite is granite. He lived by a consciousness of historical crisis, making himself theoretician, prophet, advance man, and inner critic of aesthetic modernism. The sectarianism of the radical vanguard he reenacted through the hermeticism of the artistic vanguard.

As Harold rasped along in his high-pitched voice, did he ever so much as notice who stood before him? I used to think, when visiting his studio: suppose I were suddenly to drop dead, would he stop talking? All the while he was the most ingenuous of democrats, one ear being as good as another. I would leave his studio gasping from overstimulation. If only I could "bottle" all I had heard, there'd be enough to work with for a year. But his ideas could not be "bottled," they had a curious way of evaporating into the upper air. It was as if they came alive only through his voice.

What I learned from Harold Rosenberg was not a particular idea, since he had so many, but the wonders of abundance and, still more, the satisfaction of going one's own way. In those years Harold was somewhat isolated, having remained closer to his apolitical Marxism than most other New York writers to their earlier political ideas. If this isolation bothered him, he never showed it. A man who could fill a room with his lunging, arrowed body and rivet attention through his stammer of phrases—why should he feel unhappy about his isolation?

Years later his old friend Lionel Abel would sum up the essence of the man: "That which is prior to, more fundamental than radicalism in art, radicalism in action, is the homelessness of spirit that gave rise to both. . . . Harold addressed himself to making clear that no alternative to, or ideological therapy for, our condition of homelessness has yet been found, and until something of that order is discovered, our only valid works of art, our only valid actions, must continue to express a certain distance from things, from others, and even from ourselves." Thirty years ago I could not have made so lucid a claim for this spirit of modernism, but some glimmer of it I had, and that may be why I found myself so dizzied by the hammerings of Rosenberg's mind.

Even when brief, such friendships brought lasting pleasures and rewards, but there were also missed occasions due to my muddle of shyness and vanity. Long before I thought of becoming a literary critic, I read with admiration the essays that William Troy was printing in *Partisan Review*. He was not part of its inner circle and had no apparent interest in politics, but each time he wrote— on Lawrence or Fitzgerald or Virginia Woolf—I admired his clarity. Troy was a "pure" critic and he helped—it was about time—to unsettle my provincial notions about what criticism had to be. There was an austerity to his work, a hard, undeviating concentra-

tion on the literary text, which set him apart from other contributors to the magazine: he never bothered to be merely brilliant,
he never rattled his emotions in one's ear. Several times in the late
forties I started writing him notes of admiration but always tore
them up, suspecting I might be trying to cozy up to a famous man.
A few years after Troy's death I met his widow, the poet Leonie
Adams, and when I told her of my repeated failure to write him
about my feelings, she let out a moan. In the early fifties he had
been a troubled man, uncertain of himself and his work, and the
admiration of a young stranger, she said, might have given him
pleasure. She wheeled on me: "Why did you worry so much about
your motives? Suppose they weren't pure? Don't you see that what
matters is what we *do*?" Her words shaming me as few stronger
rebukes ever have, I turned away in silence, to carry with me
through the years a dislike of that vanity which drapes itself as
scruple.

I used to think of the rise of the New York intellectuals as a
historical sport, a singular event caused by an overflow of energies
from the children of Jewish immigrants. So of course it was. But
now I also see this "singular event" as embedded in the deeper
rhythms of American culture, rhythms of shock, break, and intrusion by alien roughnecks.

Suppose we agree provisionally to look upon the history of
American culture as a grudging retreat from visions of cultural
autarchy. The appearance of the New York writers should then be
seen not just as a rude, alien intrusion—though it was that, too—
but also as a step in the "Europeanizing" of American culture.
Among *Partisan* writers there was a conscious intent, not without
touches of grandiosity, to capture the idea of Europe for America.
That meant above all the idea of *another* culture, an older culture,
one richer in moral possibilities, steeped in bloodier experiences,
and closer to the tragic than ours could ever be. Other American
writers had reached out toward Europe, from Henry James and
William Dean Howells to T. S. Eliot and Van Wyck Brooks. The
New York writers were coming at the end of a line, but even at the
end, the idea of Europe gave them a renewed energy. Themes of
cultural return figure strongly in their work: in the dissemination of
Russian modes and sensibilities, in the championing of the great

modernists, in the popularizing of Marxist ideas, in the insistence that, to be serious, literature must now be international.

Their international perspective came from a provincial experience. Most of the New York writers stemmed from the world of immigrant Jews, having come to articulateness at a moment when there was a strong drive to both break out of the ghetto and leave the bonds of Jewishness entirely. The New York intellectuals formed the first group of Jewish writers coming out of this immigrant milieu who did not define themselves through either a nostalgic or a hostile memory of Jewishness. By the late thirties Jewishness as sentiment and cultural source played only a modest part in their conscious experience. What excited them was the idea of breaking away, of willing a new life. They meant to declare themselves citizens of the world and, if that succeeded, might then become writers of this country.

The Jewish immigrant milieu had branded on its children marks of separatism while inciting fantasies of universalism. It taught them to conquer the gentile world in order finally to yield to it. By the twenties the values dominating Jewish immigrant life were largely secular and universalist, with strong overlays of European culture. Strategic maneuvers of the vanguard had first been mapped out on gray immigrant streets.

With that immigrant culture our relations were far more tormented than we could possibly know. Denial and suppression, embarrassment and shame: these words would not be too harsh. Take so simple a matter as the pen name chosen by *Partisan*'s chief editor: I knew of course what *rahv* meant, yet years passed before it dawned on me that Philip wanted to present himself as chief rabbi of our disbelieving world, choosing, in a paradox typically Jewish, to blur his Jewish identity by adopting an aggressively Jewish name. For that matter, it would be a fascinating exercise to go through the first twenty years of *Partisan Review* in order to see how frequently Jewish references, motifs, and inside jokes break past the surface of cosmopolitanism.

We wanted to shake off the fears and constraints of the world in which we had been born, but when up against the impenetrable walls of gentile politeness we would aggressively proclaim our "difference," as if to raise Jewishness to a higher cosmopolitan power. This was probably the first time in American cultural history that a self-confident group of intellectuals did not acknowledge the authority of Christian tradition. A whole range of non-Christian references was now reaching at least some American literary people, terms like Hasidism, place names like Chelm, proper names like Sholom Aleichem. *Partisan Review* printed some, if not enough, criticism of Yiddish writers—Isaac Rosenfeld on Peretz and me on Sholom Aleichem; the magazine was just starting to confront its anomalous position as the voice of emancipated Jews who nevertheless refused to deny their Jewishness. Surprising assertions broke through. I recall my shock—rather a pleasant shock —in the late forties when reading Clement Greenberg's attack on Arthur Koestler for accepting the "majority gentile view" of the East European Jews. "It is possible," wrote Greenberg, "to adopt standards of evaluation other than those of Western Europe. It is possible that by 'world-historical' standards the European Jews represent a higher type of human being than any yet achieved in history. I do not say that this is so, but I say it is possible and that there is much to argue for its possibility." Some *Partisan* writers may have felt a twinge of embarrassment before these words, but I suspect that Greenberg was also expressing part of their deeper feelings.

Little wonder that portions of the native intellectual elite, or ragtail poseurs trying to shimmy their way to elite status, found the modest fame of the New York writers insufferable. Soon they were mumbling that American purities of speech and spirit were being contaminated in the streets of New York. (When I first met John Crowe Ransom and heard that lovely man speak of "Toid" Avenue, I was stunned: had his speech also been contaminated in the streets of New York? It turned out that some Tennessee speech sounded, at least to my dull ear, like that of Brooklyn. But Ransom said "toid" without worrying about *goyim*.)

Anti-Semitism had become publicly disreputable in the years after the Holocaust, a thin coating of shame having settled on civilized consciousness; but this hardly meant that native writers priding themselves on their toughness would lack a vocabulary for private use about those New York usurpers, those Bronx and Brooklyn wise guys who proposed to reshape American literary life. When Truman Capote later attacked the Jewish writers on television, he had the dissolute courage to say what more careful gentlemen said quietly among themselves.

A sprig of genteel anti-Semitism was also entwined with the ivy of our more notable departments of English. When I tell my students that only forty years ago so distinguished a literary man as Lionel Trilling had trouble finding a job in the Academy because he was Jewish and therefore judged by his "peers" to be deaf to the "Anglo-Saxon spirit" of English literature, those students stare at me in disbelief. Their disbelief was made possible by an earlier generation's discomforts.

The New York writers introduced a new voice in American literary life: a roughening of tone, a burst of demotic speech. Here perhaps they did have some kinship with earlier writers like Whitman and Melville, who had also brought a plebeian strain into American writing, though because of their discomfort with native traditions the New York writers were slow to discover this (Alfred Kazin was a notable exception). The gentility against which writers like Theodore Dreiser had rebelled was quite beyond the reach of the New York writers clawing their way out of immigrant quarters. Gentility seemed comic. It was a device for making us squirm, reminding us of our uncouthness. And we repaid with contempt, as well as a rather ungenerous suspicion toward those of our own, like Trilling, who had mastered the art of manners (not, after all, so forbidding or impossible).

These New York writers constituted the first intelligentsia in American history—which is a shade different from a group of intellectuals. The figures near Emerson formed a community of intellectuals but not an intelligentsia—not, at least, as defined by Renato Poggioli: "an intellectual order *from the lower ranks* . . . an intellectual order whose function was not so much cultural as political." Poggioli had in mind the Russian writers of the late nineteenth century, but one can find points of similarity with the New York writers. We too came mostly from "the lower ranks" (later composing rhapsodies about the immigrant parents from whom we insistently fled). We too wrote with polemical ferocity. We too stressed "critical thinking" and opposition to established power. We too flaunted claims to alienation.

A footnote about this "Russianness" of the New York milieu

came from Lionel Abel in the forties. Invoking, or improvising, "the tradition of the *Partisan*," Abel wrote: "For good or ill, modern politics is *a school of rudeness*. . . . The exquisite aristocratic tact which subtly specified the circumstances under which things could be called by their right names is today something we know about largely from books, not from anybody's public behavior."

Insurgent groups hoping to rouse anger against established authority will always be tempted to violate rules of decorum. Rudeness becomes a spear with which to break the skin of complacency. In its early years *Partisan Review* was often rude, sometimes for no reason whatever, as if to demonstrate its sheer prickliness. But there were serious reasons, too. Rudeness was not only the weapon of cultural underdogs, but also a sign that intellectual Jews had become sufficiently self-assured to stop playing by gentile rules. At the least, this rudeness was to be preferred to the frigid "civility" with which English intellectuals cloak their murderous impulses, or the politeness that in American academic life can mask a cold indifference.

Even the ways in which New York writers earned their livings helps place them as an intelligentsia. A few scholarly figures like Schapiro and Trilling were professors. Harold Rosenberg had an enviable part-time job at the Advertising Council, where he created Smokey the Bear. (The sheer deliciousness of it: this cuddly artifact of commercial folklore as the creature of our unyielding modernist!) The others, as the Yiddish saying has it, lived mostly "off the air." The *Partisan* editors may have granted themselves modest salaries and been helped by generous wives, but their survival in the thirties and forties is still a mystery. People like Paul Goodman and Lionel Abel hung on at the margin. Clement Greenberg and Robert Warshow worked at *Commentary*. Delmore Schwartz in the late forties had about half a dozen jobs with foundations, magazines, and universities, none of which seemed to take up much time. Until the Second World War, Paul Goodman said, it had been possible for a writer to get by in "decent poverty"; later it became almost impossible to manage as a free-lancer. In the early fifties, as jobs opened up in the universities, all this changed and the *Partisan* group ceased being an intelligentsia—indeed, ceased being a group.

The story of the New York writers has curious similarities to the story of the Southern writers. Allen Tate, the most historically acute of the Southerners, remarked that "the distinctive Southern consciousness was quite temporary. It has made possible the curious burst of intelligence that we get at the crossing of the ways, not unlike, on an infinitesimal scale, the outburst of poetic genius at the end of the sixteenth century when commercial England had already begun to crush feudal England." Can we not say something similar about the New York writers? Both groups were equally cut off from the mainstream of American culture, equally assertive in affirming their minority splendor, equally ideological in styles of thought (though in New York it was called—oddly—"scientific," and in Nashville—quaintly—"poetic"). The Southerners too were on the lookout for centrality. Their relation to literary modernism was somewhat less inhibited than that of the New York writers; their politics almost as ill at ease with American liberalism. No wonder conflict melted into a gingerly friendship, plight calling to plight, ambition to ambition.

The "crossing of the ways" about which Tate spoke must always prove to be temporary, yet it is this sense of historical tremor which can give point and urgency in literary work. One thinks back, choosing and picking, to Delmore Schwartz's stories, to the early fiction of Bellow and Malamud, to Rahv's idiosyncratic criticism of American literature, to Hook's social criticism, to the London Letters of Orwell, to Robert Motherwell on modern art, to the learned incisiveness of Meyer Schapiro's critiques of Lewis Mumford and Edmund Wilson, to the brilliant drama criticism of Mary McCarthy and Eleanor Clark, to Dwight Macdonald's social journalism. Writers of alien opinion also began to find their place in *Partisan Review*: Eliot sent in "The Dry Salvages," Allen Tate his essay on Poe, André Gide pages from his journal. Nothing, at least in my lifetime, has quite equaled this.

There were limitations, too. The *Partisan* group had its tight little orthodoxies: it would have been astonishing to hear a good word for Trollope or Thackeray, a modest recognition of Arnold Bennett or E. A. Robinson. Taste had its narrow boundaries, and one took pride in the narrowness. *Partisan Review* cut enormous segments of the literary past out of its scrutiny—a parochialism of the present, as if modern literature were the whole of literature.

Connections with the American cultural past were shaky.

Rahv played a leading role in the Henry James revival, but not many *Partisan* critics were sufficiently grounded in the native cultural tradition. They didn't know enough about Puritanism and the enriched views of it provided by recent scholarship; they accepted too uncritically Henry James's notion of "a paucity of experience" as explanation for the peculiarities of nineteenth-century American writing; they failed to consider the possibility that the tradition of New England Puritanism could yield significant weights of experience, just as they failed to measure the hold upon Hawthorne and even James of the remnants of that tradition.

Not that the "paucity of literature" idea—that nineteenth-century American literature, locked into the Puritan heritage, feared to engage with social power and sexuality—was entirely mistaken. But it was inadequate to the richness of the native past, and patronizing as well. Why were the New York critics indifferent to or ignorant of Perry Miller's version of American literary history? Perhaps because they felt uneasy with Miller's probings into New England religious thought, probings that had their own element of parochialism but could have been a corrective to the views of New York. Perhaps because they were suspicious of anything coming out of the Harvard English department, which they saw as a nest of WASP gentility and literary fellow traveling. Perhaps because they saw no need to trouble themselves with "mere" academic scholarship. Whatever the reasons, I cannot recall an occasion when Miller's name was mentioned in the *Partisan* circle of the forties and fifties.

Between the New York writers and the native tradition there were barriers of taste. What could we make of all the talk, both from and about Emerson, that elevated individualism to a credo of life? Nothing in our tradition prepared us for this. The whole complex of Emersonianism seemed pale, disabling, genteel, an individualism of vaporous spirituality. Now I know better, or think I do. And perhaps we did not want to recognize what might be genuinely revolutionary in that strand of Emerson's thought which placed a central value on a shared vision of personal autonomy. In any case, I found the classical Americans, especially Emerson and Thoreau, deficient in those historical entanglements that seemed essential to literature because inescapable in life. I surely would have agreed with Henry James's judgment that Emerson leaves "a singular impression of paleness" and lacks "personal avidity." Born, as we liked to flatter ourselves, with the bruises of history livid on our souls, the New York writers wanted a literature in which experience overflowed, engulfed, drenched. So, again with the exception of Alfred Kazin, we abandoned Emerson even before encountering him; in later years some of us would never draw closer than to establish amiable diplomatic relations.

But this position could not long be sustained. Anyone who approaches American literature even casually must recognize that, except for Edith Wharton, every major American writer bears the stamp of Emerson. To evade Emerson was to evade both America and its literature. Some of the evasions turned out to be fruitful: I fell in love with Melville, found points of kinship with Whitman, yielded to Henry James; but always, the spirit of Emerson kept looming over our culture.

Yet this very "alienation" from the native mainstream contributed something valuable to *Partisan* writings on American fiction and poetry. It contributed the voice of the outsider. It contributed a skeptical European sensibility that refused to take at face value claims for the moral sublimity of our nineteenth-century literature and insisted upon the most rigorous standards—comparison with the great Russians and modernist French—in judging that literature.

My own responses were as impassioned as they were confused. At the forefront limped wily, clubfooted Ambivalence, God of Modernism, and behind straggled such lesser spirits as Eager Ambition and Self-Protective Withdrawal. More important, however, was a deep trustingness that I felt, a persuasion that the New York intellectual world really did function as a free market of ideas and talents, closer to the norms of laissez faire than any capitalist society I had ever heard of. In our little world competition was fierce, with little mercy shown to losers, and the clamor of self was incessant. Yet no entrenched monopoly was tolerated nor traditional caste privileges honored simply because they were traditional. Anyone with talent or a fresh idea could elbow into the market and set up a stall. The competitors might even help a little. There was equal opportunity to soar or tumble. There was also envy and nastiness: when Philip Rahv or Delmore Schwartz finished tearing apart a friend, little remained but a stack of bones. Still, gifts mattered, ideas mattered. Of manners there was perhaps little, of passion an abundance.

Coming into this world, I had the good sense to listen. I listened to Delmore Schwartz entangle himself in his own wit, as he declared T. S. Eliot a culture hero and ripped apart his "Christian" snobbism. I listened to Lionel Trilling slide through categories— "the will," "the moral imagination"—the exact meaning of which remained elusive. I listened to Philip Rahv chart American literary relations through lurid diagrams of power. The greatest listening was still two or three years away, the listening to Meyer Schapiro. But in my impatient, scrappy way, pocketing a phrase here and a thought there, I listened hard.

And imitated. How else does one learn? Becoming a literary critic seemed fairly easy: it was something one might pick up in a few months. Becoming a writer seemed very hard: it would take several decades. My notion about criticism was a piece of foolishness, half jokingly indulged, but my idea about writing was serious, perhaps the most relentless plunge I ever took into self-knowledge.

All you needed to be called a literary critic, it seemed, was a determination to read with charged attention and a pencil in the clutch of your fingers. Marking passages up and writing things down, you quickly discovered that reading had become spoiled with purpose. Then you tried to chart the articulated patterns of a novel or poem, its narrative line or theme, its interplay of event and character, quite as a specialist might study X-rays. You might also pick up a few semitechnical terms like "structure," "vision," and "sensibility" without inquiring too closely into their meanings. Finally you tried to locate whatever in a text seemed distinctive, some nuance of perception or tone of voice. Here, however, the whole fantasy about the easiness of writing criticism came tumbling down and you had to stare at the blinding hardness, perhaps the sheer helplessness of the whole enterprise, before which only fools and pedants thought "method" a protective shield. I remember how hard it was when I had to review a book by a new and gifted writer—say, Malamud's first collection of stories—and "all" I wanted to do was describe whatever seemed distinctive in his style.

Not once did I ever hear anyone in New York talk about "critical method": it would have been regarded as bad form. Most New York writers didn't think of themselves as critics primarily;

they thought of themselves as writers who did criticism. The difference seemed important, a difference for which our academic contemporaries never quite forgave us.

Decidedly more interesting than theories of criticism was the act of writing. I knew that my prose had a certain vigor, but was deficient in nuance, ease, modulations of tone and pace. So I decided to imitate, not the style of one or another critic, which would have been disastrous, but the common style of the *Partisan* essay. By imitating a common style, I might develop a personal style. I studied the way these writers negotiated rapid thrusts, extreme condensations, the rhetoric of antirhetoric. I played with mixtures of high seriousness and street colloquialism, a style John Hollander has called "New York Baroque." I sought that vibration of intensity which seemed the mark of our moment. But I learned that this charged, burning style would not work for anything longer than an essay.

Wondering if I could ever match the fluent wit of Elizabeth Hardwick or the rhetorical plenitude of Alfred Kazin, I narrowed my homework to simple effects. How do you begin a literary piece so as to hold attention? George Orwell was masterful at this, probably because he had none of the American literary snobbism about doing "mere journalism." Take the opening of his Dickens essay: "Dickens is one of those writers who is well worth stealing." Who but a brute or hopeless academic would not keep reading after a sentence like that? Edmund Wilson, by contrast, did not strive for striking leads, perhaps assuming that the majesty of his presence would be enough to hold his readers. Wilson saved his drama for endings, as in the essays on Kipling and Proust. Philip Rahv came on like a slow thunder of manifestoes. Trilling would begin with a simulated hesitation but soon plant a hint that a surprise lay ahead, some revelation about the ways in which "we"—"the educated classes"—were misconstruing "the cultural situation."

Such attentiveness made me aware of the essay as a form, the most natural for literary criticism. What might one make of it? Only a master like D. H. Lawrence could profit from giving way to personality or idiosyncrasy; only a semimaster like Van Wyck Brooks could manage "poetic" evocations of a text. Usually the essay required a margin of impersonality, or a showing forth of personality through indirection. You also had to learn how and when to quote—sparingly, like a pause in the flow of your voice; Tate was skilled at this, Wilson too. Most critics, I decided, had never learned how to do a plot summary without breaking the rhythm of their argument. Hardest of all was to find fresh ways of describing a writer's style, the usual repertoire of descriptives having long ago lost its freshness.

There were two main verbal resources, I concluded somewhat naively, that critical writers might call upon, and these were imagery and syntax. V. S. Pritchett was blessed with imagery. But those of us not so blessed had to keep a strict eye on our syntax, learning to shape and stretch, as a physiotherapist works with muscles. Among critics, Newton Arvin was a master of the supple, elaborate sentence, a long ribbon of thought and impression; Edmund Wilson was also skilled with complex sentences, but less for imagistic vividness than for hammering together a group of propositions. Aware that the heavenly dispenser had denied me a gift of imagery and suspecting it would be a long time, if ever, before I could approach Arvin and Wilson in their syntactical virtuosity, I looked about for other models. The idea was to imitate writers much better than oneself yet not hopelessly out of range. (One crazy evening I tried to write a critical piece in the manner of D. H. Lawrence; the next morning I stealthily dropped it in the wastebasket.) So I decided to work hard in order to write like Orwell—not, heaven knows, that I succeeded, but it made sense to try, since whatever strength of style I had lay in a certain incisiveness.

As for being a literary critic, why, come to think of it, should I want to be one? That it was enjoyable to read and write about books did not then seem a sufficient reason; now I think it is. That literary criticism apparently required no special preparation seemed at first encouraging, until the appalling thought struck me that a craft requiring no special preparation might require just about every kind of preparation. I came to see that the critics I most admired—both my own kind, like Wilson and Orwell, and those I regarded as antagonists, like Tate and Winters—were men for whom criticism mattered because it could serve as open-ended humanist discourse. Precisely what made it tempting also made it treacherous: the endlessness of possibility. The best critics of all schools took for granted that a literary text merited respect for its integrity, but saw no reason to stop there, neither the *Partisan* critics in principle nor the New Critics in practice. Obeying the command of limit, they realized that it also signified there were stretches of perception beyond that limit, which one might yet bring to bear upon the literary work.

I was stumbling upon an idea that could be traced back to Matthew Arnold and soon would be picked up by Randall Jarrell: that in a secular age literary criticism carries a heavy burden of intention, becoming a surrogate mode of speech for people blocked in public life. Unable to fulfill directly their visions of politics, morality, and religion, critics transfer these to the seemingly narrower channels of literary criticism. Precisely this spilling over of thought and passion has made criticism so interesting in our time— so perilous, too. The dominant formal claim of modern criticism has been an insistence upon treating literature as autonomous; the main actual circumstance for writing criticism has been a pressure for extraliterary connections. Ever since Arnold found that reflecting upon the place of poetry in an industrial society led him to worry about "a girl named Wragg," the most valuable critics have often doubled as cultural spokesmen, moral prophets, political insurgents. Especially in the years after the war, when so many hopes had turned to dust, literary criticism appealed to segments of the intellectual classes as a discipline in which it was still possible for the mind to move dispassionately and freely. A terrifying freedom: to make criticism into a reflection upon our most serious concerns, or to reduce criticism to undisciplined reverie, grandiose and wanton.

Unsure as I was about the place of literary criticism, I was still less sure about my own small beginnings as a critic. How seriously should I take this venture? Not too much, I told myself, solemnly on guard against solemnity. Spending one's life writing about the writings of other people seemed a fairly inglorious prospect. I used to say to friends—with a defensiveness surely transparent—that criticism was "an amiable way to pass the time." Until, that is, history beckoned me to greater callings . . .

As I came to know the New York critics and, a bit later, the New Critics, I saw that the most gifted among both groups were inclined toward a mildly ironic depreciation of the whole enterprise. All took criticism to be a secondary discipline, dependent on primary creation; if critics forgot this, they would soon be puffing themselves up with ridiculous affectations. People like Tate and Wilson, Trilling and Arvin took their work seriously enough, but all of them spoke with humor, or irritation, about the solemnity of modern criticism and its tendency to make itself a major subject for study. Trilling would talk with a sly amusement about the preening over "method" that had spread through our English departments. Wilson harrumphed the whole thing away as academic nonsense.

As for me, I was far from sure that criticism was a sufficiently urgent occupation. Nor was the approval of the New York writers, much as I wanted it, quite enough. To be accepted by them was like gaining applause for a recitation at a family party. I wanted a word of approval from the outside world, which, harder to get, seemed all the more desirable. That word came in 1952 when a letter arrived —handwritten!—from John Crowe Ransom, editor of *Kenyon Review*, saying I had been chosen for a Kenyon Fellowship in Criticism. For all one's New York cockiness, one still wanted a word, a glance, from those distant spaces beyond the Hudson.

For a moment it seemed in New York as if the life of the mind could be regarded as a "permanent revolution" of consciousness, a ceaseless dynamic of motion and change, an endless infatuation with the new. Neither rest nor retreat—that was the way. Influenced by figures as diverse as Eliot and Trotsky, the New York writers proposed to link a defense of modernist culture with a politics of anti-Stalinist radicalism. It was an attractive idea, but lacked durability.

In Europe this union of the *advanced*—critical consciousness and political conscience—had flourished only briefly, perhaps in Paris during the late nineteenth century, perhaps in Berlin during the twenties. By its very nature such an alliance could not be stable. The European Left was often middlebrow in cultural style, seldom inclined to understand or sympathize with rebellious experiments. The European avant garde was apolitical when not elitist and reactionary, sometimes lost in fantasies of hierarchical order and hermetic glory. There were exceptions. The Parisian Surrealists, led by André Breton, proclaimed themselves both modernist and radical, though how much weight to give to this example is a question. A close scrutiny of European culture between, say, 1875 and 1930 would have shown that the literary avant garde and the political Left could really not form a comfortable partnership. But here in America there was this important difference: no one in the *Partisan* circle was proposing actually to bring together people from the Left and from the literary and artistic worlds; all that was envisaged was a yoking of two sensibilities within an isolated circle. This may have represented a misunderstanding but, not for the first time, it was a productive one.

When the early *Partisan* writers were still shaking loose from Stalinism, their cultural-political program meant something at once simple and significant. It meant, between 1937 and 1946, a reaction against dogmatic views of literature, a repudiation of tendentious coarseness in criticism. Today this may seem obvious; as late as 1947 it was still a matter to fight over. In an early issue of *Partisan Review* there appeared a letter from Allen Tate commending a review Lionel Trilling had written of Tate's novel, *The Fathers*. The review showed, wrote Tate, "that it is possible for a critic to examine a work whose author holds fundamentally opposite views and yet convince that author, by moderation and intelligence, that the critic is disinterested. If *Partisan Review* can maintain that attitude, it will win the respect of all parties without yielding the essentially Marxist position that it has assumed."

This letter was a "political" gesture by an opponent, an offer of conditional friendliness; but its content was not very far from the cultural advice coming at the same time from Leon Trotsky in Mexico City, who kept repeating that "art has laws of its own" and literature should not be bent to ideological ends. Indeed, scorn for political contamination of critical judgment was an idea shared by all writers near *Partisan Review*. I'm not saying this value was never violated in the magazine; of course it was. But the fact that everyone from Rahv to Troy, Schapiro to Trilling, Rosenberg to Kazin would have found common ground at least in this belief, represented a major step in shaking off the rubbish of the thirties.

Once past this hygienic minimum, *Partisan Review* sanctioned the idea—perhaps the most powerful cultural idea of the century—that there existed an all-but-incomparable generation of modern masters who represented for our time the highest reaches of the imagination. The magazine also helped win respect for a generation of European writers—Silone, Koestler, Malraux, Orwell, Serge—not in the first rank of novelists but who served as moral spokesmen for the homeless independent Left.

The union of the *advanced*, much as it entranced and enabled, was an idea that could not long endure. Avant gardes march forward, but not necessarily to the same tune or in the same direction. By the time the *Partisan* writers came along, both the literary and political avant gardes were living off remembered glories and probably lacked the vitality needed for a shared upsurge. Modernism was not moving along a necessary line of purpose or progress. At least politically, many of its heroes were quite prepared for a backward spiral, some dreaming of re-created archaic decorums, others of enclosing themselves in aristocratic enclaves, and still others—a distressing number—yielding to authoritarianisms of Right and Left. It became fashionable in the earlier decades of this century for advanced writers—Joyce stands out as a wonderful exception!—to dismiss liberal democracy as a breeding ground of the mediocre masses and thereby an enemy of high culture. No, the union between cultural modernism and independent radicalism was neither a proper marriage nor a secure liaison, it was a meeting between parties hurrying in opposite directions, brief, hectic, messy.

The prolonged historical crisis that had provided the impetus to modernism might persist into the end of the twentieth century, even beyond, but that did not ensure that modernism would still be able to flourish. That a need for modernism might still be felt hardly guaranteed that the energies for it would reappear. Modernism, as Georg Lukacs observed, despairs of human history; it abandons all ideas of a linear development or progress; it even falls back, in more extreme instances, upon notions of a universal *condition humaine*, a rhythm of eternal recurrence, or even a blockage of the entire human enterprise. Yet within its own realm modernism signifies ceaseless change, turmoil, reaction—these, indeed, are among its defining characteristics. The more history comes to be seen as mired in endless crisis, the more must art take on a relentless dynamism—as if Hegel's "cunning of reason" had been expelled from its high place as motive force of history and exiled to culture.

How long can this standoff continue, with history grinding its wheels in the ruts of insoluble crisis, and culture ceaselessly inventing new modes of experiment? Must not a breakdown occur sooner or later, a wearying of nerves, a pull toward entropy?

It would have been hard to ask, even think of, such questions several decades ago, for precisely an acute sense of history blocked the vision of less dramatic historical options. The New York writers also discovered—it was a hard lesson to learn—that their relation to literary modernism was less authoritative and more ambiguous than they liked to suppose. Only when a backslider like Van Wyck Brooks attacked modernism for undermining the will of democracy, in his simple way anticipating the arguments later heard from the Marxist Lukacs, did the New York critics rush to modernism's defense. But the battles for Joyce, Eliot, and Proust had been fought in earlier decades and by now were mostly won. Clashes broke out occasionally with entrenched philistinism, but mostly as mopping-up operations. The New York writers came toward the end of the modernist experience, just as they came at what may yet be judged the end of the radical experience, and certainly at the end of the immigrant Jewish experience. One shorthand way of describing this situation, a cause of both their fevered brilliance and fevered instability, is to say that *they came late.*

Modernism was becoming successful. No longer a literature of opposition, it had begun a triumphant metamorphosis signifying its ultimate slow dying. What remained of authentic modernism—say, the plays of Beckett—figured like a wandering Jew of cultural life: exhausted from restlessness, yet unable to find peace in the grave. At some point in the fifties it would become clear that the problem we faced was no longer how to fight for modernism; it was to consider why the fight for it had ended in so unnerving, almost unseemly a triumph—this modernism that must suffer extinction if once it does triumph.

In 1949 these anxieties broke into the open. The jury for the prestigious Bollingen Award, which included such writers as Eliot, Tate, Auden, and Robert Lowell, voted to give its prize to Ezra Pound for his *Pisan Cantos*. Pound had spent the war years in Mussolini's Italy broadcasting for the Axis. ("Every sane act you commit," he said in a 1942 broadcast, "is committed in homage to Mussolini and Hitler.") His *Cantos*, a jumble of memories, reflections, and anecdotes—exquisite lyric and stupid rant—contained some anti-Semitic passages; indeed, one of its organizing themes is a belief in fascism. Once the award was announced, there followed an extremely bitter dispute about its propriety. This dispute reminded us that we in New York could not live at ease with some of the modernist writing we had tried so insistently to admire, and that despite growing friendships with certain New Critics, we still had our own distinctive outlooks and interests to defend.

Pound was never our poet. I had read him fitfully, dutifully, and later heard Delmore Schwartz and John Berryman speak warmly of his generosity in helping younger writers and of his major contribution to reinvigorating—"making new"—the language of modern poetry. No doubt true; but Pound never stirred my imagination as Eliot did. There was a streak of the Midwestern crank, the cracker-barrel philosopher, in Pound that finally made him tiresome. At times the *Cantos* lapsed into affecting lyrics, but the work as a whole seemed incoherent, pretentious, half-baked. Pound was *their* poet, idol of the right wing of modernist culture.

Very well, they might feel as they wished about their crank-genius. But to render him public honor a few years after word of the Holocaust reached us was unbearable. "It's a provocation," growled Philip Rahv one afternoon as we were patrolling the New York streets, and he was right. Did not the judges, all men of high sensibility, realize their decision would cause pain to Jewish literary colleagues, and indeed to others not Jewish? When John Berryman, author of an affecting story, "The Imaginary Jew," sent a letter to Meyer Schapiro asking him to support the Bollingen Award, couldn't Berryman imagine the feelings of a real-life Jew?

Why then did the judges persist? Was it a sneaking admiration for the old codger who even in Pisan captivity had kept writing his cantos? An inflexible reading of the value of aesthetic autonomy, to which both advocates and opponents of the Pound award said they were committed? "To permit other considerations than that of poetic achievement to sway the decision," wrote the judges, "would destroy the significance of the award." This wording was shrewd, for whoever wrote it sensed that most opponents of the award would still want to be regarded as defenders of aesthetic autonomy.

Two separate questions were entangled here: one, the public propriety of honoring a profascist and anti-Semitic writer even if he had written the best poetry of 1948, and the other, far more complicated, whether or how fascist or anti-Semitic matter can be lodged in poetry taken to be great. In the debate that followed in *Partisan Review*, Clement Greenberg nicely disposed of the first question:

> I do not quarrel with the esthetic verdict, but I question its primacy in the affair at hand, a primacy that hints at an absolute acceptance of the autonomy not only of art but of every separate field of human activity. Does no hierarchy of value obtain among them? Would Mr. Eliot, for instance, approve of this for his "Christian society"?

And still more tellingly:

> I am sick of the art-adoration that prevails among cultured people, more in our time than in any other: that art-silliness which condones almost any moral or intellectual failing on the artist's part as long as he is or seems a successful artist. Psychopathy has become endemic among artists and writers, in whose company the moral idiot is tolerated as perhaps nowhere else in society.

> Even if the *Pisan Cantos* did contain great poetry, an appropriate response might then be: "Yes, Pound did write the best poetry of the year, but when aesthetic standards and human values clash as deeply as in this instance, then we judge the latter to be primary. We therefore cannot extend a hand of admiration to Ezra Pound or admire his poetry with a whole heart, and we make no award for the year."

The second problem was far more difficult, meshed as it was with aesthetic issues that never have been, perhaps never can be, fully resolved. Having affirmed a belief in the autonomy of literature—the very ground on which the award to Pound was being justified—could we now say when confronted with such appalling lines as

> Pétain defended Verdun while Blum
>   Was defending a bidet.

or

> the yidd is a stimulant, and the goyim are cattle
> in gt/ proportion and go to saleable slaughter
> with the maximum of docility.

that we chose to abandon our belief in aesthetic autonomy? One way out might be to say, as Harry Levin put it, that Pound's artistic achievement was "flawed by certain problematic commitments." (What was "problematic" about them?) But Allen Tate was more candid: "I have little sympathy with the view that holds that Pound's irresponsible opinions merely lie alongside the poetry, which thus remains uncontaminated by them. The disagreeable opinions are right in the middle of the poetry." Nevertheless, added Tate, the strength of Pound's language was so great, it overwhelmed his detestable opinions.

For some of us, this quarrel over the Pound award took on an importance beyond the immediate occasion. It made us think a little more carefully about our motivating views of literature and history.

We were forced back to a reconsideration of what could be meant by aesthetic autonomy. We had meant, I think, that a work of literature has distinctive properties and must be perceived and judged according to categories distinctive to its kind. So far—phrasing aside—so good. Troubles began when we tried to specify the relation between the literary work acknowledged to be autonomous and the external world to which nevertheless it was related—the relation between literature and history. There was a view advanced by some formalist critics that a poem was not to be grasped in its essential being through references to the world of familiar experience, for the poem is not an "imitation" of that world, the poem inhabits a realm of its own. The offending lines in the *Cantos* thus would not contain a statement in the sense that an essay contains statements; those in the poem must be seen as self-contained matter.

This extreme view we could not accept—nor did its exponents write criticism consistently faithful to it. Autonomy, for us, did not signify a severance between moral precepts in criticism and in ordinary experience, though the modes of application must surely be different. Nor could a recognition of aesthetic autonomy persuade us that when Pound wrote those wretched lines he did not mean them to be statements about events within, or about the nature of, the world. "Pétain," "Blum," "yidd" all refer to recognizable figures in historical time, and refer to them in ways that may reasonably be characterized as disgusting. Pound himself, it's fair to add, had insisted on the continuity between his life and his work, his thought and his poetry.

We had to conclude, as did Karl Shapiro, the one Bollingen

judge to vote against the award, that "the poet's political and moral philosophy ultimately vitiates his poetry and lowers its standard as a literary work." We had to agree, uneasily, with William Barrett that "the category of the esthetic is not the primary one for human life, and that the attitude which holds esthetic considerations to be primary is far from primary itself, but produced by very many historical, social, and moral conditions." And we had to cultivate, increasingly, a wariness regarding the claims of the formalist aesthetic, if only because its defenders rarely wrote about literature in full accord with their own prescriptions, rarely wrote without injecting—they really had no choice—their own ideological biases.

In these violent disputes there were a few bits of comic relief. Allen Tate sent a furious letter to *Partisan Review*, saying that Barrett had insinuated "charges of anti-Semitism against the group of writers of which I am a member." This, said Tate, reflected on his personal courage and honor, and "courage and honor are not subjects of literary controversy, but occasions of action." Wonderful! A challenge to a duel—surely the first any New York writer had ever received! We were all a little jealous of Barrett, whose strength, however, did not lie in swordsmanship. When Barrett wisely sidestepped the challenge, some of us were disappointed since the thought of those two beanpoles in battle seemed delightful.

How important the Pound case was in intellectual life became clear only in later years. The collision between literary craft and moral value, if that was what we had been fighting about, could not be resolved through any formula. The uneasiness we had started to feel about some of the modernist writers now broke into the open. There would be essays in the coming years critical of D. H. Lawrence's call for "blood consciousness," his notions of the leader cult. A book by John Harrison, containing a full-scale attack on the politics of several modernist writers, became the occasion for serious rethinking. There was a notable essay by Lionel Trilling in which he admitted to mixed feelings about the very modernist writers he had long praised and taught. There was a cutting attack on Jean Genet by Philip Rahv, who felt that in the fiction of this perverse genius the compositional resources of modernism seem all but severed from moral perception. Only Harold Rosenberg among the New York critics remained unambiguously attached to "the tradition of the new," though even he had to recognize its increasing inclination to self-parody. As we entered a new cultural era that we could hardly name—I wrote an essay calling it "post-modernist," simply because I could think of nothing else—we hoped still to remain partisans of the modernism that had shaped the sensibility of our youth, but also to cultivate those critical distinctions and dissociations which the cooling of time allowed.

The same year in which the Pound controversy broke out there occurred—a piquant symmetry—the Waldorf conference, perhaps the last major effort of American Stalinism to reestablish itself as a cultural force in this country. Famous intellectuals were invited to the conference (named after the New York hotel in which it was held) and a few came; "big guns" were shipped over from Russia and Poland; war veterans noisily picketed the hotel. Philip Rahv asked me to report on the conference for his magazine, so I went there and sat at a table some ten feet from the stage where Soviet writers, musicians, and commissars were on display.

But oh, how different from the old days! Gone was the old assurance, the flowing rhetoric of confidence. Now there were no prominent writers, no John Dos Passos or Richard Wright; the sole literary star was a Harvard scholar, F. O. Matthiessen. Otherwise, worn hacks and conference-goers left over, like old furniture, from earlier conferences (those E. M. Forster had once described as "Congress-addicts who would travel any distance for their drug"). For amusement's sake there was the inevitable Popular Front clergyman, a retired bishop from Utah. I have kept some notes from the conference: "Where did they find him? He almost broke the whole thing up by droning on forever, this old fool drunk with podium-fever. When he reached his peroration celebrating God's path to peace, the Russians burst into delighted grins. They love this babbling American style."

The CP kept discreetly in the background, knowing that an open defense of Soviet policy—this was soon after the takeover in Czechoslovakia—would be unpalatable even to long-tried fellow travelers. The American speakers didn't blame the United States entirely for the Cold War, and some proposed (was it naiveté or cynicism—could a Solomon tell?) a division of the world into two spheres of influence, long a familiar imperialist idea.

A few anti-Stalinist intellectuals managed to get the floor:

George Counts, Robert Lowell, Dwight Macdonald, Mary Mc-
Carthy. Speakers being limited to two minutes, most of these critics
were ineffective—few intellectuals can say what they think, some
can't even say hello, in two minutes. Professor Counts, a historian
of education, started to document the fate of Russian dissidents; I
turn again to my notes: "Oh, these long-winded academics with
their 50-minute periods! I want to rush over and shake him, for
God's sake, hurry it up! Barely started, he has to sit down. Dwight
[Macdonald], who's been around the radical movement though
he's hardly what you'd call eloquent, is more concise. He jams in a
sharp question about dissident Russian writers." At which point the
head of the Russian delegation, a writer of sorts named Alexander
Fadeyev, brushed off Macdonald contemptuously. How many divisions does Dwight have?

I went to another panel to hear Matthiessen. Dreadfully nervous, this gifted, tragic figure seemed perversely intent at putting
his cultivation to the service of the commissars. He spoke with a
maddening simplicity, praising Melville for having made the hero of
Moby Dick a "common man." (What else could a nineteenth-
century American hero be?) Asked his opinion regarding
Fadeyev's dismissal of the question about Soviet dissident writers,
Matthiessen did not plead, as prudence might have led him to,
ignorance about Russian literary life; no, he praised Fadeyev's answer as "direct and forthright."

Throughout the conference I found myself staring at the Russians. Fadeyev was said to be a novelist, but was also a hopeless
drunk, miserable about the role he had to play. (He committed
suicide some years later.) But if miserable, he didn't show it. He
carried himself with a brutal swagger, behaving like the bureaucrat
of one's imagination, the professional Orgman, beefy and hard,
ready to crack the whip. Imagine coming before a "tribunal"
headed by this creature—or him coming before a "tribunal" headed
by another like himself!

The Russians had brought a prize, the composer Shostakovich.
Again my notes: "Thin, diffident, hands tremble, seems to wish he
were anywhere but here. His speech: squeaky bored voice, praises
Stalinist criticism of his music. An obscenity to have this composer
endorse his tormentors. [I didn't yet understand the wisdom of dictators: the bigger your victim, the better to humiliate him.] As

Shostakovich talks, a fantasy . . . the Waldorf stage is really a KGB interrogation center and Sh. is answering questions under a blinding light."

Toward the end a young literary star, Norman Mailer—still flushed with the fame of *The Naked and the Dead* and still a bit of a fellow traveler—got up to speak. His speech was good, bearing the print of a new mentor, the French anti-Stalinist writer Jean Malaquais. Mailer said both the United States and Russia were drifting toward "state capitalism," he saw little hope for peace, he regretted having to declare his pessimism. The Americans were stunned, the Russians amusingly indifferent.

The session over, I jumped up to introduce myself to Mailer—so baby-faced at close range—telling him I thought his speech "honest." He grinned with that charm of his which has since brought him to the gateway of heaven and the first circle of hell. No, he said, nobody is "really honest." Come on, I wanted to say, drop this sophomoric sincerity; but I kept quiet, and we agreed to meet again.

I wrote up my report, satisfyingly acrid, ending with a question that has kept tormenting me over the decades: "What are the drives to self-destruction that can lead a serious intellectual [like F. O. Matthiessen] to support a movement whose victory could mean only the end of free intellectual life?"

The Pound controversy and the Waldorf conference were perhaps the last occasions when the New York intellectuals could still act as a coherent group. Their earlier radicalism had been thin, anxious, problematic. They had no choice: the crisis of socialism was worldwide, and felt most keenly in countries that lacked mass movements of the Left. No version of orthodox Marxism, not even if antibolshevik, could now retain a hold on intellectuals who had suffered the trauma of abandoning the Leninist *Weltanschauung* and had come to realize the extent to which the politics of this century called into question Marxist categories. Yet if their radicalism lacked firm political foundations, it played a major role in their own history. The thirties, however much they might scorn that decade or pretend to forget it, represented their time of fervor. The radicalism of that decade gave them their distinctive style: a flair for polemic, a taste for the grand generalization, an impatience with what they regarded (often parochially) as parochial scholarship, an internationalist perspective, and a belief in the unity of intellectual work.

The representative man of this group was Philip Rahv, a Russian intellectual transported by some whim of history to American soil. He carried his "Russianness" like a flag of pride, as if it signified a decided metaphysical benefit. It meant being comprehensive, definitive, theoretical, overpowering. Russian intellectuals were serious; to be serious meant to be weighty; and to be weighty became a validation of self. At the very least, "Russianness" provided a strategy for marking out points of superiority to native-born Americans, whether literary or not. Just as some New Critics seem in retrospect to have been ministers *manqués*, their rhetoric soaring to a preacher's climax as their matter failed to keep pace, so Rahv wrote with the pleased stateliness of the Marxist theoretician, the sort who brushes aside mere particulars in behalf of the largest trends. If I lapse into a little irony here, I mean it to be affectionate, since I think Rahv's criticism often achieved bite and flavor through shadowing the motions of political argument. Pure critics are rare birds, and they seldom fly very far.

The odd thing about Philip Rahv, and what finally made him likable, was that behind his bulky body and malicious tongue lay a creature fastidious in appetite and denial. He was also, as I knew him, a somewhat timid man. His magazine excelled at infighting, but he himself was not really much of a fighter, for he shared both the anxieties of the ex-Communist and the uneasiness of the immigrant (you had to watch your step in this land of the *goyim*). But if he got you into a corner at a party, Rahv could make a fearful racket. Poking his finger into your chest, he would declare the "correct line" on some topic of the day and, his voice dropping to a confidential growl, reduce to scorn and ashes a current literary fad. All this would wind up with his tag line, "Who needs it?"—a question that sufficed to dismiss a good half of the universe. A blight of negation often fell across his talk, and he would level all human motives to a dreadful crudity, a "vulgar Marxism" in personal relations. But Rahv could also be sensitive to flickerings of mood, just as in his criticism he was sensitive to shadings of voice. Behind his air of assurance there was what we would then have dared to call "a feminine sensibility." Himself an inhibited romantic, he took pleasure in sneering at "the romantic foolishness" of his friends, yet could suddenly melt into sympathy. High theory mixed with low gossip in his talk, and even at his crudest he retained a sense of what others felt or suffered.

He was a brilliant editor, partly because he brought to the job not only energy and intelligence but a semiconspiratorial outlook he mistook for Marxism. Editors necessarily overdefine issues and overdetermine responses—and writers have to resist them. Rahv wanted his magazine to constitute a public act, a political gesture. What might give the magazine cultural weight was that it should always seem to be moving somewhere, forward or backward. The success of Rahv and Phillips in bringing this off was partly a result of their political intelligence. Let pure spirits not misunderstand: I don't mean that in *Partisan Review* literary judgments were systematically twisted to political ends, though sometimes they were. I mean that Rahv saw cultural life as if enacted in a political arena. The imagery of politics was congenital with him, an imagery of definition, conflict, alliance, exclusion. I came with a fairly similar outlook, though less inclined to notions of conspiracy, and this must have been a ground for our friendship.

Rahv's own prose often tended toward a leaden "Russian" tone, but his magazine played a considerable role in nurturing a new essayistic style, more significant for American letters than what it contributed to fiction (mainly the "Jewish American story") or poetry. This essayistic style was a style of nervousness, strewn with knotty and flashy phrases, impatient with transitions and other concessions to dullness. It willfully called attention to itself as a token of bravura, a mixture of mandarin elegance and street outcry. I think I know a few of its sources: the early Van Wyck Brooks, a superb essayist in *America's Coming of Age*; Edmund Wilson; and some European writers, too, Valéry and Eliot. But finally the *Partisan* writers *made it up*, out of their visions of what a cosmopolitan style might be. In most of these essays there was an aura of tournament, the writer as gymnast with one eye on other rings, or the writer as skilled infighter juggling knives. It was a style that easily evoked strong distaste, even fear. "Ordinary readers" were often left with the fretful sense that they were not "in," the beauties of polemic racing past their eyes, while old-line academics patronized the New York writers as "unsound."

The New York writers developed a style of brilliance, and a style of brilliance is often hard to bear. At its best this style represented a certain view of the intellectual life: free-lance dash, peacock strut, knockout synthesis. It celebrated the idea of the intellectual as antispecialist, the writer whose specialty is not to have one. It celebrated the writer as roamer among theories, as dilettante connoisseur, as *luftmensh* of the mind. It could be wonderful, it could turn rancid. Our partial assimilation—roots loosed in Jewish soil but still not torn out, roots lowered into American soil but still not fixed—gave us a seemingly endless range of possibilities. These were not really endless, of course, but it was good that for a time they should seem so. Well or poorly, we tried to live by that vision of Ishmaelite pride and independence that Melville had called the way of the loose-fish. It was a vision that could not last very long, since need and caution, realism and loss of nerve, erosion and complication would finally do it in. Decades later I still ask myself, what better than to be a loose-fish?

7

Loose-Fish, Still Flapping

Yes; but you would hardly expect a loose-fish, still flapping, to beach in Princeton, New Jersey. A coil of circumstance led me there. In 1948 my wife found a job teaching Latin at a private school in Princeton for $1900 a year, and I, semi-free-lancer, tagged along. Princeton itself I never liked, neither the town nor the university, though it wasn't until after I left in 1953 that I could admit to myself how much I had been repelled by its chilled graces and Anglophile snobbery. Every Thursday I would hurry to New York, if only to take in some city noise.

Princeton had a vital literary life in those years, centered on a marginal group near the critic Richard Blackmur. An autodidact of wide learning (though later, in Harvard Yard, I was told it was not a deep learning), Blackmur had gained a reputation as a wizard of critical analysis. He held a professorship in English, as head of a "creative writing" program, but the old-guard scholars thought him "unsound" because he had no Ph.D., not even a B.A., and they could not suppose that a man might have mastered English literature simply through private reading.

Blackmur had at his disposal an assistantship paying a few thousand dollars a year, and with this he drew to Princeton some lively young writers. John Berryman, who had not yet published his first book of poems when I became his next-door neighbor, taught now and again as Blackmur's assistant. So, once or twice, did Delmore Schwartz and Saul Bellow. All three were in their thirties, known but not famous, published but insecure, and usually hard up for money. It was whispered that they were eager for jobs in the English department, but as "Richard's boys" they stood no chance. (Years later, in *Humboldt's Gift*, Bellow would strike back at Princeton in a few pages of ferocious sarcasm.) Overawed by these glowing young stars, I felt it an honor—and it was!—occasionally to attach myself to them, marginal to their marginality.

These were my first close encounters with novelists and poets, some of them ablaze with high manic temperament. Berryman, though not always likable, was the most violently original of the trio. Wiry and tense, self-devouring in temper, ready to spin off yards of verse by heart—he had apparently memorized the whole of Yeats—Berryman cut across the Princeton landscape like a storm. His tastes were untroubled by fashion, unweighted with theory. He adored Whitman at a time when sophisticated people smiled at mention of the name; he read excitedly in Stephen Crane and Isaac Babel, finding points of kinship in these writers of pressure; he would recite stretches of Hopkins and shift suddenly to a fierce defense of Dreiser ("at his most stupid never as stupid as critics who attack him"). Brittle in voice, fantastical in humor, drawing his responses from the extreme edge of his nerves, he was a man both acutely responsive and wildly unreliable. He bewildered me, I probably bored him. One day he would scan a review I had done of Stanley Edgar Hyman's book on contemporary criticism and chortle in his reedy tenor: "This starts acid and ends still more acid!" (Acid was good.) The next day he might pass me in the street and not even nod. Three days later, eyes burning, he would drag me into the local greasy spoon, a weird place built from dirty white tiles, and deliver a finished structural analysis of *Song of Myself*, at the end of which he suddenly veered into an accusatory question: "Have you ever realized that when you read Stendhal, every other writer seems *stupid?*" (His speech was rich in italics.)

Another time we had a brief exchange that settled forever the limits of our acquaintance: "Don't you feel," he asked, "that Rimbaud's chaos is central to your life?" I was guileless enough to say no, I did not. And that, for Berryman, was the end of me: I might be a nice fellow, but I was not one of the haloed victims, not like the Delmore he adored as the suffering poet of the modern city. But I don't want to suggest that persuasions of superiority were wholly his. Berryman might have Rimbaud and chaos, but I had Marx and history, and for a time they provided equally substantial, if illusory, comforts.

I had a similar, if less "literary," exchange with Delmore Schwartz. In a quiet moment he once said to me, "Do you sometimes get up in the morning and feel that you can't even bring yourself to tie your shoelaces?" He spoke without pride in extremity, for he knew that his psychic illness was an affliction that might destroy him and, except in moments of self-pity, he resisted any fashionable toying with the benefits of neurosis. Still, there was I, cast by these brilliant young writers as a fellow with perhaps a spot of talent but deplorably, even amusingly, sane: if they wrestled with chaos, I surrendered to coherence. Nor did it help to protest that I too had bouts of depression. I resented being categorized as rational: it seemed to foreclose possibilities of glamour. We were all too young then to grasp the deadly meaning of that "difference" in psyche or temperament that Berryman and Schwartz were pointing to.

When Berryman spoke about poets and poetry, his voice rang with an edge of combativeness, an echo of romantic devotion to the inescapable conflict between society and the artist. He raised Schwartz into a poetic myth while still alive, he recognized Bellow's talent sooner than most people, and he lived—this I admired intensely—by his own tastes. He was generous in negations, barely troubling to mask his contempt for professors he sometimes had to court. Once he burst into my apartment with the lordly announcement that Carlos Baker, a Princeton professor whom I maliciously called a "buck-shoe humanist," had written "the best book on Shelley . . . ," then paused as if on the verge of some desperate act and while I stared back obligingly, roared out, ". . . this week!" Berryman, Schwartz, and Bellow formed a haughty young aristocracy of letters, devoted to the stress of their temperaments, bound together by a fraternity of troubles. Envying their inner companionship, I saw no reason why it should be within my reach.

It was Delmore Schwartz, of all the literary people I knew in the late forties, whom I loved from the start. I had read with excitement his great story, "In Dreams Begin Responsibilities," when it first came out in 1937; I heard in his stammering rhetoric, at once worldly and naive, a note almost familial; and in all his work I found, even when it started crumbling under the press of madness, a straining toward a shy nobility, what Meyer Schapiro would call in a memorial poem "the gravest musings on the human state." In these Princeton years Schwartz was often manic. He boasted he was holding down four or five jobs without working at any of them, he indulged in cruel gossip about writers I knew he admired, and somehow he managed to sound both subtle and reductive at the same time. How could this be—subtle and reductive at the same time? Philip Rahv was also like that, and so were other intellectuals I was getting to know. Later I decided, not to my complete satisfaction, that among writers coming out of the immigrant Jewish milieu there was a "natural" coexistence of high and low, refinement and coarseness.

Were there signs, in the early fifties, of Schwartz's famous crackup? Probably, but I didn't want to see them. He had become obsessed with T. S. Eliot's anti-Semitism, perhaps because he admired Eliot so much, having earlier written an extraordinary essay praising Eliot as our "culture hero." Not that there wasn't a real problem concerning Eliot and other great figures of literary modernism who revealed a streak of nasty anti-Semitism; but with Schwartz the problem took on an obsessive cast, paranoid disorder blending with ethical dismay. Mostly, however, he was still a wonderful talker, a first-rate literary intelligence—the sort who can light up the work of a poet or novelist with a single quick phrase. One evening at my house Schwartz picked up Edmund Wilson's anthology *The Shock of Recognition* (which reprints criticism by American writers recognizing the merit of contemporaries), and with a desperate abandon proceeded to compile a *Shock of Unrecognition*, starting of course with Gide's rejection of Proust. Our laughter kept prodding Schwartz to manic heights, until suddenly everyone in the room fell silent and he stopped in mid-sentence, as if stricken.

Schwartz understood my loneliness, more than personal, in Princeton, and kept trying to buoy my morale by mumbling gently —he was either a roarer or a mumbler—that an interest in politics didn't necessarily constitute evidence of philistinism. He criticized my pieces with caustic tenderness, praising my style for its "incisiveness" at a time when I felt intimidated into supposing it was merely rough, but warning me of those dangers of overassertion by which young writers try to impose their signatures.

Back in New York we had become aware of the New Critics as competitors in influence and sophistication, but possibly partners in attacks on old-style academicism. Of all the New Critics Blackmur was the hardest to make out. Small, neatly turned-out, a shade dandyish, speaking in a weighty, murmurous monotone, he was suspicious of characters like me, New York street fighters likely to cause trouble and, in any case, too political. But he was also touchingly receptive, for he wanted friendships that might break past the insulating circle of his fame.

Blackmur had no declared critical method nor much interest in declaring one. He was often praised for his close verbal analyses, but if read closely, much of his work came to seem the rankest impressionism. His essays were astonishing for their overreaching, as if to force language into doing more than it could. "Pursuing insights to their journeys' ends," as Berryman wrote in *Dream Songs*, Blackmur perfected a style chokingly intense. But he was open in mind, disconcertingly humble at times, and in one of his finest pieces, "A Critic's Job of Work," he wrote sentences I still cherish: "The worst evil of fanatic falsification . . . arises when a body of criticism is governed by an *idée fixe*, a really exaggerated heresy, when a notion of genuine but small scope is taken literally as of universal application."

Sometimes Blackmur fell back on a tiresome pretense common among American literary men, that of being a simple fellow from the countryside. How odd a mystification from a critic possessed by the dybbuk of Henry Adams! I could understand it only as a sign of his uneasiness at not having had a formal education, perhaps also the shame he felt about his pride of knowledge. There is a story about an encounter between Blackmur and Meyer Schapiro at some point in the thirties: Blackmur starts a conversation by rehearsing familiar nativist complaints that the New York writers are too intellectual, too ratiocinative, and Schapiro, for once a trifle impatient, breaks in: "Mr. Blackmur, when you use your mind, you don't use it up!" I confess to never having asked Meyer Schapiro about this story, out of fear it might turn out to be apocryphal.

Between Blackmur and me there was a temperamental and cultural distance. Recognizing it, we partly bridged it. I had admired much of his earlier work, but now when he gave me offprints of pieces written in his "late" style—a kind of cultural rumination barely touching particular texts—I could not extend him the praise he visibly wanted. (Apprentice writers patronize famous ones by being "astonished" that the latter should still need praise.) What Blackmur had once written about Allen Tate, that in Tate's poems there is "a commotion that agitates in obscurity without ever quite articulating through the surface," seemed true of his own work. But if unable to warm to his writing, I warmed to the man. He was groping for some version of intellectual order, hungering for a strain of sublimity this side of faith—a common enough hunger among American writers. Hearing Blackmur lecture once at the School of Letters in Indiana, I thought I had found a clue to his ceaseless inner churning: he spoke in a masterly hieratic style, as if offering patches of grace, and suddenly I saw before me a minister of New England from the time when the faith was full.

By arousing his suspicion I gained Blackmur's confidence. I printed a parody of his style in *Partisan Review*, not labeled as such, but he was quick to identify it and tell me it amused him. He understood that finally there was a gap between him and people like Schwartz and me, and he accepted this with gallantry, taking us— figuratively and literally—into his house.

There was another side to Blackmur: how shrewd he could be in putting his opacities to practical use! Through what must have been some very elevated talk, he persuaded the Rockefeller Foundation to finance the Christian Gauss Seminars at Princeton. He became the director and several times a year would have an intellectual or literary person deliver a set of papers followed by discussion among twenty or so guests. In 1953 the senior lecturers were Paul Tillich, Edmund Wilson, and Leon Edel; through Blackmur's generosity, I was the junior.

Wilson I had met a year or so earlier, on a visit to Cape Cod where I talked with him about a book I had begun on Sherwood Anderson. A few years earlier I had published a little essay in the *Nation* defending Wilson's criticism against attacks from New Critics. Insofar as I was growing self-conscious about my "role" as a critic, I hoped to model myself on Wilson's breadth of interest and lucidity of style. By 1953 he was in late middle age, portly and red-faced, looking, as everyone found pleasure in noting, like a cross between Henry James and W. C. Fields. He stammered, yet seemed utterly self-confident, the master of letters. This wasn't really true: no writer of any distinction is utterly self-confident, and Wilson's notebooks, published in later years, betray recurrent anxieties about himself and his work.

My interview with him on Cape Cod yielded little about Anderson, partly because he scoffed at my inability to keep up with his consumption of Scotch and partly because, on hearing I had spent the war years in Alaska, he started grilling me about Eskimos, the Alaskan economy, and Arctic weather, all the while brushing aside poor Anderson. This was part of his manner, perhaps strategy: an all-consuming curiosity about the experience and reading of other people. (Once, when studying Hebrew, he showed up with a copy of a Yiddish paper, cross as a bear because he couldn't make out the words though the alphabet was the same as that of Hebrew. When I tried to explain the difficulty, he just glared at me accusingly.)

Wilson was now giving a series of papers in Princeton on the literature of the American Civil War, later to be turned into *Patriotic Gore*, and each week I did my homework dutifully, reading the memoirs of Generals Grant and Sherman, the war poems of Melville, the sketches of Francis Grierson, the writings of various Confederate ladies about whom Wilson turned out to be inordinately gallant.

He was grave but not pompous. At parties he would float from person to person, like a bumblebee from flower to flower, interrogating them about their work, extracting bits of knowledge that he put away in some inner compartment of his mind. He was able to listen to ideas he didn't like, but then would erupt into a crescendo of grunts, rumbles, sputters, all on the way to assertion. It sometimes seemed there were several areas of space between what went on in his mind and the speech that came tumbling out of his mouth—as if his thought reached him in relays. But when aroused, he could be very quick. At one of Tillich's seminars where the theologian, charming as the devil and at least as slippery, spun out his notions about faith, those of us listening felt that the idea of a personal God—the God we had rejected, the only God we knew —kept fading farther and farther into the distance. I asked Tillich: "You say religion rests upon a sense of awe before the 'fundament of being.' Does that mean that if, on a starry night perhaps out at sea, I find myself overwhelmed by the beauty of the scene, and become acutely aware of my own transience before the immensity of things, I am having a religious experience?" My intent, of course, was to distinguish between mere cultivated sensibility and religious belief; but Tillich, suave dialectician that he was, seized upon my question and said, yes, even though I called myself a skeptic I had provided "admirably"—he grinned—a description of a religious experience. He had turned the tables on us, and we sat there uncomfortably—until from the back of the room there came the Wilsonian rumble: "Mr. Tillich, you're taking away our rights!"

These few years at Princeton gave me a sense of what it really means, and costs, to be a writer. I came to see—in promising young writers, not disappointed old ones—the nervous pressures, the psychic costs. Berryman, Schwartz, Bellow would all be regarded as "glamorous" figures, and at least the first two were. Yet as I remember, they were beset by practical troubles, anxious about their prospects, tripping up—as it was somehow right they should—on the very seriousness that made them aspire to high achievement. To be a writer was hard. It meant to be bloodied in wars of the mind; it meant to batten off the debris of self. Schwartz and Berryman, as we politely put it, were "disturbed," but they were glowingly gifted, too, and their plight made me uneasy, as if I were being pulled into some alien territory that could be neither surveyed nor controlled. Bellow was sturdier, very strong-willed and shrewd in the arts of self-conservation; he understood that while endurance may not guarantee distinguished work, it sometimes enables it.

Between the literary people who came to Princeton and the academic people who stayed, there was unavoidable conflict. Those of us outside the university were inclined self-servingly to simplify this conflict, seeing it as one between the freely creative ("we") and the routinely drab ("they"). Had Princeton hired Bellow, Schwartz, and Berryman, it would have had a dazzling literary faculty; yet a department composed of such figures could also be a nightmare—who would enter the grades and fill out the reports? It rarely occurred to me that in our disdain for the Princeton professors we marginal people had also been giving them a rather bad time. They were no fools, they sensed our true feelings. This clash between writers and professors ought to be a standard feature of literary life, but we could not afford to admit it, for we were hungry and they were not.

Part of the world's coldness touched me in Princeton, but also, in smaller part, its warmth. Princeton was another America, and surely it was time to take a few steps into that unpromising terrain. Princeton never seemed a place in which I could feel at home. Was there such a place?

Oh, to hell with Princeton! The world was big, the world was tempting, and in the early fifties it was opening up. Postwar prosperity brought modest but real opportunities for young writers. There was money to be had from publishers—no great amounts, but more than in the past. When I got a $2,000 advance for a history of the American Communist Party I was elated, though I soon realized I had been utterly foolish, the amount was not nearly enough to enable me to write such a work. There were jobs in the universities, even for those of us without advanced degrees. Little magazines began to pay, almost decently; it was with an air of lordly beneficence that Philip Rahv told me the *Partisan Review* rate was now two cents a word. Even the *New York Times Book Review*, once a fortress of middlebrow culture, was starting to admit a few serious writers. In the fifties I wrote a literary piece for the mildly liberal *Reporter* and got ten cents a word, $300 altogether: I hesitated to tell my friends about this extravagance. Some writers began to discover, perhaps too readily, that publishing a story in the *New Yorker* or *Esquire* was not a sure ticket to Satan. Others saw that the Academy, while less exciting than the Village, wasn't invariably a graveyard of intellect.

A major shift in cultural demography began in the 1950s, the dispersion of literary people from urban centers and bohemian enclaves to university towns across the continent. Even the most pedestrian universities now boasted a poet, novelist, or critic. This dispersion, while it helped writers eat regularly, brought some cultural losses. True, we had never had a Paris in this country, but the concentration of talent and the excitement of huddling together, which seems necessary if literary groups are to thrive, was becoming harder to attain. Academic jobs often meant isolation, loneliness, boredom. But there were benefits, too. Some of us were forced to learn a little about that portion of the United States beyond the Hudson. Writers, after all, should test their notions against the reality of the country in which they live; it helps.

There were New York voices, mine among them, that indulged in gloomy forebodings about this new prosperity. Out of radical intransigence or bohemian rootedness, some of us feared that entering the big, wide world would bring risks of accommodation, delusions of status, subtle corruptions gradually decreasing in subtlety. About these risks we were not wholly wrong, but we were wrong in supposing that either political radicalism or cultural seriousness required us to remain isolated in sectarian caves. Isolation and powerlessness also entailed risks, as anyone might see by considering the case of Paul Goodman, an admirable writer who stuck to his anarchist convictions through years in which he was scorned and mocked, yet who also came to seem—perhaps this was a price he had to pay—an example of asphyxiating self-righteousness.

What brought about these changes in our cultural life? Partly adaptation, a moderately conservative feeling that capitalist society, at least in the United States, was here to stay, so that there wasn't much point in clinging to yesterday's radical politics. Partly the sly workings of prosperity. But also a certain loosening of society— the remarkable absorptiveness of modern America, its readiness to abandon traditional precepts for a moment of excitement, its growing hungers for publicity and celebrity, its increasing permissiveness toward social criticism, arising perhaps out of indifference, or self-assurance, or even tolerance. The lines of separation that had defined intellectual life—lines between high and middlebrow, radical and acquiescent, serious and popular—were becoming blurred. Here and there in the fifties you could find the beginnings of petty greed or hucksterism. But no one I knew was near any big money, and the neoconservatism starting to appear was almost entirely ideological and confined to the pages of *Commentary*.

Intellectuals should have regarded their entry into the outer world as utterly commonplace, at least if they kept faith with the warning of Stendhal and Balzac that one must always hold a portion of the self beyond the world's reach. They should have known that radicalism was not simply a matter of personal rectitude; indeed, that one reason for the sterility of the American Left has been its frequent confusion of a politics of opposition with a stance of purity. What seems remarkable in retrospect is the innocence of the assumption, held by some New York writers with a mixture of guilt and glee, that whatever recognition they won was cause for either preening or embarrassment. For all their gloss of sophistication, they had not yet moved very far into the world, and the source of their discomfort lay more in their origins than their situation. The immigrant milk was still on their lips.

The fifties, people said, were an Age of Criticism, by which they meant not that great literary criticism was being written—the best of it had been written earlier, at a time when not many people noticed—but that among the "educated classes" criticism had taken on an unprecedented popularity. Randall Jarrell, biting the hand that meant to caress him, poked fun at this Age of Criticism: he told of two young friends who proposed to be married by a literary critic. And why not? What better sages did we have? "In the name of the Dissociation of Sensibility I now pronounce you man and wife."

T. S. Eliot, Yvor Winters, F. R. Leavis, John Crowe Ransom, Richard Blackmur, Lionel Trilling—these were not attendant lords waiting upon princes of imagination, these were powerful dukes and barons ruling their own demesnes. One ruled Cambridge, another Stanford, still others held cities but were weak in the countryside. And each year there poured out eager followers from the graduate schools, loyal to master and method.

Even in those years there were some literary people bemused by this burst of interest in competing critical doctrines—didn't it have an uncomfortable resemblance to earlier competitions between political ideologies, also declared by charismatic leaders and reinforced by weighty texts? Novelists and poets were still needed, if only because they provided "texts" upon which to work, but it was critics who took hold of the imaginations of the young, pretty much the kind of young who a decade later might be talking revolution and two decades later, film. Two major groups of critics, one near *Partisan Review* and the other near *Kenyon Review,* had but recently passed their peaks of achievement. In England the Leavis group claimed its true disciples. In Chicago there was a learned school of "neo-Aristotelians." Behind Yvor Winters in California and Leavis in Cambridge huddled clans that resembled religio-political sects: the proud *tsaddik* flanked by adoring *hasidim.*

By the fifties political ideologies had come to be regarded as delusions, and public life as intrinsically corrupt or vulgar. One reason for the exorbitant admiration intellectuals bestowed on Adlai Stevenson was that he sent them faint signals of concord, though as a candidate for President he couldn't quite say he shared their fastidiousness. Perhaps the most influential register of intellectual sentiment in those years was David Riesman's impressionistic sociology, *The Lonely Crowd,* which popularized the subtly conservative moods of Lionel Trilling by attaching to them shrewd catchwords. Riesman spoke about "the nerve of failure," as against the radical claim that the moment was marked by a "failure of nerve." He wanted intellectuals to admit their incapacity for public life and the consequent desirability of adopting a more modest stance. And sometimes the moderately phrased sentiments of disenchantment with earlier political hopes broke down into sheer disgust. The abominations of McCarthyism, the crudities of the Cold War were jarring to sensitive people: it seemed best to pull away and dig in.

What remained was culture, culture as surrogate faith, enclave of sensibility, sign of distinction, refuge for the nerves. For sensitive people who found employment in the universities, culture became a secret home. They sought in art and literature what they were seeking in "personal relations," a world more attractive (as Trotsky had once said), a realm of purity that might shield one a little from the ugliness of the public world. Some years later this mode of feeling was to be represented brilliantly in Doris Lessing's novel *The Golden Notebook*; still later it was to be parodied, though hardly surmounted, in Woody Allen's films. During the fifties many literary people resembled grown-up versions of Holden Caulfield, "internal émigrés" clutching their secret possession. It was a real possession, though it hardly provided the moral shield they hoped for. In any case, their favorite form of discourse—because it allowed one to reflect upon all experiences without engaging too closely with any—was literary criticism.

Criticism followed upon literature, and literature seemed exempt from (though it might portray) "the world's slow stain." Criticism allowed a wide range of moral speculation without incurring excessive risks of application. Criticism strained toward a condition of autonomy, becoming more real to some readers than the poems or novels it still had to acknowledge. Engaging emotions once pledged to religion, keeping politics at a seemly distance, opening new sources of personal inwardness, criticism came to be regarded as the special terrain of the civilized.

Such sentiments easily lent themselves to minor fanaticism. How fanatical the disciples of various critical schools could be I learned during my first venture as a university teacher. In 1952 I spent the summer at the University of Washington in Seattle, mildly terrified I would not be able to fill up all those scheduled hours of teaching. I encountered there graduate students who knew intimately the inner disputes of the New Critics—how Winters had denounced Eliot, what Ransom felt about Blackmur—quite as yeshiva students had once known the inner exchanges of Talmudic commentators. It was by no means clear, however, that these students had read Tolstoy or Stendhal or Giovanni Verga. They were very keen, eager for coherence (which they thought to find in system), and they seemed to like me because I was "fresh" in both senses of the word. But they regarded as the rankest amateurism my preference for a criticism free of methodological apparatus, often improvisatory, and finally depending on personal insight. They asked me once who my favorite critic was, and like any New Yorker I answered, Edmund Wilson. It was a good answer, I still think, but they laughed at me, dismissing Wilson as a journalist, some even as a *mere* journalist.

The prestige of the New Critics was then very high. Only Lionel Trilling among the critics living in New York did not suffer a loss of standing in those years. Edmund Wilson, who cared more about his reputation than he let on, was battered heavily in the literary quarterlies. Invoking the highest aesthetic and moral values, the New Critics seemed to justify the insularity of their academic followers and to provide a pedagogy for coping with the droves of new college students who had somehow to be trained to "read." The New Critics seemed rigorous; they certainly were serious.

Their godfather was T. S. Eliot. They looked to Coleridge, Remy de Gourmont, Henry James, Ezra Pound, and I. A. Richards, but these were mere influences and sources, while Eliot was a living, inspiring model. They found in Eliot a critic superbly gifted at locating a writer's distinctive qualities through the exact epithet, the neat comparison, the apt quotation. They found in him a critic with a profound awareness of literary tradition, perhaps the basis of his gift for making seventeenth-century poets seem vibrant contemporaries. Eliot had a flair for coining critical catch phrases that he did not define with much precision—the objective correlative, the dissociation of sensibility, the impersonality of poetry, the uses of tradition—and lesser critics circled about these phrases worshipfully.

But Eliot also had an enviable capacity for raising the shapeless concerns of his readers to the level of explicit issues, as in his reflections on "the problem of belief" (whether in an age of clashing world outlooks one must share the persuasions of a writer in order fully to grasp his work). And perhaps most important, Eliot seemed a model of serious devotion to the criticism of literature—especially in his earlier phase.

By the seventies and eighties, when their influence had lessened, the few surviving New Critics were inclined to deny there had ever been an identifiable body of theory or practice warranting the label of New Criticism. The severe moralism of Yvor Winters had, for example, little in common with John Crowe Ransom's fondness for local niceties of diction. In the vision of retrospect, it must always seem that literary or intellectual groups had little real coherence; but the mere fact that some people came together signifies that there must have been a shared intention, even if one they did not fully grasp. Yet I understand the resistance of people like Robert Penn Warren and Cleanth Brooks to being lobbed into a categorical bin.

Allen Tate once suggested that the New Criticism was distinguished by "a hostility to, or neglect of, the 'historical method.' " The remark was cogent, but there was also an ambiguity, perhaps deliberate, in what Tate said. If by "historical method" he meant the propensity of traditional scholars to flatten out the work of poets and novelists into quasi-philosophical paraphrase—X is a monist, Y a skeptic, Z a positivist—then he was surely right. The New Critics regarded such formulas as a diversion from the main business of criticism. But if by "historical method" Tate meant an interest in placing the work of a writer in the setting of his time, or tracing a line of historical sensibility within that work, then Tate was by no means entirely right. He may have been expressing New Critical doctrine, but he was hardly describing its practice, at its best more sensitive and flexible than the doctrine.

Unlike "historicists" and "positivists," said the New Critics, they proposed to read poetry *as poetry* and not as a variant or reflection of anything else. Literature was an autonomous utterance and became accessible to responsible description and judgment only insofar as the critic employed terms referring to its distinctive traits. Where all "extrinsic" schools of criticism proposed some measure of "correspondence" to an aspect of human experience, the "intrinsic" approach favored as a basis for judgment "coherence," the inner propriety and unity of the parts of a literary work.

What the New Critics wanted was to put an end to the assimilation of the poem or novel into an inert "background" of historical "forces," or into some impressionistic account of emotions aroused in a reader. Their ideal program posited—and sometimes they achieved—a close description of what a poem is: a description stressing nuances of language, patterns of form, strategies of rhetoric, refinements of tone. Seen as an excess in reaction to earlier excesses of "Marxist critics," the New Critical position could elicit sympathy. In its own right, it raised doubts. For if there are advantages to regarding a text as though it were contemporaneous, anonymous, and nonreferential, there are grave disadvantages, too. Neither static nor stable, language has its inner course of development and is constantly subject to pressures from the historical process. Not merely does one have to know the meaning of words as they were used at the time a work was written; one must try to command the complex of historical and intellectual associations accruing to words at a given time. Thus the charge to be made against much traditional academic scholarship is not that it was historical, but that it was not historical enough or had a narrow view of what "historical" meant. At the same time, there was often justice in the accusation made by sophisticated scholars like J. V. Cunningham and Elder Olson that some of the ingenious paradoxes noted by the New Critics were really read into the poems they analyzed as an unironic insistence upon irony, for example, or as violations of possible meaning in behalf of "modernist" complexities.

I used to wonder what might be left, what *could* be left, after all experiential references were stripped away. Presumably the work of literature itself. But since language has unbreakable ties to possible events in experience, can the meaning or value of a work be apprehended without some resort—be it as subtle and indirect as you wish—to historical and moral categories? If poems and novels are not, in Tate's words, "expressive of substances beyond themselves," what are they expressive of? And it's worth noting that even the evaluative terms offered by theorists of the New Criticism—terms like coherence and complexity—were heavily freighted with value associations drawn from history, psychology, morality. Is there any evaluative term not so freighted, and must not any attempt to find purely "intrinsic" categories of literary valuation wither into sterility?

As I grew more experienced in the problems of the working critic, I became convinced that critical practice is no more harmonious with critical theory than novels are with theories of the novel. The New Critics often mixed close analysis of texts with oracular pronouncements of a sort that might be described as moralistic impressionism; they released in their work ideological biases quite as strong as those of the critics whom they faulted as ideological. It is hard to imagine a serious critic entirely free of one or another bias, especially when responding to novels or poems that deal with contemporary social life or world outlooks; surely the best way of minimizing the dangers this entails is to be acutely sensitive to them. The New Critics made the rest of us sensitive, and that is to their credit, but many of them showed a startling lack of awareness that, as men and women writing in the twentieth century, they too might be advancing political and theological biases that would leave them open to Tate's charge of yielding to "the doctrine of relevance."

Consider the peculiar prestige that terms like "orthodox," "tradition," and "original sin" enjoyed among leading New Critics. In the fifties we were a little slow in noticing that "orthodox" is, properly speaking, not a literary term at all, or that "original sin" is a category of but one theology. "Tradition" is a trickier term, since it can properly be used in both literary and moral-ideological contexts. What happened, however, was that these two contexts were taken to be one or to be organically related, so that it became rather easy to assume that a sense of the literary tradition necessarily sanctioned a "traditional" view of religion or morality. There was a strong inclination to forget that the literary tradition has, for some centuries, consisted of competing, often clashing tendencies, and can be fruitfully regarded as a series of rebellions, often more than just literary, by one generation against another.

The New Critics, with the powerful exception of Yvor Winters, were sympathetic to literary modernism, and even Winters was more ambivalent, as in his tangled relation with Hart Crane, than he realized. But the New Critics appeared at a time when modernism had passed its high point of achievement, and they wrote about it in ways that tended to blunt its edge of insurgency. They came not as advocates but as conservators of modernism, and thereby, with the best will in the world, they subtly distorted its spirit. Their critical writings—as distinct, in some cases, from their creative temperaments—encouraged a preference for the static, a suspicion of novelty, a dismissal of that radicalism of voice which forms a major strand within European and American modernism. But I doubt that their doctrine mattered as much as both they and their opponents found it convenient to believe. The New Critics played a major role in American literary life because the best of them were both vivid and talented literary figures, and because in their own ways, as best they could, they grappled with central difficulties of our culture.

For many New Critics it was their experience as teachers that formed the real matrix of their doctrines. They improvised strategies for going beyond impressionist chatter, they wanted students to see how poems really "worked." (With the novel they were less successful, since the novel keeps making shameless advances to "the doctrine of relevance.") But the techniques for close reading that Brooks and Warren developed in their famous textbook could succeed only if students already had some modest stores of literacy and historical reference. When I started teaching at Brandeis in 1953, I used a loosened version of the New Criticism almost as a matter of course. With the indifferently trained but alert students at Brandeis, this method worked well, forcing them to a certain discipline and checking their fondness for grand talk. When I went to Stanford in the early sixties, the New Criticism proved less effective, since the well-trained but largely unreachable students out there quickly turned the method into just another routine for churning out papers.

Once I started teaching at the City University of New York, where the problems of mass education are acute, I had to drop whatever of the New Criticism I had earlier brought into the classroom, since CUNY undergraduates were often irritated by New Critical procedures. With them one had first to relate a poem or novel to their strong if constricted sense of life, and this was not easy—indeed, the very strength of a plebeian sensibility can be a barrier to its enlargement. These students were fearful of critical abstraction, as if all the talk about irony and ambiguity, structure and diction was a luxury they could not afford. So the New Criticism worked best with students partly educated, responsive but ill-disciplined; it usually failed, at least in my experience, with brilliant elite students who didn't need it, and with the mass of untrained students who couldn't abide it.

From pedagogic concern to cultural problem was only a short step. The New Critics seldom talked explicitly about "mass culture," as the New York literary people talked obsessively in the fifties, but finally what the New Critics were encountering in their classrooms were both the products and problems of "mass culture." And if they didn't often use terms like "kitsch," that richly expressive label for high-toned trash, finally their major concern was how to prevent the spread of kitsch. Like all conscientious teachers, they began by noticing a phenomenon I once called "the pastness of the past," how the accumulating historical distinctiveness of our lives as Americans drives a wedge between ourselves and our culture. Here the New Critics were at their strongest. Not that they wrote much of value in the larger area of cultural analysis; but what spurred them to their best work in criticism was a sharp sense of how perilous the status of the word had become, how fragile the link between the classics of the past and readers of the present, how deeply shaken the norms underlying our culture. And, rather amusingly, insofar as the most thoughtful of the New Critics found themselves increasingly engaged, even if only indirectly, with such questions, they necessarily had to violate, or at least stretch, the stricter versions of their own aesthetic. The link that some of us in New York formed with the New Critics was largely based on an unspoken sense of shared predicaments. The problem of teaching, with which the New Critics began, became the problem of civilization, with which the best of them ended. For us in New York it was perhaps the other way around, but no matter—whoever has taken this journey in one direction will soon find a way back in the other.

Populist and vulgar Marxist critics attacked Ransom and Tate as reactionaries, but if they were, it wasn't because they kept struggling to draw a line between the authentic and the false in our culture. To claim, as some muddleheads did, that an insistence upon critical discriminations was somehow undemocratic was, in Whitman's words, to confuse "democracy's convictions and aspirations" with "the people's crudeness, vices, caprices."

Intellectual fashions in America—perhaps elsewhere, too—change with bewildering, indeed vulgar, regularity; as I write these lines the New Critics are being savaged in academic literary circles quite as, a few decades ago, the lesser among them were savaging critics like Edmund Wilson. Serious people pay no attention to, or look with disdain upon, such antics. Criticize them as you wish, but recognize that the New Critics were a strong presence in our culture. There was something keen, engaged, vivid about Blackmur and Tate, Ransom and Winters. Perhaps the most vivid were the Southerners, for their culture had deposited with them a rhetoric of grandeur, a gallantry of nostalgia. Like the New York writers, they felt ill at ease with the dominant culture yet determined to engage it in battle. Less attractive by far was the savage, often benighted, hostility some of them displayed toward American liberalism; but even that grew softer with the years, and in the case of Robert Penn Warren quite disappeared.

Meanwhile, they were *there*, figures in our life, not just professors in departments. A man like Tate amusingly satisfied one's expectations of what a Southern writer should be: gaunt, fierce, melodramatic, absurdly combative, haunted by losses he could hardly name, yet without a trace of aristocratic posturing and, when I knew him in the early fifties, often slyly humorous in mocking his own persona. Ransom, whom I knew less well, at first encounter seemed like a country gentleman, perhaps the sort of lawyer who reads the classics privately. But that was a superficial impression. He knew his mind exactly, and while very kind (surely the *nicest* editor, with his handwritten notes, I ever dealt with), there was a side of him, I thought, which took a quiet pleasure in annotating the foolishness of the literary people he knew. Ideals of decorum, gallantry, courtship, styles of comeliness and courtesy flowed through his life and work, and those of us not exactly rich in these qualities had reason to feel pleasure in his presence.

These men were literary personalities, by which I have in mind anything but the coarse public posturings that have marked a number of later writers. I mean that in figures like Ransom, Tate, and Robert Penn Warren, as in New Yorkers like Rahv and Rosenberg, there was a fine grading from personal voice to printed word. And I came to feel that, clashes of opinion aside, there was something symmetrical in the situations of the writers from Nashville and the writers from New York—both groups semioutsiders starting to break into the central spaces of American culture, yet unwilling to succumb to its slackness, its small optimisms. There was enough disagreement between the two groups to create tension, enough respect to begin friendships.

By the early fifties word began to reach New York that it might be possible to find a job—no one I knew thought of it as a career—teaching in a university. A few writers like Delmore Schwartz and Alfred Kazin taught now and then. Such marginal dealings with the Academy, commonplace in later years, seemed a little disconcerting at the time. Was this perhaps a retreat from independence? If so, we had better remember that independence in New York, with its scrabbling after reviews and assignments, often meant other kinds of retreat.

Once free-lancers began to gain a foothold in some English

departments, tensions increased between "them" and "us," the professors and the intellectuals. The snobbery of at least some English professors, picturing themselves as a genteel elite, was notorious; they could hardly be expected to look warmly upon big-city invaders lacking degrees, scholarship, and sometimes, it was said, manners. New York writers repaid generously, with a scorn mixing traces of Mencken's coarse academic-baiting and Marxist sneering at people in ivory towers. But now the universities were being flooded with war veterans in search of knowledge or at least diplomas, so that some literary mavericks were allowed to camp along the perimeters of the Academy. Even Jews, until the war discreetly kept out of the more prestigious humanities departments, were now able to find a place here, a place there.

My first brush with academic life was bizarre, as if deciphered from a script by Mary McCarthy or Randall Jarrell. Seemingly out of the blue a note came in 1952 from Harold Taylor, president of Sarah Lawrence College, asking if I would agree to be "considered" for a teaching post. Uneasy about teaching "those rich girls" and knowing Sarah Lawrence as a haven for academic fellow travelers, I went up to Bronxville feeling a little nervous. The exquisite campus made me still more nervous, but Taylor greeted me warmly and in a voice of melting sincerity asked what I wanted to teach "for us." I had no idea, of course. Glancing at his desk I saw a copy of an essay I had just written on "The Political Novel" and that seemed as good as anything else. So I said, "The political novel." Wonderful, answered Taylor, simply wonderful.

I was then taken to "the gauntlet," a series of interviews with faculty members. Greenest of the green at this ritual, I wondered why some greeted me with endless questions, while others smiled politely and let me pass. A few hours later, depressed and exhausted, I reached the climax of the gauntlet: Marc Slonim, professor of Russian, *éminence grise* of the college. By then all I could think of was that he spoke English rather like Gregory Ratoff in *Ninotchka.*

"Un vat vill you teach for us, Mr. Howe?"

(*Without hesitation, by now a gauntlet veteran.*) "The political novel."

(*Gravely.*) "Dot will require a team."

"Yes, a literary critic and a sociologist."

"No, no, a team!"

(*Ratoff wants a bigger team? Why not?*) "We can add an anthropologist and maybe even a scientist."

(*By now he is red in the face, exploding.*) "A team! A team!"

(*General confusion, embarrassed gestures, as suddenly it occurs to me, idiot that I am, that he means a theme. I slink away.*)

A few weeks later I received a note from Taylor regretting that Sarah Lawrence would not be able to use my services. This was the most fortunate rejection in my life, though I hardly knew it; a few months later I learned that there had been a bloody battle at the college between an anti-Stalinist group that thought I might be a helpful ally and the fellow travelers who, unbendingly polite at the "gauntlet," knew perfectly well their reasons for not wanting me. At a disarmament conference a year or so later I ran into Taylor, who with the utmost friendliness asked me why Sarah Lawrence had not been able to persuade me to join its faculty.

In 1953 came another invitation, this one serious, from Brandeis University. To teach there would mean to have a steady job, perhaps even a vocation, and to shake off the irksome reviewing I did for *Time*. I had to consider, however, that we were now at the high point of McCarthyism—a matter to which I shall return—and that the socialist group headed by Max Shachtman, in which I retained inactive membership, was on the infamous "subversive list." So I wrote my friend Lewis Coser, who had begun teaching at Brandeis a year or two earlier, asking whether he thought its president, Abram Sachar, could be depended on to protect faculty dissidents from McCarthyite attack. Lew's answer is still engraved in my memory, since it has served for a good many other occasions: if there were minor harassments, Sachar would stand firm; but if there was a direct major assault by McCarthy, well . . .

I went up to Waltham, the Boston suburb where the Brandeis campus is located, and there encountered a miscellaneous faculty committee. Around the table sat Simon Rawidowicz, a historian of Jewish thought; Ludwig Lewisohn, who had shifted from Freudian criticism to Jewish nationalism; Joseph Cheskis, a professor of French with a thick Yiddish accent; and several scientists. Just as I had no conventional credentials, so they had no conventional questions. The session lagged, it began to look bad, until I mentioned casually that I was working with the Yiddish poet Eliezer Greenberg on an anthology of Yiddish stories in English translation. Faces broke into smiles. Rawidowicz began "correcting" my overestimation of Peretz; everyone started talking Yiddish. I relaxed happily, sure I was going to get the job.

Is there another professor of English in the country who can say that his first job interview was conducted in Yiddish?

That was Brandeis, recently started, and for the next ten or fifteen years, a remarkable place mixing college, political forum, and kibbutz, where the abundant energies of Jewish intellectuals—some of them free-lancers from New York and others refugees from Germany—found bread, speech, and audiences. Innocently, shrewdly, Brandeis didn't hesitate to hire bright (sometimes merely eccentric) people who lacked Ph.D.s or had European credentials little honored in the United States. Frank Manuel taught history, Philip Rieff and Lewis Coser sociology, Abraham Maslow psychology, Herbert Marcuse his version of Marxism. Gifted composers like Arthur Berger and Irving Fine headed the music department. The atmosphere was intense, unstarched, impudent. Not solid enough to be a first-rate university, Brandeis was brilliant enough to be a first-rate college, and while I have since taught at more distinguished schools, never have I known any place where the life of the mind was engaged with such passion.

The president of Brandeis, Abram Sachar, was an extraordinary man. The faculty saw him as a philistine, but the faculty could not appreciate that in his hands philistinism was being raised to the level of genius. Sachar had shrewdly realized that the old German Jewish money would not be within his reach—perhaps never, certainly not until after Brandeis no longer needed it. He turned to Jews of East European origin who had grown wealthy during the war years, men mostly lacking in education yet worshipful of the idea of it. Sachar milked this layer of the newly rich Jewish bourgeoisie with a skill that it would have taken a heart of gold not to admire.

At fund-raising events we faculty members were sometimes put on display, asked to say a few words in order to lend a bit of tone; sometimes Sachar would suggest with a grin that I "speak above their heads just a little," since he knew that the difficulty potential donors might have in grasping my literary gibberish would only impress them all the more. Indeed, these new millionaires were innocents who felt it an honor to be worked over by a scholar like Abram Sachar. At one fund-raiser Sachar ended his caressing pitch with an anecdote. There had been a most promising young man named Harry Widener who found himself on that fated journey of the R.M.S. *Titanic*. He went down with the ship as a gentleman should. To honor his memory, his family had a library built in Harvard Yard and now—pianissimo, the voice sinking gently— "when the students at Harvard go to the library, they don't say, 'Let's go to the library,' they say, 'Let's go to Widener.' " A hush fell across the room. One could almost see quivers of emotion journeying from soul to soul, as if the assembled manufacturers and real estate men were ruminating, "Someday maybe they'll say, 'Let's go to Shapiro!' "

What counted most at Brandeis was the students, children of the children of the Depression, children of the children of City College. Erratic, cocky, shy, arrogant, seldom well-taught but marvelously eager, the best of them formed a sediment, perhaps the last, of the best of immigrant Jewish culture. Many came from families that had climbed to some affluence after the war, but had handed down almost instinctively the quarrelsome love of politics and literature that had been handed down to *their* overburdened parents. The education a boy or girl received at Brandeis was often, to be sure, a little irregular: my colleague J. V. Cunningham once caustically remarked that you could get through the place having read Marx, Freud, and *Huckleberry Finn*.

Brandeis students—well, some of them—came to class primed for dispute. From their years of listening to kitchen debates at home, and from romanticizing the already romanticized stories their parents told about exciting movements and meetings, these students knew that education is not a matter of making oneself a receptacle into which a detached elder pours knowledge; it is an engagement in which sparring, conflict, "acting out" become a path to meaning. These young men and women knew intuitively that dialectic is a form of play—in the classroom, a simulated argument turning into authentic exchange—and that the life of the mind, precisely insofar as it summons the gravest issues, is also finally a form of play. At Brandeis I seldom lectured, but plunged headlong into the hardest and darkest questions that, say, a reading of *Middlemarch* or *The Rainbow* evoked. Sometimes I would take intellectual and moral positions the students knew I did not hold, but they understood that unless they learned to defend their beliefs coherently against my needling opposition, they had little claim to attention or self-confidence. The ability to read a text most of them already had: they had learned this not from a New Critic but from our professor of philosophy, Aaron Gurwitch, a phenomenologist who like a traditional *melamed* would study Kant and Hume with them line by line.

Teaching at Brandeis was exhilarating and terrifying. I would often come out of class with my shirt wringing wet. I never knew enough. Once I did a graduate seminar in the eighteenth-century English novel, and by the semester's end I had made my way through the entire reading list; our cultural distance from Richardson, Sterne, and Fielding became the theme of the class. Another time I assumed a stance of skepticism, breaking down interpretations of Henry James's story, "The Liar." At the end of the hour the bell rang, I said "Thank you," and started walking out—when a group of students led by Jeremy Larner, later himself a writer, came charging up to me, blood in their eyes, shouting, "You can't do this to us!" They wanted the truth.

Most of all I remember my first weeks of teaching a humanities "survey" from Milton to Virginia Woolf. (To paper the gaps in my knowledge, I borrowed liberally from Arthur Lovejoy, William Empson, Cleanth Brooks—I thank them.) When I took home the first batch of papers from students with names still unknown to me—Michael Walzer, Judith Borodovko (Walzer), Barbara Herrnstein (Smith)—a kind of terror passed through me. This prose was elegant and lucid; the thought, firm. What in the name of heaven could I teach them? I had still to learn that the best teaching consists in letting such young people move ahead on their own, perhaps supplying some bibliography (have you read Empson? do you know Max Weber on cities? Georg Simmel on the stranger?) and offering an occasional warning against purple prose.

Perhaps I am putting the Brandeis experience in too rosy a light. Wasn't there a quantity of aggression, some of it needless, in my classroom style? A former student, Martin Peretz, who later became a friend, remembers that as a teacher I was very "cutting." The daredevils in class were ready to "cut" right back, but what about those who sat in the middle of the room, got middling grades, and had middlebrow minds? Lacking weapons that "cut," they suffered at times, for the effect of my teaching could be to make them aware of their deficiencies without providing a way to overcome them. When I expressed this anxiety to my colleague J. V. Cunningham, he said that even such rude landings in consciousness were a service of sorts; but I'm not sure, I suspect that some of these perfectly harmless students were the victims of my intellectual pride.

Let me turn the question once more and half justify the methods with which I and others taught. Our Brandeis students had been raised in a culture of liberalism, they were full of that peculiar earnestness which sees no greater virtue than an open mind. In high school they had been taught that, since literature is an autonomous activity, it is gross to talk about novels or poems in political or moral terms. These students were lovely and lovable, but there came moments when one wanted to shake them into recognizing unresolvable dilemmas, hateful problems that slip past the clutch of reason. I used to ask: "Suppose you were reading a novel that showed Nazis as *characteristically* kind to Jews, how would you respond?" Instead of attacking my question—how could a sane person write such a novel? what is the point even of imagining it?— they would mumble uneasily about the need to allow writers their own terms of reference, and so forth. Then, as if on schedule, I would explode, saying that if I were reading such a book I'd throw it out the window. Hard stares back and forth, anger mounting, a break in the current of feeling between teacher and students.

The liveliest moments at Brandeis were not in the classroom at all, but at student-sponsored evening debates and meetings. Here the faculty performed, especially that segment consisting of radicals, semiradicals, pseudoradicals, and ex-radicals. There was also a tiny Far Right fringe speaking warmly of Joe McCarthy, though it was characteristic of Brandeis that the spokesman for this view should be a truculent ex-Trotskyist. Our students served as witnesses, dazed and delighted, to what they imagined was a playback to the glorious (or bizarre?) past of an older generation. It was as if we were recovering at Brandeis the vanished worlds of left-wing politics in New York and avant-garde culture in Weimar. Some of this was playacting, some an impassioned recall. There was a lot of old-fashioned inhibition, too: I remember being shocked once when Norman Mailer, up for what he called a "lecture," offered some "grass" to Martin Peretz, a young man quite able to take care of himself. To be honest, I wasn't exactly sure what this "grass" was or did.

I threw myself into the Brandeis debates with an unconsidered energy. Once, in 1956, I debated Herbert Marcuse: he, though critical of the Soviet intervention, hinted darkly that the Budapest street fighters might be reactionaries, while I supported the Hungarian revolution against totalitarian domination. Marcuse was a man of aristocratic bearing and arrogant mind, but enormously charming—one had to *decide* not to like him. His Marxism was corrupted by a streak of elitist nihilism, the contempt of the learned German for what he jokingly but revealingly called *Untermenschen*. (In the sixties, when we broke on politics, I became an *Untermensch*, as did Lew Coser; Hannah Arendt had been one for years.) Another time I debated the Harvard historian Oscar Handlin after the Israeli services had kidnapped Adolf Eichmann from Argentina, Handlin criticizing the Israeli action as a violation of international law and I defending it as a necessary moral act by the victims of the Holocaust. This debate too was heated, stirring up emotions among the students it would still be hard to sort out— bruising conflicts between their liberalism and their Jewishness, between what they took to be principle and had to recognize as feeling.

A third time I debated Howard Fast, the popular writer who in a month or two would break with the Communist Party but was still defending Stalinism. I lashed Fast without kindness or mercy. Bottled-up feelings broke out among my friends: Rose Coser kept heckling Fast repeatedly, even though students thought she was unfair. Children of their moment, our students could not understand the bitterness some of us felt toward Fast, and when he appealed to their sense of "fair play"—hack that he was, defender of the Moscow trials, defamer of the Yiddish writers murdered by Stalin!—they responded sympathetically. I could only reply that the spectacle of Fast asking for "fair play" was like a man who kills his mother and father and then asks for mercy on the ground that he is an orphan. Years later Jeremy Larner told me that for months after this debate Brandeis students discussed it heatedly. Was it right to attack Fast so violently, even though he was defending a totalitarian outlook? Was it just a tiresome quarrel between equally irrelevant old radicals? Was there a way for younger people to absorb the meaning of the earlier struggles?

A strange place, this Brandeis—brilliant, unstable, vibrant, not quite the scholarly enclave a university is supposed to be, but a home of turbulent intellectual energies, and doomed soon enough to slide into academic respectability.

The most lasting consequence of my years at Brandeis was an odd relationship with J. V. Cunningham, the poet and scholar who also came there in 1953. In his youth a heterodox Catholic, Cunningham had studied with and then rebelled against Yvor Winters, the critic-sage of Stanford. Cunningham was a learned classicist with a sufficiently wide knowledge to have taught mathematics during the war. Prickly, contentious, rudely charming, he was determinedly plebeian. If I had a New York dress presser for a father, he had a Montana carpenter, and we both felt warmth for the unions to which our fathers had belonged, both despised the genteel pretensions of many academics. Cunningham was not an easy man to be near. Inner torments could make him savage (as they could make me sullen). The way to preserve a friendship with him was to keep a certain distance.

Cunningham wrote sardonic epigrams, as well as sententious lyrics in Roman modes, and was utterly out of sympathy—at least in his declared opinions—with Eliot's modernism. The voice of his poems, though sometimes marred by an affectation of toughness, is severe, sardonic, and bruising:

> Within this mindless vault
> Lie Tristan and Isolt
> Tranced in each other's beauties.
> They had no other duties.

> Naked I came, naked I leave the scene,
> Naked was my pastime in between.

> I married in my youth a wife.
> She was my own, my very first.
> She gave the best years of her life.
> I hope nobody gets the worst.

Here lies New Critic who would fox us
With his poetic paradoxes.
Though he lies here rigid and quiet,
If he could speak he would deny it.

He also wrote learned essays, in a prose austerely sharp, on the historical contexts and limits of Chaucer and Shakespeare and Emily Dickinson. Intellectual opponent of romanticism, he struggled in his poetry, as in his life, with an ineradicably romantic temperament. A man had to live, he wrote, "divided against himself: only the selfishly insane can integrate experience to the heart's desire, and only the emotionally sterile would not wish to." Greatly ambitious, he broke himself to moments of resignation. Affecting a shuffling simplicity, though not enough to silence his wicked tongue, he sometimes came to seem—this is unfair: may he forgive me—like one of those devil figures in Thomas Mann's fiction: shabby-rakish, saturnine, bristling with irony. Cunningham lived with, believing in and suffering from, an inordinate pride. Pride was the defense a serious man put up against the world—pride and a fifth of bourbon. Pride was a sin, but an enabling sin: it helped one get through one's time.

From this man I learned that scholarship need not be the dry or trivial matter I had often supposed it to be; that if there were professors as arid as I thought, there were others for whom knowledge led to a moral exaltation. In the presence of such a man, academic-baiting seemed puerile. From him I learned to credit the historicity of literature, something that may limit the brilliance possible to criticism but encourages accuracy of description. He had written a caustic little book on Shakespeare, tearing to shreds a New Critical reading of the famous line in *King Lear*, "ripeness is all," by demonstrating through historical and linguistic evidence that Shakespeare could not possibly have meant that "maturity of experience is a final good." "It is a meaning I can enter into quite as deeply as anyone, but it is not what Shakespeare meant."

Between Cunningham and me there was an enormous gap in experience, temperament, ideas. Yet we worked easily together, amused and pleased that we could. Being professional himself, he honored me with the presumption that I too could become professional. I learned, by being with him, the value of scraping against a mind utterly unlike one's own, so that finally there could emerge between our two minds a conditional peace, perhaps even pleasure in difference. In my decades of teaching, Cunningham was the one colleague whom I regarded as my teacher.

In those years we had a young colleague named Henry Popkin, who had his reasons for not admiring either Cunningham or me. At an academic meeting, Popkin was once asked by Robert Heilman, a New Critic from the University of Washington, how those two strange characters, Cunningham and Howe, ex-Jesuit and ex-Trotskyist, got along together. Popkin flashed back: "Oh, they get along fine. They tell each other stories about the gods they used to know!" A witty thrust, but in truth we did not tell each other stories about gods we used to know; we had both, in our separate ways, learned to live without them.

It was the peculiar fate of Brandeis to be located a few miles from Harvard. The senior university, distinguished and respected, soon took a paternal interest in the junior one, which was merely fresh and avid. A few Brandeis departments became academic "colonies" of Harvard, havens for some of its less brilliant graduate students. This paternal interest was often mixed with an amused condescension, and there was, in truth, no shortage of Brandeis gaffes at which to smile. Perhaps in one or two corners of Harvard there was also a somewhat uglier feeling at work. The genteel anti-Semitism long nestling in American academic life had by now ceased to be respectable, but it was hardly at an end. Only thirty years earlier President Abbott Lowell of Harvard had openly proposed a policy of limiting by quota the number of Jews admitted. And now there they were, down the road, those New York Jewish dilettantes and German-Jewish refugees, presuming to set up a *university*!

To be patronized by Cambridge rankled me. It did not rankle J. V. Cunningham. As soon as he took over the English department at Brandeis he declared our independence: if mediocrities were to be added to our ranks they would be our own kind, preferably from the Midwest. For this show of insubordination we were not readily forgiven by Cambridge. Yet Harvard's condescension toward Brandeis was not brutal, only malicious. It took the form of an amused lift of an eyebrow regarding the antics of the new Jewish school. It was the snobbery of a benign imperialism, like that of the Englishmen in Kipling's "Head of the District" who wish the Indians no harm, but find it hard to imagine that "a native" could manage complex affairs.

At a Cambridge reception in the late fifties, I was introduced by Professor Harry Levin to a visiting Italian novelist with an elaborate flurry of suggestion: "Signor, I should like you to meet . . . aah . . . one of our more promising younger . . ." (long pause) ". . . literary journalists." The amiable Italian surely saw no harm in these words, since many European writers earn their living as journalists, but here in the United States, a land of greater purity, the term "journalist," sometimes prefaced by a withering "mere," serves as an academic putdown The erudite Levin, then the reigning prince of Harvard literary studies and a man of exquisite self-consciousness, must have known his words would cause me hurt. Indeed, since it is too late for anything but candor, I might as well add that similar academic needling would come my way, now and again, across the years.

Was this condescension, at least in part a mode of snobbery, so very different from the response of Proust's aristocrats to the lower nobility or mere commoners? The faint smile with which Levin would greet the name of some lesser scholar—was this so different from the smile of a Guermantes at the mention of a Cambremer? Proust writes that snobbery "in changing its subject does not change its accent." Yes, but it may change its stratagems. The snobbery of an aristocracy is ascribed and thereby impersonal; neither money nor talent can, in principle, subvert its standards. In a democratic society where men are not fixed in rank, snobbery must link itself to claims for notable talent, achievement, distinction. Snobbery winds, snakelike, around the highest values, and there are times when it seems almost impossible to distinguish between the two, professorial snobbery, for instance, often being entangled with a genuine devotion to scholarship.

Snobbery works only as long as the victims accept its premises. It didn't work at all with Cunningham, who knew that, even though he taught in an odd school like Brandeis, he could easily match the Harvard people in a scholarly competition. It worked with me because I felt myself a stranger or intruder in the academic milieu.

Decades later, returning to Proust's great novel, I would find myself speculating again about the various modes of snobbery. There is a sentence in one of the later volumes that seems especially touching: "Snobbery is a serious malady of the spirit, but one that is localized and does not taint it as a whole." It would be nice to think so, but is this really true? Proust had in mind that there are snobs capable of generous conduct, and this of course was as true in Cambridge as in Combray. Yet as one thinks about the damage caused by snobbery, the damage it did me and the damage I in turn have surely done others, it's hard to suppose that our moral maladies can be contained or "localized," hard to believe they do not metastasize into every part of our being.

We think of the fifties as a political decade, a time of Cold War, McCarthyism, growing conservatism—and with good reason. But even as I was getting into plenty of political disputes and helping to start a political magazine, I managed to write a good deal of literary criticism. I had a lot of energy in those days, I was still young enough to drive ahead, not yet old enough to wonder about the direction. I wrote books about Sherwood Anderson and William Faulkner, a good many reviews and essays, and *Politics and the Novel*, a study dealing with the "bloody crossroads" between literature and ideology. *Politics and the Novel* has its flaws: too great a fondness for epigrammatic sentences, some Marxist schematizing, a failure to focus in detail on an exemplary scene in the books discussed. But it also has a signal virtue. I wrote it while in the grip of an idea: how the passions of ideology twist themselves about, yet also liberate, creative energies. The price I paid was that forever after I would be identified as a "social critic." There is of course some rough justice in this description, but rough justice is finally no justice.

If, occasionally, someone introducing me at a university lecture would trouble to describe the particular qualities of my work (I enjoyed hearing my prose was "witty," though I did not hear it often enough!), I would be forever grateful. In my eyes, almost anything was better than once again being called a "social critic." But *was* I a social critic? I could hardly say. Certainly I never meant or tried to be one. I never thought of myself as having made a decision, or having gone to the method shop and picked out a method. It always seemed that I had been chosen—chosen by the time I lived in, the life I led, the visions and blindnesses that were part of my heritage and nature. With any critic at all worthy of the name, the deepest biases of temperament and strongest interests of mind are what determine the kind of criticism he writes. In my case people called the resulting work "social," and occasionally I bristled at what seemed too narrow a description, perhaps with an edge of dismissal to it. But maybe they were right, since what others *think* one is forms part of what one really is. I didn't like it but I gradually became resigned.

No, I didn't. I would ask aggressively: "Is Allen Tate really a 'formalist' critic?" The categorizers said he was, but anyone who knew him or read him had to see that what mattered in his criticism was a complex of personal biases, gifts, passions, and prejudices that broke whatever formalist scaffold he might erect. Tate himself had once protested, with his fine irritability, against such categorizing. He did resemble, he said, the other New Critics, just as in the eyes of a Mongolian, his notoriously cadaverous frame looked like that of Babe Ruth.

Still, if I could conclude there were good grounds for seeing the New Critics as a group, couldn't they feel the same about grouping me with other "social critics"? Every critic whose work has a personal accent seems closer to one kind of criticism than another. It was hardly an accident that I rarely employed Freudian categories in my own criticism. I wasn't opposed to Freudianism, quite the contrary; but it didn't engage me as a critic, it didn't stir me at those deepest imaginative levels out of which a piece of writing ought to emerge. Again, though a child of modernist culture, I wrote mainly about nineteenth-century European novelists and that group of twentieth-century writers who had gone through the ideological traumas of our age. No more, for instance, than Silone could avoid the subjects that had chosen him, could I avoid his work once it had chosen me. That in a final reckoning he would not be counted among the great writers of the century I knew quite well. It hardly mattered. I wrote about his books because his questions were also mine.

Call me "social critic" or anything else, by the fifties I knew what I wanted to do. I wanted to write literary criticism like that which Edmund Wilson or George Orwell wrote. No matter that I could never do it as well as they, that wasn't my business, judgment was for others. And most of all I wanted to be an intellectual, one of those free-ranging speculative writers who grapple with the troubles of their time yet command some of the accumulated knowledge of the past. No matter, again, that there was something naive—and vain, too—in this announced desire. It was what one might make of such a desire—the devotion or intensity one might bring to it—that finally counted.

8

Ideas in Conflict

The end of a war usually prompts yearnings for quiet and ease, a conservative fantasy of the past reassembled. But the harshnees of postwar politics made such wishes seem unreal, self-indulgent. It wasn't possible for a thoughtful person to remain still during the fifties: old systems of belief, whether conventional Marxist or conventional liberal, had clearly proved insufficient. Among many intellectuals there was now a thrust toward conservatism, and since some of these "New Conservatives" were old radicals, they found it convenient to recast their opinions by attacking those who wanted to keep a socialist kernel while dropping the Marxist shell. So, even while submitting to our own doubts, we had to fend off a barrage from the Right. A state of siege isn't the best atmosphere in which to reflect on first principles, but that was where we were.

I often suffered a kind of dizziness from the sheer piling up of political surprise. If you mobilized some resources to consider a new problem, a dozen others came tumbling down on your head, while hordes of kibitzers kept crying that the world needed "fresh ideas."

The perfecting of the atom bomb called into question not only theories of progress (they proved easily dispensable) but the very survival of humanity. The growth of Soviet power—no one had quite foreseen its magnitude—made the threat of totalitarianism seem urgent in new, perplexing ways. The Titoist heresy drained off whatever comfort might be had from theories of monolithic communism. The economies of Western Europe, refusing to abide by Marxist prescriptions, underwent an astonishing revival, as if to mock all those, both Left and Right, who in the years between wars had kept sneering at "bourgeois democracy." The Cold War now became the dominating presence in the world, blunting whatever hopes for peace had survived the hot war.

Intellectuals stumbled from fad to fad, notion to notion. It became hard to draw a line between eagerness to clarify new aspects of public experience and the coarse desire to mount a bitch goddess named Novelty. Abandoning Marxism came to resemble mass rituals of contrition—sometimes liberating, since you shook off the phantasms of ideology, but often rather sad, since you forfeited criticism, hope, commitment. And meanwhile the New York intellectuals were starting to attract public attention: articles in mass-circulation magazines, seminars at universities—a sure sign, we should have known, of reaching the end.

Much of this might have been useful, even stimulating. Some new developments were pleasing: the English Labour government had agreed to a free India, the state of Israel had proclaimed its existence, brilliant films were pouring out of Italy, Paris throbbed with fresh intellectual life, and here in New York we had that outburst of modernist art called "action painting," perhaps the richest creative impulse of our moment. Yet as I recall the mood of my friends, including those who disagreed with me politically, it was shadowed with gloom. Everyone seemed jumpy, irritable, nervous. Relief at the war's end, joy at the destruction of Hitlerism: these faded quickly, since what now overwhelmed us was the rise of communist power in the world.

During the early years of the war it had been a strain on one's nerves to hear American liberals, and even conservatives, speak glowingly about "Uncle Joe," the benign Soviet leader. But perhaps because of a residual optimism, we socialists had not really expected that Stalinism would emerge from the war as strong as it now seemed; indeed, we had usually assumed it to be a transitory or peculiarly Russian phenomenon. Until the fifties, very few political analysts thought of Stalinism as a worldwide historical force or as a new mode of social organization, distinct from capitalism and socialism, that might be moving toward world power, even world dominance. But now communist parties had destroyed Czech democracy, acquired strength in China, and established themselves as major forces within France and Italy. It was frightening. From the premise that Stalinism represented a sidetracking of "the locomotive of history," we now had to face the possibility that this locomotive had begun to race backward to a sophisticated barbarism.

The anti-Stalinist Left began to recognize—with a mounting despair—that the totalitarian curse would survive for at least the span of our lives. Whatever drove millions to the death wish of the total state, would exhaust our century. It was as if a sentence of history had been extended without limit. This meant we had to put aside the worn-out leftist notion that, on a world scale, capitalism was the sole or even major enemy. There was now a greater enemy by far—the totalitarian state, sometimes of the Right, sometimes of the Left. In 1952 totalitarianism of the Left seemed the harder to cope with and thereby, in a sense, more terrifying. Yet we also knew that this judgment, necessary as it might be, would create severe political difficulties.

Difficulties in our lives, too. How often have I cursed the fate that impelled me and my friends to spend so much time struggling against illusory "leftist" forms of the totalitarian idea! Even if we can claim a speck of credit for having undertaken this task, it is depressing to think of the waste of spirit it entailed. For even those of us never enticed by Stalinism had to suffer damage from the length and intensity of our opposition. Of course, no one in the United States was sent to a Siberian labor camp or shut away in a psychiatric hospital for adopting anti-Stalinist views; indeed, by the fifties those views were becoming a little too popular, too open to coarse exploitation. The waste of spirit I've spoken of may seem puny when compared with the loss of years, or life itself, within the Soviet Union. Nevertheless, in a milder way we did pay a price: too many enervating polemics, too great a politicizing of our thought, and too little of the composure needed for serious intellectual work.

A writer who devotes himself exclusively to politics courts the dangers of dryness, the mental undernourishment of journalism. To be sure, even the most politically conscious writers of our time have found themselves "another place"—some gaining distance from the intolerableness of the world through memory and imagination. Silone found this place in his humorous idylls about the Abruzzi peasants, Orwell in the bluff decencies of ordinary Englishmen, Octavio Paz in the labyrinths of Mexican solitude. In my own way I found "another place" in literary criticism and compiling translations of Yiddish literature. But was this really enough? Isn't there always a shrinkage of imaginative power when an "engaged" writer submits to the political moment? "The heart's grown brutal from the fare," Yeats had written, "More substance in our enmities/ Than in our love." Decades later, those lines can still evoke for me an unexpended sadness.

If there was moral ugliness in the America of the fifties, the discussion among intellectuals on the problem of totalitarianism was different: it was urgent and serious. How, we kept asking ourselves, could we account for that frightful yoking of ideology and terror, the capacity of the Nazi and Stalinist movements to sweep millions of people into their ranks?

There was perhaps a disposition to accept a little uncritically the idea of a totalitarian "essence," a sort of ideal Platonic form of which the regimes headed by Hitler and Stalin were mere alloyed realizations. Yet even those resisting this view had to admit that Hitler and Stalin had introduced something radically new in modern history. The keenest analysts—Hannah Arendt, Franz Newmann, Richard Lowenthal, Carl Friedrich—naturally focused on whatever seemed novel in the totalitarian upsurge: terror as an integral part of this new society; ideology as both mental equivalent of terror and a means of dominating the public and private lives of subjects; the breakdown of boundaries between state and society, so that "secondary institutions" could no longer play an autonomous role; the atomization of social life, with classes pulverized into a passive, anonymous mass; "permanent revolution from above," a relentless warfare of state against people; and the consolidation of a ruling elite, sanctified in the person of the Leader, claiming not just a monopoly of power or a variety of goods but the ownership, as it were, of state and society. These are elements of a totalitarian "model" driven to the purity of extreme, though there were differences of opinion, of course, about the extent to which they were present in a given society and about the weights to be assigned them analytically. Behind such questions loomed a larger one: to what extent could this new totalitarianism be distinguished from earlier modes of authoritarian dictatorship?

The two most influential books on this theme were Hannah Arendt's *Origins of Totalitarianism* and George Orwell's *1984*, the first a historical study and analytic argument, the second an imaginative foreboding. Arendt had a gift for elevating, or reducing, historical phenomena to a terror of essence. Her vision of totalitarianism was that of an insane relentlessness, a society that can accept no enduring peace but must keep driving itself toward climaxes of struggle, either against internal enemies ("traitors") or external enemies ("inferior races" and "decadent bourgeois regimes"). The "assumption that everything is possible"—which, said Arendt, was central to the totalitarian ethos—"thus leads through consistent elimination of all factual restraints to the absurd and terrible consequence that every crime the rulers can conceive of must be punished, regardless of whether or not it has been committed." A dynamic of violence and terror is set in motion: a state of total mobilization, a recurrent assault upon a population summoned to "heroic" purposes. Heinrich Himmler, head of the SS, spoke of "a selection which can never stand still."

Such regimes are revolutionary (or counterrevolutionary) not only in their methods of taking power, but still more in their methods of keeping it. The charismatic Leader calls for ceaseless vigilance, action, sacrifice. The ultimate end of totalitarianism, if there is one, appears as either world domination or apocalypse—or the two together in a sodden *Götterdämmerung*. A voracious nihilism lies at its heart. Finally this takes the shape of a hubris aiming to transform not so much society as "human nature itself." Before so ghastly a prospect, admits Arendt, the mind balks, since "in each one of us there lurks . . . a liberal, wheedling us with the voice of common sense," who regards the phenomenon of terror as an aberration and the description of it as a yielding to hysteria.

Both Arendt and Orwell performed an immense service by insisting that totalitarianism is not merely an extension of monopoly capitalism or Leninist dictatorship or even man's inherent sinfulness. All these surely contributed to the rise of totalitarianism, but what made it so powerful and frightening was precisely the break with old traditions, good and bad: precisely the embodiment of a radical new ethos of blood, terror, and nihilism. That no actual society behaved entirely in accord with Arendt's model is hardly a cogent criticism.

This model or nightmare vision, itself strongly streaked with apocalyptic elements, had a large influence on serious thought in the fifties. It made us see totalitarianism as a system that could not be changed from within or modified through conflicts among segments of its ruling elite. The implicit assumption was that totalitarianism is a society that has achieved a mode of stasis, even if one of systematized chaos. Or put another way, that it has established an equilibrium between the flow of terror essential to its survival and the energies that make possible the permanence of terror. Thereby this new mode of society comes really to signify an end to history—though here many people drew back from what seemed too extreme a conclusion. Orwell was shrewder in this respect than Arendt, since in *1984* he anticipated a gradual slackening of the unfuture, a diminution of that ferocious intensity which until now has characterized totalitarianism. But while envisioning a gradual drop from fanaticism to torpor, Orwell did not suppose this would affect the continued employment of active terror: in *1984* terror has taken on a life of its own. Orwell failed to consider that the energies making for terror might, together with ideological fervor and psychological mobilization, gradually run down, so that terror would be replaced by terror-in-reserve, which in fact has happened in the Soviet Union.

Admirers and critics alike knew that Arendt's book offered a keener analysis of Nazism than of Stalinism. The Stalin dictatorship might roughly conform to the general traits laid down by theorists of totalitarianism, but it obviously had distinct elements. It had its own socioeconomic system; it exploited the Marxist tradition; it employed perhaps a larger quotient of rationality than Nazism. One aspect of Soviet society that did not seem to conform to Arendt's thesis was the evident wish of the ruling bureaucracy, especially after Stalin's death, to enjoy habits of life generally associated with an ascendant bourgeoisie. Terror, since it cannot safely be confined to a fixed segment of the population, must frighten the rulers, too. And weary them. Besides, it was Stalin's devilish policy to use terror against the communist leadership at least as much as against the general population. In Khrushchev and his successors one could detect a yearning for "collective security," which meant a tacit understanding among the bureaucrats not to slaughter one another. Their regimes continued to be dictatorships, but sluggish ones, hardly fitting the model of "permanent revolution from above."

It became clear that if one held strictly to Arendt's theory, the Soviet regime in the post-Stalin years could no longer be called totalitarian. The ideology was there, even if in decay; the dictatorship was there, even if less brutal; but the quantity of active terror had been sharply reduced. Yet some theorists, like the sophisticated German Social Democrat, Richard Lowenthal, argued that there were good analytic grounds for continuing to call the Soviet Union a totalitarian society. As he defined totalitarianism, terror was not the central factor. Crucial in this view was the presence of a one-party dictatorship that through a mixture of ideology and unchecked power arrogated to itself complete domination over social and political life.

Did this difference of analysis matter or was it just a semantic quarrel? I think it mattered a great deal. For the point of the discussion, as it wove its way through and past the fifties, was to stress the historical uniqueness of Nazi and communist societies, while also acknowledging the differences between the two. To have used a more comprehensive term such as "authoritarian" would have been to weaken or abandon that stress upon historical uniqueness. By focusing narrowly, though brilliantly, on the more extreme and pathological features of totalitarianism, Arendt in effect abdicated her theory with regard to a society that preserved the party-state's total domination yet no longer resorted to mass killings or arbitrary terror.

Especially after Khrushchev's revelations and the Hungarian revolution, it became clear to all but Arendt's most ardent admirers that her approach had serious drawbacks. She had failed to consider that conditions of terror cannot be maintained indefinitely: all societies tend to run down. She had posited an ultimate monstrousness that constituted an end to history, but as it turned out, history did not end, it just dragged on, erratically and wastefully. Still, if we look at her apocalyptic idea historically, we may see that Arendt captured the madness, the sheer murderous insanity that drove the totalitarian regimes. She saw this not as aberration or excrescence, but as the driving power of our century. And she was right.

Inescapably this meant also to reflect upon the nature of mankind, to wonder about the limits of human malleability, whether toward perfection or debasement. Was it possible that totalitarian society might create a "new kind of man," ready to obey the Leader's commands and whims, no matter if they led to slavery or death, indeed, to obey *because* they led to death? Liberals and radicals had affirmed the malleability of human nature, though usually within bounds they did not specify; they had done so in order to oppose those who argued that the inherent limitations of the human creature rendered proposals for extensive social change implausible. Now, backs to the wall, we found ourselves stressing the intrinsic recalcitrance of human nature, its ultimate refusal of the transformations exacted through ideology and terror.

But we also had to start thinking about a matter we had paid little attention to: the actuality of "radical evil," an evil rooted, incorrigible, irreducible, not to be explained or explained away by social analysis, but part of the very nature of things. A phrase from one of Saul Bellow's novels—"evil is as real as sunshine"—lodged itself deeply in my mind.

But what could one do with this? It hardly constituted, as yet, a worked-out idea, it was merely an unshaped perception. One still wanted to oppose the conservatism that was making the doctrine of original sin a pretext for accommodation to the existing society: it wasn't, after all, as if Eve's having bit into that accursed apple had forever doomed humanity to laissez-faire capitalism. To keep in mind Bellow's pregnant sentence was to put a check on the arrogance of an earlier radicalism acknowledging no limit to its claims; was to anticipate that socialist authority, if ever there was one, would also be a power to be restrained and resisted; was even to see some wisdom in the conservative idea that politics should not be allowed to engulf the whole of human existence. Beyond that, for the moment, we could not go.

Many of these issues were canvassed in another remarkable book of the fifties, *The Captive Mind*, by the Polish émigré writer Czeslaw Milosz. Sketching intellectual figures in communist Poland, Milosz raised the possibility that the totalitarian state might be able to induce terrifying changes of belief in its subjects, or at least induce lulling adaptations to ideas which, inwardly, they might not believe. Milosz wrote about a forgotten book that had appeared in Warsaw in 1932: its author, Stanislaw Witkiewicz, creates in his quasi fiction an "atmosphere of decay and senselessness [that] extends through the entire country. And at that moment, a great number of hawkers appear in the cities peddling Murti-Bing pills. . . . A man who used these pills changed completely. He became serene and happy. The problems he had struggled with until then suddenly appeared to be superficial and unimportant. . . . A man who swallowed Murti-Bing pills became impervious to any metaphysical concerns." Linking Murti-Bing to Diamet (dialectical materialism), which also brings harmony and happiness, Milosz remarked that "Murti-Bing is more tempting to an intellectual than to a peasant or laborer. For the intellectual, the New Faith [communism] is a candle that he circles like a moth. In the end, he throws himself into the flame for the glory of mankind."

Milosz overstated his case, but with brilliant admonitory effect. Most of the people who have lived through the worst excesses of totalitarianism, including intellectuals circling its "candle," seem to emerge pretty much as they were before. We do not fully understand how this can happen, but so it is. Intellectuals in the communist countries seem not really to have believed, or seem at least in some depth of their souls to have resisted, what they were forced to say and write. Some, as victim-accomplices of the totalitarian state, went through an intellectual-emotional seizure, a mass psychosis, but once recovered, they returned to a commonplace sobriety.

This may, just possibly, offer some consolation. But even if the totalitarian state cannot complete the "brainwashing" it sets in motion and thereby transform (or collapse) our basic sense of reality, this state may also be able to reduce most of its subjects to a torpor and submissiveness serving it almost as well. If so, the totalitarian state has at least in part succeeded in transforming human nature. Happily, there is some contrary evidence. The Hungarian revolution, the rise of Soviet dissidence, the Prague spring, the wall posters in China, the mass revolt of the Polish workers—all testify that some minds refuse to submit. One reason Solzhenitsyn's novel *The First Circle* is so affecting is its rich portraiture of a traditional range of minds—locked away, it is true, in a Soviet barrack, yet maintaining a wonderful sweep of discussion. So if we cannot yet say with complete assurance that Milosz was wrong, we may reasonably suspect that he was.

These are the questions that agitated intellectual life in the fifties. Under the pressures of history, in the heat of its complexities, answers kept melting away.

Civilized if somewhat abstract discussions about the nature of totalitarianism had a way, during the fifties, of sliding into savage debates about communism and anticommunism. Here I want to draw a line of separation, like one of those dotted lines used for tearing a sheet of paper, between the debates as they actually occurred and the perceptions of them that flourished in later years.

For the few of us who still considered ourselves Socialists—that is, for those who had experienced the debacle of socialism as a central event in their lives—an unqualified and principled opposition to Stalinism was a first premise. It meant more than a political judgment, it meant an effort to salvage the honor of the socialist idea. Confronting the postwar growth of Soviet power and the possibility that communist rule might reach as far as Western Europe, we had to ask ourselves: does it still make sense to keep saying, as the Left often had, "a plague on both your houses"? Not if in one house modest improvements could be made, while in the other men and women were systematically closed into cells.

Even while remaining critical of the bourgeois order, then, we now had to "align ourselves with" or "give support to" the West in its conflicts with the Communist bloc. We could not pretend that we were spectators in a fight that was not ours. We had to make proposals regarding foreign policy that might help stop the expansion of the totalitarian states without resorting to nuclear war. What a small group of left-wing intellectuals thought about the contenders in the Cold War was, admittedly, of no great importance. We made no decisions, were far from the centers of power. But in an odd sort of way intellectuals *were* now starting to matter, for as Dennis Wrong wrote with a touch of piquant exaggeration: "When the struggle for the soul of the Left emerged as the central issue of contemporary history, the old anti-Stalinist minority woke up to discover that its knowledge of Communist history and the Marxist texts, once dismissed as quaintly esoteric, had become a national resource." I don't know that it always felt good to be "a national resource." Even our vocabulary was shanghaied: it felt strange to hear government officials speak knowingly about "Stalinists," a term that once had been largely our own.

"Revisionist" historians of later decades would argue that the fear of Communist expansion had been grossly exaggerated during the fifties. The anti-Stalinist Left, they charged, had succumbed to State Department propaganda. The possibility of a Communist takeover in countries like France and Italy, they said, was small, since Moscow understood that any effort to seize power by its supporters in Western Europe would provoke a war for which it was not ready. This was easy enough to say in retrospect—once, in fact, the danger of a Communist victory in Italy had subsided. But how could anyone in 1953, especially if profoundly shaken by the Communist coup in Czechoslovakia, hold to this "revisionist" wisdom, if wisdom it be? There was said to be a line, invisible to common folk, beyond which the Russians had been warned they could not go; but who really knew whether such a line existed or what would happen if it were crossed? The truth was that the development of nuclear weapons had made a new world war less likely, but resistance to Communist expansion more difficult.

The fear of Communist power in the ten or fifteen years after the Second World War was real. It was a warranted fear. Serious radicals and liberals held to that fear not because—surely not only because—they had succumbed to Cold War propaganda, but because their most precious values were at stake. Wherever Stalinism conquered, freedom vanished. It was necessary, therefore, to strengthen resistance among the bourgeois democratic states in Europe as they existed at the moment, and not wait for some presumed perfection of the future. This meant to support the Marshall Plan as a strategy for rebuilding the Western European economy; to help, if possible, the liberal anticommunist forces in Italy and France; and to acquiesce, though somewhat nervously, in the Western military response to the Berlin crisis.

It was an uncomfortable politics, entangling us in difficulties that a "purist" radicalism never had to face. (Purists never have to face anything.) But I think it was a correct politics. That the Communists in France and Italy never came close to taking power is by no means evidence that we overestimated the danger; I would say it is evidence of how necessary it had been to put barriers in their path. And real barriers—power, money, politics—not just articles in intellectual journals.

Like anticapitalism, anticommunism was a tricky politics. Both could be put to the service of reaction, both became prey to ideological racketeering, both carried with them moral and political perils that no one could have anticipated in earlier times. Just as ideologues of the Far Right insisted that by some ineluctable logic opposition to capitalism had to lead to Stalinist terror, so ideologues of the authoritarian Left said that anticommunism had to lead straight to the Cold War strategies of John Foster Dulles and Dean Rusk. These were arguments for the simple, slogans for dummies.

In the actuality of political life there was no pure "anticapitalism" or "anticommunism." What mattered was not so much the noun as the modifying adjective, the *kind* of "anticapitalism" or "anticommunism." And it was simply absurd for later historians to write as if in the fifties there was a single, unitary "anticommunism" endorsing all the dark deeds of American foreign policy and eliciting the support of everyone from William Buckley to Norman Thomas.

There were difficulties. A "position" could be worked out for conditional support of the West insofar as it defended Berlin or introduced the Marshall Plan or provided economic help to developing countries; but in the course of daily politics, during our efforts to influence—however slightly—the foreign policy of what remained a capitalist power, intellectuals could yield their independence and slip into vulgarities of thought and speech. Some did.

For a humane and rational mind, anticommunism could be only one among several political motives. No general principle can ever be a sufficient guide for confronting specific problems: there is never a substitute for using one's head. And there are circumstances that make it too costly to abide by even one's most cherished principles. Even intellectuals who by the fifties had swung far to the right didn't propose military intervention during the Hungarian revolution, since they too feared it might lead to a world war.

That it was hard to keep our kind of anticommunism distinct in the public mind from the anticommunism of the Right; that support of or alliances with Western powers could lead to confusions, excesses, corruptions; that among once-radical intellectuals there now prevailed a coarse version of anticommunism often ready to justify whatever the United States might do—all this can be readily acknowledged. In the last analysis, it seems no more than an acknowledgment that it would have been easier to live through the twentieth century if Stalinism had not come along to bedevil us.

But it *had* come along. No intelligent person has been able this past half century to avoid numerous, even profound changes of political opinion, but about one matter I see no reason whatever to change: those of us who cared about freedom had to speak out during the fifties—and later, too—about the meaning of communism and the terms of our opposition.

Then suddenly Nikita Khrushchev made his "revelations" at the Twentieth Congress of the Soviet Communist Party in February 1956. What excitement my friends and I felt, what shouting and laughing and inner weeping! One friend and I kept walking endlessly around the loop of lower Manhattan, telling each other that it was out at last, the truth from the mouths of the murderers. And how pitiful must those "progressive" addicts now seem who had refused to believe the truth until one of the murderers, Khrushchev himself, had spilled it out. How still more pitiful that even now these addicts believed only as much of the truth as he chose, for his own reasons, to spill. But together with this grim elation there were sadder feelings, which in our endless pacing finally reduced us to silence. It was impossible not to return in memory to all the blood and degradation that had filled the years of our youth, all the shame that had corrupted the life of the Left.

We were happy of course that terror in the Soviet Union now seemed on the decline. We had to try to gauge the long-term significance of the shift from Stalin's active terror to Khrushchev's terror-in-reserve. But we also knew that there would now again be people on "the left" who would use the changes in the Soviet Union as an argument for at least a partial conciliation with dictatorship. Writing at the time, I could not repress a note of bitterness: "Let us remind the intellectual apologists for Stalinism what it was they spent decades in saying, lest they now continue to say it for Stalin's successors."

Among the Communists themselves, at least among those who were not mere robots, the Khrushchev report created a profound consternation. One evening in 1957 I received a phone call from my friend Emanuel Geltman telling me that he had begun to get occasional visits from Joseph Starobin and Joseph Clark, both of whom had long been leading American Communists. Starobin had been the first to come, at once truculent and tormented, as if asking to be chastised. No longer a party member, he picked up an argument with Geltman they had dropped a mere twenty-four years earlier. Geltman listened quietly, wearily, allowing his emotions to break through only once—when Starobin remarked in passing that he had suspected the Moscow trials were a frame-up, had even begun to write an article saying so, but then had decided as a disciplined Communist to keep silent. "How could you—how could you?"

Clark and Geltman had grown up together in the same Brooklyn streets, but because of political differences had not spoken to each other for years. Now, badly shaken, Clark came back to talk with his old friend whom, for a full quarter of a century, he had publicly denounced as a "Trotskyist-Fascist." They kept on talking for several years, though Geltman did not introduce the new Joseph Clark until the early sixties, when he began to write for *Dissent*. As a point of scruple Clark kept insisting that he be listed as a former Moscow correspondent of the *Daily Worker*, but finally I urged him to drop it. Enough was enough.

Through Clark I came to know Starobin, a somewhat more prickly man. Slowly and guardedly, we became friends. Once Starobin, voice trembling, told me that immediately after leaving the Communist Party he had spent several months swallowing "forbidden" books, from Trotsky to Niebuhr. One day he began reading Koestler's *Darkness at Noon*. He read without a break until three in the morning and then, the last page turned, he sat alone in his room, weeping.

These men, as I came to know them, were intelligent, gentle, and liberal in their readiness to brook disagreement and doubt. Yet for a large part of their lives they had seemed hard-spirited fanatics. It was as if becoming a Communist meant becoming *another person*, meant picking out from the wardrobe of History the armor of a warrior-leader. I have no doubt that in their personal relations they had been just as sensitive and gentle during their communist years as during the time I knew them: they had chosen communism out of high, selfless motives. Yet in the very throes of their idealism, they had served as spokesmen for the Gulag, persuaded that the liberation of mankind required the uprooting of every tender feeling. Now, suffering the torments that follow a loss of faith, they were guilt-ridden, adrift, but also full of a shy intellectual eagerness. I sometimes wanted to comfort them but hardly knew what to say; I was sure only of the need to avoid moralizing, since in a milder way I too had once tasted the bitter fruits of ideological possession.

What had made possible this metamorphosis of good-hearted, pure-spirited young men into *apparatchiks* of the totalitarian idea? What infatuation with History? What delusions of Final Conflict? There was no shortage of answers and most of them I could recite, but ultimately they all seemed worn and unpersuasive, and beyond that I wish I knew, I wish I could say.

A great bedevilment of our age has been that we can no longer suppose there is but one enemy of progress. I can hardly be the only person who has felt a wry nostalgia, or supposed it would be comforting to feel a wry nostalgia, for those good old days when Socialists and liberals directed their fire solely upon capitalism, Big Business, the trusts, and so forth. Everything must have seemed so nicely simple, unshaded by ambiguity, when socialism was first ascendant in Europe and Gene Debs released his cry in America. Then I would not have had to go around irritating young and old with mumblings about "socialism being problematic"; then I could simply have pointed to the horizon and said, "It is coming, our beautiful future!" Not that I really have wanted to go back to that moment of historical innocence: it is only that in every intellectual who tries to think, there is an all-too-human creature who prefers not to.

In the early fifties we had to maneuver among bloody opponents and try to avoid being crushed in their battles. We wanted to oppose not just communism but also Joe McCarthy, we hoped to see the happy moment when not only the fascist but the communist dictatorships would fall. But a two-sided politics, however necessary, is always risky, often confusing the simple-minded and disabling the sophisticated.

It soon became clear I would have to part company with most of the New York intellectuals I admired. The problem was not so much that they were abandoning their socialist convictions: that was painful enough, though I now can recognize a fraction of truth in their complaint that I responded with stiff moralizing. But even if dropping socialism was not in itself a ground for moral judgment, still there was something shabby, even feckless, in the ease with which so many *Partisan* writers were putting to rest the persuasions of their youth. More serious was the readiness of many of them to abandon the stance of criticism which, as they had taught me, was the very raison d'être of the intellectual.

I suppose it tells us something about the intellectual life of the fifties that, on the face of it, I could be in almost complete agreement on guiding political principles with the philosopher Sidney Hook, whereas in political practice, in the responses we made to daily events, we found ourselves disagreeing frequently and sharply. Hook had a mind superbly, though sometimes only talmudically, keen in argument; also an amusing need always to have the last word—I found it amusing because I wasn't exactly free of it myself. Syllogisms dropped from his pen like the rains of heaven; he wrote with a formidable brilliance on many topics; and about the Marxism he was shedding, he still knew more than most of its orthodox defenders. Yet even his friends had to admit that something was missing in Hook, some imaginative flair or depth of sensibility that might complement his intellectual virtuosity. Within that first-rate mind there had formed a deposit of sterility, like rust on a beautiful machine. Personally Hook was amiable, even avuncular. Nature had not been kind to him: he lacked the spiritual glow of a Meyer Schapiro, the refined aura of a Lionel Trilling; he was plain and plebeian and pugnacious and he called me "Oiving," yet for all that—he was never anything but himself—I liked him. (Once, when we were both spending a year in Palo Alto and I was in a rather deep depression, Hook expressed his genuine concern by steadily asking whether I was eating enough. His wife brought some chicken soup to my place, and this classical gesture of Jewish aid moved me to speechlessness: apparently there were some things that mattered even more than politics.) Had Hook written down on a slip of paper his general principles for the fifties—oppose both communism and McCarthyism, link opposition to totalitarian systems with proposals for democratic social change—I would have stood at the head of the line to sign it. Yet there we were, quarreling bitterly.

One point of division concerned the question, should membership in the Communist Party be taken as a sufficient ground for proposing that a professor be disqualified from teaching at a university? Hook argued that the CP exacted strict discipline from its members, requiring that they use the classroom to spread propaganda; a Communist who taught history or political science was not, therefore, a free agent but a bound representative of a totalitarian apparatus. Hook intended to raise the serious problem of how much freedom a democracy can safely allow its declared enemies, but he was raising it, I thought, in a poor and mechanical way. I argued against him, in a piece I wrote at the time, that the discipline imposed by the CP might seem uniform on paper but was not so in fact; that the membership of the party was heterogeneous in character, sentiment, and loyalty; that judgments about the conduct of professors should be made individually, case by case; and that there were other organizations, both political and religious, that exacted obedience to an authoritarian world view—which, if true, would have required, by Hook's criterion, constant academic purges.

I knew quite as well as Hook that Stalinist professors sometimes propagandized outrageously in the classroom. It seemed better, all the same, to put up with whatever problems this might cause than to endanger the fragile structure of academic freedom by declaring categorical bans. I also remembered that some fifteen years earlier I had taken a difficult course in philosophy with a man who was either a member of or very close to the CP, yet taught with an exemplary fairness of spirit. What mattered was not how communist teachers were instructed to behave by their party, but how in fact each of them did behave. And so long as there was even one like that philosophy teacher at City College, Hook's position seemed wrong.*

Such differences of opinion pointed to a widening divergence in the New York intellectual milieu. Soon it would become a split between those who wanted to keep a radical perspective, and those who were moving not quite to conservatism but to a liberalism drained of militancy, tilting rightward, and not always sensitive enough to the danger McCarthyism represented for civil liberties. Guiding principles were not sufficient for determining how people responded to social crises. At least as important were temperaments inclined toward adaptation or rebellion, and honest differences of judgment.

In New York, in those years, major clashes of political opinion often led to breaks in personal relations. About 1950 I had become somewhat friendly with Diana and Lionel Trilling, and Lionel had been very generous in helping me publish my book on Sherwood Anderson. But in 1954, after I'd written an attack on his recently declared view that a desirable conciliation was occurring in America between "wealth" and "intellect" (Trilling did have a weakness for abstract nouns), I heard from friends that the Trillings were angry at what they took to be my unfair polemic. For the next seven or eight years, though a few hesitant letters were exchanged, we did not see one another. There are some who regard such conduct as appalling and claim that in England they handle these matters in a more civilized fashion, intellectuals continuing to maintain amiable relations despite harsh disputes. But among us in New York—perhaps we were less urbane, perhaps more serious—that did not seem possible. If, say, Irving Kristol and I, who had been college friends and known each other most of our lives, were to come together, we would either end with a bitter political quarrel or drop into idle chatter. It almost seemed, therefore, more civilized to stay apart until time and circumstance brought a reconciliation, if indeed they ever would.

The sudden upsurge of McCarthyism was to prove a crucial test for the intellectuals—a test, you might think, not too hard to

* "And Abraham said, Oh let not the Lord be angry, and I will speak yet but this once; Peradventure ten [righteous men] shall be found in Sodom. And he said, I will not destroy it for ten's sake." Abraham was clever in not pushing his luck.

pass, since presumably here, where our interests were directly at stake, all men of good will could agree. But the record is not glorious.

Partisan Review, then at the peak of its influence, was of course opposed to McCarthyism, but it failed to take a sufficiently strong lead in defense of freedom. It did print attacks on the drift toward conservatism, including a scatter-shot piece of mine, "This Age of Conformity," in 1954, and it had the good taste not to use anticommunism as a device for minimizing the ugliness of the domestic situation. But just when we needed most to fight, the magazine hesitated.

One reason was that many of its leading writers no longer had much taste for fighting, or felt that the domestic threat of McCarthyism seemed inconsequential when compared with the international threat of Stalinism. But there was, I think, another reason. Philip Rahv, the main *Partisan* editor, had lost his bearings, perhaps his nerve. He went "underground"—not literally, of course, but he decided that the times had become threatening and reactionary; there were now major risks in speaking out boldly (born abroad, he was an ex-CP member), so it might well be the better part of Marxist sagacity to lie low for a while. One can't pretend to precise evidence about such matters, but so it struck me at the time, during years when we were rather close.

After 1953, when I started teaching at Brandeis, I used to come down to New York every few months and visit with Rahv. We took long meandering walks through the city, and soon he would launch into complaints about the rightward trend of our intellectual friends and their failure to denounce with sufficient vigor "that bum, McCarthy." (Like the classical poets, Rahv had his fixed epithets: he never mentioned McCarthy without the prefix, "that bum.") I agreed with him, but could not bring myself to add that in a less extreme way his own magazine was succumbing to the same trend.

A curious reason for this loss of élan was Rahv's own rather crude version of Marxism. Like other Marxists and even ex-Marxists, he saw American society through categories appropriate to Weimar Germany, talking about McCarthyism as if it were the entering wedge of a mass fascist movement. Now McCarthyism was bad enough without invoking images of fascism, and the Marxist categories that Rahv and others habitually used in talking about McCarthy had the unintended effect of disabling the struggle against him. Overstating the danger made one more fearful than necessary, and by then we were all oppressed by the anxieties—indeed, the terrors—that many European refugees had brought with them. Somewhere in Rahv's imagination, I suspected, he was gathering quotations from Lenin about the need to take shelter in a storm. And as his friends knew, behind his façade of bluster lurked a delicate, somewhat timid soul. Now, several decades later, all this may seem melodramatic, but after all there was some reason for being fearful in those years and Rahv's brand of Marxism, as well as the conspiratorial bent of his mind, made for melodrama. What it did not sufficiently inspire was courage.

Far worse than anything one could say about *Partisan Review* was the approach of the writers grouped around *Commentary*. Their major stress during the fifties was not upon the struggle against McCarthyism, though of course "they too disliked it." What really stirred their blood was doing battle against the "anti-anticommunists," the few remaining (in Sidney Hook's phrase) "kneejerk liberals." The country may have worried about Mc-Carthy, but *Commentary* worried about those who profited from the struggle against McCarthy.

It was all a matter of proportion. That remnants of the Popular Front intelligentsia indulged in self-deceit (foolish cries of "terror" and "fascism"); that it was nauseating to see old CP hacks drape themselves in the costumes of the Founding Fathers; that it might have been politically and morally bracing for some of those called before Congressional committees to say, "Yes, of course I'm a Communist, and what of it?"; that there were nevertheless legitimate security concerns from which neither the defense of nor attacks upon McCarthyism should have been allowed to distract—these *Commentary* themes all had some point. But in the United States of 1952 or 1953 they were far from the main problem.

Nor was the main problem an exposure of the rhetoric of Julius and Ethel Rosenberg, convicted as atom spies and now awaiting electrocution. Robert Warshow in *Commentary* and Leslie Fiedler in *Encounter* composed withering highbrow analyses —perverse overkill—of the letters Julius and Ethel Rosenberg had sent each other in prison, letters that were then quickly published.

Warshow and Fiedler scored points: who, against the Rosenbergs, could not? Julius had written his wife that he had hung the Declaration of Independence on his cell wall so as to "read these words concerning free speech, freedom of the press, and freedom of religion," whereupon Warshow tartly noted that the Declaration says not a word about any of these matters. Very well, the Rosenbergs were entrapped in Stalinist devices; but surely at the moment what counted much more was that, innocent or guilty, they were waiting to be killed. Was it not heartless to write in this spirit, even if the Rosenbergs were indeed the poor besotted dupes one took them for? Might not the *Commentary* writers have pondered Ignazio Silone's story that his father had once punished him for laughing at the sight of a man arrested by the police since, his father explained, the man might be innocent and in any case was helpless? That the Rosenbergs were innocent I very much doubted; that they were helpless anyone could see. At least Fiedler, to his credit, closed his attack on the Rosenberg letters by saying: "Yet despite all this, *because* of it, they should have been granted mercy." In the early fifties mercy was in short supply.

The dominant *Commentary* note (once in a while there were other, better ones) was struck in early 1952 by its managing editor, Irving Kristol:

Perhaps it is a calamitous error to believe that because a vulgar demagogue lashes out at both Communism and liberalism as identical, it is necessary to protect Communism in order to defend liberalism. This way of putting the matter will surely shock liberals, who are convinced that it is only they who truly understand Communism and who thoughtfully oppose it. They are nonetheless mistaken, and it is a mistake on which McCarthy waxes fat. For there is one thing the American people know about Senator McCarthy: he, like them, is unequivocally anti-Communist. About the spokesmen for American liberalism, they feel they know no such thing. And with some justification.

In later years Kristol's friends would try to soften the shock of this passage by claiming it had been written as mere neutral description, with the remark about liberalism a tacit polemic against fellow-traveling liberals who wrote for the *Nation*. But I do not see how anyone who read Kristol's last three sentences (or knew anything about his motivating outlook) could fail to conclude that he was making a fastidious, perhaps ambivalent gesture of approval for the very McCarthy he rightly called a "vulgar demagogue"—as it were, "our" demagogue.

Just as McCarthyism was becoming a central issue in the 1952 Presidential campaign, Elliot Cohen, the editor of *Commentary*, wrote: "McCarthy remains in the popular mind an unreliable, second-string blow-hard; his only support as a great national figure is from the fascinated fears of the intelligentsia." Picture the setting: McCarthy dominates the political arena, spreading himself across the mass media, raising hell in Congress; the House Un-American Activities Committee drives people to the humiliation of becoming informers; both McCarthy and HUAC enjoy a good measure of popular support, so that people lose their jobs because they once signed a fellow-traveling petition or briefly were members of the CP; high-ranking government officials are frightened and smeared; McCarthy's juvenile bullies, Roy Cohn and David Schine, run wild both at home and abroad—and all the editor of *Commentary* can see as the problem is "the fascinated fears of the intelligentsia." If only, it appeared, the intelligentsia would learn to button its lip, all would be well.

Many of the New York intellectuals grouped themselves into an organization called the American Committee for Cultural Freedom, of which Irving Kristol soon became executive secretary. Its line was close to that of *Commentary*, with some members (Max Eastman and James Burnham) leaning toward open support of the Wisconsin demagogue, and some (like David Riesman, soon to resign from the Committee) inclined toward a stronger defense of civil liberties. On most of the issues agitating the intellectual and academic world, the ACCF kept silent, refusing to defend Communists under investigation or attack, though it could rage against people like Arthur Miller and Bertrand Russell for exaggerating the dangers to civil liberties. As Michael Harrington wrote at the time, the ACCF "was too jaded, too imbued with the sourness of indiscriminate anti-Stalinism" to devote itself to a tough fight against repression and intimidation.

Neither I nor such friends as Lewis Coser or Meyer Schapiro were invited to join the ACCF. Had we been, we would of course have refused. We were a tiny minority within the intellectual world, but we fought hard for our opinion that, while Stalinism was the major danger internationally, in domestic life it was necessary to focus energies against McCarthyism. For those who had long been Socialists, it was sad that our friend Norman Thomas should now become a leader of the ACCF. When I met Norman I tried to avoid discussing this matter, since it seemed churlish to quarrel with a man for whose life's work one felt so grateful. As for the intellectuals, well, there it was: the breakup of our camp.

Years later came the revelation that, through a series of dummy foundations, CIA funds had secretly financed the Congress for Cultural Freedom, the Paris-based organization with which the American Committee was affiliated. Some of those, it turned out, with whom one had sincerely disagreed were not even free men; they were agents or accomplices of an intelligence service, "moles" within the ranks. A sad dénouement! Most of the intellectuals belonging to the ACCF apparently had no knowledge of the CIA connection, but some who harbored suspicions hadn't troubled to investigate closely. There had been gossip in the corridors, titillating rumors about "secret funds."

The retrospective defenses of the European Congress and the American Committee were decidedly lame. Magazines and conferences sponsored by the Congress, wrote Daniel Bell, kept their intellectual freedom and even featured criticism of U.S. policies—true, but hardly to the point, since the issue at stake was not the opinions that were tolerated but the possibility of good faith among colleagues. The leaders of the Congress had deprived their supporters of the opportunity to decide whether they wished to belong to a group financed by the CIA; they had simply deceived them. Another defense, offered by Sidney Hook, was that private money was hard to find in the years when it was essential to publish journals like *Encounter* and *Preuves* in Europe. I doubt this. For the Congress to have raised funds openly would have meant discomfort, penny-pinching, and fewer plush international gatherings; it would have meant doing all the irksome things other intellectuals have always had to do. That might even have been good for their morals.

Intellectuals, even those sincerely devoted to a vision of independence, are often attracted to power; it would be foolish to deny this. The mechanisms that drew intellectuals in the communist countries to become apologists for the party-state—by now exhaustively analyzed in the work of Solzhenitsyn, Orwell, Milosz, and others—were also present, less blatantly, in the West. I suppose the leading editor of *Encounter* sincerely believed he was helping defend democracy when he established his surreptitious ties with the CIA; but was there not also a thrill of sorts for a not-very-famous editor—only yesterday a student arguing in the CCNY alcoves—to negotiate with men in power, secret figures who could overthrow governments, command private armies, and arrange the disappearance of irksome opponents? Was there not also the pleasure of knowing more than the intellectual colleagues he manipulated and deceived? And those who didn't quite know but had strong reasons to suspect—weren't they slipping ever so gently into the cynicism that is so easy to spot and denounce, when we see it in Eastern Europe?

One afternoon in the late sixties I received a visit from two leading figures of the European Congress, François Bondy and Manes Sperber. Writers of distinction, they felt the CIA connection (or was it just the revelations?) had tarnished a worthy cause and they now were asking whether I would join them in a "reformed" organization. I declined. It was too late and they knew it.

People quarreled about ways of coping with McCarthyism, and some tried to analyze what it meant. The historian Richard Hofstadter developed a subtle analysis resting on "status politics," that is, the responses and styles of social groups experiencing sharp changes of condition and therefore peculiarly vulnerable to anxiety. He focused more on the social-demographic constituencies and popular appeals of McCarthyism than its immediate place in American politics.

To the notion long put forward by sociologists that groups on the decline are likely to stiffen into rigid moralistic postures, Hofstadter added that the same may be true for rising social groups eager to confirm their respectability. Texas oil millionaires who liked to see themselves as the last apostles of rugged individualism were drawn to McCarthy because they relished his attacks on Harvard "pinkos," mushy eggheads, decadent Easterners. At the same time, said Hofstadter, McCarthy was winning support from plebeian segments of the population, especially those in the Midwest among whom remnants of populist feeling remained. Rural Americans and small-town Midwesterners still trying to live by worn simplicities felt threatened by that modernist sophistication they identified with the big cities of the East. Jealous and frustrated, they feared Eastern liberals, Eastern "internationalists," Eastern businessmen.

McCarthy took special delight in needling Harvard, for in his demonology the Ivy League occupied a place of honor. This hatred of the educated classes struck Hofstadter as having points of similarity with the rhetoric of William Jennings Bryan, though by now turned a good deal more sour. It was, said Hofstadter, the displaced petty bourgeois, the imperiled small businessman, and the country yokel who formed the backbone of McCarthy's support. Another sophisticated analyst, Nathan Glazer, noted the extent to which traditionalist ethnic groups addicted to an isolationism that had become inopportune during the war—Germans, Irish, Italians— were now resurfacing under the aegis of anticommunism.

These were genuine insights, especially with regard to the social base of McCarthyism, but such "status politics" theories finally made things a little too easy for both the intellectuals and the country at large. Such theories betrayed a growing distaste for the plebes, a readiness to dump the woes of the nation onto the backs of the hicks. (Jewish intellectuals, still numbed by Auschwitz, were becoming acutely sensitive to the anti-Semitic potentialities of plebeian movements, with the source of violence and disorder now located mainly in the social depths.) Analytically, the theories advanced by Hofstadter and Glazer may also have suffered from excessive claims. In an amusing criticism Bernard Rosenberg wrote:

> So, those going down meet those coming up, *les extrêmes se touchent*, and by their fusion they produce McCarthyism. The analysis would appear to be comprehensive since it encompasses just about all American families. A villainous role is tacitly assigned to social mobility as such. Only a static system would preclude the kind of movement in any direction that presumably has such a deleterious effect on political life.

The Hofstadter thesis offered no verifiable explanation of why McCarthyism had become so powerful at precisely this moment. It told us something about the conditions in which McCarthy's demagogy flourished, but not the causes that made it flourish. It neglected to confront the extent to which McCarthyism had become a national phenomenon, perhaps incorporating a medley of group anxieties yet also moving beyond these. Hofstadter failed to give much weight to the many respects in which McCarthyism had been prepared by repressive legislation and executive decrees under Democratic administrations, especially that of Harry Truman. I need not go into detail here about the various "loyalty programs," the "subversive list" promulgated by federal decree but often used to penalize employees in private industry, the McCarran Act of 1950 requiring "Communist-action" organizations to register their membership, innumerable state laws and regulations, and the Communist Control Act of 1954, which provided a legal basis for outlawing the CP and was in part the handiwork of the liberal Senator Hubert Humphrey.

For all its sensitivities to the textures of American society, the Hofstadter analysis saw McCarthyism mainly as a regression to a suppressed plebeian, or populist, ugliness of the American past. But a cogent critique of this view by a young political scientist, Michael Rogin, offered statistical evidence that McCarthy's main support came from the traditional right wing of the Republican Party, very far from populism, as well as from a range of urban elements aroused by the threat of communism. Commented Rogin:

Like the agrarian protest movements, McCarthy drew sustenance from concrete political issues; but his issues were not the agrarian radical issues. Populism, La Follette progressivism, and the Non-Partisan League . . . proposed concrete and practical economic reforms. McCarthy [by contrast] focused on the political not the economic order. While many McCarthy activists were in rebellion against modern industrial society, this society included—and was in their eyes dominated by—New Deal reforms of the type agrarian radicals had favored.

It was, finally, the issue of communism and the alleged "softness" of American foreign policy that impelled the McCarthy movement. If nothing else, McCarthy's brilliant exploitation of the mass media—he was perhaps our first TV demagogue—shows him to have been far more the creature of modern life than a throwback to earlier American protest.

Boozy, impudent, shameless, McCarthy seemed always intent upon violating proprieties and shocking respectable people. The outrageousness of what he said, the shamefulness of his behavior was matched, yet in a sense also undermined, by the nihilism of his every gesture: it seemed at times as if he himself barely credited what he was saying, as if he wanted to see how far he could go in reducing the Senate to a barroom, in humiliating Communists real and fancied, in making the Establishment cringe before his vulgarities. But he was not a fanatic in the Hitler style; he seemed more like a rogue who enjoyed arousing distemper. There was a touch of the Dostoevskian buffoon about him, together with the tavern bum. To gain a sense of him, look into Robert Penn Warren's novel *All the King's Men*, as it depicts the sweaty cynicism of native political hustlers.

What brought McCarthy his moment of fame was a gift for articulating the popular mood of the postwar years, a mood Dennis Wrong acutely described as one of "blocked aggression." Something about his winking nihilism, which hung about him like a trailing shirt, caught that mood. Even after his downfall he left a considerable legacy to American politics, what Wrong called "a national climate in which departures from the most elementary decencies of a democratic society are imperceptibly becoming the norm."

The endless frustrations over the spread of communist power in the world, the incapacity of ordinary Americans to grasp the meaning of Stalinism as at once reactionary and pseudorevolutionary: these, I think, were the central motifs of McCarthy's appeal. "Something uncanny," I wrote in 1954, "attaches itself to the Stalinist victories. . . . War—a full, terrible, releasing war—might be a way out, but our very progress in atomic weapons makes it too risky. . . . The result, among many Americans, is frustration, bewilderment, impotence and bursts of anger. . . . And that is the socio-psychological material from which McCarthyism is made."

McCarthy's downfall came as a result of his reckless challenge of the Eisenhower administration, which at the time meant the American Establishment. It was one thing to spread chaos, fear, repression, another to try to strong-arm the American governmental and military elite. Didn't McCarthy know it? Didn't he throw out his challenge almost willfully, as if aware it would lead to his destruction?

Long after McCarthy fell, the damage he did stayed with us. The forces he set in motion showed once again how fragile democracy is—indeed, must be; showed the explosive possibilities in yoking a national crisis to the gifted demagogue who seems always to come along at the right moment. For the American Establishment, which tolerated him for a while, he turned out to be too flamboyant, too chaotic. But among his admirers there were surely lingering regrets he was no longer available on TV, with his sullen impudence and slovenly innuendoes, his constant threat to disturb the middle-class peace of America and drive fear into the hearts of radicals, liberals, professors.

How bad was it, really, during the McCarthy years?

It often seemed as if people talked about nothing else. At political gatherings, cocktail parties, academic sessions—McCarthyism, McCarthyism, until one grew sick of it. Yet the very prevalence of talk, ineffectual as it might be, undercut Bertrand Russell's charge that in the early fifties the United States was "subject to a reign of terror" (a charge he made soon after proposing that an atom bomb be dropped on Moscow). In a reign of terror people turn silent, fear a knock on the door at four in the morning, flee in all directions; but they do not, because they cannot, talk endlessly in public about the outrage of terror.

To dismiss the more extreme characterizations of European intellectuals is not to deny that McCarthyism was frightful, disgusting, and a serious danger to American liberties. People were afraid, perhaps more than they had reason to be: but in such an atmosphere, who can be sure what constitutes sufficient reason? Sidney Hook, hardly the man to overstate the troubles of the fifties, would later write that an atmosphere was created "which made it easy for cultural vigilantes . . . to press for loyalty oaths. These were not only irrelevant to national security—no oaths ever stopped a traitor —but insulting to honest dissenters. Irresponsible charges of Communism were hurled against individuals who took unorthodox stands in the fields of morals and religion."

When I started teaching at Brandeis in 1953, I watched with a nervous fascination the behavior of academic colleagues. The professors at Brandeis were a tougher and more iconoclastic lot than at most other schools, yet even there one could witness a kind of premature capitulation. There is really no reason to expect college teachers to be more courageous than anyone else, but what I observed—and not only at Brandeis—was a pulling in, an anticipatory caution. And that of course was one of the most damaging consequences of McCarthyism: it spread a pall of fear and anxiety beyond its immediate victims.

Nor was I entirely exempt from these moods. My friends and I insisted from the start that while McCarthy was a demagogue, it was a mistake to talk about fascism. Still, I remember a discussion one evening about what to do in case I lost my job at Brandeis. Who could say how far the purges might go? How could we know if they would reach Brandeis? We decided that, since my wife was an excellent cook, we would open a restaurant in Cambridge specializing in Greek delicacies. I, at least, could manage the cash register.

Those who had wandered into Popular Front groups, or signed fellow-traveling statements, or actually been in the CP for a while, had a good deal more reason to be anxious. Some suffered terribly, and while I could not work up much sympathy for the CP leaders charged and imprisoned under the Smith Act (only a few years earlier they had supported the imprisonment of Trotskyists under the same act), I was opposed in principle to the prosecution, or persecution, of anyone for a mere opinion. And I knew people who, out of reputable motives, had wandered into the CP years earlier and were now paying a heavy price: this was a gratuitous brutality.

Still, the legend that has grown up in recent years—that almost everyone ran for cover and only a few brave souls like Lillian Hellman dared speak out against the inquisitors—has little basis in fact. Lillian Hellman deserves credit for her courage, though that is no reason to forget her record as fellow traveler. But there were plenty of other people who publicly denounced McCarthyism, plenty of liberals and radicals, and even some old-fashioned conservatives like Peter Viereck.

When we printed violent denunciations of McCarthy in *Dissent* during these years, nothing happened to us. Perhaps we weren't important enough to bother with, but others were saying, and still others could have said, much the same things. Later on, as "revisionist" historians turned to the McCarthy period, the *Dissent* group won praise for its stand against McCarthyism, but that has always struck me as rather silly. We had no sense we were taking any great risks in attacking McCarthy.

If McCarthyism was frightful and disgusting, only slightly less unattractive were those intellectuals who noted, accurately but irrelevantly, that nothing McCarthy did was as bad as what Stalin had done. By that standard, the entirety of American life could be declared immune to criticism, since nothing that anyone, except Hitler, had ever done was as bad as what Stalin had done. One of the least considered consequences of the McCarthy years was that many Americans lost their feeling for the American tradition, those strands of belief that had kept this country, despite some shameful intervals, a democracy over the decades. Perhaps this even contributed to the troubles of the sixties.

Controversies over McCarthyism seemed crucial, but in retrospect they appear mainly affairs of the surface, important chiefly as symptoms. A deeper rhythm was at work. American social and political thought was turning toward conservatism, less as ideology than impulse. This impulse would dominate our intellectual life through the several decades after the war, interrupted only during the six or seven years in which the New Left figures prominently and certain embarrassments beset the Nixon administration. There was, I think, one major reason for this turn to the right: communist politics having been a dominant force in the world since the early thirties, a severe reaction was inevitable. Those of us opposed to conservatism had to acknowledge a "rough justice" to this reaction. It was their turn, historically.

Conservative thought in the fifties, the kind that was openly declared, can seem fairly benign when compared with the rougher, meaner versions of three decades later. Only marginally political and about as far from actual power as were the few socialist intellectuals, the conservatives of the fifties did not propose hacking away at the welfare state or venturing upon eyeball-to-eyeball confrontations with the Soviet Union. Their main interest was programmatic, philosophical. Writers like Peter Viereck, Clinton Rossiter, and Russell Kirk, civilized and moderate men, were searching for general principles that in the American setting might enable them to compete respectably with liberalism and socialism. Europe had conservative ideology, but America had only conservative politicians. At least during the previous few decades there had been no coherent body of conservative thought among us. Now these writers wanted a conservatism signifying more than small-town fears, hostility to social legislation, and enmity to modernist culture. They wanted a world view justifying a politics of democratic caution, a society rooted in the past, a morality of traditionalist principle.

In ways amusingly similar to the experience of American Socialists, these conservatives had a great deal of trouble putting together a world view. In America it always seems that during periods of relative social peace, the more extreme intellectual tendencies fade into a centrist liberalism. Our radicals and our conservatives were able to retain, at most, an intellectual recalcitrance; in the fifties neither could engage actively in politics or move close to the centers of power. For the conservatives this would happen only when corporate America discovered the uses of ideology, and ex-radical ideologues the blessings of corporate America.

During the fifties I occasionally saw Peter Viereck, one of the leading conservative intellectuals. An amiable fellow, he used to send his acquaintances frequent packets of his writings, so that once you were on his mailing list you didn't have to worry about an empty mailbox. With each of his packets I would wryly measure his difficulties of self-definition against my own. Viereck was free of the raging nastiness that would characterize some of the Buckleyite conservatives, and I suspected that some of his more intransigent friends were accusing him of being "soft" on social democracy, just as my old Marxist friends thought I was.

One strand of conservative sentiment that made a notable impact on our culture was that associated with Southern poets and novelists like Allen Tate, John Crowe Ransom and, more ambiguously, Robert Penn Warren. These writers hoped for a principled rejection of industrial economy and a commitment to an ordered, hierarchical mode of social life—never real options in America, but ideas serving to sustain a myth which, through abrasion, offered a moral criticism of our culture, a little like that which nineteenth-century Russian writers had made of Western Europe. The conservative agrarianism of the Southern writers had cultural power because it touched upon sentiments deeply connected with the American past. But it was now suffering a gradual breakdown, the fading of regional consciousness into little more than willed nostalgia.

Among some literary people in the fifties one encountered

another conservative impulse, a self-conscious yearning for religious faith. (This yearning need not always be conservative, but in the fifties it largely was.) I had become friendly with the very gifted literary critic, Newton Arvin, and when visiting him once in Northampton I was surprised to hear a timid admission that on Sundays he went to the Episcopal Church. There was no reason why Arvin should have felt embarrassed, except perhaps for the memory of what his earlier, Marxist self might have said. A bit later I met others who were less reticent: Allen Tate, for example, as enchanted with his conversion to Catholicism as if he had just written a major epic.

There was a wistful reaching out toward faith, a wish to believe in the moral and aesthetic uses of faith, perhaps a hope that a declaration of faith would lead to faith itself. But at least in our time genuine faith has proved painfully elusive. Being at some distance from this experience, I probably missed its finer shadings and more authentic strivings; but to me it all seemed terribly self-conscious and willed. Philip Rahv was right in saying that most of what we saw was not religion at all but "religiosity," something "hardly distinguishable from the world-view of traditionalism, with which it is far more deeply involved than with the primary and crucial commitments of genuine belief." The God of these semi-converts was *too* ineffable. Bearded or beardless, personal or abstract, singular or threefold, He kept at a shadowy distance. Reading the reflections of intellectuals drawn to religion, many of them under the influence of T. S. Eliot's prose writings, I felt they were attracted more by the social and moral stability taken to be characteristic of past ages than by the intrinsic value of belief itself. Even skeptics might sympathize—not that we did so very noticeably—with their difficulties in saying that "he who cometh to God must believe that He is."

The strongest force in the intellectual life of the fifties was not conservatism at all, it was a liberalism increasingly conservatized, or a rightward drift of ex-radicals as extremist in contrition as once in assertion. A major sign of this occurred in a 1952 symposium in *Partisan Review,* "Our Country and Our Culture." It began with an editorial statement suggesting that its earlier radicalism had vanished, the magazine's stance of "alienation" from established institutions having been replaced by a persuasion that "most writers . . . want very much to be a part of American life." (A foolish way of putting things: had not those writers who rebelled against commercial venality and industrial exploitation also wanted to be part of American life? Wasn't "no, in thunder" as deeply ingrained in the American tradition as "well, yes"?) Of the two dozen contributors only a few—Norman Mailer, C. Wright Mills, I, and in part Philip Rahv—sharply dissented from this now dominant trend among American writers.

A mere thirty years have passed, yet many of the intellectual declarations of the fifties already seem quaint (as quaint as those of the thirties or the sixties). It was as if America had ceased to be a country with shocking extremes of power and wealth; as if our social problems, from poverty to racism, were no longer visible in 1952; as if the "permanent war economy" had nothing to do with our new affluence; as if it was no longer our business to supply fundamental criticism of the status quo. How wildly they had veered, how sadly they had fallen off, these old radicals . . .

Sidney Hook, once a leading Marxist theorist in America, now found merit in the infamous Smith Act: to be fair, he was not for its passage, he only had doubts about the wisdom of repealing it. Granville Hicks, once the leading Communist literary critic, wrote that "the good old days when it was enough to be against the government are gone . . . and the liberals have grown responsible and moderate." Newton Arvin, in a vulgarity shocking for so fine a critic, wrote that a negative response to American society "is simply sterile, even psychopathic, and ought to give way . . . to the positive relation. Anything else suggests too strongly the continuance into adult life of the negative Oedipal relations of adolescence." Mary McCarthy, perhaps intent upon avoiding "negative relations," wrote that in the America of the fifties "class barriers disappear or tend to become porous. . . . The America . . . of vast inequalities and dramatic contrasts is rapidly ceasing to exist." In America, she continued, "possessions are not wanted for their own sakes, but as tokens of an ideal state of freedom, fraternity, and franchise." Daniel Boorstin topped off this nonsense by asking, "Why should we make a five-year plan for ourselves when God seems to have had a thousand-year plan ready-made for us?" It wasn't quite clear whether God had delivered "American exceptionalism" along with the slate of the commandments or been converted to it more recently; but no matter.

In light of the traumas, disasters, and breakdowns of American society during the subsequent decades, such statements may seem bizarre. Still, that was the dominant mood of the fifties, the veiled ideology of people declaring an "end to ideology." "Everywhere," wrote Norman Mailer, "the American writer is being dunned to become healthy, to grow up, to accept American reality, to integrate himself" into society rather than dream of changing it.

The most subtle and perhaps most influential mind in the culture of the fifties was that of Lionel Trilling. He kept apart from the disputes agitating the surface of our intellectual life, but at sensitive points he spoke for the *Zeitgeist*. Cultivated people repelled by the brutishness of public life, disenchanted with earlier ideologies, and perhaps for the first time able to enjoy a modest affluence as teachers and writers, saw Trilling as their spiritual mentor. He contributed a sense of worth to the life they had chosen or the life that had chosen them, and they were appropriately grateful.

Edmund Wilson was also admired, but in a different way. Virtuoso reader and brilliant writer, Wilson did not seem especially to care whether literary people regarded him as a mentor; he wrote for some absolute Spirit of Literature, or what might come to the same thing, a handful of his peers. But Trilling, quite aware of his cultural seductiveness, tried to exert an influence upon the "educated classes," so as to shape opinion and mold tastes. Moving in the shaded area between literature and social morality, he kept steadily calling attention in his essays to "our" cultural problems and "our" premises of conduct. He had embarked on an oblique campaign to transform the dominant liberalism into something more quizzical and less combative than it had previously been.

Trilling's intellectual adversaries—among whom in the fifties I counted myself—felt that his work had come to serve as a high-toned justification for the increasingly accommodating moods of American intellectuals. When his book *The Liberal Imagination* came out in 1950, I joined in the general admiration for its literary refinement, yet something within me balked. What that was I had trouble expressing. A year or two earlier I had heard Trilling deliver a lecture at Princeton, "Wordsworth and the Rabbis," and thought I detected—less in his words than in the spaces between them—a touch of passivity, even quietism (it would reappear in some of his late essays, especially on Jane Austen). This strain of feeling, which rather oddly seemed to Trilling a conquest of the will, also helps account for his later mixed responses to literary modernism. In any case, there was something about his elegant paper that kept nudging me into what he would call an "adversary position." We talked for a moment after his lecture and I tried to put forward my criticisms, but they came out awkwardly. What I really wanted to say was that in our historical moment one had to resist, even if one were also attracted to, those allurements of contemplative withdrawal that I thought a motif in his essay. He smiled, apparently interested by my response, and now, years later, I suspect he understood what I had in mind better than I could express it. For there was another side to Trilling's mind, as in his superb essay on Keats, which led him to praise the life of activity, will, striving.

The point I had been trying to make first became clear to me upon reading in the mid-fifties an article by Joseph Frank entitled "Lionel Trilling and the Conservative Imagination." While praising Trilling's gifts, Frank found that in his criticism "the pervasive disillusionment with politics was given its most sensitive, subtle and judiciously circumspect expression." Trilling, said Frank, attacked "the liberal imagination" on the ground that most liberals assumed the complexities of reality could be adequately apprehended through the categories of politics. "Only literature, Trilling argued" —I quote again from Frank—"could truly cope with the intricacies of the moral life; and he recommended that politics appropriate for itself some of the suppleness of literature." Then came Frank's main thrust:

It is hardly necessary to say that no such politics has ever existed—or ever will exist. . . . No political ideology of any kind can compete with literature in the delicacy of its reaction to human experience. . . . Mr. Trilling's criticism of the liberal imagination revealed nothing that was not equally true of any politics that sets itself up as a total view of human reality; and he actually criticizes politics from the point of view of art—a point of view happily free from the limiting conditions of all political action. Yet by confining his criticism to the *liberal* imagination, and not extending it to politics in general, Mr. Trilling implied that his views had immediate practical and political relevance.

Yet in a way that Frank did not perhaps see, Trilling's views did have an "immediate practical and political relevance." They provided the rationale for a dominant trend within the intellectual community, they lent it an aura of ennoblement. To a generation that in its youth had been persuaded, even coerced, to believe that action in the public world was a moral necessity, Trilling's critique of "the liberal imagination" eased a turning away from all politics, whether liberal, radical, or conservative.

It is only fair to add that Trilling continued to think of himself as a liberal and felt hurt by suggestions that he was not. He adhered to the tradition of the Enlightenment, favored the values of tolerance, believed strongly in public freedoms. But if one meant by "liberal"—as in post–New Deal America one had also to mean—a militant politics in behalf of both social reform and a measure of egalitarianism, then the effect of Trilling's essays was to dissuade people from that brand of liberalism.

Did Trilling grasp the implications of his own thought? Not fully, I would guess, in the fifties, when his critique of "the liberal imagination" became an issue for polemic, eliciting sharp replies from a group at Smith College—Newton Arvin, Daniel Aaron, Robert Gorham Davis—who felt that his portrait of "the liberal imagination" was something of a caricature in that it excessively identified liberalism with the fellow-traveling mind. But in later years, I guess again, Trilling did come to recognize that there was more to the "liberal imagination" controversy than he had recognized, and this emerged in a rather curious way. His old friend Louis Kronenberger, a literary rather than a political man, wrote a gentle polemic against an essay Trilling had published about Jane Austen's *Emma*, saying that Trilling had overvalued in that novel the element of "idyll"—perhaps the same as what I have called social quietism. Some time later Trilling remarked to me upon the shrewdness of Kronenberger's criticism: it was a "hit," he said, smiling.

Through the years I would keep quarreling in my own mind with Trilling's views. I bridled at the notion that the literary life was inherently more noble than the life of politics; I bridled because acknowledging this could have been politically disabling at a time when politics remained essential, but also because I knew that it held a portion of obvious truth—otherwise, how explain my inner divisions? Perhaps also a part of me was drawn to the claims for "the relaxed will" that Trilling spoke about. Had not, after all, so entirely political a man as Trotsky once remarked that for him the world of letters was always "a world more attractive"? Yes, more attractive; but not, all the same, a world to which one could totally yield. For there remained the power of what Trilling called the *conditioned*—the demands of necessity and conscience, hard as these might be, which no refinements of "the liberal imagination" could either erase or cope with.

Wasn't it possible to bring together the dialectical reflectiveness encouraged by Trilling's criticism with a readiness to engage publicly in behalf of liberal or radical ideas? In principle, yes; in practice, not so easily. The problem obsessed me for a good many years, and when not feeling beleaguered from one direction or the other, I had to admit to myself that there must always be some disharmony between the life of the mind and the life of politics. But some connection, too! That is why I felt that, for all its pointedness, Trilling's critique provided a rationale for an increasingly relaxed and conservatized liberalism. He spoke for part of what I wanted, yet another perhaps larger part of me had to speak against him.

Writers of later decades would treat the fifties harshly, New Leftists often presenting those years as if they were merely a time of reaction and sterility. The reality was more complex, for together with a lapse into moods of conservative acquiescence there were also serious intellectual achievements—and part of conservative thought was serious, too. There was a lot of ferment, controversy, and energy in the fifties, and there was a new appreciation of American democracy—surely to be distinguished from chauvinism—which, especially for people on the left, had a genuine value.

In the culture itself profound transformations were under way. The brilliant social analyst Joseph Schumpeter had once written that Marx was mistaken in supposing capitalism would break down from inherent socioeconomic contradictions. If capitalism did break down, said Schumpeter, it would be as a result of its inability to claim people through bonds of loyalty. "Unlike any other type of society, capitalism inevitably . . . creates, educates and subsidizes a vested interest in social unrest." While no doubt pertinent for some historical moments, Schumpeter's picture of the intellectual turned out to be comically mistaken for the postwar years. He had failed to take into account—he who had insisted that capitalism is "a form or method of economic change and not only never is but never can be stationary"—that capitalism in its new bureaucratic stage would find both honored roles and high status for intellectuals. Noticing this new trend, Philip Rahv wrote that "the intellectual bohemian or proletarian has turned into a marginal figure now-adays, reminding us in his rather quixotic aloneness of the ardors and truancies of the past." Few intellectuals still thought of them-selves as a "permanent opposition" to the world of power; few writers would say with Flaubert, "Bohemia is the fatherland of my breed." Rahv called this process an *embourgeoisement* of the intel-lectuals, but I suspect it would be more accurate to speak of a bureaucratic institutionalization.

The kind of society now emerging in the West, a democratic society in which bureaucratic controls were imposed upon (though seldom very much against) the interplay of corporate interests, turned out to need intellectuals. It needed them far more than the earlier, private capitalism ever had. For this was a society in which ideology played an unprecedented part, though not quite as much as in the late seventies, when corporate America discovered that ideology really helped business. But even in the fifties one could see the start of this process. In 1954 I wrote, for instance, that "as social relations become more abstract and elusive, the human ob-ject is bound to the state with ideological slogans and abstractions —and for this chore intellectuals are indispensable." But with a crucial proviso: that while the institutional world of government, corporation, and mass culture needs intellectuals *because* they are intellectuals, it does not want them *as* intellectuals. It needs them for their skills, knowledge, inclinations, even passions, without which they would be of no use. But it does not look kindly upon, indeed does all it can to curb, their traditional role as free-wheeling critics who direct their barbs not only upon enemies but friends and allies, too. In America this once-admired vision of the intellectual

—I still admire it!—drew at least as much upon native Emersonian sensibility as upon social radicalism; but now, in the fifties, it was being dismissed as outmoded, naive, irresponsible, "romantic." What followed was the absorption, in the course of a historical turn beyond anyone's control, of large numbers of intellectuals into government bureaucracy, the industries of pseudoculture, and the corporations. As advisers, helpers, and spokesmen, intellectuals gained power, so that C. Wright Mills's description of them as "powerless people" had now to be qualified. But as thinkers and critics they lost power—the only true power they ever really had, that which had been possible when they were indeed "powerless people."

The social transformation of the intellectuals sketched here was a process hardly to be avoided. One had to eat and care for one's children; one felt that a job even in a deplored institution might be easier to bear than being a free-lance writer, which usually meant having many bosses instead of just one. The world taking shape in the postwar years could be neither flatly accepted nor rejected; it must, I said a little wistfully, "be engaged, resisted, and—who knows, perhaps still—transformed." Perhaps still.

"When intellectuals can do nothing else they start a magazine" —so I wrote once about the founding of *Dissent* in 1954. My sentence became a text for ironic commentary, as if to display still again the incorrigible futility of American intellectuals. Fair enough—no one should be exempt from irony. But might not the irony be a little misplaced? For starting a magazine, as even right-wing intellectuals would later discover, can also be a way of doing something, at least a way of thinking in common, and from thinking in common who knows what may follow? There are some who say it can change the world.

I don't see much evidence that *Dissent* has changed the world, but it may have changed some of the people who launched it. Those of us who, like Stanley Plastrik, Emanuel Geltman, and myself, had finally shaken loose from the left-wing sects felt liberated: how good to breathe the air of common life and share its quandaries! A few independent radical writers like Lewis Coser, Meyer Schapiro, and Bernard Rosenberg found in the magazine an outlet for their views. We were all young and buoyant, and we looked forward to polemical battle against our rightward-moving friends, especially those who had been less than lionhearted in standing up to McCarthyism. I suppose that for people like us, the sort usually described as the "moderate Left," it is psychologically easier to debate with right-wing opponents than with those of the Far Left, since with the Right we're at least spared the pain of hearing vulgarizations of our ideas.

First, we had to collect a little money. In our society collecting a little is harder than collecting a lot. Of all the chores that go with running a small magazine, fund-raising is always the most irksome: you have to beg, you have to smile when you'd rather sulk, and you end up sacrificing part of the very independence for which the magazine was started. But since a journal like *Dissent* can never be self-supporting, it's stick in one hand, cup in the other, and off you go.

From friends we scraped together a bit more than a thousand dollars. With the bad example before us of little magazines that had collected subscriptions only to fold after an issue or two, we decided not to begin unless we could guarantee at least a full year of publication. Then came a check for another thousand—pretty big money for Christmas 1953—from Joseph and Muriel Buttinger. He had been leader of the young Socialists in Austria once they were driven underground after the fascist coup of 1934, and she, later a gifted psychoanalyst, had been a student in Vienna working bravely to rescue endangered radicals. (Muriel was, I think, a real-life model for Lillian Hellman's "Julia.") Over the years the Buttingers would make up perhaps half our annual deficit, not as dispensers of largesse but as true comrades.

Dissent arose out of the decomposition of American socialism or what tattered bits and pieces of it remained in the fifties. Even those of us who had rebelled against sect claustrophobia still wanted to keep some of the ideas and values that had propelled us into the sects in the first place. We all agreed that, if socialism had a future as either politics or idea, there would first have to be a serious and prolonged reconsideration of its premises, but we did not yet fully realize that this crisis of socialism was by no means confined to, but only more visible in, America. Large social democratic parties in Europe kept going through the motions of parliamentary activity, but there too malaise lurked behind a façade of strength.

"Does a great historical movement ever get a second chance?" With this question I tried to dramatize our problem in an early issue of *Dissent*. "Suppose Saul of Tarsus and the rest of the original 'cadre' had been destroyed or had committed some incredible blunder, could Christianity have regained its momentum after an interval of loss and despair?" We had no ready answer, but this was the question to which we wanted to devote ourselves.

Our first issue was uneven, a mixture of academic stuffiness and polemical bristle—enough of the latter to infuriate both old-time Marxists and liberal intellectuals. In *Commentary*, then as later facing right, Nathan Glazer pronounced this first issue "a disaster." His attack, which evoked a strong defense from C. Wright Mills, delighted us, since the one thing a new magazine needs is attention.

What *Dissent* should be we were not quite sure, what it should not be we knew. We would avoid like the plague any party line. And the linked plague of scholastic pickings-over of Marxist doctrine. And the further plague of printing writers just because they were among our faithful. (It turned out not so easy to avoid all these plagues . . .) We were saying, in effect, that socialism in America had to be seen mostly as an intellectual problem before it could even hope to become a viable movement. Simply to publish a magazine might not be enough, but there are moments when patience is all—and stubbornness, too.

For some of our writers what counted most was criticism of postwar America, our repeated attacks on intellectuals accommodating themselves to the status quo. We did very well on the McCarthy issue, speaking out clearly and strongly. We might have done still better. We yielded too readily to the assumption that the United States government, or some of its agencies, "could not possibly" frame up dissidents or provoke violence through informers; we underestimated the extent to which the FBI and CIA were eroding freedoms; we forgot that in a vulgar age even "vulgar Marxists" can get at part of the truth.

For me the heart of the magazine was not its journalistic commentary but its recurrent discussions of the idea of socialism as problem and goal. After all, cogent social criticism could be written by nonsocialists, some of whom, like Dwight Macdonald, did it more skillfully than we. There was no contradiction in principle between critical journalism and political reflection, but without the latter I doubt that I'd have been willing to put up with the drudgery that *Dissent* often entailed.

In the early years the editorial work was done mainly by Lewis Coser and me; the line-by-line routine editing and rewriting (never enough, but the flesh is weak) by me. There developed between the two of us a close intellectual collaboration, later modified by circumstances but never brought to an end. Coser had grown up in Weimar Germany and as a youth had become active in left-wing politics; he carried himself with an aristocratic air that veiled a mixture of skepticism and gentleness; in our first few years, however, he wrote some cutting polemics against intellectuals in retreat. A part of him was inclined to make of his radicalism a stance primarily moral, yielding a criticism from intransigence, while another part tended to become a skilled, dispassionate sociologist. If these two sides were never wholly reconciled, it was precisely the tension between them that gave his work its distinctive note. Meanwhile for a few years the technical work—editing, makeup, and so forth—fell upon Emanuel Geltman, then making a difficult transition from socialist functionary to publishing editor. Once this work, which Geltman undertook evenings, proved to be too large a burden, we took the bold step of hiring a part-time managing editor who actually got paid (though not very much).

From the start Meyer Schapiro, the art historian, served as an editor, and while he wrote almost nothing for our pages, we were happy that so eminent a mind was ready to stand by us at a time when we were being attacked on all sides. It mattered that Meyer Schapiro attended some board meetings, speaking in his passionately lucid way about socialism as the fulfillment of Western tradition. He was a great natural teacher, in or out of the classroom, ready to provide anyone, whether close friend or casual acquaintance, with eloquent lectures on an astonishing variety of subjects. Luminously handsome, playful in his seriousness, he became for us a legendary figure. We took pleasure in his decorous sentences—only Isaiah Berlin could speak as well in this style, and he in a series of chugs, spurts, and gasps, very different from Meyer's silvered fluency. We delighted in telling stories about Meyer's erudition. One I relished was about Philip Rahv calling to check some fact and then listening open-mouthed for an hour to a lecture providing answer, background, and foreground, until Rahv turned to his wife and said, "I've just gotten an MA over the telephone!" Another time, one winter afternoon after a *Dissent* meeting, five or six of us got stuck in an elevator and, forced to wait for rescue, did not quite know what to do—until Norman Mailer slyly asked Schapiro a question (something, as I recall, about the relationship between Picasso and Matisse), whereupon we were treated to a splendid twenty-minute talk. When the repairman arrived we left, if not with the troubles of socialism under control, then at least with more knowledge about modern art.

As the magazine, to our surprise, managed to stay alive, we kept shedding more and more ideology; by about 1960 most of us no longer thought of ourselves as Marxists. At times we seemed to have almost nothing left but the animating ethic of socialism, and we knew that an ethic, no matter how admirable, could never replace a politics. But if you took that ethic seriously and persisted in struggling for modes of realization, you could have enough intellectual work for a lifetime. Still, we became gradually convinced that any expectation of putting together a new socialist system, as proud in its coherence as Marxism had once been, was not only premature, but a fantasy better to abandon. We were learning to work piecemeal, treating socialist thought as inherently problematic, quite as every other mode of political thought must be treated in our time.

A magazine with such premises is not likely to have an easy time of it. Only seldom could *Dissent* shine and gleam, only seldom brim over with high spirits. (Some people wondered why we couldn't be like the old *Masses*, the lively radical magazine of the years before the First World War, and all I could mumble in reply was that the old *Masses* had been published before the bad news arrived.) Often *Dissent* must have seemed anxious, distracted, even boring. For we had to turn in upon ourselves, questioning first principles (mostly our own), yet fighting hard against opponents who wanted summarily to dismiss those principles. We ended by pleasing only a small number of people, and those only provisionally, quizzically. To the *alte Kämpfer* of the Marxist Left we seemed to be slipping into the "morass" of social democracy. To most intellectuals on our right we seemed to be rutted in worn political categories. To the New Left of the sixties we seemed elderly nail-biters grown excessively proud of their attachment to "the problematic."

Dissent was seldom a model of journalistic brilliance, but there was good writing in almost every issue. During the fifties, when smiting the philistines, the magazine was livelier; later on it grew quieter, more reflective. One reason we printed too much "heavy" prose was that we had too many "heavy" writers, a disconcerting number of them academics with something to say but little skill in saying it. Still, in our earlier years we gained some talented collaborators: C. Wright Mills, the Texas sociologist who wanted to write like Balzac; Henry Pachter, an irascible German historian who was probably our most learned contributor; Michael Walzer, a subtle political theorist whom I first met when he was a student at Brandeis; Michael Harrington, soon to be one of the few experts on social policy the American Left has ever had. Truth is, we never had enough talent on our side, and if we managed to put out a strong issue in winter, spring was not far behind with a weaker one. Sometimes I suffered an inner conflict between my pride of craft as a writer and my conviction that *Dissent* mattered politically even if its prose didn't always sparkle. In the earlier years some of us—Emanuel Geltman, Jeremy Larner, and I—did a lot of rewriting, but as anyone with editorial experience must know, this can only make a poorly written article less bad, it cannot make it very good.

We tried to compensate by translating from European journals politically sympathetic to us, especially from the Parisian monthly *Esprit*. Through translation we brought into our pages the trenchant and melancholy voice of Ignazio Silone, the troubling speculations of Nicola Chiaromonte, the political sophistication of Richard Lowenthal. We printed the somewhat opaque essays of Czeslaw Milosz in the sixties, when no one else paid attention to him and he was many years from the Nobel Prize. Still, it wasn't enough. I envied the editors of *Encounter* and later the *New York Review of Books* their access to the best writers in English. When a piece did come from Harold Rosenberg or Lionel Abel or Paul Goodman, all writers with strongly individual styles, I felt a charge of pleasure. One wanted the interesting as well as the worthy.

A relationship that brought special pleasure was that with the novelist Richard Wright, who became a contributing editor of the magazine in 1959. I had met him in Paris at a time when his reputation and, I suspect, his morale were at a low point. The young James Baldwin had recently launched a harsh attack upon Wright's work; the friendships that Wright had made with the intellectuals around Jean-Paul Sartre had frayed; he was now a man at midpoint, famous but lonely, rootless in Paris but unwilling to go back to problems and humiliations that even a famous black man had to face in New York. Wright was interested in the new black nationalism of Africa, but critical also of its fanatical spirit. Wry and a little sad, he told me that someday Baldwin would regret his attack—a prediction, I think, that has come true. Whether he thought of himself as a Socialist I don't know, but he seemed to feel that in his homelessness he might find a ramshackle home of sorts in *Dissent*.

We had our scoops. Perhaps the greatest piece of writing *Dissent* ever published was "On Socialist Realism," by the Soviet dissident Abram Tertz (Andrei Sinyavsky), both an outcry for artistic freedom and a major text of cultural modernism. We took it from *Esprit*, which had taken it from an émigré source, and what made this all the sweeter was that we "stole" it from under the nose of Philip Rahv, who dismissed it as just another manifesto. We printed Silone's "Choice of Comrades," which through unforgettable vignettes summed up the plight of the homeless European Left. We printed two pieces by Lewis Coser and me, "Images of Socialism" and "Authoritarians of the Left," which brought our views as close to a synthesis as we could manage. We got out an issue on New York City, this one with a real journalist vibrancy, and it sold the (for us) astonishing number of 14,000 copies. That issue featured Norman Mailer's famous essay, "The White Negro," in which he spun out his reflections on hipsters and his fascination with violence. Reading the essay I felt, together with admiration for Mailer's skill, a twitch of discomfort, especially upon reaching the sentence in which he muses upon the propriety or possible good of "beat[ing] in the brains" of a fifty-year-old storekeeper as a way of articulating selfhood. Later I concluded it had been unprincipled to accept this essay for *Dissent*: I should at least have urged Mailer to drop that sentence.

Once I rejected a contribution from Edmund Wilson. Opening

the envelope, I grew excited, but upon reading Wilson's pages about Theodore Roosevelt I felt depressed, for this was Wilson at his most crotchety. Still, I would probably have suppressed my judgment had not Lew Coser put it to me bluntly: "Would you print this if it came from someone who isn't famous?" Well, of course not, but . . . Muttering about the costs of socialist conscience, I sat down to the task of writing a letter of rejection to Edmund Wilson. You think that's easy? Afterward he would chaff me about being turned down by a magazine that didn't even pay.

We certainly didn't. Though I was often asked what my salary was at *Dissent*, I can report that no editor ever received a penny in more than twenty-five years of publication. We refrained from such bourgeois indulgences as having an office; all editorial and business matters were handled on desks at home. Stanley Plastrik, an extremely able man who served as our general manager, rejected Keynesian economics not so much on principle as out of an understanding that we couldn't bear the anxiety of owing money. I can remember only one year when our budget wasn't balanced. How curious that the old-fashioned virtue of austerity, so dear to conservative hearts, should have found one of its few homes in our little socialist enterprise! During the sixties, when we would read about the wanton extravagance of the California magazine *Ramparts*, all of us felt a mixture of astonishment and disgust—no, this was not what we meant by radicalism, this was just a new brand of American con.

We tried over the years to keep good relations with writers who might not agree with us entirely but would be willing to send in their work. We had some thoughtful pieces from Daniel Bell, the polymath who defines himself as a Socialist in economics, liberal in politics, and conservative in culture (an ascending order of visibility). Harold Rosenberg and Paul Goodman were both generous. In the mid-fifties Rosenberg, that buccaneer of epigrams, was in a quiet phase, barely publishing anywhere. Lew Coser and I set to work stirring him into a more active mood—it was not very hard—and he wrote some brilliant pieces for us, the first of which, "Couch Liberalism and the Guilty Past," was a blazing attack on Leslie Fiedler's lament that "all liberals . . . had, in some sense and at some time, shared [Alger Hiss's] illusions" about Stalinism. Wrote Rosenberg:

Whom Fiedler is here describing, except possibly repentent Communists who haven't confessed yet, I defy anyone to specify. His "all liberals" is a made-up character with an attributed past. To his question, "Who is exempt?" I raise my right hand and reply that I never shared anything with Mr. Hiss, including automobiles or apartments; certainly not illusions, if my impression is correct that he was a typical government Communist or top-echelon fellow traveler.

Rosenberg later became famous as art critic for the *New Yorker*, and while we remained friendly he ceased to write for us, except for a touching eulogy on Paul Goodman. That is a fate little magazines must repeatedly suffer—the loss of talent to moneyed competitors. But Paul Goodman, though a declared anarchist at odds with us politically, remained a steady contributor to the end; he had a stronger sense of community than Rosenberg. Goodman and I never got along well personally; he thought me "dried out" by Marxism, I found his pose as sage rather tiresome. But as contributor and editor we got along wonderfully. Prolific beyond belief, Goodman could always be counted on to furnish a provocative piece whenever we ran short. It was as if he had a trunk full (he probably did) of essays on all conceivable subjects: utopian speculations and practical proposals.

Such relationships made me happy, gave the magazine a touch of distinction, showed we were not going to be ideologically rigid. But with Erich Fromm, the famous psychoanalyst and apostle of love as therapy, we had a bad time. Fromm, who called himself an ethical Socialist, was friendly in early letters from Mexico. Then in the mid-fifties he appeared one day in New York to announce that he had a "basic document" (a phrase calculated to cause a sinking of hearts among those with some experience in the radical movement). This new manifesto of his, said Fromm, would do for the twentieth century what Marx's had done for the nineteenth.

Stiff and solemn, exuding self-regard, and finally incapable of grasping the difference between a humane sentiment and a political idea, Fromm apparently wanted the *Dissent* group to elevate him to the rank of socialist guru. This wasn't exactly the role we thought destiny had cast us for, and I remember someone, perhaps Lew Coser, joking that Fromm seemed concerned about everyone's "alienated labor" except ours. For a while, nevertheless, we went along, convening a small conference at which his manifesto was to be discussed. Most of the *Dissent* people kept discreetly silent, but Norman Thomas, sharp-witted in his age, burst out: "Erich, it's a nice piece of writing and I don't disagree with a word, but you know, to me it reads like a sermon by Norman Vincent Peale!" Sitting behind Fromm I watched, not without malicious delight, the back of his neck turn beet-red. The thoughts so far from Love that must have been running through his head! Our conference collapsed and Fromm stalked out. I doubt that he was vainer than most other intellectuals; it was just that his ethical pieties kept him from recognizing his vanity.

The brush with Fromm had its absurd side, but my relationship with C. Wright Mills, at first a political friend and then a political opponent, took on a tragic cast, anticipating the crackup of friendships in the sixties. In both his person and his writings Mills was a figure of power, a fiercely grinding sort of power that came down like a fist. Though tremendously ambitious for intellectual distinction, he felt ambivalent toward the New York intellectuals. He had concluded, not without some justice, that they had given up all hope of making their opinions matter and had settled into a mere routine of display. Between Erich Fromm and me there had sprung up a mutual dislike a few minutes after our first meeting— one of the most spontaneous experiences in my life; but with Mills there was for a time a real connection, much of it deriving from our shared sense of difference. He wanted to find out what made New York Jewish intellectuals tick, and I felt the same curiosity about Texas radicals. For perhaps a decade we were friends. He was exhausting, a man whose pressures of will never let up, often forcing other people, even those who loved him as I could not, into a rigidity of self-defense. But neither when we were intellectually close nor later when we quarreled, did I ever doubt his talent, self-confidence, energy.

Mills barged into New York at the very moment the intellectual Left was falling apart. Physically large yet fragile, he seemed a robber baron of intellect, one of those native radicals neither hardened by dogma nor softened by defeat nor—but this was rather serious—chastened by modern history. A one-man work gang, he combined the spirited rebelliousness of the Wobblies with the muckraker's zeal for exposure. One reason, probably, that some of us took to him was that we had never met anyone like him before—an educated cowboy of the Left. Mills once explained to me that of the three proclaimed goals of the French Revolution he appreciated the appeals of liberty and equality but had little taste for fraternity. He was right. I never felt that he really shared our sense of the sheer terribleness of our time: he was still too much an American, insufficiently bruised.

In 1957 Mills came back from a trip to Europe and summoned me for a visit. I went reluctantly, since I had heard rumors he was in a manic state, working himself up to a new political role. Hardly two or three minutes had passed before he began to pound away: he was in a mood of exaltation, ready to break with everything that stood in its way. He had discovered reasons for hope in Eastern Europe; he was impressed by the industrial achievements of the communist countries (while I was moved by the moral strength of the dissidents); and he regarded my anticommunism as obsolete. What he proposed was a sort of Popular Front to include intellectuals sympathetic to the communist bloc.

Mills didn't become a Communist, and he didn't become a fellow traveler. He became, to employ an esoteric left-wing reference, a Deutscherite, that is, a follower of Isaac Deutscher, the Marxist historian who, though morally repelled by Stalinism, still believed that Stalin had carried through a "progressive" historical transformation. What would soon bring Mills's new ideas into coherence, and himself to an unprecedented popularity, was admiration for Castro's Cuba, the dictatorship that was presumably different. He became a hero for the New Left in its early years.

We sat there together, in a shabby lunchroom on Amsterdam Avenue, under a garish blue light and with the clatter of cheap Latin music. He hammered away, I retreated into silence. I felt myself washed over by the despair one knows when a part of one's life breaks down forever. No longer talking to me, as he used to, Mills was now exhorting and declaiming, as if he had been granted a revelation.

It was hardly news that things were changing rapidly and importantly in the communist countries. I knew we were finding new friends there, rarely among those in power, more often among intellectuals now able to speak out occasionally against despotism. Where Mills and I differed was in our historical estimate of how far the dictatorships could be expected to relax, indeed, how far they might go in undermining the basis of their own existence. We differed still more in our moral-political responses to the struggles unfolding in Eastern Europe. My instinctive solidarity went to those in Poland who, whatever their enforced vocabulary, were really liberals or Socialists at heart, while Mills identified himself increasingly with the supposedly invincible dynamic of the historical process that, he thought, would transform the communist world.

To me, his outlook was an intellectual disaster; to him, mine must have seemed like the conservatism of a radical afraid to surrender familiar positions. We parted, tense and distraught, each of us certain that far more than a personal disagreement was at stake. This kind of break between friends who care about politics can be as racking as a personal separation between people who have shared part of their lives. We had an acrid exchange in *Dissent* after Mills published his 1958 pamphlet, *The Causes of World War III*, and we never saw each other again.

In his last years Mills became a hero. He won the admiration of Castro's partisans, young people in search of a new charismatic revolution to replace the befouled image of the Soviet Union. Later there were reports that, a year or two before his death, Mills had become disillusioned with the Castro dictatorship but could not say so publicly. Harvey Swados, the novelist who was a friend of both of us, wrote after Mills's death that Mills "was torn between defending *Listen Yankee* [his pro-Castro pamphlet] as a good and honest book, and acknowledging publicly for the first time in his life that he had been terribly wrong. This would have meant . . . [admitting] that he was not a rough rider after all, but only a man of ideas who could be wrong, as men of ideas so often are. . . . I can only add that he declared to me in his last weeks that he was becoming more and more impressed with the psychological and intellectual relevance of non-violent resistance and absolute pacifism."

Mills had seemed a towering figure, one of those natural rebels who stands alone and speaks his mind. It would be comforting to suppose that finally he did, as Swados said, return to the thought that the only grounding for social hope is political freedom. But I do not know.

In the fifties, for better or worse, almost everything began that would dominate our life in the following decades. There would be neither ease nor comfort nor consistency of belief. The dominant rhythms were jagged, harsh. People of talent careened from religious revival to the joys of pot, from the "nerve of failure" to "letting it all hang out," from Kierkegaard to Marcuse, from neoconservatism to neoradicalism and back again. Poor shapeless debris floating on the waves of the *Zeitgeist* . . . What Philip Rahv had once said about our "literary periods" could be extended to the whole of our intellectual life: "In America, whose second name . . . should be 'amnesia,' the historical sense in this century chronically suffers one lesion after another. . . ."

By 1960 I was telling myself in certain rueful moments that I had some small responsibility for the endless chatter about "conformity" that was starting to sweep the country. I could hardly have known, six years earlier when I wrote my essay, "This Age of Conformity," that I was helping to make the outcry against conformity into a catchword of conformist culture—conformist not least of all in the rapidity and fickleness with which it swung from mood to mood, fashion to fashion.

In intellectual life one sometimes wins a battle too easily, and then an inner voice says no, you didn't really win at all. Of course I was glad to see the moods of the fifties evaporate, glad to see Cold War chauvinism decline and radicalism take on a provisional sort of popularity in classroom and magazine. But anyone who thought about the matter knew something was wrong. There was some deep lack of seriousness in all this wild oscillation from extreme to extreme, there was some profound disorganization of our moral life.

Still, change was in the air. By 1958 or 1959 the South began to stir. Leafing through old numbers of *Dissent*, I notice a thoughtful piece by Michael Walzer in 1960 on nonviolent resistance as a mode of protest that might break past the customary choices of reform and revolution. A little after 1960 I was writing that the "Negro revolution" was bringing us to "great and stirring days." It began to seem as if something better might lie ahead.

9
Jewish Quandaries

Wh
hen did you first become aware of the gas chambers? How did you respond to the reports from Europe that the Nazis were systematically exterminating Jews?

These questions from young friends come easily and with good faith. They have a right to know. Their questions have for some years now also been my questions, setting off a recurrent clamor of confused memories. But I cannot answer, at least as I suppose they want me to. People don't react to great cataclysms with clear thoughts and eloquent emotions; they blink and stumble, they retreat to old opinions, they turn away in fear.

It was during my years in Alaska that I first read about these Nazi atrocities, but only in a blurred, fragmentary way, certainly not with an awareness of all that we now mean by the Holocaust. Once the war was over, more facts came pouring out. But information is still very far from understanding, and only later, by the early fifties, did I even begin to grasp that I had been living through the most terrible moment in human history.

Memory points a finger: "You were slow, you were dull in responding to the Holocaust." I plead guilty, but would add mildly that now, when incessant talk about the Holocaust risks becoming a media vulgarity, we may value silence a bit more than anyone could have supposed in earlier years. Conscience scoffs: "Come, you're not really trying to say you were silent because your feelings overwhelmed you? Wasn't it more likely that your feelings were rather skimpy?"

To be human meant to be unequipped to grapple with the Holocaust. We had no precedents in thought or experience, even if we had read in our youth *Forty Days of Musa Dagh*, Franz Werfel's novel about the Turkish slaughter of the Armenians. We had no metaphors that could release the work of imagination. All efforts to understand what had happened in Europe required as their premise a wrenching away from received categories of thought—but that cannot happen overnight, it isn't easy to check in your modest quantity of mental stock.

If you ask what a sufficiently strong or quick response to the Holocaust would have been, I can hardly answer. Some friends did make halting efforts to cope with the enormity of the gas chambers, and from them I gradually learned that I had to give up the pretense that any world view could really explain what had happened. It wasn't even clear what one might mean by "explaining" the Holocaust. Perhaps it's enough to say that I should have struggled more intensely, more obsessively than I did with the "meaning" of the Holocaust, if only to conclude there was no "meaning" to be found.

What most people felt at first was sheer bewilderment and fright. No one knew what to say, no one could decide whether to cry out to the heavens or mourn in silence. We had no language. "The great psychological fact of our time which we all observe with baffled wonder and shame," wrote Lionel Trilling, "is that there is no possible way of responding to Belsen and Buchenwald. The activity of mind fails before the incommunicability of man's suffering."

Let me shift back to my years in Alaska. When I first read, in occasionally available newspapers, about Nazi atrocities, I felt an uncanny sort of fear. But I could not and probably did not even try to move from this fear to any sort of comprehensive thought. There were pictures in the newspapers of American soldiers entering German death camps piled high with corpses. The faces of these GIs, ordinary American boys, registered a stunned horror and beyond that—what was there to say? It all seemed beyond grasp or credence. There was hardly anyone in Alaska I could talk with about these matters, I didn't even know how to start talking, and no doubt I wanted to "bury" the little knowledge I had. Perhaps these stories were exaggerated? All through the thirties it had been dinned into our heads that reports of German atrocities in the First World War had also been exaggerated.

By 1946 it was impossible not to know, and sensitive people often fell into a shared numbness, a blockage of response, as if to put aside the anguish that was lying in wait. No one has described this better than Clement Greenberg in an article he wrote in 1950:

Not only is the mind unable to come to terms with the dimensions of [the Holocaust] and so resolve some of its oppressiveness, and not only does it prefer to remain numbed in order to spare itself the pain; . . . the mind has a tendency, deep down, to look on a calamity of that order as a punishment that must have been deserved. How could it have happened on that scale and in that way, if it were not? But why deserved? For what? The mind doesn't know, but it fears—fears in an utterly irrational and amoral, if not immoral, way that we were being punished for being unable to take the risk of defending ourselves. No moral considerations enter in, as there used to, to relieve our feelings when we were persecuted; we were not punished by God for having transgressed—for no people could have sinned enough against any moral code to draw down such a punishment from any just God. We were punished by history.

But surely there was still another reason, somewhat less "noble," for the tardiness with which I and others responded to the Holocaust. Some of us continued to think more or less in Marxist categories—loosened and liberalized, but Marxist still. I would not go so far as to say that a Marxist outlook foreclosed the possibility of grasping the Holocaust in its moral terribleness and historical novelty. The moral terribleness we recognized as well as anyone else; the historical novelty we did not. Writing about Nazism in the thirties, when its full criminality was not yet visible, Trotsky had foreseen it would end as "barbarism." But that was only a word, though an accurate one, which neither he nor anyone else could yet have filled out with a sufficiently ghastly content.

That in confronting a new historical phenomenon we should at first have tried to grasp it through old categories, was entirely legitimate. How else could we learn that these categories would no longer do and we needed new ones? Marxism might offer a theory at least partly helpful with regard to the origins of Nazism, seeing it as the barbaric residue of a collapsed bourgeois society. But it had little to say about the evolving *nature* of Nazism, its unbridled and "principled" sadism, its infatuation with terror, its criminal ideology justifying the destruction of an "inferior" people through scientific means. Marxism, by remaining fixed upon class analysis and social categories appropriate only to the bourgeois-democratic epoch, kept us from seeing the radically novel particulars of the Nazi regime. Neither the political course nor economic laws nor social psychology of bourgeois society could begin to explain what had happened at Auschwitz. If, that is, anything could.

We had to move toward new and, it must be admitted, somewhat frightening perceptions. Marxism could tell us a good deal about reactionary societies, but what could it say about the roots of evil, the gratuitous yet systematic sadism of the SS? I don't know that any other structure of thought told us much about that sadism either, but at least it would not try to reduce everything to a "social base" or the "death agony of capitalism." Nor were liberals and conservatives any better equipped. The beginning of moral wisdom was to admit one's intellectual bewilderment, to acknowledge we were witnessing a sharp break in the line of history. And that readiness, as I have said, could not come easily: our minds had been formed in the pre-Holocaust era and, strong or weak, they were the only minds we had.

I want to avoid the vulgarity of soliciting moral credit through abject confession. Like everyone else, I recognized the Holocaust as a catastrophe beyond measure—but it's precisely the last two words that are critical: "beyond measure." During these early years I saw it as the final evidence of the collapse of bourgeois civilization, the "barbarism" about which Trotsky had warned. There was some truth to this. And there was also good reason for insisting, in Claude Lanzmann's words, that the Holocaust must be seen as an "unqualifiedly historical event, the monstrous, yes, but legitimate product of the history of the Western world." But what I could not yet see was that, if rooted in Western history, the Holocaust had, as it were, "extended" the nature and meaning of Western history, and that we therefore had to reconsider man's nature, possibilities, and limits within that history. Most of all, I had to recognize that the Holocaust must be seen as the culminating ordeal in that sequence of ordeals which comprises the experience of the Jewish people. One's first response—not the sole response, but the first—had to be a cry of Jewish grief. For me, alas, that would only come a little later.

In the years before the war people like me tended to subordinate our sense of Jewishness to cosmopolitan culture and socialist politics. We did not think well or deeply on the matter of Jewishness—you might say we avoided thinking about it. Jewishness was inherited, a given to be acknowledged, like being born white or male or poor. It could at times be regarded with affection, since after all it had helped to shape one's early years. And clearly, it still shaped thought, manners, the very slant of being. I knew that. But Jewishness did not form part of a conscious commitment, it was not regarded as a major component of the culture I wanted to make my own, and I felt no particular responsibility for its survival or renewal. It was simply *there*. While it would be shameful to deny its presence or seek to flee its stigma, my friends and I could hardly be said to have thought Jewishness could do much for us or we for it.

So, at least, we would have said. So too it would have seemed on the surface, and the surface is never wholly wrong. So it might still seem to a stranger or scholar looking into the intellectual journals of the years before, say, 1947. Yet this impression would be partly misleading, for together with what intellectuals (or Socialists) wrote and thought there was also what we felt, and what we felt was rarely quite in accord with what we wrote or thought. In the daily course of our lives—the lives of, say, young Socialists born to immigrant Jewish parents, or New York intellectuals born to the same kind of parents—the fact of Jewishness figured much more strongly than we acknowledged in public. We still didn't "identify" with a Jewish tradition, yet in practice we grew increasingly concerned with Jewish themes. This was a kind of cultural lag, recognition behind reality. By the forties Sidney Hook was writing essays about "the Jewish problem" as in fact a problem of Christian civilization, showing how deeply anti-Semitism was entangled with strands of Christian myth. Philip Rahv often spoke acutely, with a very Jewish melody, about the extent to which re-

ceived prejudices could be detected even among high-minded gentile writers. A group of talented young writers—Bellow, Schwartz,
and Malamud among them—was starting to make of the immigrant
Jewish experience the ground of their work.

Some of us like, say, Rahv and me were a strange breed. We
knew we were Jews. We had no choice but to remain Jews, except
perhaps through devices too humiliating to consider. We took an
acute private pleasure, through jokes and asides, in those aspects of
intellectuality that bore the marks of Jewishness: quickness, skepticism, questioning. But we had no taste for and little interest in
Judaism as religion. We refused to acknowledge ourselves as part of
an American Jewish community encompassing all classes and
opinions, since we claimed that the inner divisions of social interest
and political opinion among the Jews remained decisive. We were
not at home in the organized Jewish world, and its leaders paid no
attention to us—there was no reason why they should. We had
made another choice of comrades, the straggling phalanx of the
international anti-Stalinist Left. Still, as I remember from conversations with Philip Rahv and Delmore Schwartz, we held in contempt
those Jewish intellectuals and academics who tried to pass themselves off as anything but what they were. Indeed, we took a malicious delight in poking fun at the handful of Jews who had reached
the exalted status of professor, since, we suspected, they had surely
had to pay with some unseemly evasions.

In following this ambivalent course we were by no means
cutting ourselves off completely from Jewish experience. We too
had a tradition of sorts behind us, the tradition of the estranged
Jew, which had grown increasingly strong in the life of the Jewish
people these past two centuries. It is a tradition that goes back at
least to the moment in the late eighteenth century when Solomon
Maimon, an "alienated" Jew if ever there was one, wandered away
from his Lithuanian *shtetl* to become a junior colleague of German
Enlightenment philosophers. In our own century this type has been
embodied in such leaders of European radicalism as Julian Martov,
Rosa Luxemburg, and Leon Trotsky—those who, in Isaac Deutscher's coinage, were "non-Jewish Jews." Unsatisfactory as this
cosmopolitan style would show itself to be, it was nevertheless a
familiar Jewish choice, a part of Jewish history. There was a gap
between the ideas and feelings of the Jewish intellectuals in New

York, but how enormous—and oppressive—that gap had become we did not realize until after the war. Then, starting to look around, we began to heed our feelings.

Efforts to grapple with the Holocaust, all doomed to one or another degree of failure, soon led to timid reconsiderations of what it meant to be Jewish. One of the first pieces to deal with the Holocaust came, however, from a gentile intellectual, Dwight Macdonald, in his essay "The Responsibility of Peoples" (*Politics*, March 1945). Macdonald argued against the then popular notion that all Germans were guilty, or equally guilty; but what concerns me here is something else, his recognition that "the German atrocities in this war [are] a phenomenon unique in modern history," and that "what has been done by other people as an unpleasant byproduct of the attainment of certain ends [e.g., the bombing of Hiroshima and Nagasaki] has been done by the Germans at Maidenek and Auschwitz as an end in itself." The Jews of Europe "were murdered to gratify a paranoid hatred . . . but for no reason of policy or advantage that I can see." Unsystematic as these remarks were, they had the virtue of insisting upon the uniqueness of the Holocaust—an event without precedent yet prepared for by the anti-Semitism of the West.

Macdonald was probably influenced by Hannah Arendt, who a few months earlier had published a brilliant essay, "Organized Guilt and Universal Responsibility," in the *Jewish Frontier*. Arendt wrote that "systematic mass murder . . . strains not only the imagination of human beings, but also the framework and categories of our political thought. . . . There is no political method for dealing with German mass crimes. . . . [The] human need for justice can find no satisfactory reply to the total mobilization of a people for that purpose." Again, this was a step forward in the effort to "understand," precisely as it called into question the very relevance or possibility of "understanding." (At about the same time the Yiddish poet Jacob Glatstein was writing: "Veil mir velln ksaidr munen: / Liber, tairer, heiliker numen, / Mir hubn es kainmul nisht farshtunen" (For we shall always demand: / Loving, dear, and holy Name, / We could never understand).

These essays were written while I was thousands of miles to the north, and I caught up with them only after the war, when plowing through back files of the intellectual magazines. But I shared immediately in the excitement provoked by Jean-Paul Sartre's *Réflexions sur la question juive* when it appeared serially in *Partisan Review* and *Commentary* in 1946 and 1947. There are times when a flawed piece of writing is more valuable than a "correct" one—honest confusions, incomplete strivings can stimulate others to think better. So it was with Sartre's little book. Decades later it is easy enough to spot its errors, but at the time the book came out, it was tremendously stimulating. Not only did it have the merit of describing, with that pungent detail which is Sartre's special talent, the psychology of the anti-Semite, the ragged texture of his delusions, and both the strategies of coercion concocted by "inauthentic" Jews and the desperate firmness of "authentic" ones. It also elevated the entire discussion to a theoretical level, prompting such New York writers as Sidney Hook and Harold Rosenberg (as well as, in Paris, the young Tunisian-Jewish writer Albert Memmi) to undertake sustained replies. Sartre drove his opinions, sometimes mere guesses, to melodramatic extremes, but he wrote with evident good will and even after Auschwitz that was no small matter.

"The Jew"—an abstraction he could not avoid—is defined for Sartre by his "situation." This "situation" is an ensemble of conditions and environments signifying both the relentless pressures of the anti-Semite and the tepid defenses of the democrat who is prepared to defend the Jew but not as a Jew, only as abstract "man." A Jew, writes Sartre, "is anyone who for any reason calls himself such or is called such in any community whose practices take note of the distinction." Yet, despite the persistence of this "distinction," Sartre comes to the odd conclusion that the Jews "have no history . . . for twenty centuries of dispersion and political impotence forbids [the Jewish community's] having a historical past." What creates the Jew, so to speak, and enables his twisted, precarious survival, is the all-but-universal enmity he incurs: "We have shown that the Jews have neither community of interests nor community of belief. They . . . have no history. The sole tie that binds them is the hostility and disdain of the societies which surround them. Thus the authentic Jew is the one who asserts his claim in the face of the disdain shown him."

Sartre's book offered a welcome defense, far too sophisticated to indulge in the apologetics that often afflict Jewish writing, and all this made one feel a little better. But in grappling with its brilliant if monolithic laying out of the Jew's "situation," one discovered that the book suffered from an extreme ahistoricity. It reduced both Jew and anti-Semite to bloodless, timeless essences, and failed to ask what might be the origin of anti-Semitism or, still more important, the reasons for its persistence. Sartre's conclusion, so lame after his analytic fireworks, came to little more than a version of the Marxist notion that anti-Semitism is the consequence, or index, of the social wrongs of capitalist society, and that with socialism this blight would wither away (about as rapidly, one expects, as the state will wither away). Without history or community of interest, and no longer plagued by pathological enemies, the Jews would then freely dissolve themselves into the encasing classless society. Especially intellectual French Jews, one gathered, would assimilate quickly, becoming pure Frenchmen; why the scenario could not be turned upside down, Frenchmen becoming Jews, Sartre never made clear. Perhaps he could not even imagine it.

While powerfully locating the essence of Jewish life in its relentless "situation," he failed to see that one could also, indeed always, locate its "situation" in a traditional essence. He saw the Jewish "situation" too much as a consequence of what others did and said, as the will of the powers of the world. He did not see it sufficiently as a persistent choosing of identity, a heroic self-assertion. A powerful reply along these lines came from Harold Rosenberg, and if Sartre's little book set one to thinking about the whole matter, Rosenberg's polemic prompted a distancing from Sartre's categorical excesses.

As if to echo Heine's remark that Jewish survival is "the supreme achievement of a stubborn people, made possible by their 'portable fatherland,' the Bible," Rosenberg insisted upon the unbroken presence of the Jews as a historical community. Two thou sand years of statelessness and powerlessness did not annul a history. And that dispersed community had the same right as any other to survival, whether in the actual world of capitalism or the dreamed-of world of socialism. The Jews, argued Rosenberg, found themselves not merely in a "situation" made for them by enemies and even friends; they had lived in the narrow spaces of an autonomous history and a self-affirmed tradition—narrow spaces but deep, too. Rosenberg insisted upon the hold of collective memory, the grip of origins. What else could explain the extraordinary survival of the

Jews through centuries in which self-denial would have been far more comfortable?

> The situation of the Jews does not reveal who the Jew is except when it becomes a situation that discloses his link with Abraham, Moses and David, from whom the Jewish identity sprung. . . . The continuity of the modern Jew with the Jews of the Old Testament is established by those acts that arise from his internal cohesion with his ultimate beginnings in which his future is contained as a possible destiny—the acts of turning toward the Promised Land in his crises. And these acts, *not deducible from his surroundings*, make the Jew's situation and reveal who the Jew is. (Emphasis added.)

Neither Sartre's book nor Rosenberg's criticism took much account of the modern Jews' will to declare themselves historical subjects, breaking out of their "situation" and, to an extent, their tradition as well. Neither paid attention to the emerging state of Israel; both confined the Jews to a range of options from which in practice they were already breaking free. Parisian intellectual and New York intellectual—neither could see that the Jews were finally intent upon creating a "situation" of their own.

Rosenberg's essay, nevertheless, constituted a gesture of tacit identification: it marked, for me, a turning point. Rosenberg wrote from neither a religious nor a theological premise; he wrote as a spokesman for "the partial Jew," one acknowledging links with the Jewish past, yet also forming himself through a multiplicity of identities. In his insistence upon the integrity of the inner history of the Jews, despite the absence of governments, armies, and diplomacies, Rosenberg was surely right; but had Sartre troubled to reply, he could have raised the question whether the present historical condition of the Jews would long permit them to claim or keep ties with their "ultimate beginnings." Sartre had been utterly, shockingly wrong in saying the Jews had no history—it was just the sort of thing a Frenchman might say. Later he admitted that he had written from an excessive distance and with a paucity of knowledge. Still, he might easily have modulated his views by remarking that the Jews, or many of them, were in danger of forgetting their history and abandoning their "portable fatherland." When Rosenberg wrote, "The Jews have shown that without being a race, a nation, or a religion, it is possible for people to remain together in a net of memory and expectation," Sartre might have answered, "Yes, but what if the net grows increasingly full of holes?"

So if our first response was impatiently to regard Sartre's argument as a well-meant simplification—who wants to be told that he exists only by virtue of an externally imposed "situation"?—calmer reflection warranted a recognition that the damage done to the Jews by an endless series of "situations" had been enormous. Albert Memmi, refuting Sartre, nevertheless wrote as if in partial acknowledgment of Sartre's case: "To be a Jew is first and foremost to find oneself called to account, to feel continuously accused, explicitly or implicitly, clearly or obscurely."

The debate stirred by Sartre had notable echoes and anticipations. In speaking about the Jews' "situation" as a mode of historical inexorability, was not Sartre touching at a crucial point the Zionist claim that so long as Jews remained in *galut* (exile) they could never enjoy a normal life—with the difference that Sartre saw the chimera of normality delivered by socialism, whereas the Zionists saw it delivered by a Jewish state? And in speaking of "the net of memory and expectation" as that which bound the Jews into a community, was not Rosenberg echoing a little those non-Zionist Jews, especially the Yiddishists, who argued that far from being a historical emptiness, the two thousand years of *galut* represented a rich, sometimes even satisfying expanse of Jewish life?*

The discussion provoked by Sartre's book mattered less for its particulars than the fact that a number of writers were finally breaking away from the sterilities of their earlier "internationalist" position. They were speaking now as if the Jewish question could not be reduced to a mere epiphenomenal disorder of capitalist

* Some fifteen years later, engaged in a polemic about black writing with Ralph Ellison, I found myself cast, to my own surprise, in a Sartre-like position. I had written an essay on the fiction of Richard Wright, James Baldwin, and Ellison, stressing the dominance—indeed, the inescapability—of the "protest" theme in their work. Ellison objected that I had locked the black writers into an airless box —what Sartre would call their "situation." Ellison claimed for the blacks, as Rosenberg had for the Jews, an autonomous culture that could not be fully apprehended through the lens of "protest." Surely there was some validity to Ellison's argument, yet I could not help thinking that the "situation" of the blacks had generated more traumas, more scars than he was ready to admit. Perhaps, however, it was easier for me to see this with regard to blacks than Jews. Maybe there can be no clear-cut resolution of such differences, first between Sartre and Rosenberg, and then between me and Ellison, since both sides overstress portions of recognizable truth.

society; as if Jewish identity were an implacable reality of Western history that only ideologues could ignore; and as if "we," marginal in the past to the "net of [Jewish] memory and expectation," now had to acknowledge that somehow we did have a place, uncomfortable as it might be, within that net. What mattered was not to fix "Jewishness" once and for all, but to keep alive an inquiry into its possibilities. Our dawning recognition of all this was progress of a sort.

These problems cut more deeply than I have yet been able to suggest. Our earlier failure to face them with sufficient candor had left us their victims, had made us into "inauthentic" Jews who gave the Jewish "situation" neither serious thought nor unblocked emotion. It is true that Jews who did not believe in Judaism as a traditional faith had serious problems: they were left with a residual "Jewishness" increasingly hard to specify, a blurred complex of habits, beliefs, and feelings. This "Jewishness" might have no fixed religious or national content, it might be helpless before the assault of believers. But there it was, that was what we had—and had to live with.

Touches of awkwardness, even the ridiculous, were inevitable. Some literary people, Leslie Fiedler conspicuous among them, set off on vicarious pilgrimages to Hasidism. Several *Commentary* editors held a Seder one Passover evening and invited Edmund Wilson to come; Wilson, his anthropological curiosity aroused, went. I scoffed at this innocent gathering, though I'm not sure whether because the Seder seemed a concession to religiosity or because I cherished memories of it as the loveliest of Yiddish folk celebrations, which those "Americans" over at *Commentary* could only spoil. I had no business scoffing—a smile would have been enough. Nathan Glazer—who, as I recall, was the host for this Seder—was starting to recognize that over the centuries Jewish religious practice and Jewish folk experience had been completely intertwined, so that unbelievers too, if only they acknowledged themselves as Jews, could participate in religious holidays. First the deed, then faith.

During the late forties and early fifties a number of New York writers—Paul Goodman, Harold Rosenberg, Clement Greenberg —made serious attempts to define their new, or reasserted, Jewish attachment. They wrote with some wariness, as if determined not to surrender the stance of marginality; they were fearful of even appearing to return to the parochialism of middle-class Jewish life. Greenberg disparaged a new spirit of chauvinism ("proud to be a Jew") that was becoming fashionable among American Jews in the years of postwar comfort. Rosenberg argued for the value of remaining a Jewish "semioutsider," both attached to and apart from the institutional centers of Jewish life. Goodman invoked a tradition in which "children learn certain great stories, so that, when they grow up, the puzzles of existence are recast in these great stories," then added self-consciously that "the stories of Abraham and King David have occupied, and will continue to occupy, my soul and my pen."

No one looking through such articles could fail to hear a defensiveness of voice. Now that some of these writers were making stabs at Jewish declaration, the organized Jewish community, which favors in-group solidarity above all, started to respond with more ardor than tact. Rabbis and institutional leaders began making speeches urging intellectuals to "come home," back to synagogue and community. But the intellectuals kept their distance, for they wanted to define their thin strand of Jewishness in their own hesitant way. They were more interested in Kafka than the middle-brow hacks who gained the bulk of Jewish readers; they were more excited by the historical writings of Gershom Scholem than the preachings of the American rabbis. They wanted a Jewishness of question and risk, while the American Jewish community, at least most of it, was settling into good works and self-satisfaction.

There were exchanges, pleas, remonstrances, but little serious connection. Even the handful of Jewish intellectuals whose concern with religion was genuine kept looking for fresh channels of expression, often apart from congregation and fellowship. Once Philip Roth began to publish his brilliantly abrasive stories, so wounding to the sensibilities of middle-class Jewish readers, he succeeded in deflecting the attention of the rabbis, some of whom made a virtual career out of attacking his work.

I kept away from most of these controversies for the simple reason that I had almost nothing coherent to say on Jewish themes. At the time my main intellectual journey, difficult enough, consisted of a break from an earlier orthodox, anti-Stalinist Marxism.

Yet I also read the newly "Jewish" writings of friends like Rosenberg and Greenberg with an intensity that suggested they had touched some unresolved personal involvement. I could not release my true feelings because they were blocked by worn opinions. Shapeless but strong, these feelings found their first major outlet in a literary activity that for the next few decades would become a significant part of my life—editing the translation of Yiddish stories and poems into English. This wasn't, of course, a very forthright way of confronting my own troubled sense of Jewishness, but that was the way I took. Sometimes you have to make roundabout journeys without quite knowing where they will lead to.

One day in 1953, after I had published a piece about Sholom Aleichem, I received a note from Eliezer Greenberg. He was, he said, a Yiddish poet living in New York. He liked my piece and proposed that we "become partners." Exactly what this partnership was to do I didn't yet know, but I went to see Lazer, as everyone called him, and found a vigorous man in his early fifties with a strong, squat body and a square, Slavic face. This was not the moony "folk" poet, tubercular and fragile, that Yiddish legend celebrated, but a sophisticated and sardonic writer whom the other Yiddish writers, not always friendly, called "der Amerikaner" because of his passion for unseemly English-language periodicals. Lazer knew more little magazines than anyone I have ever met (the littler the better), and he took a wry pleasure in bringing to my attention American writers—"one of yours"—I had never so much as heard of.

We became partners in the editing-and-translating-Yiddish business. It was not exactly the road to riches, but it brought me an unsystematic literary education such as few other American critics have had. Over the years Lazer and I put out six collections of Yiddish prose and poetry translated into English, and as we went along, my friendship with him grew into a central intellectual experience.

We began with a book of Yiddish stories. Once a week Lazer would haul up a briefcase of crumbling old books and we'd spend three or four hours reading, trying to imagine how a story that sounded good in Yiddish might sound in English (seldom as good), wondering whom we could cajole into the back-breaking work of translation, and later, checking the translator's script for accuracy. We had no "theory" of translation, though we soon had to modify —Nabokov's stern injunctions notwithstanding—our bias in favor of strict literalness. For we found that most literal translations turned out to be dim carbons that failed to evoke the quality of the original. What we wanted was a version that would somehow cleave to the sense of the Yiddish while satisfying the rhythmic and linguistic requirements of English. Not that we often reached so sublime a condition.

Crucial to our work was Lazer's reading aloud of a Yiddish text, but this could be treacherous also. He was a strong reader who could make a Yiddish story sound better than it really was, especially if it was a story he hoped to slip past my guard. He read with an unsentimental bark, drying out the Yiddish as he went along. Though regarded as a deviant within the Yiddish literary world because of his modernist tastes, Lazer saw it as his responsibility to maintain the integrity, which also meant the alienness, of the Yiddish tradition; my responsibility, on the other hand, was to make that tradition accessible to English readers. The differences between us were large so we would often argue, clarifying through these arguments the inescapable problems of translation.

When Lazer and I started working together, some major Yiddish writers were still alive in New York. But the truth—as we both knew but did not say—was that we were dealing with a literature close to its historical exit. A once vibrant literary criticism in Yiddish was almost exhausted. There were no young writers in Yiddish. In compiling our anthologies we were not merely exercising personal tastes, we were undertaking an act of critical salvage. This brought us into disfavor with the more parochial advocates of Yiddish, whose tastes had been formed years earlier at *mittelshul* (Jewish high school) and allowed to rest there. When we worked, for example, on our Yiddish poetry collection, I found myself resisting Lazer's entreaties to include a poem or two by Abraham Lyessin, a once popular East Side figure, not because I had anything against Lyessin but because I thought his work full of creaky eloquence and likely to seem still worse in English. The Yiddish reviewers attacked us for this omission: they remembered Lyessin, or at least his name, and that was enough. It was as if American literary taste had settled once and for all at the point of Whittier's popularity.

Whenever we reached a dry spell, Lazer would whip out a "goodie"—something special I could not resist. Once he said to me, "Sit still, be quiet, don't interrupt," and started to read, in the manner of a meditative lyric, Isaac Bashevis Singer's "Gimpel the Fool." It was a transforming moment: how often does a critic encounter a major new writer? Relishing my pleasure in Singer's story yet still intent upon clarifying the historical lines of the literature, Lazer said, "s'iz zehr idish, aber s'iz dokh nisht idish" (It's very Yiddish, but it's still not Yiddish). Years later I understood what he meant. Singer's mastery of Yiddish as a literary medium was second only to that of Sholom Aleichem, and his involvement with the prerationalist sources of Jewish folk tradition went deep; nevertheless, the world view out of which Singer wrote was strongly at odds with the nineteenth-century humanism that has dominated Yiddish literature.

I inveigled Saul Bellow, not quite so famous yet, to do the translation. Bellow had a pretty good command of Yiddish, but not quite enough to do the story on his own. So we sat him down before a typewriter in Lazer's apartment on East Nineteenth Street, Lazer read out the Yiddish sentence by sentence, Saul occasionally asked about refinements of meaning, and I watched in a state of high enchantment. Three or four hours, and it was done. Saul took another half hour to go over the translation and then, excited, read aloud the version that has since become famous. It was a feat of virtuosity, and we drank a schnapps to celebrate.

I sent Bellow's translation to *Partisan Review* and a week later Philip Rahv, his hoarse voice gurgling, called me, "Hey, where'd you find him?" (Anyone troubling to look into the Yiddish *Forward* could have "found him" much earlier.) Rahv immediately grasped the canny mixture of folk pathos and sophisticated overlay that made "Gimpel" so brilliant a story and thus became the fourth man in this chain of discovery.

Not till several months later did I meet Singer himself, still entirely unknown to English readers. At the now defunct Steinberg's vegetarian restaurant on Broadway near Eighty-second Street, we had lunch. I was a little hesitant but needn't have been, since this gnomish man eating blintzes—who looked as if he hadn't eaten anything for a year—was one of the master performers of our time. Quite as if he had a hall full of listeners before him, Singer started rolling out a carpet of wisecracks, anecdotes, platitudes, quotations, opinions that left me dizzy with amusement and dismay. I could not decide—who can?—whether I had met a genius or a comedian. This, in any case, is the story of Singer's entry into the American literary world.

Collaboration with Greenberg became for me a sustaining experience. We learned each other's secret tastes and tried to exploit them slyly—he for the sake of the Yiddish tradition in which he half believed, I for the literary audience I was by no means sure we would find. There was a pleasure in doing something absolutely pure—arguing over a recalcitrant idiom, measuring the suitability of a story for linguistic transformation, trying to cajole an underpaid translator to give "a little more blood." Our working together in the late sixties became for me a source of happiness—one day a week away from the Vietnam war and the polemics with leftist ideologues into which I had locked myself.

Greenberg ended his life a lonely man. When his friend the Yiddish poet Jacob Glatstein died, there was barely anyone left for him to talk with. In one of Lazer's poems, "Visiting Second Avenue" (I translate literally), he evokes this loneliness:

> I seldom come to see you these days,
> And except for a used-up old building
> They have managed to leave alone—
> Like some old souvenir—
> I'd never recognize this neighborhood:
> You have changed so much, Second Avenue!
> But even these trinkets abandoned by the past
> Remind me of the treasure that was ours.

With Glatstein I struck up a wary friendship. In his last years he became a poet of excoriation, though he had begun in his twenties as a modernist devoted to personal voice and experiment. No one in Yiddish has written so brilliantly at the edge of the Holocaust as Glatstein in his scourging, muted poems about God's helplessness before the destruction of the Jews. Like Greenberg, Glatstein set an example of the strength that is possible in circumstances of neglect. These writers carried themselves with barely a trace of self-pity; they knew they were closing the ranks and they went about their work. Glatstein had much the fierier temperament and a wicked talent for polemic. His irony had turned bitter, caustic. Once when I asked him what it felt like to be a major poet in a minor culture, he answered with flashing eyes, "I have to know about Auden but Auden doesn't have to know about me!"

What, I used to wonder, could be the unspoken feelings of these Yiddish literary friends? In their private talks, how did they cope with the certainty that the literature to which they had devoted their lives was approaching its end? I was a loyal ally, but still at least half an outsider. I did not share their memories and could not reach to the floor of their emotions. There was a limit beyond which they would not go, even with me; they refused, as a gesture of both honor and will, to acknowledge the bleakness of their future. Undeluded, no doubt inwardly desperate, they still felt an obligation to confront the world with a complete firmness of posture. One of the arts of life is to know how to end.

Meanwhile, where did they really live—live, I mean, in their imaginations? About some Yiddish writers there could be no doubt. The strong poet Chaim Grade resided in the North Bronx, his apartment overflowing with books he had arranged in stacks as if he were tending a library; but in the deepest part of his self he was still back in the shadowy brilliance of Vilna during the late twenties, still absorbed with the ethical severities of the Musar movement. Isaac Bashevis Singer seemed really to live nowhere at all, though everyone had an address for him. He did not quite fit into the New World or the Old, so canny was he at adapting himself to American tastes, so skillful at exploiting those tastes for his own ends. His streak of opportunism often worked in behalf of his genius, and the public clowning in which he indulged neither seriously damaged his gifts as a perverse fabulist nor lacked a touch of contempt for his American admirers.

But writers like Glatstein and Greenberg, the first a great poet and the second a minor one? They had a foot, or toe, in America. Glatstein had gone to the University of Michigan for a year in his youth, and at the time this was a matter of much consequence. He had written in Yiddish a charming essay about the early poems of Marianne Moore, and I thought there was an occasional faint similarity between some of his beginning work and her silken ironies. Greenberg had friends among American writers, he spent time working with me on anthologies of Yiddish literature translated into English, and his critical essays on Yiddish poets contain many comparisons with American writers. Both of them were well read in American poetry: Greenberg knew Frost, Eliot, and Auden well, read Schwartz, Berryman, and Lowell—only Wallace Stevens would have slipped past him. All of this signified a minor revolution within Yiddish culture, regarded with uneasiness by older writers.

During the twenties and thirties, when Glatstein and Greenberg were in their formative years, the Yiddish subculture in America was still secure enough to allow some younger writers both to feel at ease in their native tradition and to make forays into the outer, American milieu. Neither Glatstein nor Greenberg earned his living within the Yiddish world: both wanted to avoid being dependent on the Yiddish newspapers (though Glatstein did write a column for one of them, getting up at six in the morning three times a week and having his immaculate 750 words ready by eight). Both these poets found part-time employment in American Jewish organizations, where they were looked upon as cultural adornments, livening the days of functionaries. As for their forays into American culture, these were not always successful. Greenberg's criticism is marred by too heavy a reliance on notions picked up from the American literary quarterlies. Glatstein, who had the more independent mind of the two, managed to keep the realms of Yiddish and America clearly distinct.

There were personal feelings to be considered, also. Glatstein knew—he had every right to—that he was a distinguished poet who, if he wrote in any other language, would be famous, the recipient of prizes, and the subject of critical studies. It was hard for me to explain—they seldom brought it up, but I felt obliged to mention it once in a while—the utter indifference of American literary circles to the presence of a vibrant Yiddish culture that could be found, literally and symbolically, a few blocks away. Greenberg took pleasure in the friendship of Isaac Rosenfeld and Saul Bellow: it justified a little his having "strayed" from the Yiddish fold. But I knew, in truth, how profound was the chasm between the Yiddish writers and even those American-Jewish writers who had a few words of Yiddish. I still recall a remark Lionel Trilling once made to me that he "suspected" Yiddish literature; I thought there must be something profound behind those words, but later decided there needn't be at all.

After the Holocaust even Yiddish modernists felt compelled to pull back, to reaffirm the tragic grandeur of their own tradition and erect barriers of distrust against gentile culture. Glatstein wrote some poems—he was a master of rage—declaring his contempt for the *goyim* and their "American-Jewish" friends, while in his bristling journalism he adopted a tone that, not exactly chauvinist, was fiercely assertive of Jewish worth. In column after column he warred against Ezra Pound and kept savaging Boris Pasternak for asking in *Doctor Zhivago* whether the cost in blood and pain made Jewish survival worthwhile.

These writers lived in the American world, too. Once Glatstein, though fiercely anticommunist, sent me a warm note because I had written something to protest the persecution of Communists in Indonesia. Greenberg kept urging me to write a full-scale book on American literature even as we were working on translations from Yiddish; otherwise, he asked, how can you call yourself an American critic? They were often irritated at what they took to be the condescension of writers in journals like *Commentary* toward Yiddish, and by the sixties our relations were good enough for them to feel no hesitation at needling me about this. I would protest my innocence, my lack of responsibility for what appeared in American magazines; they merely smiled. They knew about "those Americans."

Only once was my friendship with these men strained, and that was in 1969 when Cynthia Ozick published her story, "Envy, or Yiddish in America." At once brilliant and malicious, this story depicts two wretched Yiddish writers who are overcome with envy of another Yiddish writer whom they call *der Chazer*, the Pig, transparently Isaac Bashevis Singer, a great success among Americans. None of these figures is let off easily: there is a hilarious bit showing the Singer-like character toying with his audience. One of the two envious writers is given a powerful speech: "I'm finished, period. We're already dead. Whoever uses Yiddish to keep himself alive is already dead." But the total effect of the story is reductive and, in the view of the Yiddish writers, demeaning. It was true, all of them did want translators, and Glatstein, a man of considerable vanity, even put up with poor ones; only Greenberg, in whom a modest talent may have enabled sharper self-perceptions, did not search for the chimera of translation. When the Ozick story came out I argued in partial defense of it, but Greenberg, though usually quite prepared to separate personal feelings from literary judgments, grew inflamed. He turned on me with anger and said, "Some things are more important than writing a good story!" Too late, I agree.

In his last years Greenberg became the editor of the once mighty Yiddish literary monthly *Di Tsukunft* (The Future). He would tell me about his struggle to get enough decent material and his pleasure in occasionally finding a gem, but later on he spoke less and less about the magazine. One day he announced that he had resigned as editor, and with a grimace sad and ironic, added: *"Di Tsukunft* iz un a tsukunft" (*The Future* has no future).

I attached myself to these writers as friend and commentator. I found strength in joining their moment of weakness. I loved them, I loved their words.

While working with Greenberg on Yiddish literature I took a somewhat austere line, telling myself I wanted to treat it with the aroused detachment of an anthropologist who is also a member of the tribe. This made sense as a reaction against that sentimentalism which floods a good many Jewish readers whenever they encounter anything Yiddish. (They protect themselves by keeping such encounters to a minimum.) But I also had a personal motive, a modest scruple. I wished not to let my work in Yiddish literature become an unearned substitute for a defined Jewishness—especially at a moment when undefined Jewishness was too readily becoming a substitute for traditional Judaism. It was all very well to work on translating Yiddish, and for me this clearly had more than just a literary interest; but in principle there was nothing to keep a gentile critic from doing the same work or even learning Yiddish to the imperfect measure that I knew it.

Still, reading more deeply in the Yiddish poets helped me to feel at ease, if not with myself, then at least with my past. It helped open memories, unclog feelings. The experiences of the immigrant world had long been left behind, and there was not the faintest chance of going back to them. My problem, as the popular phrase has it, was "to come to terms" with those experiences. What could that really mean? It meant to rid myself of the double weights of nostalgia and shame, aggressiveness and denial, so that I might now live peacefully with the idea that my years of origin were simply mine—just as the equivalent years might be for someone raised in Nashville or Duluth. That was probably asking too much—a dismissal of self-consciousness unlikely to prove attainable; but at least it set a norm, a goal.

It was in the sonnets of Mani Leib, written at the end of his life, and in the quasi-modernist poems of Moishe Leib Halpern that I heard voices recalling voices of my youth. Yiddish poetry is often a poetry of rhymed statement, addressing itself to readers, perhaps the people living next door, with an all-but-unmediated directness. Held back from ultimate sophistication by a burden of moral urgency, it is a poetry at once more threadbare and declamatory than other modern poetries. The voices of Yiddish poetry were of course richer and more disciplined than any I could remember from the immigrant years; still, the mild twilight resignation that filled Mani Leib's sonnets brought back images of elderly Jews sunning themselves in Bronx Park, and the despairing rants of Moishe Leib Halpern were like echoes of lamentations, comic in their excess, of people I remembered from decades past.

In these poems I found a fragment of peace, maybe a rekindled affection. And then, turning upon Yiddish poetry the memories it had released within me, I came to recognize how desperate had been the plight of the Yiddish writers whose work I was helping put into English. The hardness of their years, the foreseen loss of their work, the loneliness encircling them all: I saw it now with a new clarity. Between the Yiddish writers and my father growing old in Co-Op City there was a bond, though they were literary men who could quote Heine and Pushkin, while he never read anything but the Yiddish paper. That bond was simply a shared bias of feeling as it arose from a shared condition of life. Behind it lay "the stories of Abraham and Moses and King David" and also the neglected prescriptions of rabbinic Judaism, though in the life span of these writers they gave voice to another Jewish impulse, that of Yiddishkeit, split away from and yet dependent upon the Judaism of the centuries.

Getting a little closer to my father during his years of aging, I studied the frailties of his character, not unlike my own. As man and parent he grew smaller in my eyes, so that it became harder to accord the proper filial respect to whatever in his life seemed merely personal. Yet that did not make me care for him any the less. For in him, as in thousands of other immigrants, there was a force that went far beyond the merely personal, and this was a collective Jewish being as it drew upon received values and ingrained feelings. It was easy enough to see whatever was parochial in these values and feelings, but it took years to learn that they also formed the firmest moral norms I would ever encounter. Again and again I would "fail" my father through what he took to be my disordered life—a broken marriage, a sudden unexplained stay in California. But his solidarity never wavered, and I came to feel that it was a solidarity more than familial, deriving from some unexpressed sense of what a Jew owed his son. Reading Mani Leib's sonnets and Moishe Leib's poems, I learned to value that solidarity. Reading those sonnets and poems I learned where I had come from and how I was likely to end.

None of this solved for me the problem of "Jewishness." During the years between the mid-fifties and early seventies I was not even trying to solve this problem; I was hoping only to find it. Nor was I thinking of "handing down" any program for Jews younger than myself, even those also pinched into the narrowing sector of Jewish secularism: they would have to improvise and scamper about, like others before them. Besides, whatever Jews might lack, it was not programs. What they really needed in America was once and for all to end the undignified oscillation between self-assault and self-praise, after which they might settle into whatever portion of their past they could calmly accept. My own hope was to achieve some equilibrium with that earlier self which had started with childhood Yiddish, my language of naming, and then turned away in adolescent shame. Yiddish poetry, somber or wild, brought me no comprehensive views about "the Jewish problem," but it did something more valuable. It helped me strike a truce with, and then extend a hand to, the world of my father.

For some of us the path to a clarified Jewishness has to be twisted and rocky. The true journeyer is not even certain that the path is there. Along the way there were often stops marked by confusion, unclarified bursts of emotion, even hysteria. One of these was a civil war that broke out among New York intellectuals over Hannah Arendt's 1963 book on the Eichmann trial.

My first encounter with Hannah had come in 1947 when she was editor of Schocken Books, the German-Jewish publishing house recently moved to New York. She needed a part-time assistant to do literary chores (copy for book jackets, cleaning up translations, and so forth), and for the handy sum of $150 a month I took the job. With it came the privilege of visiting Hannah at her office every week. She had not yet published her major work on totalitarianism, but everyone in the intellectual world respected her and some feared her. She liked to "adopt" young people, and while I was not one of her chosen—perhaps because I was deaf to philosophy, or had been contaminated by Marxism, or was visibly intent upon resisting her intellectual lures—she would take an hour off and talk to me about Kafka and Brecht, Yiddish folk tales and American politics.

While far from "good-looking" in any commonplace way, Hannah Arendt was a remarkably attractive person, with her razored gestures, imperial eye, dangling cigarette. "Szee here," she would declare with a smile meant both to subdue and to solace, and then she'd race off into one of her improvisations. She made an especially strong impression on intellectuals—those who, as mere Americans, were dazzled by the immensities of German philosophy. But I always suspected that she impressed people less through her thought than the style of her thinking. She bristled with intellectual charm, as if to reduce everyone in sight to an alert discipleship. Her voice would shift register abruptly, now stern and admonitory, now slyly tender in gossip. Whatever room she was in Hannah filled through the largeness of her will; indeed, she always seemed larger than her setting. Rarely have I met a writer with so acute an awareness of the power to overwhelm.

Her thought leaped and whirled, refusing familiar liberal and Marxist routines. Even while appreciating her performance, I often failed to grasp its substance. Yet we did share an interest in one crucial aspect of modern political thought. Hannah used to talk about "politics per szay" and though I suspected her of an aristocratic or "supraclass" bias, I was not so foolish as to dismiss this out of hand. For her, politics signified an activity marking out whatever was distinctively human in the human enterprise—an activity by which men decided how to govern their affairs. Politics she saw, indeed celebrated, as an autonomous art free of socioeconomic debasements. Now in my own circles we were starting to recognize that in modern societies, especially the communist ones where the state has become the arbiter of the economy, it is politics that for good or ill proves to be the decisive shaper of society. So there was a meeting between the ideas Hannah put forward and the ideas I told her my friends were approaching, which came as news to her, since she had an aversion to Marxists. It was at her prompting that I went back to *The Federalist Papers* and found there, especially in Madison's essays, powerful statements about the uses of faction and the balancing of interest in a republic. Especially important was the idea that government, far from simply reflecting class interests, had to be regarded as a feat of craftsmanship, something *made* by men and thereby open to numerous variations. I learned—and for this I remain grateful to Hannah Arendt—that politics has to be scrutinized in its own right, and not just as an index of social conflict.

Hannah's attitudes toward modern Jewish life, her feelings toward the Jews as they actually lived in all their frailty and imperfection, were hopelessly mixed. She breathed hostility toward established Jewish institutions, especially Zionist ones, though in earlier years she had been closely involved with European Zionism. She felt impatient with what she took to be their intellectual mediocrity, their bourgeois flaccidity—oh, she could be very grand in her haughtiness. Yet she also knew that she stood in the main line of German-Jewish culture, and her dissection of anti-Semitism in *Origins of Totalitarianism* was a piece of high virtuosity. When her report on the Eichmann trial in Jerusalem came out in 1963, it was awaited with anticipation and anxiety. What struck one in reading *Eichmann in Jerusalem*—struck like a blow—was the surging contempt with which she treated almost everyone and everything connected with the trial, the supreme assurance of the intellectual looking down upon those coarse Israelis.

Many of us were still reeling from the delayed impact of the Holocaust. The more we tried to think about it, the less could we make of it. Now we were being told by the brilliant Hannah Arendt that Adolf Eichmann, far from being the "moral monster" the Israeli prosecutor had called him, should really be seen as a tiresome, boring, trivial little fellow, the merest passive cog in the machine of death that had so efficiently shipped the Jews to the gas chambers. This Eichmann, she said, was a cog impelled more by bureaucratic routine than ideological venom. Still more painful, as we read the Arendt book, was her charge that the Jewish Councils, or *Judenräte*, set up by the Nazis in the occupied countries were evidence of how thoroughly the Jews had collaborated in their own destruction. Again one heard a note repeatedly struck in modern thought: the victims blamed for their victimization, the helpless indicted for their helplessness. Said Arendt:

> But the whole truth was that . . . wherever Jews lived, there were recognized Jewish leaders, and these leaders, almost without exception, cooperated in one way or another, for one reason or another, with the Nazis. The whole truth was that if the Jewish people had really been unorganized and leaderless there would have been chaos and plenty of misery but the total number of victims would barely have been between five and six million.

The Eichmann about whom Arendt wrote was the Eichmann on display at the Jerusalem trial. There he seemed—as Simone de Beauvoir had said of the French collaborator Pierre Laval at *his* trial—commonplace and inconsequential, an unimaginative and feeble little fellow. (Hence the well-remembered phrase about "the banality of evil"—the killers, it seems, looked pretty much like you and me.) But even this Eichmann showed astonishing qualities, never breaking under pressure, never begging forgiveness for his crimes. Eichmann had once said, "I would jump into my grave laughing because the fact that I have the death of five million Jews on my conscience gives me extraordinary satisfaction"; Hannah Arendt dismissed this remark as mere "boasting," the big talk of a small man. But, asked Lionel Abel in a powerful reply to Arendt, "How many people have ever boasted of having killed five million people?" That kind of boast was hardly the talk of a featureless cog in a bureaucratic machine! As for the single-mindedness with which Eichmann had pursued the goal of mass extermination, surely some profound depravity of intention or monstrousness of thought had to be at its root. No merely banal creature could have conceived or executed so horrible a crime; some version of "radical evil," far from commonplace, had to be invoked here, and once invoked, it shattered Arendt's view of Eichmann. Far more persuasive was a remark by Saul Bellow that "banality is the adopted disguise of a very powerful will to abolish conscience."

None of this was so troublesome as the question of the Jewish Councils in Nazi-occupied Europe. That really rubbed raw against Jewish nerves. During the Eichmann controversy, I was close to Lionel Abel and we spent hours discussing the questions raised by Arendt. Though no more expert than Arendt herself—soon her book would be shown to contain many factual errors—Abel looked into the available literature on the Holocaust and, as best he could, tried to fight back against her theories. In a strong polemic Abel wrote that in the Ukraine, where there was no Jewish Council to collaborate with the conquerors, the Nazis had nevertheless managed efficiently to destroy more than 500,000 Jews between November 1941 and June 1942; that in some instances the Councils saw themselves as buffers between German barbarism and the helpless victims, enabling the latter to be provided with rations of a sort and perhaps thereby to survive; that similar "collaboration," at times unavoidable, occurred on the part of non-Jewish conquered peoples; that the wretched figures chosen for these Councils were seldom the earlier, elected Jewish spokesmen, but often stray and demoralized people who feared for themselves and their families; that in truth nothing the Jews did or did not do could have made any large difference, so helpless were they before the Nazi conquerors; and that nevertheless there *were* some Jewish revolts, despite the lack of arms, despite starvation, despite the absence of military experience, despite the hatred, even betrayals, of surrounding gentile populations.

The most authoritative words, however, were spoken by the Jewish historian Gershom Scholem in an open letter he wrote to his old friend Hannah Arendt: "Which of us can say today what decisions the elders of the Jews [the Councils]—or whatever we choose to call them—ought to have arrived at in the circumstances. . . . Some among them were swine, others saints. . . . There were among them also many people in no way different from ourselves, who were compelled to make terrible decisions in circumstances that we cannot even begin to reproduce or reconstruct. I do not know whether they were right or wrong. Nor do I presume to judge. I was not there."

Within the New York intellectual world Arendt's book pro-

voked divisions that would never be entirely healed. Mary Mc-
Carthy, Dwight Macdonald, and in a more subdued way Daniel
Bell supported Arendt; Lionel Abel, most vigorously, and I were
among her critics. As it seems to me now, the excesses of speech
and feeling in this controversy had as one cause a sense of guilt
concerning the Jewish tragedy, a guilt pervasive, unmanageable,
yet seldom allowed to reach daylight. There was nevertheless something good in this quarrel. At least everyone was releasing—if not
comprehending—emotions long held down. Nowhere else was
there such an intense concern with the issues raised by Hannah
Arendt. If left to the rest of the American intellectual or academic
world, her book would have been praised as "stimulating" and
everyone would have gone back to sleep. Overwrought and imbal-
anced, we at least cared. To say that one cares can easily become
an excuse for self-indulgence or theatrics, and that did happen in
this dispute—on both sides. But not to care is surely worse.

Nowhere else in the country could there have been the kind of
public forum that *Dissent* then organized in the seedy Hotel Diplo-
mat of midtown Manhattan. Hundreds of people crowded into the
hall where Lionel Abel and Marie Syrkin, a veteran Labor Zionist
writer, spoke against Arendt's thesis, while Raul Hilberg, an
authoritative scholar of the Holocaust, and Daniel Bell spoke more
or less for her. We had asked Hannah herself to come, but she did
not answer our letter. The meeting was hectic, with frequent interruptions: Abel furiously pounded the table; Alfred Kazin inter-
vened nervously at the last moment to defend Arendt; Vladka
Meed, a heroic survivor of the Warsaw ghetto uprising, passionately attacked Arendt's views in Yiddish; and I as chairman
translated rapidly from a Yiddish speech made by a leader of the
Jewish Socialist Bund. Sometimes outrageous, the meeting was also
urgent and afire.

Perhaps the most judicious words in the whole debate were
spoken by a writer not afterward to be known for judiciousness—
Norman Podhoretz. He saw Arendt's book—rightly, I think—as an
instance of that deep impulse among some Jews, especially intellectual ones, to make "inordinate demands . . . [that] Jews be
better than other people . . . braver, wiser, nobler, more dignified.
. . . But the truth is—*must* be—that the Jews under Hitler acted as

men will act when they are set upon by murderers, no better and no worse; the Final Solution reveals nothing about the victims except that they were mortal beings and hopelessly vulnerable in their weakness. . . . The Nazis destroyed a third of the Jewish people. In the name of all that is humane, will the remnant never let up on itself?"

Such controversies are never settled. They die down, simmer, and erupt again. A year after the 1963 debate I ran into Hannah Arendt at a party and stretched out a hand in greeting. With a curt shake of the head and that bold grim smile of hers, she turned on her heel and walked off. It was the most skillful cut I have ever seen or received, and I was wounded quite as keenly as she wanted me to be. Four or five years passed and we began to see each other again, talking gingerly about the Vietnam war and the New Left. Finding at least some agreement, we were still bruised, still wary, still—I like to think—sharing a faint glow of residual affection.

The reconquest of Jewishness became an important project in my life. But what, sentiment and guilt apart, did this imposing phrase mean? I had no aptitude for religion, little taste for nationalism, and rarely a wish to go back to old neighborhoods. People like me were living through a confused experience of self-acceptance, a sinking inward to that part of our being which fate or circumstance had given us. What we were experiencing might be described as an ordeal of the will, or rather a recognition of its limits. We had tried to "make" our lives through acts of decision, "programs" that thwarted the deeper, more intuitive parts of our being. We were now learning to accept the ease that might come from acknowledging and even taking pleasure in ties with a past that, in any case, had become an integral part of our being. Yet I want to add that this gradual process of Jewish self-acceptance, never smooth or straight, was not the mere consequence of having reached one's middle years. There is no ordained rhythm of youthful disaffection followed by mature return, as philistines in the Jewish community like to suppose when passing judgment on intellectuals. Potentialities of self blossom or wither in accord with historical pressures. Had American socialism not reached an impasse in the postwar years, I might have continued to think of myself as a cosmopolitan activist of Jewish origin, rather than a Jewish intellectual with cosmopolitan tastes. Had not the postwar years forced upon reflective men and women of the Left some major reconsiderations, the feelings of Jewishness that were starting to reappear might have remained dormant. These simple if unflattering truths had best be recognized, if only to keep oneself from claiming any credit for having finally acknowledged what it would have been better never to have denied. History was handing out cruel blows, teaching cruel lessons.

The reconquest of Jewishness—more a reconnoiter than a march—had some positive aspects, and one of these was a growth of feeling for the new state of Israel. It didn't happen quickly, or quickly enough; I wasn't one of those who danced in the streets when Ben Gurion made his famous pronouncement that the Jews, like other peoples, now had a state of their own. I did feel an underglow of satisfaction, but my biases kept me from open joy. Old mistakes cling to the mind like pitch to skin, we cherish them as if afraid we may not find new ones. It took some time to realize that being happy about the establishment of Israel—perhaps the most remarkable assertion a martyred people has ever made—didn't necessarily signify a conversion to Zionist ideology. Indeed, the triumph of Zionism in Israel rendered Zionist ideology in the diaspora obsolete. And suppose a little Zionism *did* creep into one's heart?*

There were serious political doubts as well. Long before the "Arab question" became a torment to Israelis, Socialists had insisted that the Arabs were a people also living in Palestine, also attached to its land and memories, also a presence to be considered. Might not the new Jewish state be sowing a future of hatred if it failed to deal courageously with this problem? A minority of Zionists had been acutely troubled by the "Arab question," but in the trials and euphoria of Israel's founding years—and as a reaction to the hostilities of the Arab states—not much was heard about this. A few

---

* One of the irritating features of American Jewish life in the decades after the war would be the prevalence of pieties about Zionism by people who had no intention whatever of buying a one-way ticket to Israel. Either you went or you didn't, and if you didn't, then you could still be a devoted friend of Israel, lobbying, writing checks, doing all sorts of things; but what sense did it make to call yourself a Zionist? The very success of the Zionist project meant there was now little place in the diaspora for Zionist declamations.

American radicals, like a tiny band of Zionist intellectuals in Jerusalem, favored a "binational state" in which Jews and Arabs would live as peaceful partners, but even at the time this seemed an unrealistic notion, since it would simply have packed into one nominal, contrived "entity" the conflicts soon to break out among the nations of the Middle East. But if the Left was dull-spirited in responding to the drama of Jewish resurgence, it was not wrong in saying that the Arab question was real, and that two national communities were locked in a tragic struggle over the land of Palestine that both claimed.

Let me admit another, less impressive reason for my "moderation" of response. In the years after the formation of Israel there swept across American Jewry a wave of simple-hearted nationalist sentiment. It really should not have been so hard to understand this and even sympathize a little. For even to Jews neither simple-hearted nor simple-minded it also seemed that in this era of blood and shame, the rise of the Jewish state was one of the few redeeming events. Still, I overreacted, perhaps because predisposed to overreact, against the public image Israel soon acquired—the image of a sunny paradise with stern pioneers on kibbutzim, rows of young trees, and the best hospitals in the world.

It was ungenerous to take seriously this propaganda of perfection, especially since the imperfect reality of Israel was impressive enough. The Six-Day War probably formed a turning point. Sophisticated intellectual or simple United Jewish Appeal contributor—who could suppress a thrill of gratification that after centuries of helplessness Jews had defeated enemies with the weapons those enemies claimed as their own? That the 1967 victory created terrible new problems, especially with the occupation of the West Bank, was also true. It might have been better, as many Israelis later remarked, if the victory had been less overwhelming. But victory it was, and I relished it.

How much easier my "reconquest of Jewishness" would have been if God, with or without a clap of thunder, had appeared one day to tap me on the shoulder and declare me his own! All uncertainties would have melted away; I would have found a peace no mere intellectuality can ever claim. But I could not melt, I would not yield. Perhaps God does not choose to come until asked.

All through the fifties I watched, at first with hostility but later with bemusement, as intellectual acquaintances tried to find their way back to God, perhaps because they thought that might ease their way back to the Jewish people. For some it became an exercise of intellectual will—a kind of ratiocinative pressing, as with Dostoevsky's Shatov—to undermine their own reluctance. For others it was an emotional journey—the more sincere, the more embarrassed—and the question of God, which for Jews had always entailed a public commitment, was now constrained to privacy, as if too fragile or precious for inspection. A few had an unblocked calling, a true gift of faith—but very few. Once religion had become an option, something to affirm or reject or return to, it could no longer have the force of a fixed imperative, such as it had presumably had in the past. Nor was this judgment a mere sign of stubbornness on the part of one-eyed intellectuals. Just as a forthright secularism was fading among American Jews, so were the temples and synagogues becoming increasingly secularized, in ways that seemed hollow and inauthentic. At least a minority of serious rabbis understood that what seemed their moment of triumph—the return of some who had strayed—might actually be a prelude to inner defeat. The better I came to know the American Jewish community, the clearer it seemed to me that it contained little genuine faith, little serious observance, little searching toward belief. The temples grew in size and there was much busywork and eloquence, but God seldom figured as a dominant presence.

Sophisticated religious thinkers insisted that religion was not an experience open to empirical test, that the old arguments for and against the existence of God were philosophically naive, that faith required a "leap" past the confines of sensory evidence. This had at least the virtue of intellectual economy, putting an end to those tiresome debates between believers and skeptics I remembered from my youth. Now there was nothing to prove or disprove, only "religious experience." You had simply to leap into the unknown, intuit a presence or power that was beyond description and yet, once encountered, utterly decisive.

This view of faith, strong among Protestants but increasingly to be heard among liberal Jews, represented a last-ditch defense. It would have been scorned, I think, when Christianity and Judaism were at the top of their strength. In putting so complete a sanction on the individual's reach toward the unnameable, was not this defense of faith moving oddly to something like the Emersonian notion (one could hardly say doctrine) of the Oversoul, dependent on a religious sensibility grown acute precisely through its longing for the "Missing All"? And if that was the best that sensitive believers could manage in this tormented century, what was to be done with those of us who could not manage a "leap," who had not been blessed with a talent for the numinous? One might still have one's rare moments of sublimity, fragments of surprise in a starry night or when calmly at sea or even dozing over a book. One might shyly near an emotion of transcendence. But surely religious belief came to more than fragile epiphanies, surely it came to a persuasion of strength. One could treat the absence of the religious capacity either in a self-serving or self-depreciatory way: be pleased at not suffering so extreme a state of dependence as to require submergence before a supernatural force, or conclude that one somehow lacked the capacity for faith quite as other people lack sight or hearing. Either way, religion was narrowed down to an "existential" option, with the authority of institutions, rituals, and theologies gravely diminished. That option unavailable, there was little one could do by way of religious affirmation other than to mobilize the will or cultivate promiscuities of myth. But I had no calling or election, and whatever grace might come to me would have to be of this world.

Some Jewish thinkers suggested that the synagogue, never proposing theological tests, had usually found a place for nonbelievers. You participated in chant and ritual and then, it was hoped, discovered faith. The argument was at once sympathetic and shrewd, and it had a certain historical validity as well; but it ignored a crucial factor: in the epoch of "total Judaism" the synagogue had been the only public register of Jewish identity, while today this was no longer true. There were other ways, fragile as these were becoming, to declare oneself a Jew. And there was also an argument from intellectual clarity: it was desirable to maintain a distinction between faith and skepticism, otherwise everything would become muddled in Jewish good-fellowship.

What I was finally left with, as "a partial Jew," was the tradition of secular Jewishness, which, as I turned back to it, was now clearly reaching a point of historical finish. Secular Jewishness, if you were sufficiently hostile to it, could be described as a strategy for keeping in touch with the rejected. Struggling against obscurantism while hoping to keep vibrant the memory of the miraculous from which it had fled, secular Jewishness still held to its line of descent from traditional Judaism. A power of negation affirmed the past. Consciously, secular Jewishness wanted to live in a state of prolonged interregnum, between the denied authority of total faith and the sterile prospects of assimilation. Consciously, it wanted to preserve a Jewish culture derived from the Judaic past yet also apart from it. By now it seemed clear that the odds against this project were overwhelming: if not physically destroyed by totalitarianism, it might be psychologically effaced by democracy. Secular Jewishness had flourished in the conditions prevailing in Poland between the two world wars, and to a lesser extent, in the immigrant quarters of America: a repressiveness sufficient to drive the Jews inward, to their own streets, institutions, and modes of life, yet not so severe as to destroy the possibility of having their own streets, institutions, and modes of life. America encouraged the illusion, at least briefly, that a secular Yiddish culture could be preserved, though the clearest minds among the immigrants, such as Abraham Cahan, realized by about 1910 that such a state of affairs could only be short-lived. Once the subculture of Yiddish was gradually dissolved under the benign pressures of "Americanization" (that "destruction of memories," as the sociologist W. I. Thomas called it), there soon had to follow a permanent crisis, indeed, the permanent crisis that is the true condition—affluence, schools, fund-raising, and temples notwithstanding—of the American Jews. At least for all American Jews except the small minority of the truly religious.

There was a certain irony in moving closer to the secular Yiddish milieu at the very moment it was completing its decline. Another lost cause added to my collection? I wouldn't dismiss this as a motive, thought I wanted to believe that was not the whole story. Or was the relationship—a kind of clinging dissociation—between secular Jewishness and traditional Judaism now being reenacted in my own relationship with secular Jewishness?

To say I felt entirely at home in the milieu of secular Jewishness, the fading world of the once buoyant Yiddishists, would be a deception. How could I, when even its life-long residents saw the roof collapsing, the walls crumbling? It was the *idea* of secular Jewishness, with its asserted marginality, that stirred me—perhaps because it was as close as anything now could be to the world that had given me shape, perhaps because it shone with a twilight beauty of its own, perhaps because it seemed to speak back to me as no other culture quite did.

So I became a friend of Yiddish poets and the dwindling community of Jewish secularists, cast by them in the role of a deplorably pessimistic enthusiast. They would ask me to speak at their gatherings, even though they were angered when I mildly expressed a conviction their world was coming to an end. Perhaps they needed to hear my obvious truths so they could have the bitter pleasure of denying them.

And yet, for me it helped. It helped me get through my time. It made me suppose I was doing something useful in editing English translations of Yiddish literature. I was content to keep what I had, savoring the goodness of the thinning tradition of Yiddish, taking pleasure in friendships with the handful of its survivors. After a time I stopped pretending that this tradition could provide answers to the questions young people asked. What I had—the fragments of a past—was enough for me, and more I could neither take nor give.

Programs, perspectives? I gave up the pretense while trying to understand how these formed part of the sustaining delusions of my Yiddishist friends. When the writer Hillel Halkin sent from Israel a powerful book arguing that the Jews in the West now had only two long-range choices if they wished to remain Jews—religion and Israel, faith and nationhood—I searched for arguments with which to answer him. But finally I gave it up, since it seemed clear that the perspective from which I lived as "a partial Jew" had reached a historical dead end and there, at ease or not, I would have to remain.

Years back Harold Rosenberg had written that in an age when traditional, organic Judaism no longer holds sway, there is validity in the idea of being "a partial Jew." That was what I had become. Rosenberg had tied this precarious state of being to the hold of a tradition, the felt "link with Abraham, Moses, and David, from which the Jewish identity sprung," and which, he continued, kept the Jews together in "a net of memory and expectation." But once that net had been ripped apart, it grew more and more difficult to define, even affirm, one's place at the inner edges of Jewish life. That I was nevertheless there, I had no doubt. Jean-Paul Sartre had written that for Jews authenticity means not to deny what in fact they are. Yes, but it also means not to claim more than one has a right to.

10
The Best
and the Worst

There are moments in history—Gershom Scholem calls them "plastic hours"—when sentiments of hope spread across the globe. People come together, talking of fraternity and betterment. The dead hand of the past will finally be lifted, and once again a journey begun to the shores of light.

In the early sixties we began to enjoy a new atmosphere of liberal openness. The zealotry of the fifties had burned itself out; McCarthyism, for all its damaging consequences, had not proved to be the advance guard of American fascism; fears of a communist victory in Western Europe were abating. The Cold War came to be regarded more as wearisome burden than prelude to apocalypse and this, one hoped, might give dissenters on both sides a little room for maneuver.

If John F. Kennedy did rather little in his brief term as President, his presence enabled others to do more. Though he had none of Franklin D. Roosevelt's talent for mobilizing popular constituencies, Kennedy was admired by the liberal intelligentsia quite as much as Adlai Stevenson had been a few years earlier. To literate Americans, a literate President seems a luxury beyond words. What Kennedy gave us was a glimmer of imagination and style. The glimmer helped. People bored with the flaccidity of the Eisenhower years, students recognizing they could now experiment with new ways of living, blacks looking for some national figure to bless their new militancy—all, you might say, made Kennedy into an emblem of their hopes. And went further than he ever would have.

Freedom Riders fanned across the South, pilgrims of equality. Blacks demanded the simplest of rights, say, the right to sit next to Whitey at a lunch counter. Reporting on a visit to North Carolina colleges, Michael Walzer wrote in 1960 that the black students were not afraid, they were ready to die if necessary—and that meant they were serious. In 1963 A. Philip Randolph, the black labor and socialist leader, organized the enormous March on Washington at which Martin Luther King told of his "dream" of American fraternity. White students, some risking and a few losing their lives, poured into the South to help blacks register and vote. There were heady moments when it began to seem we might really be entering "an era of good feeling."

(A far-off echo: in 1963 a few students and teachers organized a rally at Stanford, the first on that sleepy campus in years, to declare solidarity with the black children bombed in Birmingham. Hundreds came, moved by that belief in "fairness" with which some Americans still grow up. At the rally's end I made a fund appeal for the Birmingham families, drawing upon memories of leftist soapboxers and Fourteenth Street pitchmen, neither exactly familiar to the Stanford imagination.)

The young civil rights movement brought a fresh idea to American society: nonviolent resistance, sometimes shading off into civil disobedience. (Nonviolent resistance need not entail breaking a law, civil disobedience often does.) By declaring themselves at once morally outraged and personally vulnerable, the Southern blacks hoped to elicit shame from the white majority; the strength of their protest depended on invoking values that most whites said they accepted even if they frequently violated them. Nonviolent resistance, wrote Michael Walzer, "is not revolutionary precisely because it is *civil*—that is, it is orderly and public, it involves no conspiracy, it does not require the total renunciation of the established social order." Where resisters broke a law, say, a local Jim Crow ordinance, they were prepared to accept the punishment of the courts. Now, from the retrospect of disillusion, we can recognize how frail the hope for racial reconciliation actually was, and how quickly it would be shattered by the failure of American society to satisfy expectations aroused among the blacks. But the mood of the early sixties was bracing. "Plastic hours" glow.

Intellectuals were stirring themselves, too. In 1960 Paul Goodman published *Growing Up Absurd*, a first-rate book about the distortions of value and the psychic costs that the worship of "success" brought the young. Goodman's was the best kind of utopian thinking, that which rested on close attention to daily life; it helped release the good-tempered activism of the early sixties. David Riesman, who had earlier drifted along with the conservative tide, now sponsored a Council for Correspondence, linking intellectuals who worried about the nuclear impasse. Michael Harrington, a gifted young Socialist, documented in *The Other America* the large stretches of poverty remaining in the United States; there were rumors that President Kennedy himself had looked into and been touched by the book. *Commentary* found itself a new editor, Norman Podhoretz, who steered it sharply toward the left. What America needed, he wrote, was "an unremittant effort to keep a vision of the good society alive. . . . A commitment to such visionary ideals, no matter how utopian they may seem, is the best conceivable safeguard against being taken in by the lies of politicians and ideologues." I read these lines with pleasure.

Since the war a deep change had occurred in both the thought and condition of American intellectuals. When I first came onto the scene in the late forties, it was assumed as a virtual New York patrimony that we were obliged to keep a stance of critical independence at a healthy distance from governments and institutions. By the fifties this idea was being called into question, and those few of us still faithful to the older tradition were elbowed to the outer edges of intellectual life, sometimes even persuaded through sheer repetition that we had become futile, irrelevant, outmoded. (In America nothing is worse than to be outmoded.) The historian Stuart Hughes wrote a wistful speculation that in advanced societies the intellectual vocation was becoming obsolete: state bureaucracies and giant corporations needed specialists who would contribute intellectual or semi-intellectual skills while at the same time surrendering their independence. Perhaps there was no more social space for free-lance critics and radical dreamers.

Now, in the early sixties, a major change was under way, though not, we can see in retrospect, as deep a change as we then supposed. Dozens of books appeared criticizing "conformity," the "Orgman mentality," and so on—stringent about surface failings of American society, timid in social analysis. The Kennedys liked to have a scatter of intellectuals on their premises, it added a touch of color; but whether they paid much attention to Arthur Schlesinger and John Kenneth Galbraith is another question. The intellectual ferment of the moment was lively but superficial, pleasing in spirit but not very penetrating.

Stuart Hampshire, an English philosopher visiting the United States in 1963, noted some uncertainties of thought and posture that were troubling American intellectuals:

Paul Goodman humorously remarks that he is treated by the present American authorities as a jester, and is urged by Washington to keep up his cries of dissent. . . . He is a member of the intelligentsia, and dissent is what the authorities expect from an intelligentsia, just as they expect battle plans from an admiral. . . . From the centers of power the radical intellectual can be viewed with complacency, as an ornament of culture in a free society. He does not threaten property.

It was exactly this diversionary role of a freely speculative and morally concerned intelligentsia which aroused Karl Marx's destructive rages. He understood very clearly why the ruling classes would always feel safe as long as radical thought was kept in these speculative, philosophical, spiritual channels. . . . Reading Mr. Goodman and sometimes also *Dissent* and *Commentary*, the German utopian radicalism of the 1840s seems to have come alive again, with one significant difference: that with most of the American new radicals, concepts derived from clinical psychology have replaced the concepts of Hegelian metaphysics.

Even while acknowledging Hampshire's accuracy, I felt a certain irritation upon first reading his remarks. Did he really suppose he was telling us something new, something we hadn't mulled over endlessly? If there had been a political movement in America with which democratic radicals could align themselves, even one so unglamorous as the British Labour Party, many of us would have been glad to do so. But there wasn't. Reduced as intellectuals were to "mere" criticism, we had been driven back—as Hampshire said —to a position somewhat resembling that of the nineteenth-century utopian Socialists: isolated critics without a social base. Perhaps this was our distinctive American fate, perhaps a condition that would soon prevail throughout advanced industrial society. All we could do was take some small comfort in the remark of Harold Rosenberg that seems to serve as a refrain for this book: "The weapon of criticism is undoubtedly inadequate. Who on that account would choose to surrender it?"

Hopeful as the public mood was, for me these were hard years. Thirty-nine, D. H. Lawrence once said, is a dangerous age. It marks the middle of the journey, raises fears of a decline in strength and potency, signals the end of that animal vigor which is the gift of youth. My "thirty-nine" came at forty-one, when fantasies of a grand metamorphosis, a willed transformation, overwhelmed me. Yet the irony of it all was that my upheavals—the collapse of a marriage, the breakup of a family—should occur at the start of our "plastic hour," as if to thwart hopes for public life and action.

Not from any philosophical curiosity, I started brooding upon the "deep" questions of life: what does it all mean? To get up each morning became an ordeal of the will. Everything I had striven for seemed pointless. *Weltschmerz* returned, a weight on the heart. I grew disdainful of the routine passage of existence, the ordinary exchanges of courtesy and commonplace. In my misery I swelled with pride—pride *in* my misery. I kept squirming in a private eschatology, my own shallow secret of an end to days.

The great American fantasy overtook me: a new life, a second chance! I was no different from all those other Americans, piling anger and anxiety onto the slender frame of "personal relations." In the years after the war "personal relations" had become the religion of sensitive people, the credo of the cultivated. I took this to be an inadequate credo, but could not escape its stamp. And then, once "personal relations" collapsed—as they had to, given the sheer weight imposed on them—all that remained was my grasping, greedy American soul: *I want, I want, I want* . . . another chance.

Only in our talk can private trouble and public disarray be kept distinct. Stumbling in private life, I was soon overcome by doubts about vocation. I could not reconcile my desire to be a writer with remembered fantasies about public action. I had written books just good enough to mark the limits of my talent. I chafed under the crossed frustrations of literary critic and socialist editor:

frustrations of secondary exegesis and unheeded complaint. Problems of the public self fed upon and aggravated intimate troubles. Had there nevertheless been a vital communal life where such problems and troubles might be worked out, it's possible I could have avoided a lot of pain. But there was no vital communal life available to me, and pain and delusion had to be borne alone, quite in the American way.

Whereupon I awoke one morning in Palo Alto, professor at Stanford University, holding a lease on an antiseptic utility apartment in which a bed came popping out of a closet like a furious cork. At last I was free, night and day. Free and miserable.

My two years in California have the makings of a gloomy farce. A kindly English department hoping to staunch my wounds of cultural transplant, though a few skeptics take side bets on how long I will last in the Pacific balm . . . Graduate students curious about this distracted, methodless teacher whose estrangement from all things Californian enables him to achieve moments of sincerity in the classroom . . Disconsolate evenings in Palo Alto: where are the sidewalks, the pedestrians, the taxis, the crowds? . . . A grudging surrender to California nature, the starkness of the coast, the rounded hills of the peninsula, the calming grandeur of the redwoods . . . And beyond this comedy of a cosmopolitan provincial unmoored, accurate perceptions that something about California, softening the mind, makes it finally a second-rate culture, self-satisfied and self-adoring.

After months of idleness, when even my compulsion to work had weakened, I chanced to read Doris Lessing's novel *The Golden Notebook*, and its humorless surrender to obsession brought a kind of relief, the sterility it evoked providing an antibody to my own. I was going at the time to a therapist in San Francisco, who practiced upon me a perilous method of dry mockery. During my first visit, to make sure he would acknowledge my intellectual virtuosity, I remarked that his name in Hebrew means "dog." "You really think," he quickly turned, that "you're the first one to notice that?" A recognition that I had been neatly put in my place eased me toward that objectivity which is as close as most of us come to health. Good work, Dr. Dog! A bit later I came in complaining I felt so bad, I ought to be hospitalized. His compassion untainted by mercy, he asked what had happened to me that week. Well, I had written a little, though badly, and had had an encounter with a woman, not too bad; still . . . He leaped up in a gleam of mimicry: "A little creativity, a little sexuality—my God, who can stand it?" I rose and, seeing his grin, grew white with anger, clenched my fists, prepared to smack him—and broke into laughter. He worked at the edge of peril, this therapeutic tormentor.

Still, to what absurdities of desperation might I have been driven, had I remained in California! Become a dealer in dope? A speed racer? Set up as transcendental guru? Beat poet? Stanford dean? The providence in which I disbelieved again proved merciful: a job offer came from the City University of New York and I scurried back home. If there is a "plastic hour" once in a rare while, you surely don't want to spend it in Palo Alto.

I found a ratty apartment in the West Village, a few doors from a truculent liberal Congressman named Koch. Teaching at Hunter College—no longer a nest for brilliant Jewish girls, but not yet an academic chaos either—I took pleasure in the students, the best of whom still hungered for thought. Girls from Slavic, Polish, Greek, and Ukrainian families were coming to Hunter, and I was often moved by their willingness to work even while shaken by the extent of their ignorance. They seemed without any sustaining culture, the communities from which they came having lost their ties with the Old World while keeping primly aloof from the New. Some of them, children in limbo, opened nervously to the charms of a poem, the force of a novel.

New York literary life had crumbled into success. Not much was left of the acrid intransigence that had lent it a distinctive flavor a few decades before. Plenty of talented people remained, but I could find no sense of shared purpose. It was now everyone for himself, on the lookout for reputation. The tradition of the New, as Harold Rosenberg called cultural modernism, had acquired wrinkles and a paunch, though in two of the arts, painting and ballet, New York could still claim to be a cultural capital.

With an amateur's mute attentiveness, I began to look at the abstract expressionist paintings about which Rosenberg and Clement Greenberg had been writing. There was a strict critical line on these "action painters," and it would have taken nerve to challenge it. Painting was now a spontaneous act, free of image or allegorical shadowing, unmarred by literary alloy, broken at last from the grip of nature. "At a certain moment," wrote Rosenberg, "the canvas began to appear to one American painter after another as an arena in which to act—rather than as a space in which to reproduce, redesign, analyze or 'express' an object, actual or imagined. What was to go on the canvas was not a picture but an event." This idea was elaborated in Rosenberg's essay on Arshile Gorky: "Attempts to 'read' [his] pictures for disclosures concerning the pathos of the flesh or the destiny of man seem ill-advised. . . . Not in his metaphors but in the action of his hand in fastening them within their painting-concept lies the meaning of his work."

Bewildered or entranced, perhaps both, I stood before the swirling lines, the drips of color, the "unreadable" forms of this new painting, and at first Rosenberg's description seemed apt—a radical naming of a radical art, without unseemly haste to judgment. Yet uncertainties persisted. I showed a regressive tendency to do exactly what Rosenberg warned against, that is, to " 'read' . . . for disclosures concerning the pathos of the flesh or the destiny of man"— indeed, for *something* beyond the sheer grapple of paint. And I kept wondering why some of these painters affected me more acutely than others, why Franz Kline's thick black bands worked so keenly on my nerves and Mark Rothko's melting fields of color held an aura of contemplative mystery. I had to confess, but only to myself, that I was indeed "translating" these paintings into unmarked psychic states. If this was "ill-advised," it was also the habit of a culture. Perhaps, too, something in the work of Kline and Rothko solicited my heretical responses, perhaps some touch of the "romantic" or "metaphysical" that other "action painters" had put aside. I did not know. But Rosenberg would sometimes allow deviations from his own precepts, acknowledging for example that Rothko's pictures had "a conclusive insigne of a disembodied absolute."

During the late sixties I came to know Rothko a little, and later, when a retrospective show of his work was held at the Guggenheim Museum, I came across a statement in which he said that "there is no such thing as good painting about nothing . . . the subject is crucial and only that subject-matter is valid which is tragic and timeless." What he meant by "subject" is not very clear, though I suspect he wanted to hint that if his painting was an "act," it was also something more. Meeting him during summers at Cape Cod, I was drawn to this man who seemed to be staggering under some vast burden of Jewish woe but also, I fancied, harbored a strong inner light. Some tremor of kinship—a remembered nod of our grandfathers?—passed between us. It's hard to believe that this artist could ever have been indifferent to "the pathos of the flesh or the destiny of man," in or out of his work.

New York was changing, seldom for the better. The city had lost some of its plebeian easiness, there was a new air of menace hanging over the streets. It was no longer comfortable to go up to the Apollo Theatre on 125th Street for the Saturday night show. It was dangerous to sit, alone or with a woman, in Central Park on summer nights. Appetites of irrational violence were building up, and not much solace or protection was to be had from either one's old habits of liberal tolerance or Norman Mailer's catchy theories about the iconography of hipsterdom.

I no longer loved the city, I only remained hopelessly attached to it. Even its abrasiveness could quicken life: this was the place to start again if you had to. Eudora Welty, as far as anyone could be from the city, had once written: "Location is the crossroads of circumstance, the proving ground of 'What happened? Who's here? Who's coming?' and that is the heart's field." In the discords of this city I could again listen to myself. Even when heartsick, I knew it was my heart's field.

All such questions, all such thoughts were soon to be swept away by a new American politics, a radicalism at first innocent and sweet-tempered. It would not remain either innocent or sweet-tempered for very long, but so, in the early sixties, it seemed.

In 1962 several leading figures from Students for a Democratic Society, then a tiny, obscure organization, paid a visit to the *Dissent* editorial board. I remember among them Paul Potter, Tom Hayden, and Paul Booth, bright and eager young men who would become important in the politics of the sixties. At this meeting two generations sat facing each other, fumbling to reach across the spaces of time. We were scarred, they untouched. We bore marks of "corrosion and distrust," they looked forward to clusterings of fraternity. We had grown skeptical of Marxism, they were still unchained to system. We had pulled ourselves out of an immigrant working class, an experience not likely to induce romantic views about the poor; they, children of warm liberals and cooled radicals, were hoping to find a way into the lives and wisdom of the oppressed. ("I live in Newark among the rats," said Tom Hayden proudly to a fourteen-year-old stepson of mine, who looked up to Hayden with awe, as at a decorated hero.)

Both sides in this encounter favored social criticism, both had no taste for Marxist-Leninist vanguards, both held to a vision of socialism as a society of freedom. It seemed at first as if there might be a joining of two generations of the Left.

The SDS visitors kept using the term "participatory democracy," by which they meant a society in which masses of people wouldn't just vote once every few years but would become active and articulate citizens, thereby endowing the democratic "forms" with popular substance. That seemed fine with us, until they started juxtaposing this envisaged "participatory democracy" with the "representative democracy" in which we lived, as if somehow the two were contraries. We winced. It sounded a little too much like the fecklessness of our youth, when Stalinists and even a few Socialists used to put down "mere" bourgeois democracy. At least as troubling was the readiness of SDS people to excuse the lack of freedom in Cuba, a country that seemed to them the home of a better or more glamorous kind of communism. They, in turn, made quite clear their distaste for our "rigid anticommunism" and our lack of responsiveness to the new moods of the young.

Wise after the event, I now see that we mishandled this meeting badly. Unable to contain our impatience with SDS susceptibility to charismatic dictators like Castro, several *Dissent* people, I among them, went off on long, windy speeches. Might it not have been better to be a little more tactful, a little readier to engage in give-and-take rather than just to pronounce opinions? No doubt; yet a clash was inevitable. We simply could not remain quiet about our deepest and costliest conviction: that if socialism still has any meaning, it must be set strictly apart from all dictatorships, whether by frigid Russians or hot Cubans. There is the value of tact, but also the value of candor.

I liked the evident sincerity of the young SDSers, and still more the gentleness of some of them. As our talk continued, it turned into polemic and it soon became clear that the most brilliant among them was a boy named Tom Hayden. But also the most rigid, perhaps even fanatical. Pinched in manner, holding in some obscure personal rage, he spoke as if he were already an experienced, canny "political"; after the meeting a number of *Dissent*ers remarked spontaneously that in Hayden's clenched style—that air of distance suggesting reserves of power—one could already see the beginnings of a commissar. All through the sixties I kept encountering Hayden, each time impressed by his gifts yet also persuaded that some authoritarian poisons of this century had seeped into the depths of his mind.

The meeting broke up, our relations broke down; but one kept hoping. Something good, an undogmatic native radicalism, might yet blossom in this new student movement. The early SDS statement adopted at Port Huron still strikes me as a fresh exposition of an American democratic radicalism. And equally attractive were the new radicals' sense of style, their feeling for community, their readiness to take risks.

I attended one or two SDS board meetings, sitting through interminable and structureless sessions. Two ideas were being tested here: that decisions be reached not by vote but consensus, and that the role of leaders be kept to a strict minimum. Attractive as these notions were, it soon became clear they had not been thought through. In the blur of fraternity nothing was thought through.

For some of the SDS people the ideal polity seemed to be a community without or beyond rules, an anarchy of pals, in which anyone dropping in at a meeting could speak as long as they wished, whether upon the topic of the moment or not; then, out of this chaos of good feeling, concord would emerge. But to me it all seemed a chaos favoring manipulation by tight sects and grandiose charismatic leaders; the SDS theory of organization did not take enough account of people as they actually are and are likely to remain. To talk out differences endlessly was all very well; but what if the differences persisted, as in the frailty of the human condition they always do? Didn't the SDS procedure put an improper kind of pressure on minorities to give way, so that all might end in public ceremonies of affection and harmony?*

---

* George Orwell writes in his essay about *Gulliver's Travels*: "In a society in which there is no law, and in theory no compulsion, the only arbiter of behavior is public opinion. But public opinion, because of the tremendous urge to con-

Friends who had gone South in organizing drives reported that an attractive "movement" leader named Bob Moses refused on principle to sit up front at meetings: he wished to avoid the arrogant postures of the *apparatchik*. An admirable motive; yet some of us argued that what Moses was doing had an undemocratic potential. There is good reason for putting leaders up front: to position them as targets for criticism.

Still, the SDS was brushing against important matters in its talk about "participatory democracy." The malaise it wished to treat had earlier been designated as the "mass society," one in which populations grow passive and atomized, coherent publics based on clear interests fall apart, and man tends to shrink to a consumer, mass-produced like the products, diversions, and values he takes in. No serious advocate of this theory would have claimed it was more than an alarming possibility, but as popularized by the New Left this view of modern society ("one-dimensional man," in Herbert Marcuse's phrase) tended to treat the cartoon as if it were an actual photograph. The early SDS style—a mixture of student bull session, Quaker meeting, and group therapy—had its uses for young people with lots of time and no pressing need for sleep; but it could seldom contribute to solving problems of democracy in societies where the sheer number of citizens and the complexity of clashing interests require some system of representation.

In 1965, after I had given a lecture in New York, a young writer named Sally Kempton came up and with all good will asked whether I favored representative or participatory democracy. I started to stammer that choosing between the two would be foolish, but suddenly fell into depressed silence. I thought I knew how to cope with error, but innocence left me baffled. Ms. Kempton must have thought me rude.

Suppose the United States had not become so deeply embroiled in the Vietnam war—how might this have affected the New Left? Probably toward a more gradual and harmonious develop-

---

formity in gregarious animals, is less tolerant than any system of law. When human beings are governed by 'thou shalt not,' the individual can practice a certain amount of eccentricity; when they are supposedly governed by 'Love' or 'Reason,' he is under continuous pressure to make him behave and think in exactly the same way as everyone else."

ment. Its growth would have been less rapid, but it might have found a path to a democratic radicalism suitable to the American temper. We will never know, for the Vietnam war soon eclipsed everything else in American life.

If the fifties had been marked by a contagion of repressiveness soon infecting large portions of official society, then the years of the Vietnam war constituted a time of structured deceit. Lying now became a systematic "necessity" of the war—lying about the nature of the regime we were propping up in South Vietnam, lying about the attitudes of the Vietnamese people, lying about the methods used by American troops. For the poisonous atmosphere blanketing the country, the Johnson and Nixon administrations were mainly responsible. They knew the puppet regimes in Saigon neither enjoyed nor merited much support among the Vietnamese. They knew the scare talk about "falling dominoes"—let Vietnam go communist and Malaysia will fall soon, to be followed by Indonesia and India—was at best a speculative notion, at worst a cheap intimidation. They knew that some methods used by government agencies to infiltrate and incite antiwar movements were illegal. No one in power told the truth.

What gave these years a special aura of sleaziness was that the language of liberalism was often employed to justify the war. Rhetoric from the days of the Marshall Plan was reheated for Vietnam. The economic aid to Western Europe after the Second World War had been a major achievement of American policy: it really helped save democratic societies. But no one could argue seriously that helping the corrupt dictatorships of Diem, Ky, and Thieu formed a legitimate continuation of that earlier policy. When liberals like Hubert Humphrey tried to justify the Vietnam war by recalling a strategy that had been beneficial to European freedom, they caused grave damage to American liberalism. Young people outraged by the war tended to identify the liberal idea with liberal politicians, and liberal politicians with American policy in Vietnam; it was impossible to persuade them this was a simplification almost as gross as those of the people in power.

Within the antiwar movement, the simplest opinion was that a victory of Hanoi and the Vietcong would advance the "progressive" cause. Or a shade less simply, that only a leftist authoritarian government could be both radical and ruthless enough to further national independence and capital accumulation in Third World countries. The assumption here—a curse of our age—was that political liberty is a luxury that developing nations can, or must, do without.

A more authentic response was that of people, mostly non-political, who felt morally repelled by the war. The war seemed to them unjust because it constituted an attempt by a great power to impose its will on an oppressed people. This was a strong judgment, but it needed to be buttressed by a political analysis of the struggle in Vietnam. That our side committed atrocities was cause for shame; but could it really be argued that the other side did not? Was there a reliable measure with which to compare magnitudes of atrocity? (Communist atrocities in Indochina reached their culmination only after the war was over.) That nonintervention should be a strong moral principle or disposition is certainly true; but could it be an absolute principle, an unqualified premise in a century that saw the rise of expansive totalitarian states? The moral argument against the war was strongest when it rested on considerations specific to *this* war, and did not merely invoke a generalized pacifist sentiment. But it was an argument that could be secured only through a strong link to political analysis.

As the war dragged on, wearying and depressing everyone, many people, especially in Washington, who cared little about either moral issues or political analysis came to the "pragmatic" conclusion that the cost of continuing it was simply too great. No national interest, they hastened to say, required a victory in Vietnam. Even conservatives, at least those not drugged with ideology, came to see the point.

As for liberal and socialist opponents of the war, by the mid-sixties we had concluded that the most to be hoped for was a negotiated truce enabling American troops to leave Vietnam and delaying somewhat the impending communist victory. That victory now seemed certain, and the more America plunged into the war, the less likely was even an appearance of compromise. We saw the war as partly an inherited colonial struggle, with the United States taking over the imperial role of France; partly a civil war between two orders of society within Vietnam; and partly a reflection of the worldwide conflict between the two superpowers. As early as the mid-fifties it had become clear that the conflict in Vietnam had acquired an all-but-irreversible political character that precluded the Saigon government's winning mass support among the Vietnamese people. The Communists had appropriated the historical energies of Vietnamese nationalism; they were superbly organized; they were ready—and inspired a readiness among their followers— to fight hard and risk death. About few other Vietnamese could this be said.

By, say, 1965 or 1966 there was consequently no real choice but to accept a communist victory or keep the war going endlessly, with terrible consequences both in Vietnam and, in lesser ways, at home. This political judgment lent a sad sort of cogency to the moral argument against the war, since it helped explain why the American intruders, in themselves neither more nor less moral than other people, were often guilty of outrages during their "pacification" campaigns. What they could not do politically, they tried to do through sheer military weight—and of course failed.

It never was necessary to defend the communist regime in Hanoi or the Vietcong guerrillas in order to oppose American intervention. Some of us had hoped during the mid-fifties for the emergence of a Vietnamese "third force," capable of rallying the people through land reform in the countryside and democratization in the cities. This now appears to have been a vain hope: there simply were no political forces strong or coherent enough to move in this direction. Vietnam had been fiercely polarized by the French who, unlike the British in India, allowed almost no freedom for the early Vietnamese nationalists. This, in turn, made it virtually certain that moderate or liberal tendencies among these nationalists would be rendered helpless and that the better-organized, more combative Communists would take over leadership of the nationalist movement.

Working for a measure of freedom in Third World countries does not strike me as futile, even though authoritarians of Left and Right often take a peculiar delight in sneering at the idea. But it is, I admit, difficult. The policies of the United States, usually tilted toward support of old-style autocrats, constitute one major reason for the difficulty. Soon the Vietnam war would settle into a struggle between the totalitarian government of Hanoi, skilled at exploiting nationalist traditions and peasant needs, and the authoritarian government of Saigon, precariously kept in power by foreign money, arms, and troops. Even if one judged the Saigon regime to be a "lesser evil," the reality in Vietnam was that once the civil war began, support to Saigon meant assuring the victory of Hanoi. And so it did.

All through the late sixties antiwar demonstrations were mounting in size and intensity, and for the democratic Left this posed some perplexing choices. We too thought it calloused to prolong the war. We too wanted to demonstrate against it. But we took the trouble to read the materials issued by the organizers of the antiwar demonstrations, and what we saw dismayed us. Always a double standard: harsh criticism of Saigon and either silence about or approval of Hanoi. The tens of thousands who came to these demonstrations paid about as much attention to the manifestoes as most citizens to the platforms of the major parties; but for Socialists to have yielded to this American nonchalance would have been to break with all our training, all our habits.

Segments of the antiwar movement were starting to talk about proposals for forcible resistance: stopping troop trains, blocking induction centers, "storming" the Pentagon. This was mostly talk, but of a kind that could easily become dangerous, inducing delusions of revolutionary coups, providing government provocateurs with opportunities to incite violence, and leading to confrontations with the government that the movement could not win.

Here is Staughton Lynd, one of the cooler New Left leaders, writing about an antiwar demonstration in Washington: "It was unbearably moving to watch the sea of banners move out toward the Capitol. . . . Still more poignant was the perception that . . . our forward movement was irresistibly strong. . . . Nothing could have stopped that crowd from taking possession of its government. Perhaps next time we should keep going, occupying for a time the rooms from which orders came." Under whose mandate, some of us asked Lynd, were the marchers to "occupy" the government? And if "next time" they did manage a coup, even if only for five playful minutes, how did he propose to keep other crowds, other causes, equally moving and sincere, from doing the same "perhaps the time after next"?

A strong case could be made out for conscientious objection and civil disobedience to the war. Many people felt the usual methods of political protest were no longer adequate. But what was not legitimate was to use tactics that looked like civil disobedience yet really constituted "uncivil" and prerevolutionary acts. "Stopping" troop trains—I leave aside the question of whether anyone could— is a basic challenge to the authority of the state, and it makes sense only if undertaken as part of a revolutionary sequence. Otherwise, it must seem ineffectual playacting. The rhetoric of the New Left escalated, and there was plenty of provocation from a government that kept lying about the war. For that very reason it was important that the methods used in opposing the war not give enemies of liberty a plausible excuse for destroying both the protest and democratic procedures. So at least my friends and I argued, though with little success.

We were stuck, those of us who opposed American involvement in Vietnam yet did not favor a communist victory. We had no happy ending to offer. By the mid-sixties, and probably for some time before then, no happy ending was possible. If our protest did not seem quite as single-minded as that of others, it was because we were caught in a trap: we thought it would be good to end the war, but knew that no good was likely to follow in Vietnam. Our opinions, perhaps too shaded to be effective, were swept aside. The tacit or open allies of Hanoi prevailed, their slogans captivating a good many of the young. The truth seems to be that in moments of crisis those who try to speak with some awareness of complexity are likely to be disabled politically. A depressing thought.

In 1963 I became somewhat active in the moderate peace organization called SANE. You could find there the usual assortment of activists, from liberals to fellow travelers, from hard pragmatists to soft pacifists. None of these interested me greatly: I was too well acquainted with them all. What I did find absorbing was a certain type of protester whose response to the Vietnam war was an unqualified personal testimony. Not necessarily radical, often no longer young, and seldom or only by accident close to the New Left, these protesters seemed to me thoroughly in the American grain, moral voices from the nineteenth century bedeviled by the twentieth.

American intervention in Vietnam, they believed, was wrong, even criminal, and on this conviction they rested their testimony. If anyone raised the question of inadvertent or unforeseen consequences of our antiwar activity—a communist victory in Vietnam? a reactionary backlash in the United States?—they responded with irritation, sometimes anger, since it seemed to them that even to consider such possibilities might compromise their opposition to this evil war. Marked by high earnestness and suspicious of any tendency to accommodate—accommodate with enemies in Washington, accommodate with colleagues in SANE—these spiritual children of Thoreau had engaged themselves with issues utterly political, yet ultimately they were not interested in politics. Thoreau in his *Journals* had praised such individualistic men of principle: "They attend no caucus, they make no compromise, they use no policy."

There has always been among us a strong tradition of moral absolutism, setting conscience above community. Emerson urged his listeners "to cast behind you all conformity, and acquaint men at first hand with Deity." The best place for making that acquaintance turned out to be within the self. Thoreau regarded freedom as an absolute, nonsocial state of being, in contrast to the view, necessary to all democratic thought, that freedom is a consequence of regulated arrangements between authority and citizens.

"Any man more right than his neighbors," Thoreau had said, "constitutes a majority of one already." But what if there were many such majorities of one, each persuaded, as of course it always must be, of its rightness? How could conflicts among them, or between them and ordinary mortals, be managed except through the shabby rules of politics?

Now, in the sixties, I was encountering people who spoke with the accents if not the eloquence of Thoreau. They were admirable people and I often admired them. They brought fervor to the antiwar movement, and I was often glad of that. But I did not really like them. It was hard to work with such people: they carried themselves with an air of righteousness not very far from fanaticism.

The anarchist vision in its Thoreau form can always excite our imagination, even if we don't accept it because our primary loyalty is to a democratic order. But in the day-to-day affairs of a group like SANE, I often found myself at odds with the moral absolutists. Tactical adjustments seemed to them the devil's work; alliances of convenience such as American democracy mandates, they took to be a sellout. Too often, they moralized instead of thought. Politics requires more than rectitude; it requires skill, intelligence, compromise, sometimes even a little cunning.

The posture of the moralists kept them from acknowledging the complexities of the Vietnam war, or from facing the grim possibility that, if "our side" in the American debate won, there might be consequences that could leave us deeply unhappy. They cared only for their dualism: it was right against wrong and they knew they were right. I came to feel that so fixed a moralism might entail a touch of selfishness, as if all that matters in life is keeping oneself pure. Yet I knew that in any American insurgency such people were necessary. They were right to warn against the lures of accommodation, the kind of politics that starts and ends with a surrender to politicians. The moment might come, perhaps it already had, when political opposition to the Vietnam war would seem insufficient and we would have no choice but an unbending moral witness. But in the mid-sixties I still thought a large public protest could be mounted to bring about a change of policy in Vietnam, whereas the bearing of moral witness was a last resort to fall back on only when democratic options failed.

Had I thought to look into Max Weber's great essay, "Politics as a Vocation," I might have gained a keener perspective on these moral protesters and my ambivalent feelings about them. Weber distinguishes between those who act from "an ethic of responsibility" and those who act out of "an ethic of ultimate ends." The latter cleave to the maxim, "The Christian does rightly and leaves the results with the Lord." But ordinary people wanting to live by "the ethic of responsibility" know it will not do to leave things with the Lord; too often He seems not to be paying attention. It is we flawed human creatures who must take responsibility for what we do. All human action, suggests Weber, contains a tragic split between reality and desire, fact and value; yet he adds that "an ethic of ultimate ends and an ethic of responsibility are not absolute contrasts but rather supplements, which only in unison constitute a genuine man—a man who *can* have the 'calling of politics.' "

The "genuine man" I already knew: his name was Norman Thomas. Years earlier he had been mostly a public voice, the silver booming of socialist promise, often eloquent, sometimes weary.

Public voices have a way of seeming distant, and even some of Thomas's friends occasionally complained he was too impersonal. But now he was no longer so winning or handsome as in his days of public fame. He was an old man, arthritic, lonely, sardonic, yet selfless to the end—always on call to speak or write, debate or protest. I would drop in at his Nineteenth Street office, a shabby box from which he sent his bulletins and letters as a one-man agency of conscience. Coming to know him more closely, I grew familiar with his stoical passions. I felt overwhelmed, sometimes shamed, by his complete discipline in continuing to do his, perhaps the world's, work. He was still a public man—the style of a lifetime could not be changed—but in my visits I learned to watch for his sudden breaks into candor, his touches of shyness, his fierce impatience with meanness (even more than stupidity), and those moments when he would sadly look back upon what he regarded as a lifetime of failure.

His party was a wreck, but he stood fast. In a style oddly linking the brusque and the gentle, he would dismiss any indulgence in self-pity of the Left such as I, for instance, sometimes yielded to. Bah! there were things to do, people to help, evils to expose, and if you didn't do them as a party leader you did them as a solitary figure. In truth, sometimes it was easier that way (fewer tiresome meetings). Our condition might be hard, but that was no reason to whimper. Yet even as he said these things, Thomas knew our condition *was* hard. He'd ask how *Dissent* was managing, could we pay our bills? By now he had largely exhausted the few financial "angels" still responsive to him, but whenever he snared a new one he'd try to pass him or her along. These encounters with Thomas became precious to me, though I had to get used to his habit of orating (not preaching) even in personal conversation. He couldn't help it: that had been his life. And I was moved, at times, by realizing that the oration was just for me, a personal oration, so to say.

Once, hurrying through an airport, I saw him at a distance, an old man limping, really toddling, off to speak at some meeting. I wanted to run over and say a few words of gratitude for his unspoken decision to see his commitment through to the very end. The words did not come. Nor did it matter, since Thomas had grown tired of "tributes," most of which came from people hurrying to abandon him politically. What he wanted was collaborators, comrades ready to join in the work still to be done.

Max Weber's phrase, "a calling for politics," nicely yokes the religio-moral vocation with the tainted action our world requires. The two were uneasily linked in Thomas's career—not that he brought them into balance or union, because he didn't. Mostly he had failed and he knew it. Now, almost alone, he kept struggling with the warring demands of politics and ethics, responding warmly, sometimes uncritically, I thought, to moral protesters while remaining alert to the chances for realistic action. Part of him still throbbed to cries of intransigence, another part wanted allies and tried to influence men in power. These rival ways of public life tore him apart, and some of Thomas's critics, like Daniel Bell, saw his political failure as rooted in an inability to adjudicate between them. Perhaps so; but I also came to think that Thomas's readiness to live with his inner divisions was a sign of strength.

There wasn't a touch of pontification, rarely a lapse into that self-aggrandizing "wisdom" that makes elderly people tiresome. (At one of his last speeches Thomas limped slowly to the podium, cane in hand, and rasped to the audience, "Creeping socialism!") His socialism now consisted of a loose egalitarian creed, a stubborn refusal to accept the given as immutable. His mind grew more caustic with age. I recall a *Dissent* forum at which Michael Harrington, then still a semiorthodox Marxist, indulged in pieties about "the role of the working class," whereupon Thomas, speaking next, launched a snorting assault on this notion. He liked Harrington and saw him as a successor, but that didn't keep Thomas from lashing out at intellectual sloppiness. And the nice part of the story is that Harrington would remember this incident with a wry sort of affection, knowing that a bit of verbal roughing-up can also be proof of comradeship.

Among those who were turning from him politically it became fashionable to praise Thomas as a kind of saint. He was nothing of the sort. I knew him as something better than a saint—as a troubled, sometimes irascible, but strong and fearless old man. He could be short with fools. He would twist your arm if he wanted something done for a cause. (During a dispute within SANE in which

Thomas and I were on opposite sides, I sometimes evaded his phone calls, knowing how hard it would be to resist his pressures even when I thought him mistaken.) He could be sharp and sour; after a debate with William Buckley he did a very funny imitation of Buckley's drawling superciliousness. He despised snobs.

Here he is, close to the end, as Dwight Macdonald describes him speaking at a rally against the Vietnam war:

So now he is 82 and he has to be helped to the speaker's stand, but once there, in the old, familiar stance, facing the crowd—they are on their feet applauding, calling out to him—he takes a firm grip on the rostrum, throws his head back, and begins to talk in a voice that is quavering. . . . For ten minutes he baits the President, modulating from irony to polemic to indignation to humor to fact to reasoning, speaking in a rapid business-like way without rhetorical effects. . . .

He winds up briskly, professional brio, as how many times, how many times? We get to our feet to clap, to cheer timidly, to smile to one another as members of the same family do when one of them acquits himself well in public. The old man endures the applause politely for a reasonable time, then begins to make his way back to his seat.

Even after he died Thomas remained, so to say, in my head, setting a standard of right action, pointing to the elusive path where the "ethic of ultimate ends" and the "ethic of responsibility" join. When I did something unworthy in politics, it was to his memory I had to answer; when I acquitted myself well, it was his approval I would most have wanted.

Scenes of turbulence, the mid-sixties . . . Professors who the day before yesterday were the milkiest of liberals or disdained politics entirely, now take avidly to revolutionary rhetoric. Students plaster their rooms with photos of Guevara and Castro. "Confrontations" with spongy university administrations become training sessions for revolution. Enthused academics, recharged intellectuals—I call them, uncharitably, "guerrillas with tenure"—keep telling me, "The kids are turning the country around!" Turning it where, to what end?

• A polite young man dressed in elegant jeans challenges my mild defense of trade unions at a meeting on the Ohio State campus. Unions block the path of revolution. Unions give the workers a pittance. Unions induce "false consciousness." Be patient, I tell myself, be patient—you're not effective when you lose your temper. (The angel dispensing patience with the heavenly eyedropper skipped right past me.) I try to explain why small gains can lead to class confidence, and why, in any case, it's inhumane to dismiss the daily needs of workers. Talk to the wall! The polite young man in elegant jeans stares at me with a cool contempt, as if seeing before his eyes a candidate for reeducation on one of Chairman Mao's manure piles.

• An invitation comes for me to speak at a symposium on foreign policy, to be arranged by the Student Council at the University of Kansas. The fee is a whopping $1200. Other invited speakers are Tom Hayden and a Columbia professor of political science named Zbigniew Brzezinski. I ask the Kansas students if they want a formal presentation; one ought, after all, to do some work for $1200. The youthful voice on the phone answers wearily—he can't bear these hang-ups of his elders—that they don't believe in formal presentations, but that if I must, well, no more than five minutes. Five minutes to analyze American foreign policy!

It's an enormous meeting—some fifteen hundred students crowded into a gymnasium, in the middle of which clusters a group of perhaps seventy-five, greeting Hayden with cheers and me, before I can even start my hard-won five minutes, with a volley of boos. I taunt Hayden into talking about the recent Soviet invasion of Czechoslovakia, and he says he isn't prepared to condemn the Russians since there may well be "counterrevolutionaries" among the Czechs. We spar viciously. The audience is mostly with Hayden. Professor Brzezinski, worldly and detached, sits back in evident amusement at the whole spectacle, only occasionally saying a few words, and once leaning over to whisper in my ear that I'm "doing well." Thanks.

• Perhaps the largest mobilization against the war in Washington—thousands of young people sprawled on the lawn, sleeping, hugging, playing catch, enjoying a bit of grass, doing everything but listen to the speeches from the loudspeaker. Awed by the size of the crowd, Stanley Plastrik and I do listen as David Dellinger, a "pacifist" who admires Castro, unleashes his inflamed rhetoric. Suddenly Stanley turns to me, laughing at our incorrigible habits: "In this whole crowd is there anyone but you and I paying attention to what that bastard is saying?"

• It's 1969 and I'm at a "think tank" near Stanford. Each afternoon I drive to the campus to eat lunch with my wife. One day a group of SDS students led by a fellow named Cohen forms a semi-circle behind us, chanting hostile slogans. They mean to carry the battle against decadent liberalism to the heart of the enemy. This continues day after day. Go elsewhere for lunch? My pride won't allow it. So each afternoon we are followed across the campus, objects of a kindergarten confrontation. Then one day I wheel about and shout at the insufferable Cohen: "You know what you're going to end up as?" The question startles him, and before he can resume his chanting I cry out, "You're going to end up as a *dentist!*" Cohen blanches—the insult is simply too dreadful—and I march off in miniature triumph.

Ah, Cohen, wherever you may be, are you really pulling teeth?

• The American Jewish Committee sponsors a conference on "Jewish intellectuals and the New Left." Whether anyone needs this conference is a question, but about twenty-five people show up. The intellectuals, reading from right to left, include Seymour Martin Lipset, Irving Howe, and Paul Goodman. Spokesman for a New Left contingent is an old acquaintance, Paul Jacobs, blessed since the thirties with an insatiable appetite for agitation. He attacks the sponsoring organization as part of the Establishment, wondering out loud whether he and his friends should even deign to talk with its representatives. Rising to the bait (one of my gifts), I answer that Jacobs was not obliged to come unless, of course, he has come simply to announce his departure. A rustle of tension. Paul Goodman, sitting near me, pats my arm and says quietly to Jacobs: "You know, when people come together and sit around a table, the only thing they can do is talk to one another."

• The New Left is not without its victories: it takes power in the Modern Language Association, electing as president Louis Kampf, a teacher at MIT. About a year after Kampf's triumph he and I speak at a professorial forum in Philadelphia, and I quote some of his extraordinary statements: he cannot tolerate Jonathan Swift, who he is sure would not have had him to dinner; the study of Proust at a time when students are liberating campus buildings is an idle luxury; he rejects the "counterrevolutionary acceptance of fate" imbedded in the Western "concept of tragedy." Unfazed by my ridicule, Kampf continues with his amiable version of what in the Soviet Union is called "Zhdanovism"; yet I know Louie, he isn't really a commissar, he wouldn't hurt a fly, he has simply been driven out of his wits by the *Zeitgeist*. I remark that even from a Marxist point of view he is talking nonsense, since the Marxist tradition has always insisted that the heritage of Western culture be made available to masses of people unjustly deprived of its benefits. It's all hopeless, we talk right past each other in what Camus once called "a dialogue of the deaf."

• Encounters with the other side, too. I speak at a symposium with Frank Trager, once a Socialist of the Far Left but now a defender of American policy in Vietnam. The audience consists of Jewish trade unionists, "old Socialists" as they still like to call themselves, worthy people who have done worthy things but are now locked into a single passion: a coarse, monolithic anticommunism. There are plenty of good reasons for being opposed to communism, but these people no longer trouble to make distinctions; they keep talking about "the Commies" and something about that phrase strikes me as marking a collapse of standards, a vulgarity of mind that will soon prompt some of them into alliances with the Far Right. They're not interested in analyses of the Vietnam situation—they're anticommunist and that's enough.

More sophisticated people succumb to the same vulgarity. Here's an old friend, Miltie Sacks, the boy theoretician whom I first encountered when he peddled the *Daily Worker* at Bronx subway stations, then came to know within the anti-Stalinist Left; now, after having become a Brandeis professor specializing in Vietnamese history, he prattles on about "winning Vietnamese hearts and minds," quite as if he were at the very center of the State Department. We argue violently in a shouting match that will surely exhaust me first. Like the old Stalinists who are turning into admirers of William Buckley, Miltie now brings his passion for world revolution to a defense of Lyndon Johnson's policies in Vietnam. What is it about old radicals—it barely matters which kind—that makes them so indifferent to the cautions of liberalism? Why must they oscillate so wildly, now to the left, later to the right? Ah Miltie, so sharp in mind and hot in temper, what a strange journey you have made!

A conversation with George Kateb, a subtle political theorist teaching at Amherst. Himself a liberal, Kateb admits an attraction of sorts to the hijinks of the New Left. "The trouble with your social democratic politics," he says amiably, "is that it's so boring!" I bristle, yet the remark stays in memory. What I think Kateb meant is that, even for a rational mind, there are occasions when the power of the irrational is greater than that of rationality, and that the Fabian gradualism of the social democracy fails to take this into account. Call it liberal, call it social democratic, a politics devoted to incremental reform even while still claiming a utopian vision—how can such a politics satisfy that part of our imagination still hungering for religious exaltation, still drawn to gestures of heroic violence, still open to the temptations of apocalypse?*

Kateb's remark keeps haunting me through the years. Between my political beliefs and the dark reaches of our century there is obviously a gap. I tell myself that the character of our time forms a decisive argument in behalf of a politics avoiding total ultimates, but there is no way for me, or anyone else, not to be affected by those passions of innocent blood that periodically sweep across modern life. Who, looking upon the experience of our century, does not feel surges of nausea, a persuasion that the very course of civilization has gone astray? Who does not sometimes wish to join in the jeremiads against all humanity is and all it has?

But we must not allow ourselves to. No matter how acute our discontents, the civilization that creates them remains precious to us ("states of nature" thrive only in the heads of civilized people). Kateb's remark probably points to a very serious difficulty for socialist or social democratic movements, but if a reformist politics is sometimes "boring"—negotiating for better social security can hardly be as exciting as storming the Winter Palace—the alterna-

---

* Perhaps it was recognition of this fact that led the leadership of the European social democracy in the years just before the First World War to maintain some of the "revolutionary" symbols and language of early Marxism, though their parties had ceased to be revolutionary in any serious respect. Intuitively they grasped that the parties they led were not just political movements but, in some sense, branches of a "church." Their followers needed to believe that the immediate gains won by the social democratic parties and the trade unions were steps toward a complete restructuring of society, indeed, a complete renovation of humanity. No one will sacrifice life for a ten-percent wage increase. Once social democracy lost this belief to the Communists, its appeal to the idealistic and/or desperate young sharply declined.

tive is likely to be murderous. Yielding to the hunger for apocalypse too easily slides into moral suicide.

About the new radicalism of the sixties I found it hard to settle into a dispassionate judgment. I cared too much. I was too close for detachment, too far for engagement. I grew dizzy before the sight of old mistakes renewed. Each day the New Left kept moving away from its earlier spirit of fraternity toward a hard-voiced dogmatism, from the ethic of nonviolence toward a romantic-nihilist fascination with a "politics of the deed." In the years of the Vietnam war the New Left grew rapidly, mostly as a center of opposition, but by locking itself into a politics more and more like that of the old left-wing sects, it made certain that in the end it would do no more than reenact their collapse.

Sometimes the New Left resembled a society for resurrecting The God That Failed. It had never been so foolish as to worship that God, it knew little about his theology, yet it seemed bent upon dredging up the least savory of his dogmas. To see Stalin's theory of "social fascism" refurbished by SDS leaders as a theory of "liberal fascism," played hell with one's nerves. To see the Leninist theory of a "vanguard party" transformed into the New Left strategy of "confrontation politics," made one suspect nothing ever is learned from history. To see the Leninist-Stalinist contempt for liberal values elevated to Herbert Marcuse's haughty formulas about "repressive tolerance"—formulas used to rationalize the break-up of opponents' meetings by some New Left groups—made one despair of any authentic Left in America.*

The authoritarian debauch was soon all-encompassing: ideol-

* Tolerance, wrote Marcuse, "is administered to manipulate and indoctrinate individuals who parrot, as their own, the opinion of their masters." This tolerance proves to be "repressive," since "it protects the already established machinery of discrimination." To be historically authentic, tolerance would have to endanger the established order, even if that might require the use of "apparently undemocratic means." Nor did Marcuse flinch from specifying those means:

They would include the withdrawal of toleration of speech and assembly from groups and movements which protect aggressive policies, armaments, chauvinism, discrimination on the grounds of race and religion, or which oppose the extension of public services, social security, medical care, etc. Moreover, the restoration of freedom of thought may necessitate new and rigid restrictions on teaching and practises in the educational institutions which by their very methods and concepts, serve to enclose the mind within

ogy hates free spaces. "Those who controlled the New Left," wrote a former adherent, Peter Clecak, "tended toward ever more bizarre notions of liberation, until at last the distinction between capitalism and civilization blurred." In the late sixties the strategy of confrontation politics—semiviolent disruptions and clashes with police, choreographed to feed the mass media's hunger for sensation— found intellectual support in Herbert Marcuse's thought: we live in an advanced capitalism that provides bread, circuses, and technology; this has tamed the opposition and thereby undercut hopes for "transcendence" (the workers seem in no hurry to make a revolution). Since all efforts at reform are inherently superficial and the prospects for revolution dim, the only recourse, suggested Marcuse, is a series of raids or adventures, perhaps to usurp, perhaps to unsettle established power. Society might yet be shaken through such attacks by the neglected poor, the alienated hippies, the oppressed blacks, the rebellious students. The aim was to "polarize" the population—in plain English, to shock a minority of liberals into radicalism while demoralizing and neutralizing the rest.

Young people assigned themselves tasks of assault and sacrifice, sometimes for a semester, sometimes for the whole of their lives. That the New Left had no support in the American working class; that it had not tried to elect a half dozen representatives to Congress; that most Americans, for reasons good and bad, detested it—such calculations were simply dismissed as signs of liberal timidity. After the 1968 sit-ins at Columbia, Tom Hayden advanced a concept of power: "Columbia opened a new tactical stage in the resistance . . . from the overnight occupation of buildings to permanent occupation; from mill-in to the creation of revolutionary committees; from symbolic civil disobedience to barricaded resistance."

Some years later such statements must seem delusionary, yet Hayden was by no means a fool. What then was really going on in

---

the established universe of discourse and behavior—thereby precluding a priori a rational evaluation of alternatives.

Since such "withdrawal of tolerance" would seem to be required for a majority of the American people, there was a logic of sorts in Marcuse's frank admission that he favored "an educational dictatorship." Has anyone ever proposed another kind?

his head and in the heads of thousands like him? How could New Left leaders drift into such self-defeating absurdities? One reason, I suspect, is that the New Left was so utterly American. It took to the arts of publicity like Tom Sawyer to games of deceit, offering the mass media the verbal, sometimes actual violence on which it dotes. Bayard Rustin talking sense about the relations between blacks and potential allies is too rational, too dry for the seven o'clock news. Rap Brown scowling that "violence is as American as cherry pie" —that's the ticket! And each triumph of publicity chipped away at the slender remains of good sense.

Another reason for New Left delusions is that radicalism in America had suffered a rupture of continuity during the forties and fifties. Young people of the New Left showed little interest in learning from the experiences (mostly mistakes) of earlier leftist generations. When I sat down in 1968 to write a few paragraphs about the way talk of "liberal fascism" repeated the stupidities of "social fascism," I realized I had first to explain what Stalin's theory had been and how greatly it had damaged prospects for resisting Hitlerism.

A deeper reason for the turn to confrontation politics was the guilt-ridden submissiveness that white student leaders felt toward the rapidly changing black movements. SNCC was abandoning its creed of nonviolence; the Black Panthers were talking very tough, with bloody results for themselves and sometimes the police; new black leaders—cool adventurers like Stokely Carmichael, sullen desperadoes like Rap Brown—were winning the allegiance of militant black youth.

Perhaps the most impressive of the new black leaders was Malcolm X, in the eyes of rapt intellectuals an American equivalent to Frantz Fanon, the black writer in Algeria whose book *Wretched of the Earth* proposed a therapy of violence to burn out the inferiority complex of colonial peoples. I heard Malcolm X speak in 1965 at a Trotskyist rally and found him at once powerful and repellent. He spoke with a bitter sarcasm that offered blacks the relief of finally releasing hatred, contempt, defiance. He said he would go to Mississippi, not unarmed, if the blacks there asked him to come—a promise that could only leave him safely up North, since the last thing Mississippi blacks needed was military guidance from Malcolm X. Never did he descend to details of alliance, maneuver, compromise. His verbal intransigence, so thrilling to the audience of white Trotskyists and black nationalists, masked a nihilism of thought, and the two together—intransigence and nihilism—gave his speeches their alienating forcefulness. Malcolm X's rhetoric, soon leading to the slogan of "Black Power," touched a segment of young blacks deeply. It also moved some whites to feelings of exhilarating guilt, which they took to be a first step toward a "radicalizing" of thought. If the boldest of the blacks were now talking revolution, surely their white brothers could not lag far behind.

Finally, the Vietnam war must account in good measure for the disastrous turn of the New Left. The country was being ripped apart by the war; atrocities committed by American troops could not be tolerated morally or stopped politically; sentiments of desperation drove young people to hurl themselves against the prevailing deceit. Sacrifice and turmoil might yet bring a vast eruption, or at least prepare an American cadre for the moment when the Third World would rise to destroy the decadent West.

No wonder most New Leftists refused to support Eugene McCarthy when he started to campaign in 1968 for the Democratic Presidential nomination on a platform opposing the war.* I thought their response a blunder, though by then it was too late to argue. The McCarthy campaign provided me with my first chance for wholehearted electoral work since my undistinguished soapboxing for Norman Thomas. It was a pleasure to speak, write, even raise money. Once McCarthy lost the nomination, however, he seemed permanently to lose his bearings; he went into a prolonged sulk, abandoning his seat in the Senate as well as the thousands who had rallied behind him and who, had he persisted, might have formed the basis for a renewed liberalism. Some disastrous streak of cultural snobbism or intellectual perversity overtook this very intelligent man. The several times I met McCarthy I was impressed by his charm and lively mind, but whatever it is that goes to make a political leader—strength of will, self-assurance, sheer hard work—

---

* "Tom Hayden began to discuss revolution with Norman Mailer. 'I'm for [Robert] Kennedy,' said Mailer, 'because I'm not sure I want a revolution. Some of those kids are awfully dumb.' Hayden the Revolutionary said a vote for George Wallace would further his objective more than a vote for RFK." (*Village Voice*, May 30, 1968)

he didn't have. Still, in 1968 his campaign led one to hope that we could bring the war to an end through action within the democratic process. Most New Leftists rejected this view as naive or worse; they were by now beyond such "liberal illusions." The sectarian disasters of American radicalism are apparently fated to repeat themselves again and again, generation after generation.

Tragedy, farce, brutal fantasy, delusionary pathos—all came together in the concluding phase of the New Left. It is merciful to be brief. One SDS faction turned to Maoism, another, the Weathermen, to terrorism, as if to reenact on American soil the Nechayevan madness Dostoevsky had captured in *The Possessed*. Here is Mark Rudd speaking at Columbia: "I've got myself a gun—has everyone here got a gun? *Any*one? No? W-e-ll, you'd better fuckin' get your shit together." When members of the two SDS factions met, said Rudd, "We sometimes beat them up and they beat us up. What we usually do is beat them up when we find them." (*New York Times*, Sept. 26, 1969)

The pathology engulfing Weathermen politics emerged with classical finish in a speech by its leader, Bernardine Dohrn:

Dohrn characterized violent, militant response in the streets as "armed struggle" against imperialism. "We're about being a fighting force alongside the blacks, but a lot of us are still honkies and we're still scared of fighting. We have to get into armed struggle."

Part of armed struggle, as Dorhn . . . laid it down, is terrorism. Political assassination—openly joked about by some Weathermen—and literally any kind of violence that is considered antisocial were put forward as legitimate forms of armed struggle. . . .

"Honkies are going to be afraid of us," Dohrn insisted. She went on to tell . . . about Charles Manson, accused leader of the gang which allegedly murdered a movie star and several others. . . .

"Dig, first they killed those pigs, then they ate dinner in the same room with them, and they even shoved a fork into a victim's stomach. Wild!" said Bernardine Dohrn. (*The Guardian*, Jan. 10, 1970)

Allied to this "theory" was the "praxis" of West Eleventh Street in New York City, where several young Weathermen destroyed themselves trying to manufacture bombs (in an elegant townhouse—no Newark rats there!). That only a small minority of the New Left went along with this madness, is true. Yet there was some connection between the rhetoric increasingly employed by the New Left and the sordid dénouement of Weathermen terrorism. Only six or seven years had passed since that little meeting between the *Dissent* group and the early SDS leaders, but it felt like decades. What still remained of the hope for "participatory democracy"? Of any hope?

In the late sixties I felt politically beleaguered, intellectually isolated. I kept throwing myself into conflicts with New Left spokesmen, but with very little profit or success. Why didn't I simply pull away and wait for time to sort things out? Whatever common ground there had once been for debate was steadily shrinking, and after a while political encounters took on a predictably ritualistic character. Yet something within me—sentimentality, conscience, stubbornness—kept murmuring that I had an obligation to speak. And I felt genuine sadness at seeing the early idealism of the New Leftist youth turn sour.

Part of what had gone wrong with the New Left seemed an extreme instance of what had always been wrong with American radicalism. Their mistakes were not new; some I had participated in a few decades earlier. The trap in which I found myself was this: if the New Left registered victories I couldn't share in them, but when it suffered defeats I would probably have to bear at least some of the consequences. True, with the passage of time there occurred a growing dissociation, and for the fascistic Weathermen I felt nothing but hostility. Yet there were still a number of young New Leftists sparked by a genuine idealism, and they stirred in me painfully mixed and thwarted feelings.

There was something peculiarly wounding in the New Left attacks on older liberals and radicals. I felt that some of its spokesmen wanted not just to refute my opinions—that would have been entirely proper—but also to erase, to eliminate, to "smash" people like me. They wanted to deny our past, annul our history, wipe out our integrity, and not as people mistaken or even pusillanimous but as people who were "finished," "used up." (Lenin in 1907 explained his attacks on the Socialists: "That tone . . . is not designed to convince but to break ranks, not to correct a mistake of the opponent but to annihilate him, to wipe him off the face of the earth.") When New Left students painted the slogan "Up against the wall, motherfuckers!" on campus buildings, they had in mind not just the corporate state or the Pentagon or the CIA; they had in mind the only "enemy" they knew at first hand, their liberal and socialist teachers; they had in mind parents of the New Deal generation who had raised them on the deplorable doctrine of "repressive tolerance."

But before someone else does, I had better put to myself the question: wasn't all this a case of unrequited love? Hadn't middle-aged Socialists like you set for yourselves the role of mentor to the young, and weren't you now reeling from blows of rejection?

Yes; I see no reason to deny that this is part of the truth. We had, after all, been waiting a long time, almost as long as Beckett's pair for Godot. If all we had wanted was the admiration of the young, we could easily have chosen the paths Marcuse and Chomsky took, and for a while Paul Goodman. We need only have said, at some expense to our convictions, what the New Left wanted to hear. Goodman had been a guru to the Berkeley students, though in 1969, as soon as he published an essay criticizing his disciples, they thrust him aside with contempt, another "used-up" intellectual.

Perhaps I should not have gotten so emotionally entangled in disputes with the New Left. But I did. Perhaps I should have eased my way into the paternalism that some intellectuals adopted. But I could not. I overreacted, becoming at times harsh and strident. I told myself that I was one of the few people who took the New Left seriously enough to keep arguing with it. Cold comfort.

Friends began to hint in the kindliest way that I was becoming a little punch-drunk. I found myself wondering why Michael Harrington, who expressed criticisms of the New Left close to mine, was not regarded as so dastardly an opponent. The generous-hearted Harrington was a Christian of sorts, while I was a polemicist in the old style. So, in a conversation painful to both of us, Michael Walzer gently told me. Couldn't I make my criticisms more temperate? Someone should, I could not.

The truth is that the "kids," as the phrase goes, "got to me." I might score in polemic, but they scored in life.

Among intellectuals there was a rush to celebrate a radicalism of gesture—the "herd of independent minds" was turning about-face. Hard-won defenses of skepticism fell; critical faculties were suspended. The *Zeitgeist* triumphed quite as decisively as in the conservative fifties, and we were treated to an "instant radicalism" among literary people who had never before troubled to entertain a political thought.

Susan Sontag pronounced America to be "a doomed country" with "the most brutal system of slavery in modern times," and still more remarkably, "the white race [to be] the cancer of human history." Robert Lowell contributed prestige and sincerity to demonstrations shaped politically by leftist authoritarians like David Dellinger—a carelessness Lowell would never have condoned in literary matters. Mary McCarthy, after a short visit to Hanoi, wrote a book notable for its amiability toward the Vietnamese communist leaders. Leonard Bernstein arranged a chic reception at his home for Black Panthers. Norman Mailer, locating self-realization in acts or fantasies of violence, provided a foundation for at least part of the "counterculture." Philip Rahv praised the New Left as "a school for politics." The *New York Review of Books* printed on its cover a diagram explaining how to make a Molotov cocktail, in case, apparently, its readers in English departments were preparing to become urban guerrillas.

Some intellectuals were swept away by their outrage over the Vietnam war. A few were excited by the rekindling of old Marxist sentiments they had supposed would never again be put to use. While I felt little admiration for these people, I could at least understand what made them behave as they did. The intellectuals who infuriated me were those who kept their heads sufficiently to scorn the ideological vagaries of the late sixties and yet, from a wish to stay on good terms with the spirit of the times, assumed an avuncular benevolence toward the New Left.

Personal relations grew strained in such an atmosphere. I had been friendly with Norman Mailer since the late forties, and even after he came to regard *Dissent* as fuddy-dud conservative, he kept his name on our masthead. Once a year, in Provincetown during the summer, we would go out to dinner, and he would always wear a jacket for these diplomatic occasions, perhaps as a good-natured jab at my "squareness," perhaps as a sign of affection for his "bourgeois-socialist" cousin. He had a certain gallantry that made you like him regardless of what he said; he wouldn't hit someone who was down, and in those years we of *Dissent* were down. I also suspected that within the noisy public Norman there was a reflective private Norman, who kept a skeptical eye on the former's recklessness of speech and wondered whether there might be a speck of truth in the cautions of his liberal and socialist friends.

With Philip Rahv I had another kind of entanglement. Suddenly and, as it seemed to me, out of nowhere, Rahv in 1968 printed a harsh political attack on Michael Harrington and me. It was as if the previous two decades—with all Rahv's silences, retreats, hesitations—had never happened. Presenting himself as a veteran Marxist and praising the SDS decision not to "exhibit or stress anti-Communism," Rahv dismissed Harrington and me as mere Social Democrats: "Howe's attempt to set up anti-Communism as the supreme test of political rectitude on the left strikes me as a terrible blunder. It leads him to ill-timed thrusts at the militant New Leftists. . . . Presumably a democratic socialist, Howe puts such illimitable emphasis on the adjective 'democratic' that in consequence his 'socialism' appears wide of the mark."

Had I been wise, I would have sent Rahv a postcard with his favorite tag "*Who needs it?*" and kept quiet. I was not wise. I wrote a reply in the *New York Review*, arguing that his softening of opposition to communism was a betrayal of principle. I also, it must be confessed, needled him personally: "After nearly twenty years of painful circumspection, appears Philip Rahv offering . . . Little Lessons in Leninism. A delicious spectacle for the theatre of the absurd: Rip Van Winkle wakes up and fancies himself at the Smolny Institute."* These remarks were not meant to be kind: they provoked Rahv to a strong reply again declaring the bankruptcy of liberalism and social democracy. So things remained between us. We exchanged a few gingerly letters but never saw each other again.

I have since tried to think through what really happened: was this just another intellectual brawl, worth five minutes of attention, or was there, at least for me, something notable about it? What troubled me was not so much that Rahv had decked himself out in a vanguardist costume, as if a veteran of 1917; it was the feeling that this old friend was being personally disloyal. Even if all he said about me was true, *he* was not the one to say it. Now this appeal to personal relations would have been regarded in many advanced

---

* The Smolny Institute was the headquarters of the Bolshevik Revolution in 1917.

circles as an archaic sentiment, having more to do with E. M. Forster than Chairman Mao. Very little in the political and intellectual traditions that Rahv and I shared had prepared me to feel at ease with such a sentiment or prepared him to give it serious consideration. But that was the way I felt, and still do.

Behind or beneath such bickerings a vast mutation of culture seemed to have begun. No one could fully understand it.

For more than one hundred and fifty years there has been a line of Western thought, as also of sentiment in modern literature, which calls into question not one or another moral commandment or regulation, but the very idea of commandment and regulation; which insists that the ethic of control, like the ethic of work, should be regarded as spurious, a token of a centuries-long heritage of repression. . . .

Now, even those of us raised on the premise of revolt against received values . . . did not—I suppose it had better be said outright—imagine ourselves to be exempt from the irksome necessity of regulation, even if we had managed to escape the reach of the commandments. Neither primitive Christians nor romantic naifs, we did not suppose we could entrust ourselves to the beneficence of nature, or the signals of our bodies, as a sufficient guide to conduct. . . .

By contrast, the emerging new sensibility rests on a vision of innocence: an innocence through a refusal of our and perhaps any other culture. . . . This is a vision of life beyond good and evil, not because these experiences . . . have been confronted or transcended, but because the categories by which we try to designate them have been dismissed. There is no need to taste the apple; the apple brings health to those who know how to bite it; and look more closely, there is no apple at all, it exists only in your sickened imagination. (From my 1968 essay, "The New York Intellectuals")

About one thing all thoughtful people agreed: that the upheavals of the sixties, international in scope, were more than just political in character. Some writers concluded that they represented significant breaks in our culture, deep fissures in our civilization. Those of us who wrote about a crisis of civilization were probably exaggerating, and soon the immediate symptoms of this crisis faded away; but I think that in one or another form both the crisis and the symptoms are likely to recur. For we were witnessing the birth of a "new sensibility" and, approve or abominate, it was decidedly more than just a fashion of the moment.

The new sensibility posits a theory that might be called the psychology of unobstructed need: men should satisfy those needs which are theirs, organic to their bodies and psyches, and to do this they now must learn to discard or destroy all those obstructions, mostly the result of cultural neurosis, which keep them from satisfying their needs. This does not mean that the moral life is denied; it only means that in the moral economy costs need not be entered as a significant item. In the current vocabulary, it becomes a matter of everyone doing "his own thing," and once all of us are allowed to do "his own thing," a prospect of easing harmony unfolds. Sexuality is the ground of being, and vital sexuality the assurance of the moral life.

. . . [But] one is troubled by the following problem: what if the needs and impulses of human beings clash, as they seem to do, and what if the transfer of energies from sexuality to sociality does not proceed with the anticipated abundance and smoothness? The new sensibility . . . falls back upon a curious analogue to laissez-faire economics, Adam Smith's invisible hand, by means of which innumerable units in conflict with one another achieve a resultant of cooperation. Is there, however, much reason to suppose that this will prove more satisfactory in the economy of moral conduct than it has in the morality of economic relations? (Ibid.)

The German social democratic theorist Richard Lowenthal and the American anarchist writer Paul Goodman both published major essays in 1969 trying to place the New Left. Perhaps remembering Marx's famous remark that historical events repeat themselves, "the first time as tragedy, the second as farce," Lowenthal saw the New Left as a misshapen but significant byblow of traditional radicalism, a result of "the disintegration of the Marxist-Leninist doctrinal synthesis." That disintegration had led to a gap in political life and now there emerged a half-educated intelligentsia marked by "a dissociation of revolutionary passion and action from the Marxist belief in the rationality of history. . . . New Left movements have come increasingly to reject the link between the progress of industrialization, the growth of the working class, and the utopian goal [socialism]. Instead they are looking for support to the peoples of the underdeveloped 'countryside of the world' whose revolutionary ardor has not yet been dampened by material comfort."

Nor was the New Left alone in this search for fresh sources of revolutionary energy. Almost everyone on the left, but the Marxist remnants especially, was fervently on the hunt for a "substitute proletariat"—some agency that might yet undertake the historical mission assigned to the workers by Marxism. Some turned to the blacks, some to Asian and African peasantries, some to the intelligentsia, some to lesbians and gays and—in the last, mad days of the Weathermen—even high school students. Revolution was ripped out of historical context, becoming a mere function of sacrifice and daring, all now dependent on the will of a self-chosen vanguard.

If Lowenthal placed the New Left in the setting of twentieth-century historical expectation and failure, Goodman minimized the political claims of the New Left, seeing it as part of a larger impulse in our culture to break away from Western rationality. "Dissident young people are saying that science is anti-life, it is a Calvinist obsession, it has been a weapon of white Europe to sub-jugate colored races, and scientific technology has manifestly become diabolical." In talking to young radicals Goodman came to realize, he said, that "they did not really believe there was a nature to things. Somehow all functions could be reduced to interpersonal relations and power. . . . There was no knowledge, but only the sociology of knowledge. . . . To be required to learn something was a trap by which the young were put down and coopted. Then I knew that I could not get through to them."

Nor could I. My own encounters with the insurgent young led me to credit Goodman's view that many of those drawn to New Left politics were really trying to satisfy formless religious hungers. Goodman remarked, "The extraordinary rock festivals at Bethel and on the Isle of Wight are evidently pilgrimages. Joan Baez, one of the hierophants, ecstatically described Bethel to me, and the gist of it was that people were nice to one another. A small group passing a joint of marijuana often behaves like a Quaker meeting waiting for the spirit. . . . In the end it is religion that constitutes the strength of this generation."

Perhaps so; but if religion was the strength of this generation, it was ill equipped to use it. A yearning for religious experience dissociated from organic tradition, secure institutions, and disciplined belief could too easily waste itself upon antinomian zeal and discounted novelties. Trying to satisfy religious needs through radical politics represented a confusion of realms damaging to both. It is not really possible for everything to be everything else.

The sixties were political to the very marrow, and no serious person could avoid the noise, the heat, the dirt, the excitement of polemic. Still, part of me resisted. I continued to see politics as a central human activity, yet I had learned that it can drain the spirit and thicken the mind. Lenin had demanded that his followers give "the whole of their lives" to politics, something possible only for those intoxicated with ideology. For me there was no movement to which full allegiance could be yielded, and if I regretted this intellectually, I made peace with my regrets once I looked around at the movements that were flourishing. I was settling into an ambivalence toward politics that would remain with me to the end—an ambivalence perhaps rooted in any democratic persuasion. I wanted, in Isaiah Berlin's terms, to be a fox, but a fox who upon need could pass for a hedgehog.

There were things in life other than politics. There were stretches of the commonplace, the flow of hours that men and women give to work, domesticity, pleasure, talk. Whatever evaded positions, categories, statements gleamed with a new attractiveness. Perhaps I would even discover a therapeutic benefit in the boredom I usually associated with ordinariness, but that far I hadn't yet gone.

I kept teaching. At the Graduate Center of the City University of New York there were students who cared to read Jane Austen and Henry James, even during the nerve-racking days of the American invasion of Cambodia. I kept writing. Across two summers at Cape Cod I completed a small book on Thomas Hardy, and in those benign months Tess and Jude, Sue Bridehead and Michael Henchard were utterly real to me, while Dean Rusk and Herbert Marcuse seemed mere apparitions of the *Zeitgeist*. Literature regained brought a purification through detachment. Cape Cod became my pastoral, and its pines and sand a restorative of sanity.

I knew what I wanted from my friends. I wanted instances of that poise which enables a writer to engage with the passions of the moment yet keep a distancing skepticism. I wanted examples of the ability to keep two, perhaps three, ideas in mind at the same time. I wanted people who might show me how to pull back a little from my obsessions. These aids and teachings I found in a friendship with the American historian Richard Hofstadter. By ordinary judgments, ours was not an intimate friendship: we never exchanged private fantasies, or rated our wives, or vented upon each other overflows of despair. Nor did our friendship rest on political concord. I thought he had veered too far toward a conservative brand of liberalism, and he thought my polemics with the New Left showed I hadn't yet freed myself from youthful delusions. It hardly mattered. Ideas, says George Eliot, form a poor cement for friendship. The one between Dick Hofstadter and me rested in a shared affection for the life of ideas, which is rather different from being captive to a particular set of them.

Dick Hofstadter became for me a model of what the scholar-intellectual ought to be, and I tried to learn from him. The way to learn was to be near him. He would have said he was neither quite a scholar nor an intellectual, only a historian with a developed taste for prose. He worked hard and wanted to write good books, but he was wonderfully free of that grating aggression which is so frequently declared the spring of American success. Modest and humane, but above all without the need to impose himself that seems a special curse of intellectuals, Dick Hofstadter set an example that might yield a moral education. There was profit even in his silence.

Giving off a mild glow of charm and sanity, he had reached a security of being I could only envy. How, I used to wonder, could someone so quiet and unassertive wield so large an influence on everyone who came near him? What I was wondering about was the mystery of goodness which, the bias of our culture notwithstanding, is finally a greater mystery than that of evil.

This question haunted me, and there was profit in staying with it. I decided that Dick was by nature a gentleman—a category of culture not deeply rooted in American life. But why not? How would our moral rectitude or radical politics be threatened by the idea of a gentleman? Dick was our Mr. Knightley, though far less stiff in opinion and manner than Jane Austen's figure. (You could hardly imagine Mr. Knightley making high comedy out of a Ping-Pong game with the children of his friends.) A gentleman by nature, Dick seemed largely free of the obsessions I had come to suppose intrinsic to intellectual life. He had no interest in casting himself in the historical roles that stirred the fantasies of intellectuals. Think of the repertoire: one wanting to be Eliot, another Trotsky, a third Valéry, a fourth Matthew Arnold, and a fifth a mixture of Emerson, Reich, and Genet. But Dick had no taste for an identity that comes out of dramas of reenactment.

I cannot say that knowing him improved my character or changed my ideas. What it did was to ease my judgments and perceptions, opening me to ranges of feeling I had previously not allowed myself. Perhaps it made me a little bit gentler. I suppose I'm trying to evoke a quality that can be called liberalism of spirit, a quality that seemed intrinsic to Dick Hofstadter even though I knew that with him, as with everyone else, it had to be learned.

This quality figured more self-consciously with Lionel Trilling, as standard or perhaps as program. Trilling strove—think only of his essays on Keats and Austen—imaginatively to encompass extreme states of being that in his own moderate life he might never encounter directly. If he found something attractive in the heroic strivings of writers as diverse as Keats and Isaac Babel, he was also drawn, a little bashfully, to the relaxed passivity that is evoked by Jane Austen. And if the "liberal imagination"—that shadowy ghost of his mind, at once cherished and chastised—did not manage to connect with these extreme visions of life, then it would surely slump into mediocrity.

In the fifties Trilling and I had had a falling out over politics. Now, silently accepting that our disagreements persisted, we began to see each other again. It was a hesitant friendship. There was hardly any point in rehearsing political disagreements, for in these years politics had become too rigid and predictable, everyone knew everyone else's "position." As for Trilling himself, he seemed depressed by the inability of liberalism to muster any strength at a time when that "polarization" of opinion favored by both Far Right and Far Left was becoming a reality. It was a relief to talk for an hour or two about other things. We would test unexpected kinships of taste, proceeding quickly to that half-formed sentence which comes from the heart of one's feelings. On the surface this was mere literary talk, but actually we were engaged in fathomings of value, self-consciously but with humor, too. I used to think that in these conversations there were four of us: he, I, and the two of us watching.

That each of us should independently have become passionate admirers of *Kim* was a topic of playful talk—playful, as it were, about the literature of play. We were being attracted, each in his own way, to the idea of a literature of ease and pleasure, for me the equivalent of those paintings of Vuillard and Bonnard I had come to love. There would be less moral critique, fewer worked-over texts. We had both written, again in different ways, about our uneasiness with the heritage of cultural modernism, and envisioned an art of moral ease and sensual candor that would move beyond but not repudiate modernism. I now suspect that this was really a utopian notion, impossible to our century, but perhaps that was what made for the intensity of our desire.

Our conversations had a characteristic rhythm of hesitation, thrust, and retreat. "Why is it," I once asked, "that among the intellectuals we know, friendships seem to thrive between women but seldom between men?" A quick tilt of his thick eyebrows, expressive at once of reserve and recognition: "That bothers you? I've wondered about it for a long time, but wasn't sure anyone else had. Really, we must talk about this." And then, as if to reinforce the point of my question, we never did.

Other friendships were older and closer, but in the late sixties it was these two men, Hofstadter and Trilling, who left a strong imprint on my consciousness, though as far as I can tell they didn't especially influence my thought. Of course this sounds like a simplification, since anyone leaving an imprint on consciousness must influence thought. There were some younger "leftist" literary people who looked glumly at these friendships, especially the one with Trilling, seeing them as evidence that my radicalism was waning, I was being subverted by the subtle charms of these liberals. The idea of either of these two men subverting anyone is wildly comic, though each certainly exerted cultural power—Hofstadter casually, and Trilling with a keen awareness of his authority. In any case, I had to go where my deepest impulses led me, and that was toward a liberalizing of radicalism. But what mattered most for me in the presence of Hofstadter and Trilling was the sense of ease and grace they radiated. From them I learned about a life of the mind that can keep some distance from competitiveness and clamor. I still believed there is an urgent need for public struggle, which means often enough a life of clamor. But I also felt that somehow, if I could, I would like to share in that liberalism of spirit which these two men embodied.

> I take it for granted that The Movement is dead. . . . Some of my friends have become cultists: as isolated as the sectarians who preceded us on the left. . . . Some work in the cities . . . hoping to find a "constituency" that their efforts will either serve or move. More, as time passes, go back to work, or take up training for professional careers their political involvement delayed. . . A few are underground, institutionalized, or dead.
>
> —Eleanor Langer, a New Left activist, writing in 1973

One day there was a movement able to rally hundreds of thousands of people for demonstrations in Washington; the next day, a squabble of sects picking at their own bones. The decline of the New Left, when it occurred in the late sixties, seemed astonishingly rapid, like the sudden end of a summer storm.

Few of the New Left leaders stopped to ask what had gone wrong. First, there came from them assurances of quick recovery, then efforts to blame governmental repression, and finally promises of eventual recovery. Still later, they scattered to other interests. Tom Hayden, having denounced Harrington and me for presenting the Democratic Party as an arena in which radicals could function, entered the Democratic Party because it was an arena in which radicals could function. As for other celebrities of the New Left, Rennie Davis joined a spiritualist cult, Jerry Rubin clowned his way to Wall Street, Todd Gitlin wrote thoughtfully about old mistakes, and others dropped out of sight. The response of many New Leftist leaders to the collapse of their movement was quintessentially American: don't look back, start up again, behave as if nothing had ever gone wrong.

There were of course explanations for the sudden breakup of the New Left. It had been consumed by a factionalism so extreme as to make old Marxists look like Trappist monks. It had been a one-issue movement, and when antiwar protest no longer seemed urgent, many people dropped away. It had been cut up by government provocations and repressions. All these explanations had some validity, but I want to propose still another.

In 1969 I was speaking about the New Left at Wayne State University. A student, obviously serious and not at all hostile, rose to ask: "Do you *really* mean you don't expect a revolution in the United States in the next two or three years? You really mean that?" Yes, that was exactly what I meant. He shook his head, more in disbelief than anger, puzzled at my blindness to the assured course of history.

There were thousands like him. Some were caught up in a fever of expectation, others granted themselves a private skepticism even as they yielded to the fever, and still others expected not a revolution but cataclysm, perhaps native fascism, that once and for all would bring down the rickety frame of liberal democracy. Did they really believe such things? Well, "believe" is a tricky word: one can believe and disbelieve at the same time, one can be swept away by emotions of a multitude while inwardly tormented by doubt.

By the late sixties the most passionately self-deluded segments of the New Left had whipped themselves into a fury so exalted they could no longer subsist on the nourishments of daily life. Some inner momentum—call it vision, call it madness—drove them along an upward curve of excess. And then they shattered themselves on the peak of their strength. Like Sabbatians counting the end of days, like Bolsheviks in 1920 awaiting the revolution in Europe, the extremists of the New Left—and by now it was hard to find any other kind—could see nothing but images of their own projection. Yes, factionalism had made things hard and government repression had been damaging; but finally the New Left burned itself out in the ecstasy of its own delusions.

For the third time in our century, a radical movement in America had come close to being a major force. Then, in a twinkling, it vanished. People with New Left convictions would remain, but not the movement. This extraordinary rise and fall seemed to follow a recurrent rhythm of American radicalism. There is a gathering of energies, a fusing of discontent. A movement springs up, buoyed by evangelical expectations. An encounter follows with American politics—its corruptions, its recalcitrance, its opportunism—and then a profound lapse into despair. For what is to be done with a movement neither attuned to gradualism nor equipped for revolution? Splits follow—they must.

The waste of energies that could have gone into working for social change! The painful repetition of the errors of Debsian socialism and the inanities of American Stalinism—posturings of rectitude, fantasies of violence, a complete incapacity to attend the pulse of American experience!

The question that haunts me is whether the rhythm of utopian enthusiasm followed by sectarian crackup is "built into" the very nature of American radicalism. Is this really our fate? Two great historical pressures are at work here: that of nineteenth-century America and that of twentieth-century Europe, the first a quasi-religious fervor disdaining the petty affairs of politics in the name of a total transformation of consciousness, and the second a hard-spirited ideology prepared to destroy freedom in the name of a total transformation of society. Is it possible, then, to create a radical movement both politically realistic and morally firm, devoted to the needs of the moment yet bringing to bear a larger vision of the good society?

Looking back at the history of the American Left, I am not overwhelmed with hope. The sixties speak mostly about the spillage of idealism, the draining of energy. "The waste," says William Empson in one of his poems, "the waste remains and kills."

11
Fragments of
a Decade

Try to retrieve the seventies and memories crumble in one's hand, nothing keeps its shape. I can summon a roster of Presidents and politicians, recall hours spent watching the Watergate hearings on television, patch together a sequence of public events. But the decade itself lacks a distinctive historical flavor. It's as if the years had simply dropped out of one's life and all that remains are bits and pieces of recollection.

In the early seventies I began to meet a new generation of militant feminists, and naturally there followed conversations, disputes, sometimes anger. I came to expect that sooner or later these ardent young women would half jokingly—which often meant, quite seriously—spring the question, "So who does the dishes in *your* house?" I knew the answer perfectly well, yet for some exasperating reason could never quite cope with the question.

By that point in our dialogue I would already have indicated my agreement with most of the immediate objectives of the feminist movement. But also, my reservations about the ideologues of "radical feminism," the extremist wing that was then especially articulate and influential. Matriarchy in primitive societies was not a topic to set my blood pulsing, and theories favoring the abolition of the family struck me as feckless. So we would grind to an impasse, whereupon the young feminist would often switch from speculations about matriarchy to inquiries about the dishes. Could I reply, what was indeed true, that I was a tested veteran of soapsuds and Brillo? Not really. For while the question bore a strong personal charge, it did not invite a mere factual answer. Yet I didn't think it a silly question. It came from a deep sense of hurt, touching intimate relationships while also invoking persuasions of inequity almost transhistorical in scope. And the intention behind the question was clear: to test my authenticity as a man claiming friendliness to the women's movement. The test wasn't a very good one, since many male chauvinists have also plunged their elbows into soapy water. Good faith required that I take the question symbolically even when it was being put literally, and perhaps that explains my hesitations in answering.

By the early seventies it was becoming clear that this new movement would be both significant and enduring. Its appeals were comprehensive, and the issues of justice it raised seemed so cogent that to evade them was a mark of dishonor. But I also thought the women's movement flawed, an opinion that won me few friends.

One reason women started speaking out was that the welfare state enabled new styles of complaint. Previously quiescent or ill-organized groups now felt "entitled," and thereby free to express their grievances. But there was also a more immediate reason, the partial continuity between the disintegrated New Left and the newly confident feminists. Angry young women were learning that the discrimination they had recently suffered among radicals wasn't very different from what they experienced in the outer world. This link with the New Left had distinct advantages: it gave the feminist movement energy and brought a number of experienced activists into the ranks. But it also lowered upon the movement a heavy weight of ideology. Insurgent groups, at least when starting up, seem to need comprehensive world views that enable their followers to believe they are in rhythm with the inner course of history. That belief can excite the ranks for a while, but it also exacts a price in moral righteousness and intellectual rigidity. In the early seventies there were people who might have greeted the new feminism warmly, but who were put off by the ideological writings of Kate Millett and Shulamith Firestone, popular advocates of a radical feminism that propounded an implacable and seemingly interminable war between the sexes.

Some leaders within the feminist movement understood that if it was to become a major force in American politics, it would have to focus on such concrete problems as equal pay for equal work, the right to legal abortions, day-care centers, and so forth. These were demands that could be won short of revolution or an equally improbable transformation of human character. Yet it was my strong impression in those years that for the more ardent feminists such proposals seemed pedestrian, even boring—quite as for earlier generations of Marxists anything short of the "seizure of power" was trivial.

In their deepest feelings these young feminists seemed most engaged with ideology, with a multitude of theories anthropological, historical, and metaphysical regarding the place of women in both the mists of prehistory and the glare of utopia. Was male supremacy really an inexorable presence throughout the course of civilization? Might there be primitive societies offering instances of matriarchy that form exceptions to the grim prevalence of male power? Was the domination of the male inherent in the family structure, and if so, ought we not to be courageous enough to consider proposals for an end to the family? But what could an end to the family mean? Would not such thinking leave the movement at a dead end, since most American women had no desire to abolish the family, indeed, could hardly imagine what that might signify?

It wasn't hard to understand why intellectual women would find it more stimulating to discuss such questions than to start campaigning for equal pay. Many feminists were professional and middle-class women whose grievances, while real enough, were not merely or even primarily material. The questions exciting these sophisticated women were, however, difficult to formulate precisely —that was what made the questions interesting—and still more difficult to answer in a dispassionate, scholarly way. Adding to the problems of this early feminism was the fact that a good many of the feminist writers often took unbending ideological positions:

they felt, for example, that to concede that differences in behavior between the sexes might have a biological source was to make inadmissible concessions to sexism. Whoever at this point spoke with accents of certainty, brushing aside doubt and nuance, was the most likely to gain a hearing.

Difficulties that had torn apart the student and black movements reappeared among the feminists. One problem they had to confront was deeply interesting and of a kind that had often beset American radical movements: their largest possibilities for success lay in a patient engagement with immediate issues such as could gain the backing of many women not in the feminist ranks, whereas the energies of their most active members were often directed toward something quite different—a vision of sweeping transformations of the human condition.

For the younger feminists there was still another area of concern. The life of private feelings, the terms of marital relation, the chores of the kitchen, the habits of the bedroom—in short, how people managed their lives together—agitated them deeply. As well it might, at a time when few certainties of value and style were evident. Such ardent young women turned to the looming themes of ideology with a hope that, somehow, these might yield answers to the dilemmas of personal life. They were neither the first nor the last to do this.

But then a perplexing question had to be asked: could you have a movement oriented toward public issues that also tried to transform radically the intimacies of personal life? What equality meant in the work place was reasonably clear; but what it might mean in the relations—familial, romantic, sexual—of men and women was decidedly less clear. You could agitate for the right to legal abortion, but could you set up a campaign for those subtle and profound transformations of conduct that women wanted both among themselves and in their dealings with men? Sensing this difficulty, the feminist movement shrewdly organized "consciousness-raising" groups to provide women with that collective reinforcement which might enable them to restructure their lives. But alas, it was not that easy. An enormous gap between the reinforcement and the restructuring soon showed itself, even in the experience of women who sincerely joined the consciousness-raising groups.

So the movement kept experiencing difficulties in aligning its planes of concern: how to cope simultaneously with ideological discussion, political issues, and personal problems. Lines of understanding were often crossed. When a young feminist shifted abruptly from matriarchy to the dishes, I might find it bewildering, since to me the connection between the two wasn't self-evident; but to her there was a powerful logic in moving from the one to the other, since she felt that ideology, public policy, and private responses were all closely related.

In those early days, it had better be acknowledged, there was a good deal of playacting. Bright middle-class women took up the cry of writers like Kate Millett that throughout history women had been "vassals" and "chattels." But who, encountering these lively, self-assured young women, could suppose them to be anything of the sort? Protest movements in our country seem often to require historical costumes. They must claim for themselves humiliations borrowed from other cultures, other continents; they must dress up in the rags of an adversity not genuinely their own, if only to persuade themselves that their suffering is real. Their suffering *is* real, and they do not need those rags.

It was as if there could be no escape from the worn historical melodrama called "looking for a substitute proletariat." Just as white students from affluent homes had absurdly described themselves as the "niggers of the university," so women with college degrees spoke about themselves as a class eternally oppressed—"chattels," wrote Kate Millett in her best-selling book, "who in exchange [for] domestic service and [sexual] consortium" put themselves up for "barter" or sale to the ruling masculine class. Students had legitimate complaints and women suffered from serious discrimination, but the former weren't "niggers" and the latter were seldom "chattels." I wanted sometimes to find a nice rooftop and cry out, "There is no substitute proletariat!"

When Kate Millett wrote that "sexual domination [is] perhaps the most pervasive ideology of our culture and provides the most fundamental concept of power," it bore the musty smell of that "vulgar Marxism" which reduces a multitude of social phenomena to a single "base." Who could believe she was describing the actuality of our lives? That a woman laboring in the Midland mines some decades ago could be regarded as at all the same sort of "sexual object" as the bourgeois ladies of Matisse's Paris? Or that the American pioneer woman or the Jewish immigrant mother was, to quote Millett again, "customarily deprived of any but the most trivial sources of dignity and respect"? Didn't social class play at least as crucial a part as gender in determining the destiny of women? Couldn't one find humane feelings and even loving companionship in the marital relations of many Americans? And why were the radical feminists so determined to undervalue everything in the life of women that required unmediated personal involvement, while placing so high a premium on impersonal success in the world of commerce, much of it meaningless and some debasing?*

Far more bothersome than one or another point of disagreement was a certain hardness of tone in the utopian assertions of the radical feminist writers, an all-too-American contempt for the life of the past, for everything men and women of earlier generations had painfully managed, or failed, to do. It was as if history had started yesterday and nothing before then was worthy; as if no one had thought to aspire to personal freedom and sexual equality before 1968; as if the struggles and even compromises of our parents and grandparents were simply tokens of "sexism" and "false consciousness." It was hard to trust a future constructed by those who knew so little about the past.

Once polemic was exhausted, the fact remained that feminists spoke for genuine grievances. Anyone who had spent some time in American universities had to know there was persistent discrimination against women—sly, paternalistic, even good-natured, but discrimination nonetheless. Anyone who had spent time in left-wing movements had to know that even there, despite the rhetoric of equality, sexual condescension was frequent.

What persuaded, indeed, shook me into recognizing the new significance of feminism was not so much its formal statements or ideological constructs, but the depth of anger many women now felt free to release. You simply had to pay attention to this. If you

---

* An intricate dialogue followed here between the sexes. Men wearied by the "rat race" of American business would react with irony to the eagerness some feminists showed for plunging into that "rat race." But such men were in danger of repeating a mistake high-minded liberals made in the sixties when they looked down their noses at blacks striving for material success. The rewards of American commerce may well be illusory, but no one wishing to reach for them ought to suffer discrimination. Besides, it's notably easier to scoff at "materialism" when you have a cozy bank account than when you're not sure you can pay next month's bills.

cared to, you could find uncharitable explanations: these women didn't want to take on the irksome responsibilities of being mothers, they were using slogans of protest to propel a shrewd bourgeois advancement, they were in rebellion against their own natures. (And men were not? Isn't it a premise of civilization that we rebel against our natures?) What finally mattered was the strength and genuineness of the feelings women were now displaying—a crucial testimony. Women were sick of the type-casting to which they had been confined. They were bored and irritated by the condescension, the avuncular petting that had often been their "privilege." They wanted not just to gossip about children and clothes while men discussed politics; they wanted also to make for themselves a life of initiative and decision. They wanted, as they said, their "full humanity."

Well, that was rather a problem since few men had "full humanity" either, and surely more than just sexism blocked its attainment. The social injustices and debasing values that stood in the way of "full humanity" operated in our society quite as harshly, if also somewhat differently, for men as for women. I think the feminists sometimes fell into a melodrama of gender, hoping through relatively blunt public action to remove difficulties of private life that were subtle and perhaps intractable. Their movement didn't quite yield a comely anticipation of "full humanity." Yet justice was on their side.

So we had good reason to respond warmly to the turmoil of debate set in motion by the movement. Strategically, it made a lot of trouble for itself by linking public and private experience; but morally this was a genuine strength, since the movement demanded from its adherents that their conduct have at least some relation to their vision.

I had to notice within myself habits of condescension that women had no doubt noticed long before but were only now combative enough to criticize. When this happened to me, I didn't like it. I wasn't prepared to admit that in my pure heart—socialist heart of hearts!—there could be so much as a grain of sexual bias. But of course there was. I remember conversations among intellectuals and academic men about women colleagues: "Why is it that when you start a discussion with women they will stand up [man to man?] for their opinions, but when pressed, fall back upon their charms and wiles?" That women sometimes did behave in this fashion, is true. But what the men smugly making such remarks failed to consider was the confusion of standards, the severe cross-pressures to which even the most intellectually secure women have been subject.

All of us have "regressive" tendencies. Part of me is moved by that vision of feminine beneficence Virginia Woolf drew in Mrs. Ramsey, a radiant figure of caring and response. We can hardly expect young feminists to model themselves on Mrs. Ramsey, though it would be a pity if they simply dismissed her. In a world where all of us will have reached our "full humanity," perhaps there will also be a place for Mrs. Ramsey.

The condition of women, I suspect, has more inherent difficulties than most feminists like to acknowledge. The more grandiose feminist visions may turn out to be blocked by barriers of nature that no cultural transformation is likely to remove.* I don't know, and neither does anyone else. But this margin of doubt is surely no reason for not moving toward a fundamental change in the status of women. A greater candor and transparency in the relations between the sexes; an end to prejudice and condescension; a fairer division of social and familial burdens; and someday our "full humanity," I hope with elements of the humanity we have already achieved—such goals we ought to set and try together. Two cheers, then, for liberation: I say two because no public movement quite merits three.

Going to the ballet seemed at first a diversion, as good for tired writers as Matisse said painting should be for tired businessmen. But soon I started caring for ballet as an art and came to think that being witness to Balanchine's gift was one of the privi-

---

* Witness Marianne Moore: ". . . experience attests/that men have power/and sometimes one is made to feel it." And Elizabeth Hardwick: "No comradely socialist legislation on women's behalf could accomplish a millionth of what a bit more muscle tissue, gratuitously offered by nature, might do. . . . Any woman who has ever had her wrist twisted by a man recognizes a fact of nature as humbling as a cyclone to a frail tree branch. How can *anything* be more important than this?"

leges of our time. That an elegant lift or heroic leap could be exciting, hardly explained the flood of pleasure ballet brought me. Friends teased that I had succumbed to an "aristocratic" art, but remembering Big Bill Haywood's apothegm that nothing is too good for the proletariat, I would reply that a Socialist addicted to the ballet was simply claiming a rightful heritage.

I chose to remain an amateur spectator. Once, in 1971, I did write a piece about attending the ballet, which showed that my resistance to knowledge of technique had been entirely successful. But the piece didn't claim to be criticism, it was just a report on how an enthusiast yields to a complex art.

When I first started going to the ballet I was shaken by the skills of virtuosity: the brilliance of a jump, the precision of a turn, the silken flow of a woman dancer, say, Violette Verdy, raised in the air and then smoothly lowered. When someone like Edward Villela began to race across the stage, an almost primitive excitement filled the hall. Ballet must finally consist of more than such display, but it rarely proceeds very far without an abundant virtuosity, the sheer power of the body to do astonishing things. Yet anyone with my cultural background was likely to feel some uneasiness about these feats of virtuosity. A grown man surrendering to gymnastic capers?

I sometimes found old Tolstoy sitting next to me as together we watch Suzanne Farrell and Peter Martins in *Chaconne*. He turns to me, old Tolstoy, ablaze with anger: "Is this what you have come to, you who were at least a serious man, even though completely mistaken in your opinions? What is the ethical import of all this elegant prancing? How does it affect our convictions about the relation between man and God?" I try to parry, but of course he sees through my devices. Again he speaks angrily: "Fellows like you, peacock intellectuals, honor me no end, prattling about my genius; but there is one possibility you will never consider—that I may be right in what I am saying."

That makes me pale: have you ever tried arguing with Tolstoy? All I reply is that there are kinds of beauty before which the moral imagination ought to withdraw, and that in my lifetime these kinds of beauty have been served well by Balanchine.

I liked best those of his ballets that had neither narrative overlay nor symbolic reference, but were devoted simply to configurations of movement. I came to think of ballet as an art in which the controlled execution of bravura plays a special role, an art embodying a direct sensuous appeal through strength and grace. I read the critic Edwin Denby and was delighted by his mild suggestion that ordinary viewers ignore technique and relax into enjoyment. Nor was this quite so routine a piece of advice as you might suppose, for these days we place an enormous value on *talking* about culture. For me, however, the "civilized happiness" Denby said a Balanchine performance could bring was quite enough.

Had Balanchine, I sometimes wondered, read the sentence in the Preface to the *Lyrical Ballads* where Wordsworth speaks of "the grand elementary principle of pleasure" as constituting "the naked and native dignity of man"? Did Balanchine ever come across the sentence in Matisse's *Notes of a Painter* favoring "an art of balance, of purity and serenity devoid of troubling or depressing subject matter, an art which might be for the mental worker, be he businessman or writer, like an appeasing influence, like a mental soother"?

Still, that old devil of "meaning" cannot be kept down so easily and there are times when I return to Tolstoy, nudging me in the next seat about the frivolity of it all. My head goes out to him, partly, and ultimately I might want to be in accord with him. Yet I am determined not to let myself be intimidated by the old bear. There is a time for prayer and a time for chatter, a time for talking and a time for watching. At Lincoln Center it was a time to watch.

The day my father died I felt almost nothing. I stood near the hospital bed and stared at the shrunken body of this man who never again would greet me with an ironic rebuke. I saw nothing but inert flesh, a transformation beyond understanding. Then came a sequence of absurd tasks—notifying my father's *landsmanshaft* (fraternal society) to arrange for a grave; deciding whether to buy the more expensive coffin, ornately carved, or the bare wooden coffin that my father would have chosen, sullenly, while preferring the expensive one. These rituals which, honor them or not, I had to get through, served at least to blunt grief.

Even before my father died I had made him into a myth.

Myths are wonderfully convenient for blocking the passage between yourself and your feelings. Now into his mid-eighties, my father steadily grew feebler and complained, even whined, a good deal—I judged this to be a "weakness," partly out of fear that I shared it with him. To see your father lose masculine force is an experience profoundly unnerving, like watching your own body disintegrate. To see him fall because he could no longer walk, was unbearable, and then I would berate myself for the cowardice that kept me from bearing it. Had my father become senile it might have been easier. But his mind grew keener as his body decayed, and he would describe his plight with a self-pitying exactitude.

What did he want from me? To move in with him, yielding entirely to his needs? No, he said, he didn't want that at all. He wanted nothing from me, there was nothing I could do for him, his complaint was not directed to me or indeed to anyone. He sat there in his apartment in Co-Op City, staring at the walls but still—I knew him as I knew myself—fearful of death. Had my father used my kind of language, he would have said all this is simply in the nature of things and there is nothing to do but submit. Submit, yes, but not without some noise.

When I took him to the hospital, he still had enough strength to argue against my proposal that we hire a private nurse. He didn't need one. And what could a nurse do, make him young again? His eyes glinted as he said this, waiting to see if I would record his last stab at paternal irony.

Oh, the unmeasurable willfulness of these immigrant Jews, exerted to their last moment in the service of self-denial! My father had saved, literally from years of sweat, some forty thousand dollars, but that had to be kept . . . for what? He didn't say, but didn't have to. I understood: *the night cometh when no man can work.* The last dike against helplessness is a bankbook.

So he was right again, my sardonic Pop, as so often he had been about my ways, my women, my life. I hired a private nurse and, to no one's surprise, my father accepted her without protest. His obligation had been to argue against hiring her, mine to hire her. It was my turn to pay. He had never before allowed it, but now it was all right—no, it was right.

I did my duty. I ran up to Co-Op City in the northeast Bronx, to Montefiore Hospital in the northwest Bronx. I did all a son is supposed to do, but without generosity, without grace. It would take me three hours to get to and from the hospital, but in the hospital itself I could not bear to stay more than twenty minutes. I spoke to the doctors, scheduled the nurses, brought my father food, and all the while could not look at his wasted body, for I knew myself to be unworthy, a son with a chilled heart.

I could not speak words of love because I did not love my father as a man. I had discovered, long ago, that he was "weak," too dependent on women—an affliction that seems to run in our family. Yet I was overwhelmed with emotion at the thought of his decades of suffering and endurance. Even while still breathing he had become for me a representative figure of the world from which I came, and I suppose a good part of *World of Our Fathers* is no more than an extension of what I knew about him.

Close to the end he told my son that finally I had been a good son. He did not say a loving son. Was there a difference in his mind? Could I doubt his gift for discriminations? Whereas he, perhaps not such a good father, had been a loving one, always ready, after his opening sarcasm, to accept my foolishness and chaos. The words he spoke in praising me, which I knew to be deeply ambiguous, finally brought the tears long blocked by my hateful addiction to judgment.

I knew the end was close when one day I came to his room and saw he no longer troubled to cover his genitals. Like most immigrant Jews, he had been a severely respectable man, shy about his body, even wearing a tie and jacket in the August heat. Now it no longer mattered. I could pay for the nurse, he could leave himself exposed.

In death he seemed terribly small, and I kept thinking back to all those years he had spent over the press iron, the weariness, the blisters, the fears, the subways. In the space that circumstances had thrown up between us there still remained a glimmer of understanding, a tie of the sardonic. To make a myth of the man I should have mourned as a father, to cast him at the center of the only story I had to tell, was to reach a kind of peace between generations.

Andy Warhol said that everyone in America is famous for fifteen minutes. My fifteen came in 1977 when *World of Our Fa-*

thers, to the surprise of both me and my publisher, reached the best-seller list for some weeks. I had published a good many books before then—some, I think, good ones—but the income from all together would not have equaled a year's modest salary. Now I was making some money, appearing uneasily on talk shows, and being interviewed in newspapers. It would be pious to claim that the money made no difference, even though I had lived for years with the sacred persuasion that the poor sale of my books was a sign of virtue.

Some of the talk shows were dreadful, humiliating. Brassy young women who had not read a line in any book since junior high school ("I don't know too much [*that is, anything*] about your subject, Mr. Howe, so could you give us a two-minute summary?"), and not-so-young men bored to distraction by the thought that anyone could have the gall to write still another book: these left me feeling used, foolish, soiled. A TV encounter with Edwin Newman eased my shame, for he prepared himself diligently, asked keen questions, and made me think that perhaps—just perhaps—TV was not entirely hopeless.

It was pleasant to anticipate royalties that could yield more than a spaghetti dinner for two. The money mattered because I had just seen my father die and come to realize how important it is to end one's life with a minimum of squalor—an expensive undertaking in our society. But I can't say the money brought me much pleasure. It came too late, long after habits were formed and denials ingrained. Marks of youthful poverty, as Chekhov and Fitzgerald both knew, lie forever imprinted on one's soul. The ease of being that seems a privilege of inherited wealth is not to be acquired in middle age.

Once while I was sitting in a restaurant with a relative, a complete stranger came over and asked for an autograph. It never happened again, and that startled relative may well suspect the incident was staged for her benefit. Sitting down in a restaurant I am again simply a stoop-shouldered man with a bald spot. The fifteen minutes are over.

But the success of my book: what could that mean? That a good many people, most of them probably Jewish, hurried out to buy it could be explained, I suspect, not by any authentic desire to "find their roots" (they hardly had to wait for me, if that was what they wanted), but by a readiness to say farewell in a last fond gesture. *World of Our Fathers* enabled them to cast an affectionate backward glance at the world of their fathers before turning their backs upon it forever and moving on, as they had to, to a world their fathers would neither have accepted nor understood. My book was not a beginning, it was still another step to the end.

"We cancel our experience"—this astonishing line from a late Clifford Odets play could stand as an epigraph to the life of culture in America. Racing nervously from decade to decade and from doctrine to doctrine, fearful of "falling behind," clutching the latest news from Paris, American intellectuals seem capable of almost anything except the ultimate grace of a career devoted to some large principle or value, modulated by experience and thought, but firm in purpose. Creatures of short breath, they bend and turn. From the tepid conservatism of the fifties to the utopian frenzies of the sixties, then back to a conservatism more virulent than any we have ever known: who can discover any coherence in all this, any deep, sustained seriousness?

Perhaps it is unavoidable. A disruption of certainty has been the fate of all serious political thought, and this in turn prevents anyone from enjoying the sort of organic development intellectuals once dreamed of. There are some who scoff at the very claim for organic development, insisting that in an age of crisis we have no choice but broken effort, shifting direction. Still, the vision of a lifetime devoted to an abiding value is hard to give up. I remember Harold Rosenberg once saying, "If you change your mind after a certain age, you get sick." I dismissed this as one of Harold's home-made apothegms, but now I think he was on to something. For there is such a thing as being true to one's experience, even one's mistakes—which doesn't at all mean to repeat them.

The extreme discontinuities of our culture, the inclination of writers to run in packs, the vulgar gropings after publicity: all make it hard to work by a tradition that one has chosen—or better, that has chosen one. I admire writers like Thomas Pynchon and J. D. Salinger who maintain strict privacy; at least in this regard they offer a better example than Norman Mailer. But Pynchon and Salinger are talented artists, while those of us who traffic in mere opinion cannot enjoy their luxury of withdrawal. We have to submit to the discontinuities and incoherences we know to be damaging, we must yield to whatever conflict of ideas takes place at a given moment. After having lived through four or five intellectual "periods," each in wild contrast to the others, I feel some weariness, a sense of *déjà vu*, at the prospect of still more quarrels and polemics. But there is no choice, at least if you think democracy the least of political evils.

This is a moment—the early eighties—of peculiar sordidness. It's as if the spirit of the old robber barons had been triumphantly resurrected, as if the most calloused notions of Social Darwinism were back with us, as if the celebrations of greed we associate with the late nineteenth century were reenacted a century later—the very ones I remember from the lips of those tattered, jobless young men who in 1934 kept arguing in behalf of "self-reliance" against my socialist soapboxing. Visions of community that were to relieve the heartlessness of a moneyed society—does anyone recall them? The "no, in thunder" of the great American writers of the nineteenth century—are there no echoes? The Spirit of the Market, which if only sufficiently appeased will shepherd us all to bliss—does this now form a free man's worship?

Christopher Lasch has described the *Zeitgeist* as a kind of narcissism, but this pertains only to portions of the educated classes. What one finds in the country at large these years is a terrible coarseness of feeling, a contempt for the vision of fraternity, a willed brutality of value. Gradgrind and Bounderby, Pecksniff and Veneering, Bumble and Merdle—all are back with us, these phantasms of Dickens now made flesh.

How long will it last? Seven or eight years? And then another of those abrupt oscillations, with a new "herd of independent minds" announcing itself to be terribly radical? It's as if in each turn of intellectual fashion we are fated to suffer another corrupted version of Emersonianism: either absolutist posturings of rectitude or cynical puffings of self-interest. But the spirit of community seems unable to thrive among us, even if it remains too enticing a dream to abandon completely.

When I think of the intellectual careers I admire most—both friends and adversaries—I am struck by the sheer difficulty of living a coherent life in this time and place. Those of us who have tried to resist the tug of fashion have paid a steep price in piety and stiffness. There is really no virtue in staying with a single set of opinions throughout one's life: it's only the fact of living in America that inclines one to think so. For then, at least, one could say, "I have not canceled my experience."

A Song of Meetings

I sing a song of meetings,
Of meetings held to plan future meetings,
And meetings to discuss the failure of earlier meetings,
Of meetings to counter the dark consequences of enemy meetings,
And meetings to commemorate the uncounted meetings we have
    been strong enough to attend.

I sing a song of meetings,
Of explanations that start with creation,
And interruptions fueled by indignation,
Of agendas stretched and padded,
Confusions enjoyed and added,
And climactic declarations denouncing those so weak
    as not to stick it out to the end.

I sing a song of meetings,
Of the need for further clarification
If we are to avoid the world's termination,
Of passionate denunciation
And all but outrageous accusation
    —by people unimpeachable in goodness.

I sing a song of meetings,
Declaring factions to end the blight of faction
And endless speeches on the need for action,
Abrupt insistence on calling the question,
Speakers begging for a two-minute extension,
And mortals made of common clay, fading flesh,
    who marvel at their own endurance.

We stare suspiciously, sniffing old odors. We
    know where we have met, we

Who are survivors. A wince, a tremor, see
    the marks of finger, foot, and knee
That speak of meetings gone and failed. As for me
I cannot look them in the eye, these aging children
    of meetings.

The years of my life coincided with the years of socialist defeat. Step by step, we suffered a dislodgment of received ideas even as we tried to retrieve their moral core. Serious people of other persuasions knew similar crises of belief; those who claimed to be exempt from them were mere fools passing through the twentieth century without experiencing it.

The children of the thirties were latecomers. We had never been able to enjoy the early enchantments or delusions of the socialist hope; we adhered to it mostly through violent negations of its traducers. In the early forties some of us began a journey that would take years fully to comprehend, as we moved from Marxist system to a quizzical and undogmatic attachment to socialist values.

The disadvantages of having been educated in a school of defeat are numerous and grave. But there is one advantage: we tried to be honest with ourselves and submit our thought to self-criticism. We learned a lot from liberalism (at least its classical tradition) and, I should add in fairness, something from the more serious conservative thinkers. We didn't remake an ideology or rebuild a movement, but we did recognize the need for turning our old answers into new questions. This irritated veteran comrades, both ex-radicals who thought it time to drop the whole business, and true believers for whom socialism had become a kind of talisman.

All of which meant, of course, discarding ideological baggage. Socialists are no longer persuaded that by itself nationalization of industry brings us much nearer to the good society; we now see it as a neutral device capable of being put to desirable or retrograde uses, with all depending on whether such measures are integrally related to democratic controls, what the Europeans call *autogestion*. We recognize the difficulties and limits of centralized economic planning, and while a measure of such planning seems inescapable in any advanced society, its value depends on the social forces that sponsor it and the democratic checks that control it. We find interesting the notion of "market socialism" in which prices would not be set by decree, so that autonomous elements of the society could come into a fruitful interplay. In short, we are learning.

The notion that as soon as "we" take power, all will be well; the notion that democracy, even in its debased forms, is anything but a precious human conquest; the notion that social change will occur through the automatic workings of the economy, just like the opposite notion that history can be forced through the will of a sacrificial band—none of these can be taken seriously by thoughtful people, none ever should have been.

I am now inclined to think the case for socialism must be made increasingly on moral grounds: democracy in the work place as fulfillment of political freedom; an end to extreme inequalities of socioeconomic condition; the vision of a humane society as one that requires a setting of cooperativeness and fraternity. But such moral arguments have their moral perils. A twisted or fanatic idealism can be put to ghastly service; from moral righteousness to the usurpations of terror there is a well-worn path.

Will socialism in America ever again be more than a marginal phenomenon? I hope so, but am far from certain. Perhaps it does not finally matter. What matters is that the moral impetus that drove people to become Socialists should find expression, with a fresh vocabulary, in behalf of a fresh radical humanism. What matters is that, no matter what they call themselves, democratic Socialists remain, devoted to a problem or to a memory that gives rise to a problem. Just as there would be an especially acute need for abrasive critics, both anarchist and conservative, in a socialist society, so there is a special need in capitalist society for socialist critics offering an alternative vision of human possibility.

Turn back in memory across the decades. At a meeting of workers in Berlin a century ago the Social Democrat August Bebel speaks. He tells his audience that men who work with their hands need no longer be subordinate and mute. They too count—in their numbers, their joined strength, their readiness to sacrifice. The mute will speak, the shapeless mass will cohere into a disciplined class, the objects of history will become subjects prepared to transform it. In England too—in the night schools for workers, the labor colleges, sometimes the edges of the dissident chapels—such words could be heard. In France, through the traditions of Jacobinism and the Commune. Even in America . . .

The socialist idea is no longer young or innocent. It cannot thrive on a reiteration of simple slogans. But a living core of belief remains. At one point that core overlaps with liberalism: a devotion to the widest political freedoms. During the late seventies I wrote an essay proposing "articles of conciliation" between socialism and liberalism; it was not much noticed, perhaps because for some it contained a surplus of truisms and for others a surplus of heresies. But the conciliation about which I spoke had already begun in many branches of European social democracy. My own idea of socialism rests on unbreakable liberal values, and if at any point a socialist proposal were to conflict with the fundamental values of liberalism, I would unhesitatingly opt for the latter. With liberty you can struggle for greater equality; equality without liberty is a new mode of enslavement.

But the socialist idea also contains something beyond traditional liberalism: the expectation that the plebes, the common workers, can gradually rise to articulation and authority. This is much derided these days, though it has received a superb if tragic confirmation in Poland. But if you deny it you threaten not only the hope of socialism but the basis of democracy. We believe that the democracy more or less prevailing in our political life should also be extended deeply into economic life. The interpenetration of state and society, government and economy is ultimately an irrevocable process in the modern era. Will this occur under corporate auspices, as part of a bureaucratized state capitalism, or can it be subject to popular controls?

A few years ago a neoconservative writer charged that my socialist attachment was "religious" in character. I was supposed to be devastated by this charge, but I was not. If by "religious" one means here a faith for rational men and women, in behalf of which they can devote their best efforts even while remaining aware that the ultimate goal may never be fully realized, then yes, you can say a socialist belief has a "religious" component. But then, so does any other serious political view.

Our burden is to live by the values of both the visionary and practical, the far and near. "It may well be," writes Robert Heil-broner, "that each attack [upon power and privilege] succeeds only to fail . . . that the ultimate goal of a transformed—indeed, transfigured—man is only a chimera . . . [But] taking socialism seriously means understanding that it is the expression of a collective hope for mankind, its idealization of what it conceives itself to be capable of." There I rest.

Past sixty, I think frequently about death. Sometimes I think in response to bodily messages: an arrow through the chest, a creaking in the hips. Sometimes I think out of greediness for time: another book to be finished, another tyrant's end to be celebrated. So people delude themselves into supposing their hunger for life has some objective validity. The truth is, one simply wants.

I think about death because it seems proper at this point in life, rather like beaming at the children of younger friends. But how absurd to suppose there is any sort of propriety in such matters! Perhaps I mean that the time has come to get ready for what no one can ever be ready for. The contemplation of death, says Montaigne, helps us "withdraw our soul outside of us and set it to work apart from the body, which is a sort of apprenticeship and likeness of death." A wonderful sentence, but who can follow its disciplines?

This thinking about death is a decidedly curious experience since, think as one may, it yields no thoughts. Who would care to add a line to Montaigne? In the end I hope not to disgrace myself with panic or a deathbed conversion, but as for thoughts about death—rattle this skull as you wish, you won't find any. But perhaps what we call thinking about death is not really thinking at all. It seems more like a slow unclenching of the will, a readiness to wait for the angel at the door. This much acknowledged, one submits to the wand of comedy: not all your wit nor guile can help.

I think about death because I fear extinction, total and endless. My fear is not equally intense from day to day; apparently the deepest terrors are as short-lived as the keenest ecstasies. But even when dulled, my fear persists. The thought that I won't be here in, say, the year 2000 hardly troubles me; what troubles me is the thought of never coming back. A fatal heart attack next week seems far less frightening than eternal extinction. This precious consciousness of mine, coaxed through so many trials and now at last showing a few signs of worth: must all this now end as nothing?

A serious person who has spent a lifetime without religious faith must accept the idea of eternal nonbeing. Having taken pride in skepticism, I must have the courage of its consequences. That doesn't, however, keep me from a bemused interest in notions of reincarnation, since no one would mind a thousand-year sleep if at the end, knuckle to one's eye, there were a prospect of waking.

Death, says Wallace Stevens, is "the mother of beauty." He says this in "Sunday Morning," the poem for unrepentant naturalists, a credo molded out of voice and countervoice such as one sometimes hears in one's head. Yet in its penultimate stanza even this credo breaks down:

> Supple and turbulent, a ring of men
> Shall chant in orgy on a summer morn
> Their boisterous devotion to the sun,
> Not as a god but as a god might be.

It won't do. No chanting in a "ring of men," not for me. Either you chant to a god or you don't; but who has any interest in chanting to "a god [that] might be"?

"To be silent; to be alone," says Mrs. Ramsey, and then, all our doing done, "one shrunk, with a sense of solemnity, to being oneself, a wide-shaped core of darkness, something invisible to others."

I like the way she uses the word "shrunk." Learning to savor the time that remains, I recognize it not at all as an invitation to sublimity. I do not merge with godhead, I do not become enlarged, I am not a transparent eyeball, I seek no transcendence. No, I shrink pleasantly. A quiet hour, an ease of minutes, as if nestling in the hand of being. It doesn't happen very often, it goes against the grain of restlessness. But I am in training.

In Jerusalem, the summer of 1980, I lived a few houses away from an Israeli writer named Yuri Orlev. He is a little fellow, rather solemn, with a brush mustache and a very straight back—looks somewhat like a miniature Polish colonel. Orlev grew up in War-saw, the child of emancipated Jews, and in early adolescence was locked into the Nazi camps. Withdrawn, not afraid of silence, he shows little taste for talking about the Holocaust. He prefers to ask questions about my childhood in America; the Bronx seems to interest him more than Bergen-Belsen. Or he starts to reminisce about curious events in his adult life, such as one that led to the breakup of an earlier marriage.

But once, as we sit in his elegant shabby house, Orlev hands me a little notebook. He says no word of explanation. The notebook is worn, the cheap paper from which it was manufactured has turned a deathly gray, and I cannot read the minute spidery script that crowds its pages. Finally Orlev starts to talk a little. As a boy in the camps he traded several days' worth of food for this notebook, and in it he secretly wrote poems in Polish. Somehow he managed to keep the notebook with him through all the years, from the camps to Jerusalem.

I weigh the little book in my hand, silently rubbing a finger against its eloquent surface.

> The twentieth century—more homeless still,
> a haze where terrors hide beyond our ken.
>
> —ALEKSANDR BLOK

If these pages yield a common thread, it can only be the idea that we have been witnesses to an age unique in its terribleness. Now, this is a perilous claim and we cannot be certain it is true. Nor can anyone disprove the counterclaim that some decades from now people will have no difficulty in placing our century within a larger sequence of historical disaster. The idea that ours has been a unique time opens us to historical vanity and self-pity, and there are people who dismiss all such claims as modernist rhetoric, prepared to point out that many died in the Black Plague, too.

Yet I want to affirm what I cannot prove to be true: that our century has been marked by a special terribleness, robbing not only life but death of value. Only through the perception that the age of Auschwitz and Gulag bears a unique stamp of dread can we find some faint meaning in our lives. Nor does it matter which world view we start or end with, since what distinguishes those who have listened to the time in which we live from those who have been deaf is not at all the world view they hold. Those who have listened reveal a certain generosity of confusion, a readiness to admit bewilderment, fright, and awe.

The names of the writers who have meant the most to me—I put forward an odd yet by no means arbitrary list: Eliot and Brecht, Solzhenitsyn and Orwell, Kafka and Silone and Nadezhda Mandelstam—are not necessarily those of the greatest writers. But they are the names of crucial witnesses. It is with their testimony that, along the margin, I want to identify. Along the margin, because no American can possibly be more than a witness to witnesses.

Old Tolstoy having come unbidden, let me bid four writers of my own time to an imaginary but not wholly unimaginable meeting. They sit in my apartment: Octavio Paz, the Mexican; Milan Kundera, the Czech; V. S. Naipaul, the Trinidadian; George Konrád, the Hungarian. We talk about the fate of literary generations. Why, with the utmost good will, is it so hard for writers of one generation to connect with those of another?

I read aloud two passages. One is from the ending of Ignazio Silone's *Fontamara*, where the peasants of the Abruzzi, defeated by the Fascists and landlords, keep asking, "What are we to do?" The other is from André Malraux's novel about the 1927 Chinese revolution, *Man's Fate*, in which Kyo, a militant of fine consciousness, confronts the Shanghai police chief. "Do you want to live?" the police chief asks. "It depends how," answers Kyo. "What do you call dignity?" asks the police chief. "The opposite of humiliation."

When I first read these books decades ago I already knew that Stalinism was an overpowering blight, yet it was still possible for me to feel that Silone and Malraux were evoking the pathos of an authentic revolt. But today? Can you still be stirred, I ask the assembled writers, by passages such as those I have just read?

They respond warily, with suppressed irritations and excitements. Paz, the oldest, grasps most readily what I am struggling to ask—perhaps just because he *is* the oldest. He fought on the republican side in Spain and there, as he writes in *The Labyrinth of Solitude*, found "a desperate hopefulness. . . . The memory will never leave me. Anyone who has looked Hope in the face will never forget it. He will search for it everywhere he goes." Yet, Paz suggests quietly, the passage of time cannot be undone, the books from which I have read are embedded in their historical moment, and the most one can feel toward them is a kind of fraternal distance.

Konrád, a writer who lives in Budapest, tolerated but distrusted, is too young to have "looked Hope in the face"; what he has seen is the face of that God everyone knows to have failed. He wonders, nonetheless, whether some residue of Kyo's hope might yet survive in the ashes of its destruction. Naipaul speaks next, his voice caustic and his sentences brilliant: he is impatient though not unfriendly. Aren't you trying, he says, to keep alive a last spark of illusion that might better be snuffed out? And then Kundera, the Czech refugee living in Paris, talks in his wonderfully complicated way, laughing, mocking, plunging into sudden gloom, for he knows how strongly men can yearn for "the unity of their circle." In the ensuing conversation someone rescues a sentence from Kundera's *Book of Laughter and Forgetting*: "Totalitarianism is not only hell, but also the dream of paradise." Everyone nods; we know what he is saying.

And that is all?

God died in the nineteenth century, utopia in the twentieth. The writers gathered here, all endowed with a keen political sense, have sung the dirge of utopia. Their voices ring with skepticism, doubt, weariness: they are poets of limitation. But could their skepticism weigh so heavily upon them, had there not been an earlier enchantment with utopia—that of the generation of Silone and Malraux? Now, what separates these two generations is not just a few decades but a historical chasm.

There is utopia and utopia. The kind imposed by an elite in the name of a historical imperative—that utopia is hell. It must lead to terror and then, terror exhausted, to cynicism and torpor. But surely there is another utopia. It exists at no point in time and space, it is never merely given, it cannot be willed either into existence or out of sight, it speaks for our sense of what may yet be.

Or may not. But whether a real option or a mere fantasy, this utopia is as needed by mankind as bread and shelter. "The golden age," Dostoevsky once wrote, "is the most unlikely of the dreams that have been, yet for it men have given up their lives." A utopia for the sober, a utopia for skeptics, a utopia for unyielding democrats who still want to say that dignity is the opposite of humiliation? I put the question to my four writers. They stare, they smile, they shrug, and they start to answer . . .

ACKNOWLEDGMENTS

One special pleasure in writing this book has been that I was able to ask some of its actors also to be its critics. Chapters have been read by a number of my friends: Lewis Coser, Rose Coser, Emanuel Geltman, Jeremy Larner, the late Stanley Plastrik, Judith Walzer, and Michael Walzer. To all of them I am profoundly grateful. My most thorough readers and stringent critics have been my son, Nicholas Howe, and a young friend, David Bromwich, and to them I am still more grateful.

Drenka Willen, my editor, has contributed generously of her time, attention, and intelligence—she has reminded me of what a true editor can be. And finally a word of thanks to my wife, Ilana, who brought to bear upon this book a deeply valued critical judgment.

Note: In a few sections of this book, I have drawn upon passages from essays that I have written over the years. But in all these instances the passages have been reworked, in accord with the development of my thought and feelings.

Index